Penelope Hall's social services England and W

Edited on behalf of the Sociology Department of Liverpool University

by

John Mays
Formerly Eleanor Rathbone Professor
Department of Sociology
University of Liverpool

with

Anthony Forder
Department of Social Work
Liverpool Polytechnic

and

Olive Keidan
Department of Sociology
University of Liverpool

Routledge & Kegan Paul

London, Boston, Melbourne and Henley

The tenth edition, ed. John Mays
first published in 1983
by Routledge & Kegan Paul Ltd
39 Store Street, London WC1E 7DD,
9 Park Street, Boston, Mass. 02108, USA,
296 Beaconsfield Parade, Middle Park
Melbourne, 3206, Australia and
Broadway House, Newtown Road,
Henley-on-Thames, Oxon RG9 1EN

Photosetting by Thomson Press (India) Ltd., New Delhi
and printed in Great Britain by
Hartnoll Print, Bodmin, Cornwall

The Social Services of Modern England
by M. Penelope Hall was first published in 1952
Second edition 1953
Third edition 1955
Fourth edition 1959
Fifth edition 1960
Sixth edition 1963
Seventh edition, ed. Anthony Forder, 1969
Eighth edition 1971
Ninth edition, ed. John Mays, 1971

Library of Congress Cataloging in Publication Data

Hall, Penelope, 1904–1966.
Penelope Hall's Social services of England and Wales.

Includes index.
1. Social service—Great Britain—Addresses,
essays, lectures. I. Mays, John Barron. II. Forder,
Anthony. III. Keidan, Olive. IV. University of
Liverpool. Sociology Dept. V. Title. VI. Title:
Social services of England and Wales.
HV245.H33 1981 362'.942 82-15021

ISBN 0-7100-0837-6

Contributors

Anthony Forder Head of the Department of Social Work, Liverpool Polytechnic.
Graham White Lecturer in Sociology, Department of Sociology, University of Liverpool.
Ken Roberts Senior Lecturer in Sociology, Department of Sociology, University of Liverpool.
Kathleen Pickett Senior Lecturer in Sociology, Department of Sociology, University of Liverpool.
Olive Keidan Lecturer in Social Administration, Department of Sociology, University of Liverpool.
Eileen Holgate Lecturer in Social Work, Department of Sociology, University of Liverpool.
Clive Davies Lecturer in Sociology, Department of Sociology, University of Liverpool.
Robert Stevens Senior Lecturer in Social Work, Liverpool Polytechnic.

Contents

Charts

Tables

Preface to the fourth edition

A writer rash enough to call her book *The Social Services of Modern England* is in the position of Alice in the grip of the Red Queen. Run as hard as this unfortunate child might, still the Queen cried 'Faster! Faster!' and when at last they paused, and she was able to look around, she found herself in exactly the same place as before. 'If you want to get anywhere else you must run twice as fast as that,' remarked the Red Queen acidly. Similarly at the end of each successive attempt to catch up with current legislation and research, I find myself, as always, a little behind the times, conscious that, like its predecessors, the newly revised edition contains statements of fact that were correct when the manuscript was written but which have become out of date during printing, and opinions which might have been modified had the findings of a government enquiry or piece of current research been available a little earlier. The way out of this dilemma is with the reader. If he wishes, as he should, to get 'anywhere else' he must himself consult the government publications and other original and specialist writings to which, as stated in the Preface to the First Edition, this book is intended as an introduction.

The present revision has been more thorough and extensive than previous ones and several chapters have been entirely re-written. I am grateful to those colleagues and friends who have helped me with it by their advice, criticism and encouragement. For the errors and inadequacies which still remain despite their generous help I must take full responsibility, and can but trust that they will be rectified by the student's further reading, observation and practical experience.

September 1958 M.P.H.

Editor's preface

It is a great privilege once again to be able to edit this new edition of Penelope Hall's *Social Services of England and Wales* and to contribute a Preface to a work which, since its first publication in 1952 under its original title of *The Social Services of Modern England*, has become a classic of its kind. For over a quarter of a century this book has been read by several generations of university and college students and has been a special boon to those preparing themselves for a future career in some branch or other of the social services. Its readership indeed has been world-wide and over the course of many years its reissue has brought considerable lustre to Liverpool University's Department of Social Science, as it used to be called before, in 1971, we decided to fall into line with other universities and adopt the more generally understood name of Department of Sociology.

This change of title of the Department should not, however, be interpreted as a breach with Liverpool's long established tradition of involvement with the whole field of social administration and of social work training and with what is generally known as problem-centred research. It is still true that many of our graduates go on to careers in social work and to allied posts in welfare, education and social administration. In most other universities as a matter of deliberate policy there has been a sharp split between the teaching of sociology and the teaching of social administration as a result of which an unfortunate division between the so-called applied and the mainly theoretical courses has occurred at both the teaching and research levels. I am glad that we in Liverpool have so far avoided such a schism and in so doing remain comparatively faithful to the aims of our founders, who, at the beginning of the century, sought to establish a new department of the university which would concern itself with the many problems facing the surrounding community and in its own way strive to help to discover what might be done to overcome these problems and in so doing discharge some of its debt to those who had worked to bring it into existence. The fact that our two professorial chairs are named after Charles Booth and Eleanor Rathbone serves to underline this very significant aspect of the Department's history. Many of my colleagues, though perhaps not all, agree with this emphasis and would hold with Durkheim that any neglect of the theoretical must be to the detriment of the practical and vice versa, and that one, at least, of the main purposes in studying society is in order to be in a better position ultimately to shape our communal destiny and overcome, or at least reduce, some of our social and human problems.

Such a view would, I am sure, wholly recommend itself to Penelope Hall herself and the regular republication of her well known book helps to keep green the memory of a greatly respected friend and colleague whose personal integrity, devotion to teaching and scholarship were an example to all who knew her or who had the privilege of working with her in Liverpool. But she was more than the disinterested scholar. She was, above all, a committed individual who in her own life strove to live up to the ideals implicit in social welfare work and Christian responsibility. It was this spirit, indeed, which gave the earlier editions of her book that stamp of moral enthusiasm which raised it high above the level of the run of the mill academic textbook.

Pen Hall was an outstanding member of a generation of university teachers that has almost passed away. This was the generation of men and women who had grown up during the bleak decades of the 1920s and 1930s, who had survived the rigours of the Second World War and who, drawing on these challenging experiences, were determined to try to make Britain a better land for the average citizen to live in. They sought to achieve this end not so much by political activism as by the development of social administration as an applied academic discipline which might lay bare the roots of our social problems and make positive contributions to general well-being in every relevant field of social and family life. They were people who were, in the late Professor Titmuss's phrase, 'committed to welfare'. Richard Titmuss indeed was the doyen of that older generation. Throughout his working life he strove to make social administration both academically respectable and socially valuable, combining in his own personality and example 'that uncommon mixture of intellectual excitement and practical usefulness' which Pen Hall and others in their own humbler ways have sought to follow and exemplify. For such individuals social administration is not, to quote Titmuss again, 'a messy conglomeration of the technical *ad hoc*', but an intellectual study whose 'primary areas of unifying interest are centred in those social institutions that foster integration and discourage alienation'.

Some of today's younger social scientists might vigorously challenge the validity of such a philosophy and those more especially who are steeped in Marxism would no doubt dismiss it as merely a misguided attempt to buttress up a rotting social order. But the development of the Welfare State during the last hundred years and its associated values cannot be so lightly put aside. Those, moreover, who seek to reduce the extent of public welfare and who see its development as necessarily inimical to individual choice, freedom and responsibility will also dislike a consensual approach which eschews radical political solutions and stresses the need for an enlightened and generous attitude on the part of the whole community towards those who suffer from various misfortunes, sometimes as a result of their own but just as often of society's defects and deficiencies. Some of our economic surplus surely must be reserved to assist the less able and the less fortunate—the vital question is one of the right balance between the justifiable claims of individual aspiration and communal responsibility. This is at heart as much a moral as a political problem, one of the will as well as of organisational skill. Indeed the effort to achieve a moral consensus of the middle ground is perhaps the main issue that lies before us today, the central problem upon whose solution our national future depends.

Not all those writers who have contributed to this volume would subscribe to such a view, and I hasten to absolve them of any guilty complicity.

In conclusion I wish to pay the warmest possible tribute to Olive Keidan who has not only contributed separate chapters but has been very actively engaged with me as a co-editor of this book. To Anthony Forder, too, I extend my own and the department's thanks for the contributions he has again made to this reissue of a work of which, after Pen Hall's death, while a lecturer here, he became for a time the principal editor. Apart from two, all the authors of the individual chapters are present members of the Department of Sociology. Their collaboration and efficiency has made my own task an easy one and my co-editors and I are greatly in their debt. Although we have brought this new edition up-to-date at the time of writing, it may well, while in the hands of the printer, have been overtaken by new events and fresh legislation. Such is the tempo of change in modern society. The way out of such a dilemma, as Pen Hall said in her preface to the Fourth edition, 'is with the reader'. He himself must try to keep up-to-date with current legislation and government reports as they flow from the press. Alice is thus forever in the clutches of the exigent Red Queen!

John Barron Mays

The authors have aimed to make this volume up to date at September 1981. Some legislation and reports after that date may be referred to in the text or in notes, but the reader should assume that events after September 1981 are not included.

TABLE 1 *Public expenditure in 1969 and 1979 expressed in £ million and as a percentage of the gross national product*

		1969		*1979*	*1969–79*
	£m.	*% of G.N.P.*	*£m.*	*% of G.N.P.*	*change: % of G.N.P.*
Education	2,250	5.6	9.542	5.8	0.2
National Health Service	1,733	4.3	8,863	5.4	1.1
Personal social services	204	0.5	1,733	1.1	0.6
School meals, milk, and welfare foods	162	0.4	544	0.3	– 0.1
Social security benefits	3,571	8.9	18,497	11.3	2.4
Housing and environmental services	1,935	4.8	9,261	5.6	0.8
Total: Social Services and housing	9,855	24.5	48,440	29.5	5.0
Military defence	2,289	5.7	9,057	5.5	– 0.2
Other government expenditure	6,864	17.2	27,409	16.8	– 0.4
Total Government expenditure	19,008	47.4	84,906	51.8	3.4
Gross national product	40,131	–	163,936	–	–

Source: *Annual Abstract of Statistics*, HMSO, 1981 Tables 14.1 and 14.18.

The gross national product is the total monetary value of all goods and services produced within the economy in a given period, usually a financial year from April of one year to March of the next. While there are many limitations to the figure, it is the best crude indicator of national productivity and national income. The increase in the monetary value of the GNP in the last line is almost entirely due to inflation, although Chart 1, which provides comparative information using uniform prices, indicates that there was some increase in the real value over the period 1970 to 1978, despite minor fluctuations and a slow recovery from 1975 to 1978. The same inflation affects the figures for expenditure on individual services, but by expressing the figures as a percentage of the GNP it can be seen that there was a real increase in government expenditure, and an even greater increase in the expenditure on social services because of a reduction in military and other expenditure. The largest increase was in social security benefits, some of which was due to increases in the numbers receiving benefits, particularly the unemployed, but some of it represented a real increase in the value of long-term benefits as is shown in Chart 2.

TABLE 2 *Post-war cycles in the British Economy*

	I	*II*	*III*	*IV*	*V*
Period	1952–7	1958–61	1962–5	1966–70	1971–3
Duration	6 yrs	4 yrs	4 yrs	5 yrs	3 yrs
Real GNP rise (%)	16.4	12.1	13.4	11.2	10.9
Peak unemployment*	1.8	2.0	2.2	2.3	3.7
(% average for year)	(1952)	(1959)	(1963)	(1968)	(1972)
Peak inflation†	5.3	3.4	4.7	6.4	9.2
(% year-on-year)	(1955)	(1961)	(1965)	(1970)	(1973)
Peak payments‡ Deficit	0.91	1.12	1.29	§	2.07
(% of GDP)	(1955)	(1960)	(1964)		(1973)

* Unemployed in GB excluding school-leavers and adult students.
† Change in average retail price level between calendar years.
‡ Current account in calendar years.
§ Masked by 1967 devaluation.
Source: Peter Jay in *The Times*, 1 July 1974.

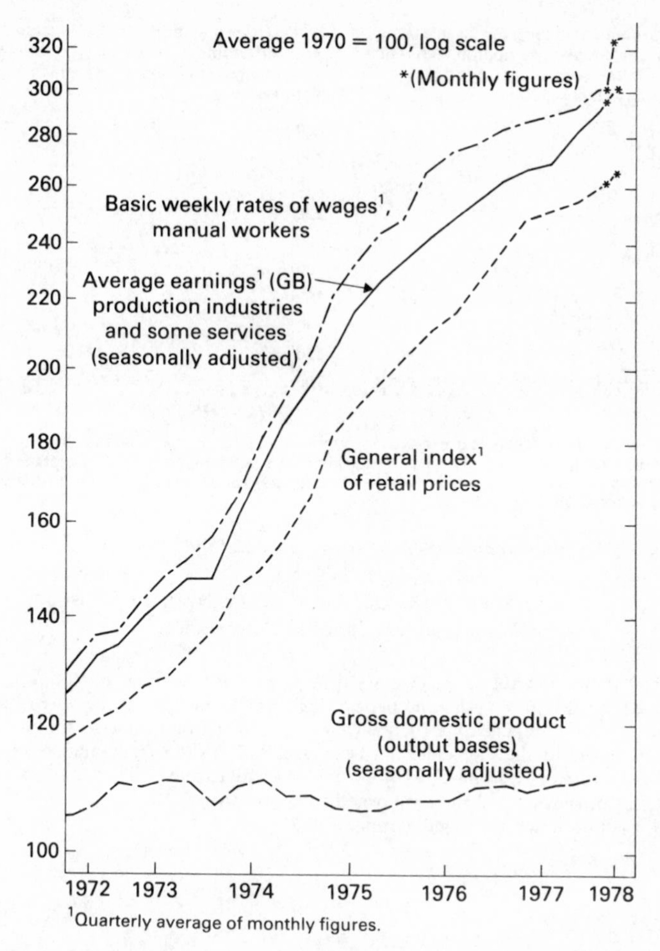

CHART 1 *Prices, wages, earnings and the Gross National Product 1972–8*
Source: *Economic Trends*, 1978.

Chart 1 shows the relationship between increases in the general index of retail prices (often referred to loosely as the cost of living index), increases in certain wage indices and the gross national product at uniform prices. The graphs are presented on a semi-logarithmic scale, which accounts for the progressive decrease in the distance between points on the vertical scale. The advantage of this form of presentation is that one can compare the rates of change of different variables, which are indicated by the slope of the graph. Lines running parallel show the same rate of increase. One can see in this graph how increases in the wages of manual workers and of workers in productive industry have more than kept pace with increases in the index of retail prices since 1970.

1 Ordinary and long-term scale rates (married couples) compared with retail price index (excluding housing) (January 1973 = 100)

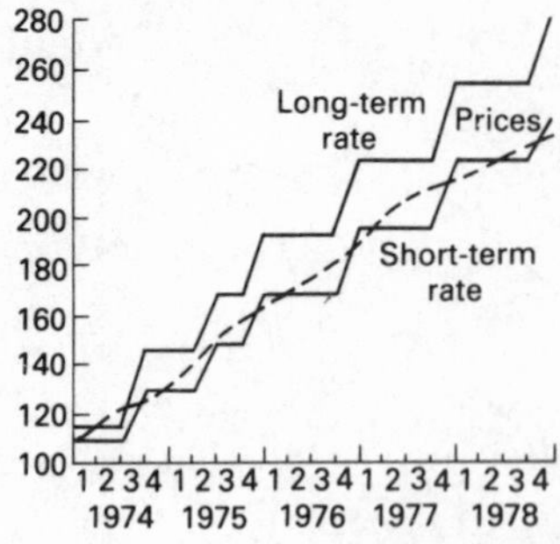

2 Ordinary and long-term scale rates (married couples) compared with average net earnings* (married male manual worker) (January 1973 = 100)

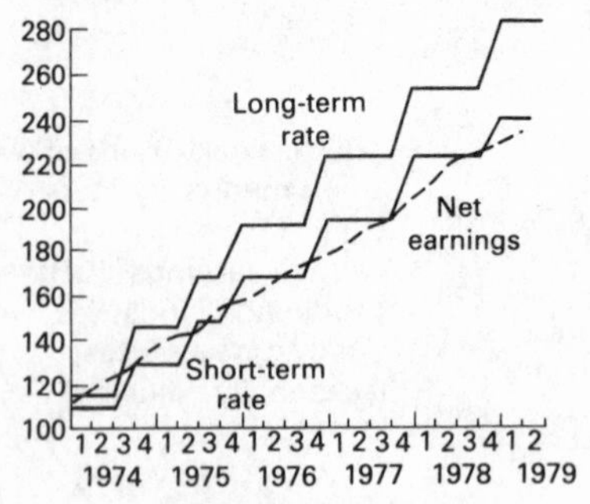

*Net earnings are taken as gross average weekly earnings for full-time male manual workers, less income tax (personal or married man's tax allowance only as appropriate), NI contributions and estimated average rent and rates for each household type. Earnings for December 1978 are provisional.

CHART 2 *Supplementary Benefit scale rates and indices of retail prices and net earnings 1974–8*
Source: *SBC Notes and News*, as. 14, April 1979, issued by the Supplementary Benefits Commission

Chart 2 shows how the supplementary benefit scales for married couples have changed in relation to prices and net earnings of male manual workers. Earnings are shown less compulsory deductions and estimated rent and rates, which are covered in full by the supplementary benefit scale. The short-term rate has kept level with prices but dropped slightly compared with earnings. The long-term rates, for pensioners and those on benefits for over two years, have increased faster than both net prices and earnings.

Population of the UK: data used below

Age group	1951		1961		1971		1979		2001		2011	
	mill.	%	mill.	%	mill.	%	mill.	%	mill.	%	mill.	%
0 - 15 years	12.0	23.7	13.1	24.7	14.2	25.5	12.1	21.5	12.9	22.0	11.8	20.0
15 to retirement age	31.8	62.7	32.2	60.8	32.4	58.2	34.2	61.2	35.9	61.6	37.1	63.0
Over retirement age	6.9	13.6	7.7	14.5	9.1	16.3	9.7	17.3	9.6	16.4	10.0	17.0
Total	50.7	–	53.0	–	55.7	–	55.9	–	58.4	–	58.9	–

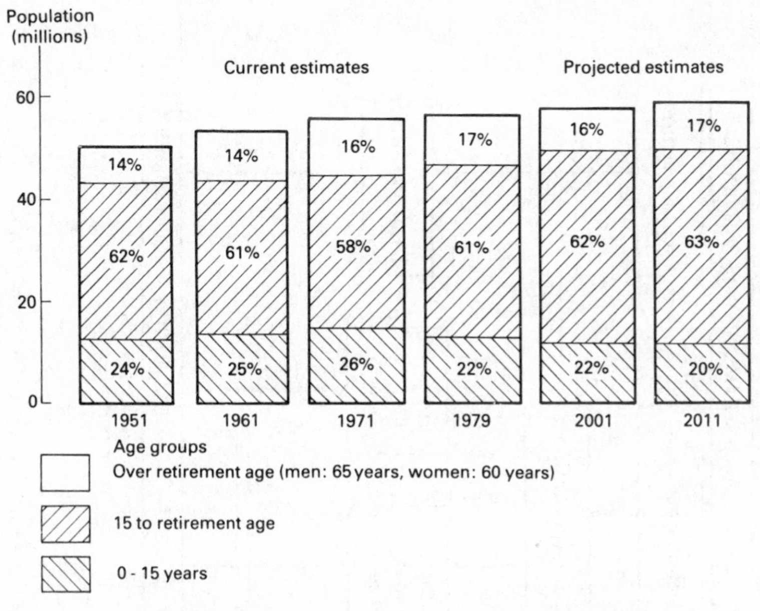

CHART 3 *Population of the United Kingdom: Registrar-general's estimates for* 1951, 1961, 1971, 1979, 2001, 2011

The chart shows how the proportion of the population in the productive ages between the statutory school-leaving age and retirement has varied in relation to other age groups since the Second World War and how they are expected to vary over the next thirty years. Projections are more reliable for the elderly than for children, and alternative projections based on higher and lower estimates of fertility are available. The chart shows that there has been an increase in the absolute and relative numbers of the elderly, but fears of further vast increases are unjustified and are likely to be compensated by reductions in the proportion of children in the population. It should, however, be noted that the chart fails to show a substantial increase in the very small numbers of very old people who make exceptionally high demands on services.

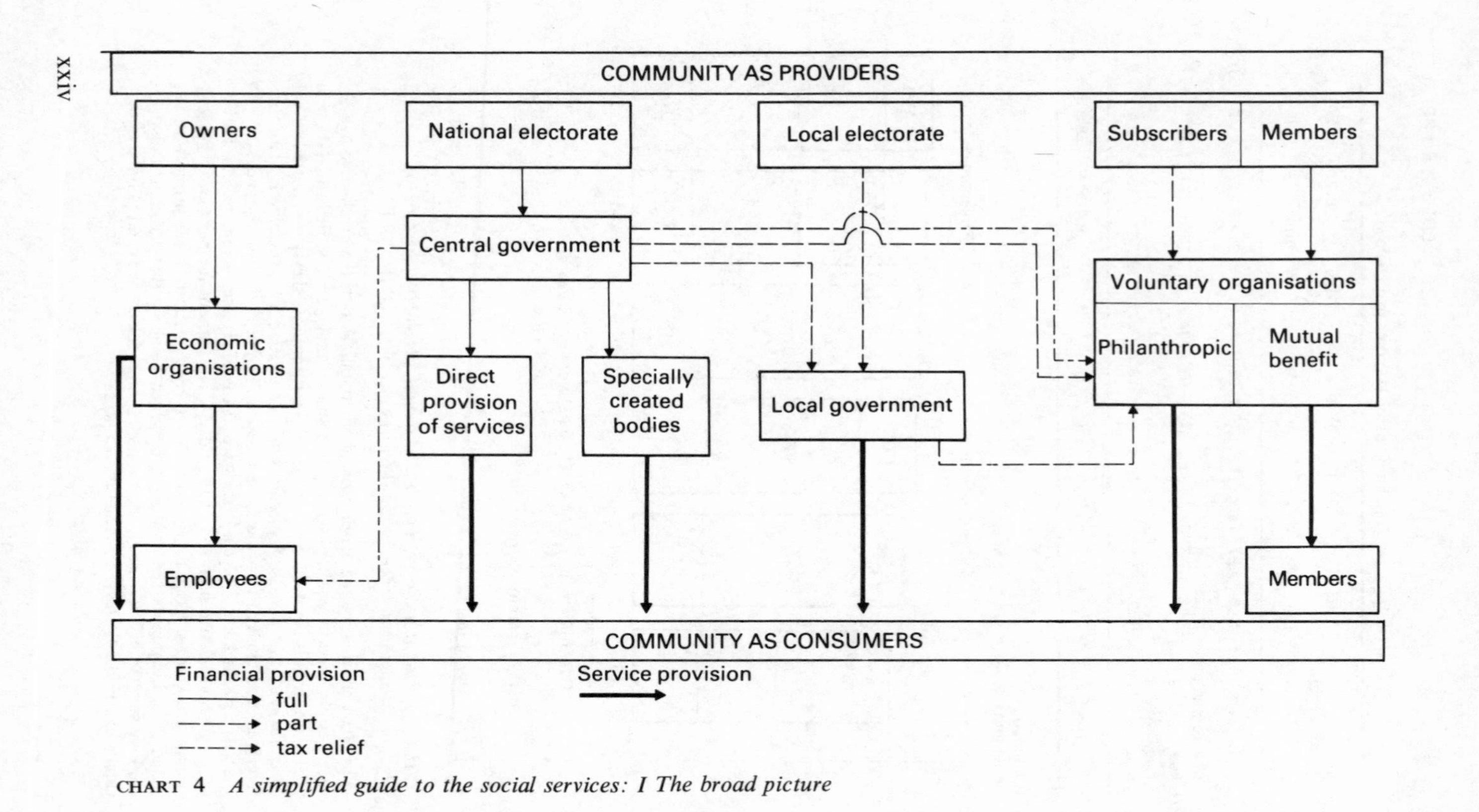

CHART 4 *A simplified guide to the social services: I The broad picture*

CENTRAL GOVERNMENT

	Education and Science	Home Office	Employment	Treasury	Health and Social Security	Environment††	Lord Chancellor
Departments*	Education and Science	Home Office	Employment	Treasury	Health and Social Security	Environment††	Lord Chancellor
Services administered directly by Central Government Departments		Prisons Immigration	Employment exchanges Industrial rehabilitation units Skillcentres	Taxation	War pensions Social security Reception centres Special hospitals		Courts
Services administered by semi-independent bodies	Higher education**	Probation and after-care Police† Race relations	Redundancy payments Industrial Training Boards		Health authorities		

LOCAL AUTHORITIES

	Education	Social services	Environmental health	Housing
Services administered by local authorities (see chart 6)	Schools, further and higher education Youth Service Careers Service Education welfare	Social casework Residential and day care Home helps, etc.		Town planning

*Administering or giving oversight to services below. The Welsh and Scottish Offices are omitted from the chart.

**Universities should be considered as voluntary bodies, but the University Grants Committee comes in this category.

†Responsibility shared with local authorities.

††Has a general responsibility for the oversight of local authorities.

CHART 5 *A simplified guide to the social services: II Government services*

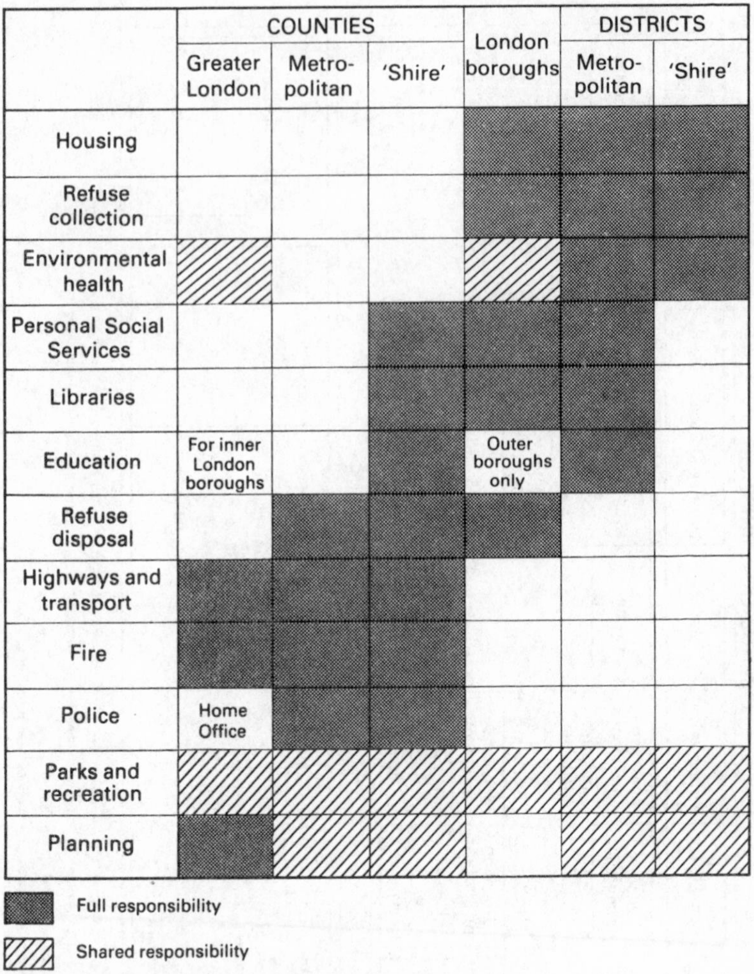

	COUNTIES			London boroughs	DISTRICTS	
	Greater London	Metro-politan	'Shire'		Metro-politan	'Shire'
Housing						
Refuse collection						
Environmental health						
Personal Social Services						
Libraries						
Education	For inner London boroughs			Outer boroughs only		
Refuse disposal						
Highways and transport						
Fire						
Police	Home Office					
Parks and recreation						
Planning						

Full responsibility

Shared responsibility

CHART 6 *A simplified guide to the social services: III Distribution of local authority responsibilities*

1 Introduction

Anthony Forder

There is no general agreement on the definition of what is a social service.[1] There are, however, three implications of the word 'social' which help to set the boundaries. 'Social' in this context refers to the fact that the service is provided through collective action. Second the social services are designed to meet 'social' needs, that is those needs that are dependent for their fulfilment on the effective organisation of social relationships. Finally, it contrasts those services that are provided for a 'social' motive and those provided for an 'economic' motive, thus excluding many services provided for profit or primarily to meet the needs of trade and industry.

On this basis the definition of the social services is very wide and certainly much wider than the services covered by this book. Nevertheless the selection of these particular services for study is not without its rationale. They are services whose manner of operation directly affects the lives of individuals and is in turn affected by their reactions. Attitudes are at least as important as techniques in determining their effect. On this basis one can justify the omission of such services as sewage disposal, fire services and road construction. Somewhat less justifiable is the omission of discussion of such matters as library services, and the relationship between the public and the police, and the limited attention given to the penal system and the integration of minority groups into the community. These have all been omitted on grounds of space rather than reason.

However, in this introduction it is important to consider in more general terms the circumstances in which social services have grown up in this country and the factors that have affected the form they have taken.

Table 1 shows the proportion of the gross national product used in recent years for social services provided by the state in Britain. It also shows that this proportion was still higher at the end of the 1970s than it had been ten years earlier despite increasing economic difficulties.

An extended provision of social services is characteristic of all, or almost all industrialised countries today whether capitalist or communist, although the form of these services varies considerably according to government ideology and national culture. In some ways this is not surprising. Greater specialisation of function and greater physical proximity among large populations increases the dependence of individuals on each other for the satisfaction of their needs. Higher standards of behaviour and skill are demanded of people; higher expectations are raised by increased resources and new technologies. The individual in an urban industrial society faces hazards that fall to some extent at random, encouraging the sharing of risks. This is as necessary for the rich as for the poor, though there will be a difference in the risks they face and their attitudes to them. At the same time society as a whole needs literate, healthy citizens, able and willing to act responsibly in a variety of roles, as workers, voters, trade unionists, parents and so on. Thus 'enlightened self-interest' provides support for humanitarian impulses springing from the sense of identification of one human being with another or from the recognition that one has contributed, however indirectly, to another's misfortune. This support is necessary, because human capacity for sympathy is limited and unreliable, and also because even when sympathy is aroused there is too often a breakdown between humane impulse and humane action.

Having said this it is necessary to warn the reader against viewing the origins of the social services as springing in some simplistic way from a recognition of needs. This cannot be justified whether needs are seen in personal terms and the social services as being provided because of the operation of a social conscience, or needs are seen in terms of the efficiency of the social system, and meeting them as a rational response to the recognition of such problems. The recognition of social problems and the decision to take action on them are complicated social processes in which culture, ideology, the availability of relevant techniques and resources, and, above all, the relative strengths of different political groups all have a crucial role to play.[2]

The development of social services in England 1830–1939

In England in the mid-nineteenth century the rationalism of the Benthamite tradition favoured reforms,[3] but the main target of reform was the vested interests of the landed aristocracy which had for years supported legislative stagnation in the face of mounting social changes. The same rationalism, when allied with the individualistic philosophy which was characteristic of protestant religious leaders and free-thinking philosophers alike, produced a strong opposition both to government control and to collective action. Additional support for this policy of *laissez-faire* came from a deterministic economic theory which stressed the inability of government action in the long term to change the position of the poor.

However, even at the height of the influence of Benthamite liberalism, there were other tendencies operating. Rationalist philosophers opposed unnecessary suffering. Evangelical Christians believed in a God of love.[4] Both philosophies had an essential humanitarian element. Tories believed in the value of paternalism, while among 'the labouring classes' and some of their supporters faith in the effectiveness of collective action remained strong. Throughout the nineteenth century each of these elements struggled for expression in legislation. The most notable example was the agitation which produced the procession of Factory Acts from 1802 to 1898, giving increasing protection first to women and children and later to men in industry.

Gradually these humanitarian elements were reinforced by the pressure of events. The squalor of the poor areas of the growing towns was the breeding ground of crime, vice and disease that spread beyond their own boundaries to threaten the security of the prosperous. An amusing example is the persistent concern of Parliament up to 1857 for the effect of the stench of sewage from the Thames on its work.[5] Services to protect the public health and more effective crime prevention were among the first to receive government support, together with education which was necessitated by both the extension of the franchise and industrial development. From the second Reform Act, 1867, to the end of the century a whole series of laws was enacted by both political parties extending the role of government in the regulation of social conditions, and the protection of the weak, and sanctioning collective action by the working classes. At the same time more effective administrative institutions were being developed in central and local government to cope with the extension of activity in these politically sensitive areas.

However, even at the end of the nineteenth century the problems of poverty and of meeting the needs of individuals in distress had hardly begun to be tackled. From the point of view of today it is easy to be critical of the Victorians for their failure to face this problem—though not so easy now as it was twenty years ago when even well-informed people were convinced that the problem of poverty had been solved in this country. There is little doubt that today poverty could be eliminated if the people of the country as a whole were determined enough. In the nineteenth century the size of the problem, the lack of understanding of its nature and causes, and the absence of the tools needed to tackle it all combined to place its elimination beyond the capacity of the country. Faced with this situation the Victorians tended to assume that economic 'laws' made preventive action impossible. Alternatively, responsibility was laid on individual failure. Both attitudes were supported by the *laissez-faire* and individualistic philosophies of the time.

One instrument was available to the state, not for dealing with poverty as such, but with 'paupers', individuals who were 'destitute', i.e. lacking the means of subsistence, and who by virtue of the receipt of relief were given an inferior status as citizens. This was the Poor Law.[6] It was inherited from the Elizabethans by whom it was created as an instrument for making the prevention of destitution the responsibility of the local community. Administered in a humane, paternalistic manner in the early years of the century, the Poor Law had manifestly failed to meet the conditions that were developing. The Poor Law Amendment Act, 1834, attempted to limit demand by an approach which, in the hands of people whose main concern was economy, became frankly deterrent. Those who accepted relief were stigmatised as paupers. Relief to the able-bodied was only to be given in institutions in which the regime had to be more unpleasant than the conditions which were generally endured outside these 'workhouses'. Contrary to the intentions of the Act the same conditions were applied to other destitute persons. The circumstances which made people destitute were very varied, including as well as unemployment, physical and mental illness, old age, and the loss by children of parents. Because destitution was regarded as the primary problem, only gradually and to a limited extent were different methods and institutions developed to meet these varied needs. Even in 1944 the Curtis Committee was horrified to find some children in the care of local authorities in all-purpose workhouses of the type developed in the nineteenth century.[7]

Such a deterrent system could only be morally justified by the belief that the individual was responsible for his own condition. It was recognised that for some at least this was not true, but it was believed that the state could not provide separate treatment for these. The needs of such people were left to private philanthropy, which could relate assistance to individual need in a way that the state could not. This philanthropy was the major outlet for the humanitarian impulses of the middle and upper classes. But philanthropists too had to limit demand, and did so by emphasising the distinction between the 'deserving' and the 'undeserving' poor which was the justification for so limited a state provision.

By the end of the century the thesis that the majority of the poor were responsible for their own condition was no longer tenable in face of the evidence against it. In particular the surveys of Booth and

Rowntree had finally shown that the greatest causes of poverty were low wages in relation to the size of families and the risks of interrupted earnings through sickness, unemployment and old age.[8] When these discoveries were supplemented by anxiety about the level of physical health and nutrition among recruits for the Boer War, the door was opened for a more energetic state campaign not only against poverty itself, but against those ills, such as squalor, disease, ignorance and crime, which were most closely connected with poverty. In 1904 a Royal Commission was set up to consider the operation of the Poor Law. This provided a sounding board for the various views on the causes and cure of poverty, and for information on the subject. The commission eventually produced a majority report, and a minority report reflecting mainly the views of Sidney and Beatrice Webb. The former recommended the retention of the Poor Law with modifications; the latter proposed the break-up of the Poor Law and the institution of a series of services to meet particular needs. Neither report was directly implemented, although the minority report was more accurate in its forecast of future developments, but the commission did clarify the need for change, and add to the impetus.[9]

The result of these various pressures was a remarkable programme of legislation particularly under the talented Liberal government of 1906 onwards.[10] It included measures for cheap meals and health inspections for school children; for health and unemployment insurance; for old age pensions; for the probation of offenders, the reform of juvenile courts, and the institution of borstal training; for the setting up of employment exchanges and the resettlement of the unemployed; and for the care of mental defectives.

Most of these reforms were based on the imaginative adaptation of methods developed by charitable organisations and voluntary associations in earlier years. Thus the system of health and unemployment insurance, while owing much to an examination of the German system created by Bismarck in the 1880s, made use of the voluntary Friendly Societies that had grown up for a similar purpose in England. The provision of school meals for necessitous children was an extension to the state of a service first pioneered in Liverpool by the Liverpool Food Association. The development of probation involved the legal incorporation and extension of the work of the Police Court Missionaries. Voluntary organisations were seen as the pioneers of services, but they were also preferred as the channel for providing state services because they were felt to be able to provide an individualised, caring service that the state could not give. Thus it was regarded as an essential element of the probation system that the probation officers should not be directly employed by the state.

These measures enabled large numbers of people to receive

assistance in time of need without enduring the stigma of the Poor Law. There were, however, many gaps, particularly as state intervention concentrated on the welfare of school children and employees, two groups for whom state help was most easily justified in terms of national need. Some of the gaps were stopped by further legislation on similar lines in the period between the two world wars. However, throughout this twenty-year period England suffered an almost continuous industrial depression in which unemployment sometimes reached 20 per cent of the working population and was rarely below 10 per cent. The effect of this on the social services was complex. On the one hand the shift in power in favour of the working classes, which might have been expected as a result of the growth of the Labour Party and the trade unions, was largely nullified by their weaker bargaining position in times of depression. The limited availability of resources tended to result in reduced growth or even cuts in the social services. The fear that demands for assistance would again outstrip the availability of resources helped to sustain the Poor Law attitude to the giving of relief. On the other hand the nature and extent of the unemployment, so clearly a product of the economic system, showed the inappropriateness of the Poor Law for dealing with the problem, while the large numbers that suffered meant a growing pressure against deterrent measures. The immediate result was that unemployment assistance was completely removed from the ambit of the Poor Law by the setting up of the Unemployment Assistance Board, though the old attitudes often remained in its administration. This was symbolised by the 'household means test' under which every earning member of a household was held fully responsible for the maintenance of the other members. In the long run the depression meant that the rout of the Poor Law in 1948 was the more complete. It was no accident that the legislation of the 1940s took the form it did in the hands of the leaders of those who had suffered most in the inter-war period.

Post-war developments in social policy

In the Second World War a tremendous effort was required of the nation, combatants and civilians alike. The creation of national unity, which wars in any case tend to engender, was a conscious objective of government. Policies, such as rationing and price control, were developed to ensure a fair distribution of limited resources among civilians. The decision in 1941 to set up a Committee for Reconstruction to begin planning for after the war was both an outcome of that sense of unity and a support for it. There was a determination that peace should bring the rewards of victory to all.

Above all, mass unemployment and the indignities of poverty in the inter-war period were to be abolished.

The first fruit of this planning was the Beveridge Report on *Social Insurance and Allied Services*, which set the pattern for later thinking. 'The scheme proposed here,' said Beveridge, 'is in some ways a revolution, but in more important ways it is a natural development from the past. It is a British revolution.'[11] This description could justly be applied to all the legislation which set up the social services from 1944 to 1948, whether it was passed by the wartime Coalition, or the post-war Labour government.

The revolution lay primarily in the acceptance by the state of a much fuller responsibility for the determination of social policy. Social development was no longer to be left as a by-product of economic development, with the state filling in the gaps left by private enterprise. There were two major prongs of this 'revolution'. First there was the management of the economy so as to maintain full employment. Second there was the abolition of the Poor Law and the development of a system of 'universal' social services, that is services available to all who needed them without regard to their income. The continuity with the past lay in the use made of methods already tried and accepted, like social insurance, and, whenever possible, of well-established institutions.

Management of the economy

The acceptance by government of responsibility for the maintenance of full employment was required partly to avoid the damage to the welfare of the unemployed and their dependants resulting from the breakdown of the normal methods of income distribution in an industrial economy. But equally influential was the need of a highly capitalised industrial system for continuity of the production to provide an adequate return on past investment and the confidence to invest in the future. Maintaining full employment means managing the economy to an unprecedented extent, the full implications of which are only gradually beginning to emerge.

For twenty-five years the maintenance of full employment was achieved with remarkable success by all post-war British governments. The national average rate of unemployment rarely exceeded 2 per cent of the insured population before 1967 or 3 per cent before 1970 despite much higher figures in some depressed areas.[12] Indeed, the economy was rather hampered by the relatively slow growth of the labour force, which was only partially counteracted by immigration. This was combined with a sustained growth in the economy, which was marred only by the knowledge that Britain's industrial competitors were almost all doing substantially better. The price of this success seems to have been continuous and rising inflation coupled with an intractable problem in balancing accounts with the rest of the world.

Inflation has been a world-wide problem and this has helped to lessen Britain's difficulties except in certain critical periods. Moreover the worst effects can be mitigated by such measures as building inflation-proofing into wage agreements, pensions and other contracts and by relating benefits to the retail price index through regular reviews[13] (Charts 1 and 2 on pp. xxi and xxii). But the problem of the balance of payments has been particularly severe for Britain because when incomes rose, imports rose even more. So every significant rise in the rate of production has produced a corresponding crisis in the balance of payments. Now British governments before 1979 responded in a similar manner. Balance of payments crises were met by severe curtailment of demand (except for a disastrous attempt by the Heath government in 1971–4 to 'spend itself out of the crisis'). As the balance of payments improved they tried to stimulate demand to improve investment and production and the cycle was repeated. This has become known as the 'stop-go policy'. At the height of the crisis successive governments were reluctantly led to try to control inflation by controlling wages and prices.[14] These controls, by operating at a specific point of time, tended to fix relative incomes in an arbitrary manner and then to change them arbitrarily by operating more effectively on some incomes and prices than on others. The result in each cycle was mounting discontent which ended in a wage explosion that gave a new fillip to inflation.

These recurrent cycles tended to become successively shorter and more severe in their effects (see Table 2 p. xx), until in the second half of the 1970s a combination of a stagnant economy and high inflation ('stagflation') presented a new and even more disturbing phenomenon. Since 1976 unemployment has not been below 5 per cent. By April 1980 it had reached 6 per cent, and a year later 10 per cent (though it is worth remembering that Beveridge had thought in 1942 that he should estimate for an average level of 8½ per cent even if government was committed to a full employment policy).[15] Inflation has been up to 27 per cent per annum in 1975 and an annual rate in single figures has proved an elusive target. If the balance of payments and the exchange value of the pound have been less of a problem this has been largely due to the temporary windfall of North Sea oil. Entry into the EEC, on which many hopes were placed in the early 1970s, seems to have provided little help for these basic problems, and indeed the high contribution of Britain to the EEC budget, largely to subsidise European agriculture under the Common Agricultural Policy, has been an additional heavy burden [16]

Since the Conservative government under Mrs Thatcher came into power in March 1979, the situation has deteriorated further. In efforts to control inflation and make industry more efficient in its use of resources the government has reversed previous Keynsian policies and attempted to influence the economy mainly by controlling the money supply and cutting back on government expenditure, particularly in the social services. The result has been that in a period of severe world depression, British industry and employment seems to have suffered a greater contraction than those of any other industrialised country. Interest rates have remained very high and inflation has not yet been reduced below 10 per cent, although this was the main target of policy. Cuts in expenditure fell first and most severely on housing but are affecting to greater or lesser extent all other services except those supporting law and order.

The social services

In the new structure of universal social services, four services were central. The Education Act, 1944, was designed to provide equality of opportunity for children of all classes. It was based on the report of the Hadow Committee in 1926. The National Health Service was created by the Act of that name in 1946. Four Acts dealt with family allowances and social security.[17] The Town and Country Planning Act, 1947, was to enable the government to control the physical environment in which people lived. The problem of housing was not seen as requiring a universal social service in the same way. Instead reliance was placed on the continuance of wartime controls to ensure that resources went to the housing departments of local authorities.

The provision of universal social services received the support it did partly from the sense of national unity which persisted for a time after the war. This can be seen in the way in which the extension of wartime controls into peacetime was accepted by the community. Severe food rationing, for example, was continued until 1954, and then only abolished with misgivings on the part of many. At the same time political leaders were united temporarily in agreement about the necessity for new legislation, although individually they saw it as a stepping stone to different ultimate goals. Beveridge, for instance, saw the provision of a basic minimum income for all as the foundation for a policy that would leave the maximum opportunity for each individual to improve his own lot. On the other hand some Labour leaders saw the social services as a step towards greater equality among the people as a whole.

The sense of achievement in the country at the post-war developments in the social services was epitomised in the descriptive phrase 'the Welfare State'.[18] However, behind the general use of this term were some important misconceptions. Most people thought, and many still do, that the generous provision of social services was a peculiarly British phenomenon. The fact that other European countries, including our greatest competitors, France and West Germany, had developed similar institutions was largely ignored. As a result many people regarded the provision of social services not as a necessity of industrial development, but as a luxury that could be reduced without damaging the social structure.

It was also generally believed that the new services represented a transfer of resources from the middle classes to the working classes. This was only partially true. Research has since shown that in the fields of education and health the greatest gains were made by the middle classes who received services free which had previously only been free to those with lower incomes.[19] The advantages gained by the middle classes were a natural consequence of making the social services universal and free. The misconception about the nature of the transfer may have been strengthened by the relative decline of the incomes of professional and white-collar workers, which had taken place at the beginning of the war independently of the development of the social services.[20] Large-scale publicity given to inadequate statistics also created the impression that taxation had had a very substantial effect on differences in income between different classes.[21]

The structure of the social services[22]

A broad and simplified picture of social services structure is given in Charts 4, 5 and 6 (pp. xxiv–xxvi). Chart 4 shows the interrelationship of the main types of institution involved in the provision of social services with special reference to the role of governments. Chart 5 gives more detail of the statutory services and can be seen as an enlargement of the central area of Chart 4. Chart 6 shows the distribution of responsibilities within the local authority system.

A quick glance at the charts shows that the structure is both complex and fragmented. One reason for this is the pragmatism which has preferred to make use of established institutions rather than develop new ones. But there are also issues of political principle involved. The increasing proportion of the gross national product channelled through government could have resulted in a dramatic increase in the power of central government as controller of the economy, provider of services and as employer. It could also have produced a stultifying rigidity that killed individual initiative. Fears of this encouraged a policy of delegation using existing institutions, setting up *ad hoc* bodies, and developing the work of the statutory local authorities. At the same time those who worked in the services, particularly professionals, have striven for a measure of autonomy through the vertical segmentation of the services on the basis of occupational skills.

Use of existing institutions

Before the widespread involvement of the state, the provision of services and the distribution of resources were undertaken by several different kinds of institution. These included the institutions of the economic market through trade and employment, families, local communities, philanthropic organisations and mutual-benefit or self-help associations. Religious bodies were at one time particularly important, combining the roles of mutual-benefit associations, local communities and philanthropic organisations.

The state has made use of all these types of institution, sometimes by encouragement, sometimes by compulsion and sometimes by providing financial support, with or without conditions attached. For example, the Poor Law placed responsibility for support of the destitute on local communities. The first Acts did so by exhortation, later Acts by compulsion. The local authorities in turn enforced family obligations and only assisted where these could not be fulfilled.

In general the autonomy of these institutions has been valued and respected by central government. It has been reluctant to intervene in their internal affairs except to prevent exploitation and to curb damage to society. Examples are the protection of children, the regulation and inspection of homes and institutions, and the regulation of employer-employee and landlord-tenant relations. Even when financial assistance is channelled through these institutions, surprisingly few controls are applied. This is particularly true where the assistance is given through tax concessions, like the allowances on covenanted subscriptions to charities or on superannuation contributions. But as the issues involved become politically more important, central government is likely to tighten its control. So Griffith in his study of the relations between central government department and local authorities found that the method and extent of central control tended to be influenced not by the efficiency or inefficiency of the services, but by their political importance.[23]

Each type of institution has its own pattern for the distribution of power and its own principles for the distribution of resources. For example, employing bodies, which hire labour through the economic market, tend to allocate power on a hierarchical basis, and income and conditions of service tend to follow the same pattern. Thus the terms of employers' superannuation schemes tend to be more favourable to those with higher status in the organisation. In contrast, mutual-benefit associations, families and philanthropic organisations base their provision on the ideal of meeting need, although their power structures vary. Mutual-benefit associations are governed by committees accountable to members who are also the consumers of the services; philanthropic organisations are paternalistic with accountability to subscribers; and families are paternalistic with a very high measure of autonomy. When the state uses these institutions it has to accept these basic patterns, which it can modify only to a limited extent.

Local government

Local authorities differ from the institutions already discussed in their accountability to a local electorate composed of those who pay for the services and those who use them. This accountability is considered to justify giving the authorities a large measure of autonomy in the exercise of very considerable powers and the control of large resources raised through their own taxes or received as subventions from central government. They also undertake a very wide range of tasks. Such delegation should make possible a flexible response to local needs and local opinion and the co-ordination of services at a local level. On the other hand it may make it more difficult for central government to ensure the maintenance of adequate standards in services over the country as a whole and may also interfere with national planning of the use of resources.

The pattern of local government that has recently been superseded was first instituted in 1888. It was based on the principle that the interests of town and country were separate, which was largely true at that time.[24] In the country areas, which were mainly rural and generally covered extensive areas with large but scattered populations, a two-tier system was introduced, county councils in the first tier, with urban districts, rural districts and non-county boroughs in the second tier. London was also made into a county with a second tier of London boroughs, with their own special powers. In other densely-populated urban areas, a single tier of all-purpose county boroughs was created. This system produced authorities of varied size in terms of geographical extent and population at all levels.[25]

It had long been recognised that shifts in population, changes in mobility and the structure of communications, and extension of the responsibilities of local authorities, had made the principles underlying that structure inappropriate. As people with work and interests in the towns have chosen to live outside their boundaries, and country dwellers have made increasing use of the cultural and economic facilities of the towns, the interests of town and country have converged. At the same time, it was also generally agreed that extreme variation in the size of authorities has made it difficult to define their responsibilities appropriately.

For many services there are technical factors which set a minimum size for efficiency. In some cases there is a minimum population that must be served to make it economical to provide a sufficient variety of institutions and services. For example, with education a local authority could be relatively small if it had responsibility only for primary education (though special education for categories of the handicapped would be a problem). But secondary education, with a greater variety of subjects and standards, requires a larger catchment area, and higher education a larger one still.

Geographical factors may also be important. In areas with a low-density population, the minimum population size for economical provision may have to be sacrificed in the interests of accessibility and democratic influence. Transport, water and river control are also influenced by geographical factors.

The minimum size for efficient operation of different services will tend to vary, and so may the optimum size. But, if the boundaries for different services are allowed to vary to meet these criteria, co-ordination becomes difficult, as in the different branches of the health service before 1974.[26] Any boundary will, therefore, represent a compromise, and within very broad limits there is no evidence that one compromise is better than another. On the other hand, if the authorities are larger rather than smaller, it may be possible to cope with the problem of remoteness by the creation of administrative districts of a smaller size but without the independence of a second-tier authority.

The size of authorities also affects relations with central government. A multiplicity of local authorities makes communication difficult. Griffith[27] found that communication with central departments was easier for those authorities near London and was carried on on a much more equal basis when larger authorities with chief officers and councillors of national standing were involved. Central departments had more confidence in larger authorities and some departments were more restrictive in their procedures generally in order to maintain effective standards in the weaker authorities.

If there was more confidence in the ability of all local authorities to act responsibly and efficiently, it would be much easier to remove what is at present the greatest limitation on the freedom of local authorities. This is the *ultra vires* rule, under which local authorities cannot provide any service, however desirable, unless they are specifically authorised to do so by legalisation, except within very narrow financial limits.[28]

These problems were examined in the reports of three Royal Commissions for Greater London, England and Scotland, and in two White Papers on local government in Wales.[29]

Generally four levels of administration were recognised below the national level. These were regional or provincial, 'county', district, and 'local' or neighbourhood level.

The regional or provincial level was seen as involving some five to eight provinces in England together with the countries of Scotland and Wales. The impetus for a regional tier of government has come from four directions; the need for strategic planning over areas wider than those covered by local authorities, congestion at the centre, demands for the democratisation of a rapidly growing regional bureaucracy and perhaps most important the perceived threats by nationalist movements in Scotland and Wales. The issues are well summed up in the Report of the Royal Commission on the Constitution,[30] which was set up in 1969 primarily because of the pressure for constitutional change in Scotland and Wales and to a lesser extent the English regions. The Commission reported in October 1973 and nationalist successes in the general elections of 1974 quickly brought its recommendations for Scotland and Wales to the forefront of a prolonged political debate which culminated in the Scotland and Wales Acts, 1978. Governmental consultations regarding devolution to the English regions revealed a lack of support for major reform and in November 1977, the government announced its intentions not to proceed with such reform in England. Just over a year later the fact that less than 40 per cent of the Scottish and Welsh electorates were prepared to support devolution in referenda held early in 1979 has made effective regional government very unlikely. This was confirmed in August 1979 by the Conservative government's abolition of the Regional Economic Planning Councils. These Councils created by a Labour government in 1964, were among the more influential of a number of bodies that have at different times and for different purposes taken into account the regional dimension. Still remaining are the Regional Economic Planning Boards composed of civil servants representing the regional interests of central departments with a general co-ordinating function in economic matters, and some regional bodies for specific services like the Regional Hospital Boards and the Regional Advisory Councils of the DES.[31] Some of these, like other 'Quangos', are under threat of abolition.

Administrative bodies at the lowest level, the neighbourhood or parish, were generally regarded as representing communities too small to carry responsibility for essential services, but all the reports recognised the importance of this local level because it is here that people are most likely to feel a sense of belonging to a community,[32] so that citizen participation in local government can be more easily stimulated.

From the point of view of the administration of the social services it is the two central levels, county and district, which are of most immediate significance. In the various reports referred to, three approaches to county-district organisation were put forward. In areas with the highest population densities in England a two-tier structure was proposed, with major environmental planning functions in the upper tier and most of the personal social services in the lower tier. In areas of low population density in Wales and Scotland a two-tier structure was proposed with most of the social services in the upper tier, but with some functions such as housing management, environmental health and recreational facilities in the lower tier. Third, for areas of intermediate population density in England and Wales, unitary authorities were proposed with responsibility for all these functions.

In the event the Conservative Government of 1970–4 decided on two-tier authorities throughout the country based on the first approach for metropolitan areas, similar to that already created for London in 1963,[33] and based on the second approach for all other areas. A rough guide to the distribution of responsibilities between counties and districts in the Greater London Area, metropolitan counties and the 'shire' counties is shown in Chart 6.

Some of the advantages of delegation to local authorities have been lost through traditions that have developed in local government. The Maud Committee on management in local government[34] was set up because of concern about apathy in local government and the failure to attract able people for positions of responsibility as councillors and principal officers. It commissioned a series of most useful studies of councils, councillors and the attitudes of their constituents. Its broad conclusion was that despite much excellent work, the country was not getting full value for the time and money spent on local authority services. The most important reason for this was that councillors concerned themselves too much with the day-to-day details of administration. As a result, decisions tended to be pushed up to the highest levels, overloading councillors and their principal officers with detailed decisions, and leaving no time for the examination of policy. The heavy burden of routine decisions discouraged the recruitment of able people and left councillors with too little time to make contact with their constituents. At the same time, the work was fragmented between too many separate departments without effective co-ordination at any level.

To meet these problems the Maud Committee recommended a clearer division of functions and responsibilities between councillors and their officers and the adoption of 'the guiding principle that issues are dealt with at the lowest level consistent with the nature of the problem'.[35] It also recommended a much more centralised structure involving a small management board of councillors, like the central government cabinet, responsible for policy to the council, with a chief executive to whom other principal officers would be accountable.

This strong central control was unacceptable to many people, and the issues were given further consideration by a study group on local authority management structures which prepared a series of recommendations to guide the councils of the new authorities.[36] These are known by the name of the chairman of its Working Group as the Bains Report. There is evidence that its recommendations have been very influential in determining the way many of the authorities have planned their structures.[37] In particular the new authorities are more likely than the old to have fewer committees and departments, a policy committee with sub-committees for personnel, land and finance, a chief executive with formal authority over other chief officers and no departmental responsibilities of his own, and a management team of officers holding regular and frequent meetings.

The determination of the Conservative government to reduce public expenditure has resulted in a running battle between central and local government. Central government has reduced intervention on how local councils use their resources, but has taken new powers to control their total expenditure. Failure to reach required reductions in expenditure is to be met by reducing central grants. This reduction can only be met by increasing the local rates. Many local authorities seem prepared to maintain expenditure despite this effect, and the government is now threatening to take new powers to control increases in the rates. Local accountability would be very seriously threatened.

Ad hoc bodies and direct provision

It has already been pointed out that the most important reasons for using existing institutions to provide services are political. This is particularly true in the subsidising of voluntary organisations. The absence of direct accountability to a popular electorate is regarded as making it easier to pioneer new developments and to meet the needs of some of those who are in conflict with state institutions or the standards of society. Where a suitable voluntary body does not exist the state may set up semi-autonomous *ad hoc* bodies fully financed by central government. Examples are the Race Relations Board, the Community Relations Commission, and Regional and District Health Authorities of the National Health Service.[38]

These *ad hoc* bodies have been christened 'Quangos'—Quasi-Autonomous Non-Governmental Organisations. Attention has been focused on the opportunity that these bodies provide for government patronage through the appointment of full-time and part-time members. Concern has also been expressed about whether their cost is justified. There are over 3,000 Quangos and they are estimated to cost almost £8 billion a year to run. The present Conservative government planned to disband many of them, and to make substantial cuts in others, but there is little evidence that it has managed to make more than marginal changes.[39]

It is really only as a last resort that social services are provided and administered directly by central government. Thus Beveridge justified central provision of social security benefits on the grounds (a) of the importance of uniformity of rates, conditions and procedures; (b) that social justice required that costs be met nationally, and this in turn required that expenditure should also be controlled nationally; and (c) on the grounds of economies of scale.[40] In addition he was probably influenced by the political importance of the issues involved requiring tight central control. Similar factors have tended to justify central administration of such services as the prisons, and the special hospitals for criminals who are mentally ill or subnormal.

This list of reasons justifying central provision serves as a reminder of the problems created by a policy of delegation to independent institutions. Broadly, while making possible greater flexibility, delegation also makes control more difficult to exercise. This in turn results in discrepancies in the provisions in different areas and problems of co-ordination between organisations with complementary functions.

Vertical segmentation of the social services

A policy of delegation results in horizontal discontinuities in the administration of services. But it is also evident that the British social services are divided vertically as well. This segmentation is based on the categorisation of needs in relation to the skills and knowledge required to meet them. The principle involved was clearly enunciated in connection with the division of responsibilities between Area Health Boards and local authorities, when the National Health Service was about to be reorganised:[41]

> After carefully considering the contrasting views expressed on these questions, the Government has decided that the services should be organised according to the main skills required to provide them rather than by any categorisation of primary user.

In other words, medical services should be provided through the National Health Service, social work services through the local authority social services departments, and these should be separated from other services such as education and environmental health provided by the local authorities.

In putting forward this principle the government was giving formal recognition to a long-term trend, which is particularly clearly seen in the departmentalism of local authorities. This phenomenon was discussed in the Maud Report. First the law requires local authorities to appoint certain officers and certain committees with specialist functions. But beyond this, with the growth of specialisation, there is a tendency[42]

> for specialists who do not head departments to seek principal officer status which, apart from considerations of pay, is often seen as providing:
> (a) an apex for a career structure for those specialists;
> (b) a degree of professional independence;
> (c) direct access to members in committee to whom professional advice can be proffered.

Thus departmentalism and vertical segmentation more generally are seen as proceeding in part at least from professional pressures for autonomy and influence. The department provides a territory within which professional knowledge and skills can be effectively employed and professional values given expression. Access to the committee gives opportunities for influence over policy and in the demand for additional resources. The career structure is seen as an added attraction for the able entrants that every profession needs. In this connection it is worth noting that the skills given recognition in separate organisations are the skills of those with relatively high status, who control in these organisations a large number of people with other skills with less prestige. In the health service doctors are outnumbered by other auxiliary workers; so are social workers in local authority social services departments.

Apart from the benefits to the staff of the services, segmentation on the basis of skills or processes does assist the development of services. A specialist service is able to define its values and goals—and therefore its priorities—relatively clearly, so that decisions can be made more quickly on the basis of consistent principles. It also ensures that the specific needs met by those specialist skills are not neglected. Unfortunately, the very advantages that such a structure creates also have their reverse effects. The focus provided by skills and processes is narrow in terms of the totality of human need, and provides the basis for conflict between departments both at policy level and in the services provided to individual consumers.[43]

At consumer level it leads to inadequate diagnosis and inadequate treatment. Specialists tend to diagnose a problem in relation to what they themselves can offer. If the kind of treatment they can offer seems to provide any hope of improvement they are likely to try it; if, before or after such a trial, they feel they cannot help, they are likely to turn the client away. They generally know too little about the skills and assistance available from other sources to be able to make effective referrals, or to compromise their own criteria for determining action in order to make a joint attack on a problem.[44] Many, perhaps even most, of the problems that face the clients of the social services require a combination of different kinds of assistance for their solution. To ensure that the right combination is in fact provided at the right time requires co-ordination, and this in turn seems to need the presence of a person with the authority to ensure that co-operation takes place. In a segmented structure like that of the British social services, there is unlikely to be anyone with formal authority at the right level to take such decisions. The emergence of someone with informal authority in any particular case is a matter of chance. In general the co-ordinator's role is left to the client, who usually lacks both the knowledge and the influence to perform it.

At policy level similar problems tend to arise. In particular externalities arise in the decision-making process, that is to say the decisions of one department fail to take into account the costs and benefits that their decisions create for other departments. Thus decisions in the hospital service to concentrate on patients who present the likelihood of improvement, and discharge chronic patients, may put additional costs and burdens on community services and on families which they may not be able to meet; while the failure of local authorities to provide adequate hostel accommodation may result in a more expensive form of care in hospitals.[45] Similarly within a local authority inadequate provision of sheltered housing by one department may throw higher costs on social services departments. This is a useful reminder that putting separate functions in the same organisations will not result in co-ordinated activity unless appropriate administrative machinery is instituted. There is little indication that bringing together the separate Ministries of Health and Social Security has resulted in common policies. In contrast, in the same department a real effort seems to be being made to relate health and personal social services through, for example, 'Policy Divisions', which attempt to identify the needs of particular groups such as the elderly and mentally handicapped persons, and to find ways of meeting their needs 'regardless of service boundaries'.

Two alternative approaches to these problems of co-ordination have been proposed and in some cases implemented. Where a single authority has diverse responsibilities a more centralised management structure has been considered appropriate with greater emphasis on management techniques in decision-making and the monitoring of results. This can be seen in the proposals of the Maud and Bains Reports discussed earlier. It is also evident in the reorganisation of the National Health Service[46] and in the thinking of the Fulton Committee on the Civil Services[47] and the Seebohm Report on local authority personal social services.[48] The alternative approach is to retain separate organisations and to encourage co-ordination through joint committees, cross-representation on committees, and joint or seconded appointments. This is the approach that has been necessarily adopted with regard to co-operation between the local authorities and the National Health Service[49] and is recommended by the Bains Report with regard to other issues.

It is not surprising that the problems of co-ordination revealed in the statutory services are even more in evidence in relations between the large number of independent voluntary organisations. The National Corporation for the Care of Old People in its annual report for 1973 noted 'the incredible patchwork of local bodies and branches of national organisations . . . with varied accessibility and vast differences in expertise'. It pointed, too, to the difficulties created by the persistence of voluntary organisations that lose touch with their subject, and are ill-equipped to perform any function, having no knowledge of the needs and conditions prevailing in their locality, and no communication with other voluntary organisations. Lack of communication can lead to competing activities with consequent waste of resources, and the poaching of volunteers will lead to bad relationships between agencies. The ideal situation as outlined in the report is one where the statutory services are matched by voluntary organisations that earn respect because of their expertise and involvement.

The National Corporation is one of a number of national bodies which aim to co-ordinate and promote the work of voluntary agencies. Others include the National Association for Mental Health, now called MIND, and Age Concern England, while the National Council of Voluntary Service has broad responsibilities, promoting cooperation between agencies at local and national level.

At local level there are similar bodies, often affiliated to a national body. Local councils of social or voluntary service have been set up in many areas. Considerable impetus was given to this movement recently, when the changes in local authority boundaries were affected. Voluntary agencies that had formerly enjoyed local authority or council of social service 'support' were faced with the need to establish new relationships in newly defined areas. Furthermore, the requirement that voluntary organisations should be represented on the Community Health Councils made it imperative that there should be some organisational machinery through which the agencies could arrange for representation. Councils of voluntary service already established were able to advise and assist the formation of new councils in their own areas, while the national body adopted as advisory and supportive role.

The European dimension

Before concluding this chapter some comment must be made on the influence or potential influence of British membership of European organisations on its social policy.

The first attempt to inaugurate a political union in post-war Europe was the establishment of the Council of Europe in 1949. Perhaps the most enduring result of that initiative was the signing of the European Convention of Human Rights and the setting up of the European Court of Human Rights to enforce its provisions.[50] Britain is one of the signatories. The convention covers civil and political rights derived from the United Nations Universal Declaration of Human Rights of 1948, Articles 3 to 21. It covers such matters as the right to fair trial, freedom of expression and assembly, the protection of privacy and the rejection of inhuman or degrading treatment or punishment. Petitions may be submitted to the European Commission of Human Rights by individuals as well as organisations and states. The Commission or the government of any state subscribing to the convention may refer a matter to the European Court of Human Rights. Most matters raised have concerned the administration of criminal justice.

The most far-reaching European organisation is, however, the European Economic Community (EEC) which, together with the European Coal and Steel Community and Euratom, Britain joined in 1972. The EEC, as its name indicates, was originally set up for economic purposes, although many people see its ultimate goal as some sort of political union. In the period in which it was set up, the dominant economic philosophy of Western Europe was one of *laissez-faire*, although the maintenance of full employment on a Keynesian model was seen as both necessary and possible. Thus social policy was seen as secondary to economic objectives.

The Treaty of Rome which inaugurated the EEC places certain obligations on its member states with regard to their internal administration.[51] These are enforced by the states' own courts, although the latter can refer issues to the European Court of Justice for rulings on the interpretation of Community law. The most important obligations are concerned with ensuring free movement of goods, capital, persons and services between member states. In particular the Treaty forbids any action that would result in discrimination against nationals of another member state with regard to employment, social security and health provisions.

Member states are also required to ensure equal pay for men and women in similar employment. The Commission of the European Communities must also concern itself with such matters as labour law and working conditions, prevention of occupational accidents and diseases, basic and vocational training, the right of association and collective bargaining between employers and workers. This is partly to ease mobility, but also, no doubt, to prevent unfair economic competition.

The Treaty also had to recognise that the development of a free economic market between member states would make some groups vulnerable to economic disaster. The two groups whose needs were originally recognised were workers displaced by the rationalisation of production (an issue first raised in the earlier European Coal and Steel Community) and farmers. For the former a Social Fund was established. The incomes of the latter were protected by the Common Agricultural Policy (CAP). However, by the end of the 1960s it was becoming clearer that other groups were also paying a price for the increased prosperity of the Community as a whole. Certain areas, like southern Italy and south-western France, were suffering a severe relative decline. Some people, whose work was marginal to the needs of the economy, like immigrant and handicapped workers, women and some older and younger people, were also suffering deprivation. To avoid social and political friction the *laissez-faire* economic policy had to be counter-balanced by social policies supported by the Community.[52]

In response to these pressures, a social action programme was prepared and approved in January 1974. The programme was primarily concerned with employment including the development of training schemes, equality of opportunity between men and women, worker participation in management, safety at work and the protection of workers' rights. There was also provision for supporting regional development. But a few proposals were less directly related to industry. These included proposals for the control of environmental pollution and to establish pilot schemes to combat poverty.

The actual achievements since 1974 have been minimal, and the expenditure on the CAP has continued to exceed by far expenditure on other social objectives. It is still difficult to see whether the importance of the EEC contribution to social policy will increase. On the one hand maintaining the unity of the EEC will require that more account is taken of the social effects of its economic policies; on the other hand the pressures of recession may drive individual members to take defensive action which will make common policies more difficult to achieve.

Further reading

History to 1948

In attempting to cover more than a century and a quarter of history in a few thousand words, the truth is inevitably distorted by the absence of detail and by the personal elements in the selection of material. It is therefore particularly important that students should supplement this chapter by further reading on their own account. The literature available is massive, so there is an inevitably arbitrary quality about the books selected for this list.

For a general introduction to the ideological background of reform in the nineteenth century Dicey is a classic that is short, easy to read and stimulating, although it has been criticised for over-emphasising the political importance of *laissez-faire* doctrines.

Bruce (1968), Fraser (1973) and Marshall provide narrative accounts of the development of the social services with varying amounts of detail. Marshall is the shortest and easiest to read, and Bruce the most detailed. Such books can usefully be supplemented and made more vivid by collections of extracts from original contemporary sources such as Bruce (ed.) (1973), Evans (ed.), Mayhew, Rose (1971) and Watkin. Rose (1972) gives a short and stimulating account of the knowledge available on attitudes to poverty and its relief in the period while Fraser (ed.) (1976) is a collection of scholarly essays on the Poor Law in practice. Rowntree's study of York is another classic that is brief (it can be read in about an hour) and well worth the time spent on it for the insight it gives into life and attitudes in the period. Heasman and Gosden throw much light on the voluntary sector which was so important in preparing for future state services.

Jones tackles a specific problem, immigration, in three periods, and in doing so throws considerable light on general social policy from the mid-nineteenth century to the 1960s. Her second chapter provides an excellent summary of the various explanations given for the development of social policy at different periods.

For the inter-war period Mowatt provides a very useful historical background and gives good coverage to the social services. Gilbert examines the policy-making process in that period in more detail. Titmuss (1950) and Ferguson and Fitzgerald are essential reading for developments in the Second World War.

M. BRUCE, *The Coming of the Welfare State*, 4th edn, Batsford, 1968.

M. BRUCE (ed.), *The Rise of the Welfare State*, Weidenfeld & Nicolson, 1973.

A. D. DICEY, *Law and Opinion in England in the Nineteenth Century*, 2nd edn, Macmillan, 1914.

E. J. EVANS (ed.), *Social Policy 1830–1914: Individualism, Collectivism and the Origins of the Welfare State*, Routledge & Kegan Paul, 1978.

S. M. FERGUSON and H. FITZGERALD, *Studies in the Social Services*, History of the Second World War, UK Civil Service, HMSO and Longmans, 1954.

D. FRASER, *The Evolution of the British Welfare State*, Macmillan, 1973.

D. FRASER (ed.), *The New Poor Law in the Nineteenth Century*, Macmillan, 1976.
B. B. GILBERT, *British Social Policy, 1914–1939*, Batsford, 1970.
M. GOSDEN, *Self-Help—Voluntary Associations in Nineteenth Century Britain*, New York, Barnes & Noble, 1974.
K. HEASMAN, *Evangelicals in Action—An Appraisal of their Social Work*, Bles, 1962.
C. JONES, *Immigration and Social Policy in Britain*, Tavistock, 1977.
T. H. MARSHALL, *Social Policy*, 3rd edn, Hutchinson, 1970.
HENRY MAYHEW, *Voices of the Poor*, ed. Anne Humphreys, Cassell, 1971.
C. L. MOWATT, *Britain Between the Wars, 1918–1940*, Methuen, 1955.
M. ROSE, *The English Poor Law, 1780–1930*, David & Charles, 1971.
M. ROSE, *The Relief of Poverty, 1834–1914*, Macmillan, 1972.
B. SEEBOHM ROWNTREE, *Poverty—A Study of Town Life*, Macmillan, 1901.
J. B. SMELLIE, *The History of Local Government*, Allen & Unwin, 1968.
R. M. TITMUSS, *Problems of Social Policy*, History of the Second World War, UK Civil Services, HMSO and Longmans, 1950.
B. WATKIN, *Documents on Health and Social Services, 1834 to the present day*, Methuen, 1975.

Background to the post-war period

Most of the literature on developments in this period is related to specific services and is referred to in the relevant chapters. Theoretical and conceptual works are listed together at the end of the final chapter. The list here is confined to three types of books—those on government, those on international comparisons, and two books on the British economy.

It is important that students of social administration should understand how local and central government in Britain work. On local government, Richards gives a good straightforward account of how it came to be reformed, and how it operates now, making use of recent research and government reports; Stanyer provides a more analytical approach based on systems theory; and Donnison provides case studies which give a vivid picture of the complexities of local policy change.

On central government, Hall, Land, Parker and Webb is exceptionally useful. Case studies of policy change at national level are preceded by a thorough examination of the evidence about structure and processes in central government and of the theoretical issues involved. The subsequent analysis also has practical implications for those who want to encourage change. Smith provides a systems analysis of central and local government. Griffith's case studies of central and local government relationships and his analysis have been used by many subsequent works (see pp. 11–13 of the text) although the first chapter is somewhat out of date. Shanks is a useful account of EEC social policy.

D. V. DONNISON, V. CHAPMAN *et al.*, *Social Policy and Administration: Studies in the Development of Social Services at the Local Level*, National Institute for Social Work Training and Allen & Unwin, 1965; *Social Policy and Administration Revisited*, NISW and Allen & Unwin, 1975.

J. A. G. GRIFFITH, *Central Departments and Local Authorities*, Allen & Unwin, 1967.

P. HALL, H. LAND, R. PARKER, and A. WEBB, *Change, Choice and Conflict in Social Policy*, Heinemann, 1975.

P. G. RICHARDS, *The Reformed Local Government System*, 2nd edn, Allen & Unwin, 1975.

M. SHANKS, *European Social Policy, Today and Tomorrow*, Pergamon, 1977.

B. SMITH, *Policy-Making in British Government—An Analysis of Power and Rationality*, Martin Robertson, 1976.

J. STANYER, *Understanding Local Government*, Martin Robertson—Fontana/Collins, 1976.

The literature on comparative social administration is rapidly growing. The value of it is that it provides a useful perspective for national studies. Its difficulty, for both writing and reading, is that there are so many complex variables to be considered, such as differences in history, culture and governmental institutions. Here are some examples:

A. HEIDENHEIMER, H. HECLO and C. T. ADAMS, *Comparative Public Policy: The Politics of Social Choice in Europe and America*, Macmillan, 1976.

M. KASER, *Health Care in the Soviet Union and Eastern Europe*, Croom Helm, 1976.

B. N. RODGERS, with J. GREVE and J. S. MORGAN, *Comparative Social Administration*, Allen & Unwin, 1968.

Economic policy provides an essential background to the development of the social services. Two books cover British economic policy over this period, Hackett up to 1967 and Stewart from 1964 to 1977.

J. and A. M. HACKETT, *The British Economy: Problems and Prospects*, Allen & Unwin, 1967.

M. STEWART, *Politics and Economic Policy in the UK Since 1964: The Jekyll and Hyde Years*, 2nd edn, Pergamon, 1978.

2 Education

Graham White

Historical introduction

Social histories of England and Wales illustrate the increasing role taken by central and local government in the management of people's lives. In taking over education the state assumed traditional socialisation functions of family and church, and from the struggles which ensued education came to be seen unequivocally as a social service. There is a continual reciprocal interaction between education and the other social institutions, such as the economy, the family, religion, politics and social class. An historical view highlights the complexity of that relationship and its effects upon education.

For most of the nineteenth century, education resembled moral training rather than the schooling of today, and was provided by voluntary bodies, mainly the churches,[1] who depended on subscriptions to finance building and running of schools.[2] Many of these were small and ill-equipped. Attempts to assist them financially from the rates provoked bitter arguments based mainly on the nature of the catechism taught at the various schools.

The Elementary Education Act, 1870, was a compromise which kept the voluntary schools, but empowered the government to 'fill the gaps'. In districts where no voluntary school existed, or where provision was inadequate, local School Boards were elected with power to levy a rate in order to build and maintain elementary schools providing a basic education only. The churches were allowed one year's grace to fill the gaps themselves, after which time any schools they might build competed with state schools subsidised out of public funds. The religious traditions persisted into the twentieth century and were a feature of R. A. Butler's presentation of the Bill leading to the Education Act, 1944.

Elementary education was compulsory up to the age of fourteen, and ran parallel with secondary education for several years without there being any fruitful contact between the two systems. The former provided an education suited to the needs of manual workers, the latter being appropriate for those destined for 'white-collar' jobs or for higher education. Inevitably, more powerful parents were able to use such a stratified educational provision to enhance the occupational opportunities of their own children.

In 1907 the Board of Education required all secondary schools maintained or aided by the local authority to reserve a percentage of places, usually one-quarter, for children from the elementary school who were awarded scholarships by their local authority. This was an attempt at creating equality of opportunity, but it was found in practice that it tended to benefit the children of artisans and small shopkeepers rather than the children of unskilled workers, a feature of the differentiation by social class that persists in education to this day.

Previously major reform had come with the Education Act, 1902, which (a) made available to voluntary schools money from local rates as well as taxes—which gave rise once again to bitter sectarian disputes; (b) replaced the School Boards with general purpose county and county borough councils, together with some smaller authorities, with the statutory *duty* of ensuring adequate provision of facilities for elementary education; and (c) gave permissive powers to the county and county borough councils to provide and grant-aid 'education other than elementary'. The fact that these powers were permissive meant that some authorities made generous provision whilst others made none at all. These disparities between districts have been inherited by our present educational system.

Towards the end of the nineteenth century 'higher grade' schools had grown up under the School Boards, providing a quasi-vocational technical training to complete the structure of elementary education for selected pupils. Poverty and malnutrition formed a barrier to achievement even when opportunities were there. The Education (Provision of Meals) Act, 1906, empowered local authorities to provide meals and milk for children in elementary schools. This was the first time that benefits in cash or kind had been given outside the machinery of the Poor Law. It heralded the breakdown of that system and the coming of the 'Welfare State'. Although the meals and milk service was provided not as an end in itself, but only in order to ensure that state-subsidised education did not merely involve the instruction of children but also extended to social care for them. Subsequent Acts soon compelled local authorities to provide medical inspection and treatment for the children in their care.

The Hadow Report of 1926, *The Education of the Adolescent*, recommended that at the age of 11 all children should enter a second stage of education which would be geared to their needs as adolescents. It suggested that the term 'grammar school' should be extended to include not only the older foundations, but also the county and municipal secondary schools which had been founded after the 1902 Act. These grammar schools would have a higher leaving age and a predominantly academic curriculum. Secondary education outside the grammar schools was to be provided in 'modern schools' with a less academic curriculum and with freedom of experiment. The report emphasised that these modern schools should be given parity of treatment with the grammar schools in terms of accommodation and equipment. Successive governments failed to raise the school-leaving age to 15, or to ensure suitable conditions for the development of secondary modern education. The Spens Report of 1938, *Secondary Education with Special Reference to Grammar Schools and Technical High Schools*, recommended a further diversification of the secondary system by including the junior, technical, commercial and trade schools which had been in existence for the some time.[3]

This 'Tripartite System', although it was not specifically enforced by the Education Act, 1944, became the pattern on which most local authorities based their immediate post-war planning of secondary education. Few technical schools were ever built, and by the beginning of the 1960s this tripartite outline was further blurred as secondary modern schools were offering academic courses and were entering their pupils for the General Certificate of Education examinations.

The Education Act, 1944, abolished fee-paying for local authority schooling and aimed to provide secondary education for all children according to age, aptitude and ability. The removal of the economic barrier was believed to make the social status of the family irrelevant to the child's chances of educational success. However, little was done about the 'public' or independent schools which continued to prosper outside the local authority system providing an elite sector for an educational syllabus which included the training in character, manners, speech and values many parents in the professional occupations seemed to prefer for their children.

The 1944 Act tried to solve the religious question by ascribing aided or controlled status to voluntary schools, and by implementing a regulation for religious instruction according to an agreed syllabus.[4] On the whole the denominations came out of the 1944 Act needing only to show willingness to meet costs of building, maintenance and improvements to be able to retain control.[5]

For two decades after 1944 the unsettled co-existence and sporadic co-operation between local and national government continued, without any serious challenge to the general principles laid down by

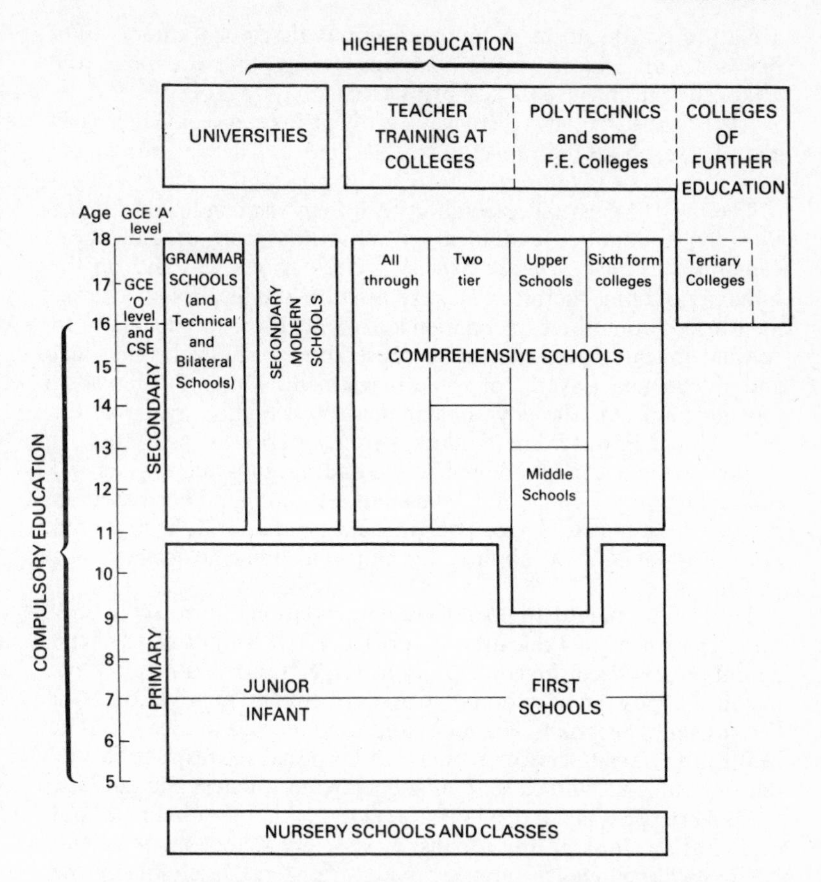

CHART 7 Educational provision in England and Wales. This diagram shows the main elements in the provision of maintained schools and of higher education in England and Wales. Source: *The Educational System of England and Wales*, HMSO, 1978, p. 41.

the Education Act, 1944. The Act left two Ministers responsible for educational policy, but the variety and scope of schools was left to local initiative. No effective coercive machinery was built in whereby central government could ensure control in crucial issues and the main decision-maker in educational policy was financial rather than legal. In spite of this imprecision there were only occasional organisational squabbles, until in 1964 the discontent about selection at eleven came fairly sharply to a head.

In recent years development of comprehensive schooling has been a feature of education in England and Wales. Such schools offer places to all children within an age group, and are now well established in most local authority areas.

Also during the 1960s there was a growing insistence, albeit largely speculative, about the impact of so-called cultural deprivation on the school careers of children.

The most influential research in this area was conducted for the Plowden Committee and forms a substantial part of the report *Children and their Primary Schools.*[6] Great stress was laid on the influence of home factors in any explanation of educational achievement. The committee recommended compensatory education to combat educational disadvantage caused by the physical, emotional and intellectual poverty of the environment. Upon the Plowden recommendations the government made £16 million available for Educational Priority Area buildings over a period of two years.

Plowden in a sense made public the findings of psychologists and sociologists in the 1950s and 1960s that selection methods based on inaccurate tests placed great weight on a child's social background and the wastage of ability through selection inefficiency was enormous.[7]

The Report made a number of recommendations aimed at not only the Department of Education and Science (DES), but at teachers, parents and indeed the community at large. The recommendations included allocation of resources to areas of cultural deprivation. As a forerunner of Seebohm, Plowden supported the idea of area teams of health and social service workers with specialists responsible for school problems, and closer contacts between teachers and parents.

Many suggestions were incorporated in relation to primary school organisation, looking for expansion in many school facilities and flexibility about ages of pupil entry and transfer. On school size the Report suggested 240 children on average for a first school, and 300–450 children in middle schools.

The committee was divided on religious education, and no changes were advised in that respect. Regular national surveys of attainment were supported, as was the total abolition of physical punishment in primary schools. Suggestions were made in detail about requirements for the training of nursery assistants, teacher aides and for fabric improvements. The committee also stated the need for clarification of the instruments of school management, and recommended the inclusion of teachers and parents on management bodies.

Other proposals echoed the desire for flexibility of organisation, including combinations of individual and group work in class, and variable school days, terms and years. Streaming was discouraged.

The committee felt there was a need for more generous staff-pupil ratios and considered part-time teachers and teacher aides as essential for expansion of the service, and also stressed the need for a full enquiry into teacher training.[8]

The White Paper *Education: A Framework for Expansion*[9] presented to Parliament on 6 December 1972 contained a ten-year programme for the development of education in England and Wales.[10] The rates of development were acknowledged to be variable but the hope was that central government, the local authorities and the various voluntary groups would co-operate to implement the plans framed under five headings in the White Paper. As in the past, central government offered tentative guidelines only. These have been variously summarised,[11] but briefly the five areas for increased expenditure were:

1 a new programme for the development of nursery education;
2 expansion of school building programmes for primary and secondary schools as well as a plan for special schools;
3 expansion of the teaching force to improve pupil–teacher ratios in schools;
4 reorganisation and improvement of preservice and in-service teacher training in pursuit of the James Report;
5 expansion of higher education opportunities, including the introduction of a two-year course leading to a new Diploma in Higher Education.

Many aspects of these aims were sacrificed to economic necessity during the later part of the decade, so that, for example, the expansion of the teaching force proposals were replaced by efforts to reduce numbers of students in initial training in colleges. However, slow progress was made in certain areas, and by 1977 there were over seventy centres with DES approval to offer courses for the Diploma in Higher Education.[12]

Structure of the present system

The law at present states that children must receive schooling from the age of 5. Since 1 September 1972[13] the minimum age for leaving school is 16.[14] Parents may send their children to a publicly maintained school, free of charge, or pay for the children to receive another recognised form of tuition. Financial assistance is generally available to any student choosing to continue his education beyond school.[15] The number of children attending full-time education in the maintained sector is shown in Table 3.

Nursery education

Children under 5 may be catered for either in nursery schools or in nursery classes within infant schools. Following the 1972 White Paper

TABLE 3 *Schools and their pupils*

Number of full-time pupils in maintained primary and secondary schools[a]

Age of pupils	*Jan. 1978*	*Jan. 1979*	*Jan. 1980*
Under 5	426,000	422,000	409,000
5–10	4,120,000	3,996,000	3,850,000
11–15	3,530,000	3,542,000	3,525,000
16+	275,000	283,000	293,000
Total	8,351,000	8,243,000	8,077,000

Number of maintained schools

	Jan. 1978	*Jan. 1979*	*Jan. 1980*
Nursery	593	593	596
Primary[b]	21,372	21,309	21,242
Secondary[b]	4,711	4,694	4,680
Total	26,676	26,596	26,518[c]

[a]Including pupils at immigrant centres, but excluding pupils at maintained nursery and special schools.
[b]The figures for primary and secondary schools include those schools deemed 'middle'.
[c]The total number of school closures approved in 1980 was 112.[16]

Education: A Framework for Expansion large resource allocations were made to local authorities for expansion of nursery provision, and programmes of research and development were announced by the DES. No detailed proposal was laid down and directions were flexible in order to allow plans to reflect local needs and resources. Nevertheless it was hoped that priority would be given to areas of social deprivation and to children with special needs. Nursery provision was planned generally on a part-time basis, and the hope was that play-groups and other schemes should expand alongside maintained provision.[17]

By the summer of 1976 almost half the local authorities in England and Wales had relinquished all or part of their allocations and the nursery education programme was being scaled down. Paradoxically further research projects were still being sponsored bringing the total in 1976 to six.[18]

From 1980, as economic stringencies began to bite, the future of local authority provided nursery education was threatened by a late amendment to the Education (No.2) Bill which received Royal

Assent on 4 April, removing from local authorities the obligation to provide nursery education. However, any plans for nursery school closure had to be referred to the Secretary of State for prior approval, a caveat which made more than one authority rethink hastily conceived policies.

In January 1980 there were 215,800 children occupying maintained nursery with a further 213,500 4-year-olds going to infant schools, more than half of these being 'rising fives'.

There is considerable nursery provision in the private sector, where places are fee-paid, and where well over half the children attend part-time.

Primary schools

The first stage of compulsory education takes place at the primary school. The majority of primary schools accommodate children of both sexes from 5 upwards. Other schools are Infant only (5–7) or Junior only (7+upwards). Generally primary schools cater for between 100 and 300 pupils each. Of the 2,000 Welsh primary schools those in Welsh-speaking areas instruct in the Welsh language and there are also bilingual schools in some English-speaking parts of Wales.

Middle schools

To enter secondary school pupils leave the primary phase at 11, but in many areas middle schools have been developed. These vary in the age ranges catered for according to the preference of the local authority concerned, with intakes of 8–12-year-olds, 9–13-year-olds, or 10–13-year-olds. Although middle school units did exist in larger comprehensive schools, Wallasey was the first authority, in 1968–9, to begin changing to middle schools in the 9/10–13 age range, with upper schools for 13–18-year-olds. The DES paper *Launching Middle Schools* traces their development in one West Riding area, and it was at Bradford that the first purpose-built middle school opened in January 1969. As with all comprehensive schooling there is a great variety of middle schools though they all represent the general enthusiasm of the early 1970s for the trend towards unstreamed teaching.[19]

Secondary schools

Comprehensivisation being incomplete means that a great mix of available schooling exists. This makes it almost meaningless to think of *a* system of secondary education. However, by 1980, 88 per cent of secondary school age children (approximately 3 million) attended the 3,647 comprehensive schools.

In July 1965 the Labour government of the day had issued a circular[20] requesting local authorities to reorganise their secondary schooling on comprehensive lines, and including plans of six schemes, already proposed or in operation, for local consideration. The schemes adopted reflect the resourcefulness and initiative, or lack thereof, of local education authorities, rather than any government direction. In consequence, without any legislative teeth, the responses of local authorities led to a total picture that was at best confused. Nevertheless, by 6 October 1967, the *Times Educational Supplement* could show that 159 of 194 local education authorities had submitted reorganisation schemes in response to Circular 10/65. The mixture of schemes so proposed went largely unchallenged by the DES even where plans which Circular 10/65 had advised against were included—especially proposals for middle schooling. The lack of clarity about what was intended persisted so that no clear statement was made, for example, about the position of direct grant[21] schools, and the implication was that this should be left to local decision. The anomalies so presented were alarmingly exacerbated by the introduction in June 1970 of Circular 10/70 by the new Conservative government without the customary consultation. Circular 10/70 allowed Secretary of State Thatcher to 'free' secondary reorganisation to become the responsibility of local authority enterprise. It had been recognised too late that only by law could comprehensive reform take place and the 1970 Education Bill was interrupted by the General Election and nothing reached the Statute books. The cumulative effect of Circulars 10/65 and 10/70 was to pin the debates about comprehensives to the local level and fitfully the growth of comprehensive schools has gone on. Without central direction no comprehensive *system* emerged. In March 1974 the minority Labour government issued a further circular in the saga. This repeated the election promises to end selection in education, though by the General Election in October 1974 legislation had still not been introduced. The bite in the circular came with the undertaking that only building programmes designed for comprehensive schooling would be supported.

The comprehensive schemes outlined in Circular 10/65 were as follows:

1 The 'all-through' school taking children from eleven to eighteen. This was the pattern favoured by the Wilson government since it had already been a success in some local authority areas[22] and it came to be regarded at the time as the 'orthodox' scheme.

2 Tiered schools of broadly three kinds; first those where all pupils transfer at 13 or 14 from a lower school or tier to an

upper one; second a parallel-tiered model where only some pupils, by choice or selection, go on to a higher tier; and third a type where at 13 or 14 pupils may opt, or be selected for, a long or short course.

3 The standard 11–18 format may be divided into a lower 11–16 school followed by either a sixth-form course or a junior college.

4 Middle schools, as described above, leading on to one of the secondary comprehensive models.

The Education Bill requiring all local authorities to introduce a system of non-selective comprehensive education received Royal Assent on 22 November 1976. At the time eight recalcitrant local authorities were pressed to submit proposals for comprehensive reorganisation within six months. Encouraged by Conservative Party pledges to repeal the Act upon coming to power, Tameside local authority notoriously continued to defy the government in the summer of 1977. On 18 April 1978 Shirley Williams, the Secretary of State for Education and Science, told the Commons that only six local authorities had failed to abolish selection in secondary education, or had not submitted plans to do so. Little over a year later, Mark Carlisle, the Secretary of State in the newly elected Thatcher administration, whilst recognising the extent of commitment in some areas to comprehensive schooling, still repeated his party's intention of permitting local authorities to implement the secondary school system of their choice. The Education Act of 1979 gained Royal Assent in July and effectively repealed Labour's 1976 moves to press home comprehensivisation. Thus were local authorities released to withdraw the earlier mandatory proposals for secondary school development along comprehensive lines and to retain existing divided provision, or even, if they so wished, to split comprehensive schools back into the old grammar and modern schools again.

Many observers believe that comprehensive schools, by drawing all their children from one geographical area, emphasise differences between social classes, and that even where the social classes do mix in such schools, it is the working-class pupils who move downstream whilst others press ahead towards 'O' level examinations.[23] Therefore any provision which continues to segregate children from different social groups is regarded as undesirable. Nevertheless, whatever the prevalent arguments around this issue in relation to comprehensive schools, one aspect of educational privilege clearly persists in the presence of the independent schools.

Independent and voluntary schools

A number of independent schools, particularly those that are members of the Headmasters' Conference, the Governing Bodies

Association or the Governing Bodies of Girls' Schools Association, are known as public schools. The title public school is a misleading archaism as these schools are mostly independent, and are very exclusive in their intake. Originally the title appears to have referred to those better boarding grammar schools which attracted pupils from a wide area, and so were 'public' by comparison with others which were bound by the terms of their foundation to take only local children. Though many public schools are grant-aided in some way or another, the title still carries great prestige value, and received a certain official recognition when the President of the Board of Education set up the Fleming Committee[24] in 1942 to examine the relationship of the public schools to the rest of the education system. The Public Schools Commission, 1968,[25] found public schools to be socially divisive in recruiting and segregating a special group of children from the majority, a finding echoed by many individuals and pressure groups who believe that the public schools are the strongest remaining bastion of privilege in the educational system and who wish to bring them into the maintained sector whilst at the same time preserving their educational excellence.

By the summer of 1981 the DES had published a list of 229 independent schools offering places under the Assisted Places Scheme. This scheme was designed to allow clever children of less well off parents to receive their secondary education at an independent school, and after having received a stormy passage through Parliament the regulations applying to the Assisted Places Scheme were approved by the Commons on 30 October and by the House of Lords on 4 November 1980. This meant that assistance was now available to be calculated according to a means test scale based on parental gross income up to £10,000 per annum, and in certain cases, depending for example upon the number of other children in the family, beyond this figure. Councils not agreeing to publicise or otherwise refusing to co-operate in the scheme were threatened with a possible change in legislation to deny them their legal right of refusal. It is in the early 1980s, a matter for bitter contention that funds in the order of £70 million of public money should be available for assisted places which appear to be based on the premise that only independent schools are able to offer appropriate education for the best pupils, and that correlatively schools in the maintained sector are not.

Action had earlier been taken to phase out the direct grant schools. The 174 of them existing in 1975 received a *per capita* grant in return for an allocation of at least one quarter of their places to pupils from maintained primary schools. The local education authority had then to pay the standard fee for such pupils. The remainder of the direct grant school intake was of children whose fees were paid, partly or wholly, by parents. On 5 May 1975 the DES informed these schools that no further money would be paid in respect of pupils taken on after 1 August 1976 unless by 1 January 1977 plans were in hand to become part of the maintained sector. In spite of concerted objections, direct grant schools began to be phased out during that year, 51 of them indicating their choice to enter the maintained sector, the rest either closing down or 'going independent' (48 of 51 Roman Catholic direct grant grammar schools going to the maintained sector).

Within the maintained sector there exists a number of voluntary schools. In January 1981 there were about 8,300 such schools, and of these some 3,500 were of controlled status. Controlled schools are those where the facilities are the property of the voluntary body—being in most cases affiliated either to the Church of England or Roman Catholic Church—but where recurrent and capital expenditure is met by the local education authority. Restrictions are imposed on the composition of governing bodies of such schools. In aided schools playing fields are provided and internal repairs are undertaken at the expense of the local education authority but other repairs or alterations are the responsibility of the governing body and have to conform to set standards.

Further and higher education

Further education is a term used to embrace any form of education which takes place after the school career has ended, but may exclude universities and colleges of education, which are regarded as centres of higher education. It is the duty of local education authorities to ensure sufficient provision of facilities for full- and part-time education for people over compulsory school age. Each authority, having taken into account any local university or similar provision, adheres to a working plan for further education in its area which the Secretary of State must approve.

The field of further education is one of considerable scope, and courses in vocational as well as academic subjects are offered to craft or professional qualifications, to O- and A-levels, and to first and higher degree standard, the equivalent of higher education qualifications from the universities.

Diverse provision allows for considerable flexibility. There are no age restrictions and basic or advanced courses allow individuals to work up to whatever standard they can achieve. This is reflected not only in the wide range of courses but indeed in the variety of further education institutions. These include the new polytechnics which are now the main centres for higher education qualifications within the further education provision, and colleges of commerce and arts, agricultural and technical colleges as well as the evening institutes. Attendance at these centres has increased steadily in recent years. By 1980 there were around 350,000 students on advanced programmes of various kinds. As well as full-time or sandwich courses, which have periods at college alternating with practical on-job training, study may be part-time, e.g. one day a week (day release) or for days or weeks at a time (block release) or on an evenings-only basis.

In addition to the local authority controlled colleges there are some colleges serving specialist interests. Many of them receive financial support from the DES, whilst others, like some secretarial or correspondence colleges, remain independent and largely rely on fees.

Liaison between local authorities and local industry and commerce in matters of further education is common. Firms favour a day or block release programme, often associated with formal in-work training. The qualifications for which such trainees study include the certificates of the City and Guilds of London Institute, and the regional training bodies. Occasionally specialist full-time short courses might be arranged to suit the needs of a particular group or industrial concern.

Polytechnics developed rapidly during the 1970s and now offer courses which are wide ranging in both content and intake, and provide teaching towards degree level or its equivalent as well as professional and higher national qualifications. Degree courses may lead to external University of London degrees but increasingly they relate to the degrees for the Council for National Academic Awards.[26]

The Secretary of State for Education ensures sufficient resources for teacher training. Where necessary a local authority may be directed to make provision for teacher training and other authorities may be required to assist in the expenses incurred.[27] It is necessary for teachers to be qualified in order to teach in maintained schools. The initial course of training lasts for three years, but after any form of training course, teachers taking up first posts in maintained schools have to serve a probationary period of one year to demonstrate their practical classroom ability. Graduates used to be accorded qualified teacher status without undergoing a course of training, and this also applied to possessors of advanced specialist qualifications other than degrees. Such people qualifying in between 1970 and 1973 could only teach in secondary schools, and since 31 December 1973 all graduates wishing to teach are required to follow a one-year course of teacher training.

Four-year courses leading to B.Ed. degrees include professional qualifications, and one-year post-graduate training is available at twenty-eight university departments of education. Thirteen art training centres offer similar courses for students with advanced qualifications in art, and there are four colleges specialising in one-year training for those graduates intending to teach in further education. In many instances validation of courses and examinations at the various institutions of higher education remains the responsibility of the education or college studies section of the local university.[28]

Recent development of the polytechnics has been closely associated with the re-structuring of the colleges of education. In January 1977 the Secretary of State accepted the proposal by the Advisory Committee on the Supply and Training of Teachers for a severe reduction of initial teacher training places by 1981. This ultimately meant closure for 20 of the 163 colleges and polytechnic departments of education. Others would be called upon to take on a wider spread of courses, sometimes alone, but more often in a merger with the polytechnics.

In 1974 the first amalgamations took place. By November 1976 the future of only sixteen colleges remained to be decided and the Advisory Committee was recommending that teacher training provision for 1981 should be reduced to 45,000 places (including 10,000 for in-service training) capable of stretching to accommodate 60,000 students if necessary. At that time, over 7,000 trained school teachers were registered as being unemployed. When the last entry to non-graduate certificate teacher training courses took place at the beginning of the academic year 1979–80 the estimated total of teacher training places was in the region of 43,500, a contraction which has been designed to match expected future needs of a declining school population. Institutions have been asked to give priority to recruiting students to main courses which correspond to the areas of teacher shortage in schools, and to favour those intending to teach in secondary schools.

Universities

The British universities operate on a national basis so that suitably qualified people from any part of the UK may, if admitted, go to any of the universities in England, Wales, Scotland and Northern Ireland.[29]

Full-time university undergraduate courses to first degree level are generally of three years duration. The 250,000 or so students in 1980 were distributed between arts, science and medicine in a ratio of 50:41:9. Plans for future rationalisation of the universities, drawn up under the influence of the Thatcher administration, should change the ratios to 48:42:10 by the end of 1981. About 20 per cent of full-time students are post-graduate, either working for higher degrees and diplomas or engaged in research. Compared with the education system in general a favourable staff-student ratio exists in the universities, at present averaging about 8:1. Within individual universities or departments there may be considerable variations in this figure, and as economic cut-backs take effect the overall figure is becoming less favourable; a consequence partly of the introduction of full cost fees for all overseas students other than those from EEC countries.

In addition to the conventional universities[30] the Open University offers part-time courses leading to degrees. Instruction is carried on by correspondence, short residential courses, tutorials and through the radio and TV media. The Open University differs in other respects in that there are no formal academic requirements of entrants, and qualifications are awarded on a credits system. Six credits are needed for the ordinary BA degree and eight credits for an Honours degree. Courses and credits may be combined in a variety of ways to cater for students' abilities, though for a degree with Honours a minimum of two credits must be at the higher grades 3 or 4 of academic content.

In 1978 there were more than 60,000 students registered as undergraduates of the OU and plans were well in hand to equal that number in the continuing education sector by 1995.

Adult education

The range of provisions of facilities for people over compulsory school age is extremely wide. Local education authority provision, extra-mural departments at universities and Workers' Education Association centres predominate, though HM Forces, the trade unions, the YMCA, the National Federation of Women's Institutes and other responsible bodies also make provision.

Courses range from full-time of one- or two-year duration, at residential centres like Ruskin College or Coleg Harlech, to short sessions provided by special organisations. Fees charged do not cover the cost of provision, in order to encourage all who wish to study to take part.

By 1980 there were about 1,650,000 students enrolled at adult education centres and local authority evening institutes, a low level of enrolments not matched since the early 1970s.

The adult literacy campaign, begun in 1972, achieved remarkable success. Within the first five years of operation almost 100,000 adults with difficulties in reading and writing had received tuition. The Adult Literacy Resource Agency formed in 1975 was replaced in 1978 by the Adult Literacy Unit, financed by the DES, which acts as a focus for adult literacy, commissioning special projects, and channelling funds to voluntary bodies engaged in this kind of work. This in turn was replaced by the wider remit of an Adult Literacy and Basic

Skills Unit for an initial period of three years from 1 April 1980. The bulk of their financial allocation goes to employing staff to assist local authorities in the furtherance of the campaign, all of which authorities offer tuition facilities. In 1980 the number of voluntary helpers in the scheme was around the 35,000 mark, a fall over previous years reflecting the growing emphasis on group rather than individual tuition.

Special schools and education welfare provisions

Special schools

The Education Act, 1944,[31] laid down that special educational treatment should be provided either in special schools or provision made within ordinary schools elsewhere for pupils suffering from disability of mind or body. Some handicapped children may attend ordinary schools, or other maintained special schools, including hospital schools for in-patients, whereas others may go to non-maintained special, mostly boarding, schools of which there are some 110, where fees are paid in full by the local education authorities.

Special schools exist for certain categories of handicapped children, where the handicap is of such a nature and degree as to prevent the child from benefiting from primary or secondary education alongside normal children.[32]

Special educational treatment is provided for pupils who are blind, partially sighted, deaf, partially deaf, educationally subnormal, epileptic, maladjusted, physically handicapped, delicate or suffering from speech defects not due to deafness.

The Education (Handicapped Children) Act of 1970 provides that certain severely mentally disabled children be regarded as needing special education. From 1 April 1971, the education service took responsibility for the 30,000 or so children concerned. Before that date these children were regarded as being unsuitable for education, and care and training arrangements were left to local health authorities.

The intention of special schooling is to provide a stimulating and diverse educational environment to endeavour to overcome the learning difficulties of the handicapped child, aiming at a degree of self-reliance and responsibility in adult life. Special schools are comparatively favourably staffed and in certain cases provide speech therapy, physiotherapy and other specialised treatment as well as special teaching facilities.

Of the maintained special schools about 75 per cent are day schools, although in some cases of severe handicap where day schooling is inappropriate or where long journeys to and from home may be necessary, boarding accommodation is provided free of charge. In circumstances where to remain at a special school beyond the age of sixteen is clearly an advantage this can sometimes be arranged.

The largest group in receipt of special schooling is that of the educationally subnormal. These are pupils who 'by reason of limited ability or some other condition resulting in educational retardation require some specialised form of education'.[33] They are children who are not necessarily intellectually backward, but who may suffer educational difficulties as a result of illness, environmental or emotional problems.

Identification of children in need of special education is the duty of the local authority. Any child of two or over may be called for medical examination; a legal notice may be served on parents if necessary, requiring them to submit the child for examination.

On the basis of the medical officer's report, with information from the educational psychologist and the teacher, the educational needs of the child are then determined. The parents' wishes are considered and should they disagree with the local education authority's decision they can appeal to the Secretary of State. Decisions regarding special schooling can only be made on an individual basis bearing in mind the social and psychological needs, as well as the educational and physical needs, of the child and the resources of the authority. The needs of the individual must be balanced against the needs of the group; a disruptive slightly handicapped pupil may be more in need of special school care than a stable but more severely handicapped child. The DES encourages provision in ordinary schools wherever possible in the belief that the more normal the environment in which the child develops the more easily will he find his place in the adult world. The Education Act 1976 stressed the desirability of such provision, unless it is impracticable, against the educational interests of any children involved, or would incur unreasonably high costs. In January 1980 there were 125,000 pupils in special schools of all kinds including about 4,700 in hospital schools. About 16,000 handicapped children were attending special classes in local authority and voluntary schools. In addition, nearly 7,500 pupils attended independent schools catering for the handicapped.

In addition to traditional special education a few children are educated at home or in small groups. This work is undertaken by the local education authorities. Special provision may also be made for further education and pre-vocational training and guidance for young people who are blind or suffer from certain other physical handicaps. Vocational training may then be available through the Department of Employment. In many cases today disabled persons are able to attend courses at ordinary centres of further or higher education. The White Paper *Education: A Framework for Expansion* recommended an increase in special schools building, particularly for the mentally handicapped. An increase from £11 million in 1972–3 to £19 million in 1976–7 was proposed to cover new building costs and the improvement of established premises. By 1976 government economy measures curtailed these plans, and no major building programme for special schools was undertaken for 1977–8.

Following the report of the Warnock Committee in May 1978, a White Paper, *Special Needs in Education*,[34] was published announcing Government plans to widen the definitions embracing children with special educational needs, and to replace the existing somewhat restrictive and precise categories. Parents of handicapped children were to be given more opportunity to express their preferences as to whether their children should receive education in ordinary or special schools. Unfortunately no mention was made of any further funding for this part of the service, nor of the situation regarding the education of handicapped students in colleges or universities.

Ancillary services

The Education Act, 1944, extended the powers of local education authorities to assist children whose education might suffer as a result of poverty or ill-health.

The School Health Service is discussed in chapter 6, and education welfare provisions, including meals, milk, clothing, grants and maintenance allowances, are included in the chapter on income and need.

In addition to the provisions described elsewhere, local education authorities have a duty to provide free transport for fit children below the age of 8 who have a distance of more than two miles to travel to school, and for older children with a journey of three miles or more between home and school; they are also empowered to provide it for shorter distances. Special services may be made available, but where public transport exists the local authorities may use it by paying the necessary fares.

Since 1973 the DES has been attempting to make new statutory arrangements for school transport, probably to include the withdrawal of free transport. In the face of opposition from various quarters new ways of approaching the issue have been under discussion since 1977.

On 31 March 1978 a report, *Home to School Transport*, was published by the DES. The report revealed the wide variations in provision between local authorities, and whilst making no firm recommendations it provided factual information for a new Consultative Document aimed at resolving the thorny transport question. By 1980 the issues were still not resolved and the relevant clauses related in the Education No. 2 Bill were excised at the House of Lords reading. So, for the time being at least, transport responsibilities remain as before: the Secretary of State announcing to Parliament on 18 March 1980 that the government would not seek the reintroduction of clauses 23 and 25.

Boarding education may be provided where the authority and the parents think it desirable. This may be free, or a charge may be made according to the means of the parents.

Children who are so unsuitably clothed that they cannot make use of their schooling may be supplied with clothing by the local authority. This provision exists for pupils of all maintained schools and all special schools, whether maintained or not. The authority is expected to recover clothing costs wholly or in part from parents who are not in financial hardship.

The Education Welfare Service

Education Welfare Officers—the one-time School Attendance Officers—deal broadly with problems of absence from school, as well as with assessments for educational benefits, transport attendance for children at special schools, and other welfare-related tasks. Such work is closely associated with social work and the Seebohm Report recommended that the service be incorporated into local authority social service departments. In the main such amalgamation has not taken place. Education welfare officers, and indeed appropriately trained teachers, could greatly facilitate liaison between home, school and local authority social services. The welfare officers do not have a thorough social work training and such qualifications as are available to them do not confer professional status commensurate with the job they do. As a result the Education Welfare Service is more often regarded as an enforcement agency than one of understanding and help.[35]

The Youth Service

This service, always regarded as part of the education service, has never attracted the attention, glamour or finances of the other areas of education provision. Local authorities maintain their own youth centres, and assist voluntary agencies with youth work within their areas, so that the service is essentially one of co-operation between local authorities and voluntary organisations. In 1971 the report of the Youth Service Development Council[36] was not accepted by the government; the Secretary of State decided that the service should continue on its existing basis but that there should be 'certain changes of emphasis which should be reflected by corresponding changes in the financial support given by the Department'.[37]

A simplification of the grant-aiding system was felt to be needed, with more help being channelled into less prosperous areas and into experimental youth work. Since April 1972 new arrangements for capital grants have applied, local authorities becoming responsible for the finance and administration of projects to receive support and the DES then making grants proportional to the total cost and the local authority's contribution.

A report was commissioned by the DES[38] in 1968 to describe the use made of the Youth Service and assess the facilities provided. It published its findings in June 1972, its most significant one being that the number of young people not attached to a club were fewer than previously believed. This finding might be partly explained by the definition of 'club' used by this report differing from that of the Albemarle Committee and other earlier reports.

During 1975 the DES held discussions with interested parties in order to identify future needs for Youth Service provision. In December 1976 the resulting Youth Service Forum met to consider how young people themselves might influence policy, how the Service might relate to the local community, and whether or not restructuring of the organisation would be desirable. The Forum was axed late in 1979.

In 1980 Youth Service Partners published a survey report, *Local Authority Expenditure and the Youth Service 1979–80/1980–81*[39] which showed that plans to reduce expenditure on the youth services were widespread in local education authorities. Many of the proposed cuts were to be in the region of 10 per cent, and this, coupled with the existing imbalance in provision between local authorities, left the Youth Service in something of a sorry plight.

Education of immigrants

When in 1973 the DES stopped collecting statistics on numbers of immigrant pupils in schools there were about 280,000, representing about 3½ per cent of the total school population.[40] Such statistics were dropped as the category used became increasingly irrelevant. More recently the DES has again considered the question of collecting statistics on ethnic minorities in schools. In July 1977 their consultative document on ethnic minority children was issued in response to the report on the West Indian Community undertaken by the Select Committee on Race Relations and Immigration.[41] This is in the spirit of the Secretary of State's affirmation that the education service has important contributions to make to the general well-being of immigrant communities.

Within schooling itself programmes dealing with language difficulties and ethnic minorities have been one valuable area of activity. Increasingly, however, it has become necessary to recognise forms of racial discrimination which may operate in the education system. It is important to point out that the majority of black youngsters facing educational problems today are indigenous blacks, and not immigrants at all.[42]

It is already well known that many children of West Indian origin are achieving well below the rates for indigenous or Asian children.[43] Language difficulties may continue to be part of the problem, but many interested parties now draw DES attention to low performance expectations by teachers, irrelevant curricula, cultural and economic deprivation, and the failure to establish good pupil/teacher relationships. Whatever the true nature of this issue, Little seems to sum it up adequately when he observes that our most immediate problem is how far the education system has failed to 'respond effectively to the needs of minority communities'.[44]

Gypsy education

This topic has commanded considerable attention in recent years. Since the Plowden Report commented that gypsies were 'probably the most severely deprived children in the country'[45] Lady Plowden has herself helped to form the National Gypsy Education Council. This and other interested pressure groups (such as the Gypsies and Travellers Education Council), studying the educational needs of the different gypsy groups, have witnessed the provision of the on-site Liverpool Travellers' School, an autonomous unit within the local education authority, with six specially appointed staff working flexible hours to suit the needs of the gypsy community, the West Midlands Travellers' School, and school-attached classes for gypsies such as those at Blackburn and Sevenoaks.

The National Gypsy Council Report on Gypsy Education published in June 1978 found that gypsy parents preferred their children to be educated with other children in ordinary schools. This claim is contrary to the cultural segregation preferred by the National Gypsy Education Council, and the Advisory Committee for the Education of Romany and other Travellers. The West Midlands scheme, which provides full-time education for gypsy children in the area, was applauded by the report, which also commented that gypsies tend to reject outside interference in their way of life by certain otherwise well-intentioned groups or individuals.

Administration of the education service

Education in the public sector is administered through a combination of national and local government bodies.

The 1944 Act made it the responsibility of the Minister of Education to ensure the comprehensive provision and development of education in England and Wales. This involved the collaboration of local education authorities in implementing national policies for the education service. On 1 April 1964 the Secretary of State for Education and Science took over these duties and, in addition, responsibility for the universities of England, Wales and Scotland, which until then had been administered by the Treasury.

The Department of Education and Science has the Secretary of State for Education and Science as its political head. He is a senior Minister of the Crown who would usually have a seat in the Cabinet. He is assisted by two Ministers of State and two parliamentary under-secretaries. The department is staffed by civil servants whose appointments are non-political, their work being to deal with schools, further education and teachers in England and Wales, and with the universities throughout Great Britain. There are also specialist branches providing information and advice on particular topics, such as health, buildings and statistics. The Department's responsibilities in Wales are looked after by the Education Office for Wales, and after 5 November 1970 the Secretary of State for Wales took over responsibility for schools in Wales from the Secretary of State for Education and Science, who is now responsible for all education in England, for the universities in Scotland and for all post-school education in Wales.

Central Advisory Councils

Two Central Advisory Councils, one for England and one for Wales,[46] advise the Secretary of State, usually on matters referred to them regarding the theory and practice of education but also on those matters which in their opinion should have his attention.

Not all forms of education come under Department of Education and Science control: education in the Armed Forces, or in community schools or borstals, falls outside its competence. It has only an indirect influence on university education through the University Grants Committee, and it does not yet have any powers to control the growing industry of private 'correspondence courses'.

Since 1969 correspondence colleges have been able to apply for course recognition from the Council for the Accreditation of Correspondence Colleges. From 1978 to 1981 the CACC received £5,000 a year from the DES in order to strengthen the Council's administration and to encourage more applications for accreditation.

The DES does not run any schools or technical colleges, engage any teachers, or prescribe textbooks or curricula. The Department is primarily concerned with the formulation, interpretation and execution of national policy as laid down in Acts of Parliament and Regulations. Its functions also comprise the following:

(a) control of the rate, distribution, and nature and cost of educational building;

(b) control of teacher training and supply, and of the principles governing qualification for entry into the profession;

(c) the settlement of disputes, e.g. between a parent and a local education authority or the governors of a school;

(d) the payment of certain education grants from central government funds, e.g. in scholarships, for educational research, or through the Arts Council;

(e) the administration of a teacher superannuation scheme;

(f) with local authority consultation, predicting local authority expenditure to be considered when determining rate support grants;

(g) the administration of grants support to some special education institutions.

Since 1964 the Schools Council for the Curriculum and Examinations has advised and encouraged research programmes and development projects which schools may support if they choose. Composed mainly of teachers, it nevertheless represents the whole spectrum of the educational service, including the universities and the DES.

In 1976 the Council recommended a common system of examinations at 16 plus to replace existing O-level GCE and the CSE examinations. These proposals were reflected in the White Paper *Secondary School Examinations: A Single System at 16 plus* of 23 October 1978. In this the government announced its support for a new General Certificate of Secondary Education to be introduced in the mid 1980s.

The Secretary of State for Education and Science has the power to create *ad hoc* committees to advise him on particular problems. He is represented on various autonomous bodies, such as, for instance, the National Foundation for Educational Research, which are often subsidised by the Department. Finally, the Department frequently consults, both formally and informally, the local education authorities, the churches, the teachers' organisations, and any other bodies which would be affected by a proposed course of action.

Although central government controls the overall nature of education, albeit in some measure through local education authorities, it does not control curricula in schools. A communication channel to schools is kept open by the 411 HM Inspectors of Schools whose job is to report to the Secretaries of State on work in maintained schools and colleges.[47] The inspectors are Crown officials and, although for administrative purposes this is merely a nominal distinction, it does symbolise a real tradition of independence in the inspectorate. Their principal function is the inspection of educational establishments other than universities, all schools being open to their inspection. They can only criticise, recommend and advise; they cannot give orders to teachers, governors or local education authorities. They report direct to the Secretary of State, but must discuss their report with the school authorities before submitting it. Any teacher who is adversely criticised must be shown a copy of the report and be given a chance to reply to it. Once written, the report cannot be altered by anyone other than the writer—not even by the Secretary of State himself.

The inspectors are also responsible for approving independent schools for recognition as efficient. In addition the inspectorate gives professional educational advice to the Department and to local education authorities; provides a focus point for information on educational developments; conducts courses for serving teachers; and prepares advisory literature for teachers and the general public.

Local government

Following the Local Government Act, 1972, reorganised local authorities took over their new responsibilities on 1 April 1974. Of the 45 new counties, all but 6 are responsible for education. In those 6 counties, 36 metropolitan districts have responsibility for education, and with the 8 new Welsh counties plus the existing local education authorities the total number of local education authorities in England and Wales is 105.[48]

Each such authority appoints an education committee, a majority of the committee members being by law members of the authority, but also including co-opted members who have 'experience in education and persons acquainted with the educational conditions prevailing in the area'. This illustrates the tradition in English government that legislative decisions should not be entrusted to specialists but should be made by ordinary citizens who have been elected to represent the community and who can assess the opinions of specialists against broader issues.

The education committee in its turn appoints sub-committees to deal with special areas in the field of education, such as primary schools, secondary schools, and further education.

'A local education authority may authorise an education committee of an authority to exercise on their behalf any of their functions with respect to education, except the power to borrow money or to raise a rate.' However, councils differ widely in the extent to which they delegate powers to their education committees.[49]

Education authorities have to provide schools, employ teaching staff, local inspectors of schools and education organisers. They must ensure sufficient equipment and provide education to meet all needs within the community. Costs for such provision are met from rates and the rate support grant, which is paid from Exchequer funds by the Secretary of State for the Environment. Except for housing and trading services all local authority services share in the grant although education is the largest of the services so financed.

All schools in the maintained sector have a governing body. The general educational character of a maintained school is decided by the local education authority. The general direction of conduct and curriculum is the responsibility of the governors in consultation with the head teacher who is usually given effective control over the day-to-day running of the school by the rules of management or articles of government. In practice the professional status of the class teacher means that he has considerable independence inside his own classroom.

The governors of county schools are appointed by the local education authority (or by divisional executives to whom it may have delegated the necessary powers). A varying proportion of the governors of voluntary schools is appointed by the voluntary body concerned according to the status of the school, the remainder by the local education authority.

In controlled schools two-thirds of the governing body are nominated by the authority, which also meets all costs and appoints the teachers.

In an aided school two-thirds of the governors represent the voluntary body who are responsible for repairs, improvements, enlargements or alterations to the school fabric. Central government grants are available for up to 85 per cent of approved capital expenditure including the work of providing new schools or extensions to existing schools not previously eligible for grant. The local authority pays the teachers though their appointments are the responsibility of the governing body.

Special agreement schools, for whom local authorities pay between one-half and three-quarters of the cost of new building, also have two-thirds of their governors provided by the voluntary body.

On 20 September 1977 the Taylor Committee Report, *A New Partnership for our Schools, Report of the Committee of Enquiry into the Management and Government of Schools* stressed that school governors should be collectively responsible for the work of their school, good relations within it and with the wider community, and that governors should have a greater contribution to make in taking decisions affecting the school. The teacher organisations were critical of the report, fearing what they believed to be outside intervention in internal school affairs and matters of discipline, curriculum and day-to-day organisation.

Nevertheless the Open University was granted £90,000 to provide courses of study for school managers and governors to begin in October 1980, the Taylor Report having recommended that all governors should undergo initial training and in-service training regularly thereafter.

A DES publication in September 1978, *Progress in Education: A Report on Recent Initiatives*, promised the legislation which now allows parents and teachers to participate in the government of schools, a feature in operation for many years in some local authority areas.

Most further education colleges are local-authority maintained, and in some cases by more than one authority. Fees may be charged of students in further education but these do not cover actual course costs and are generally remitted. Students taking degree equivalent courses are in any case grant-aided. Further education is co-ordinated by ten regional advisory councils which include representatives of colleges, universities, industry and commerce as well as from the local authority.

The governing bodies of polytechnics and further education colleges, which may include a student representative, are responsible for the general control of the institution, the principal overseeing internal organisation and discipline. The academic board plans, co-ordinates and develops the high-grade academic courses.

Since the establishment by Royal Charter in 1964 of the Council for National Academic Awards, colleges may devise curricula and syllabuses of suitable standard leading to a CNAA degree or other qualifications and determine their own admission requirements and run their own examinations.[50]

Higher education in Great Britain falls into two categories. There is an autonomous sector of universities with a fair degree of academic freedom to decide the number and quality of the students they will admit, the appointment of staff, the subjects taught, what degrees to award and on what conditions to award them. They have their own internal system of government, exercised in most universities by a court which is formally the supreme governing body, the council which administers finance, and the senate which is the chief academic authority. Faculties control day-to-day academic matters and are usually composed of departments representing different, though related, fields of study.

Oxford and Cambridge are self-governed, by senior members of the university, and self-financed by taxes and endowments. The ultimate authority at Oxford is Congregation and Cambridge the Regent House.[51]

Candidates for first admission to a British university—other than the Open University—submit their preferences to the Universities Central Council on Admissions which sends the application to the universities concerned. Graduate applicants apply direct to the universities, who are quite free in all cases to admit students according to their standards and resources. Ninety per cent of students in the universities receive assistance from public monies. Undergraduates are normally financed by an income-related[52] local education authority grant. At postgraduate level government departments and research councils generally make grants, though these are diminishing in number and scope. Since September 1967 DES bursaries may be available for students in fields where other financial assistance is not forthcoming. The government exercises its financial responsibilities in universities through the University Grants Committee. The committee's members are appointed by the Secretary of State from the academic and business worlds, though the universities are not directly represented. The main functions of the committee are to collect and diffuse information on university education in the UK, especially with regard to overall financial needs, and to advise the government on the use of Parliamentary grants, and to help in the preparation of plans for the development, and currently (1982) the curtailment of university education. Grants made on the advice of the University Grants Committee represent about 18 per cent of the universities' recurrent expenditure, and about 90 per cent of their capital expenditure.

Recurrent grants, almost half of which go to pay academic salaries, are assessed quinquennially. Non-recurrent grants meet expenditure arising from government-approved annual building programmes.

Tuition fees have undergone frequent increases in recent years. The 1981 rates for university students were £1,320 for postgraduates (£3,000 for overseas students) and £900 for undergraduates (£3,200 for overseas students).

As a result of the overall reappraisal of university finances the Secretary of State has increased student grants to £1,535 maximum, £410 minimum for students living away from home. Special rates apply for mature students.

Parental and educational associations

These groups are taking an active part in shaping the development of the education system. Teachers and parents, as well as taking part in school management wherever possible, have formed associations in an effort to link the values and difficulties of home and school to the ultimate benefit of the child. The Plowden Report stressed the worth and the National Confederation of Parent-Teacher Associations encourages the development of such ventures. The Confederation of State Education, comprising over 100 local associations, seeks to co-operate with local education authorities in developing closer ties between school and community. A forum and information service is provided by the Advisory Centre for Education with its stimulating and well-informed periodical *Where*? and the Confederation for the Advancement of State Education has often expressed itself strongly on the serious gaps and deficiencies which still remain in our educational system.

Teachers and teacher education

The payment of full-time teachers in maintained schools and institutions of Further Education follows a national scale determined by machinery established under the Remuneration of Teachers Act, 1975. Salaries are negotiated in committees, known as Burnham Committees, composed of representatives of the DES, of the local education authorities, and of the teachers. In the event of disagreement there is provision for independent arbitration and the arbitrator's decision is binding on both sides unless set aside by Parliament. The remuneration of the teaching staff in colleges of education used to be decided at the national level by the Secretary of State for Education and Science on the basis of recommendations made by the Pelham Committee representing staff and employers. Since 24 February 1976 Pelham has been superseded by the Burnham Further Education Committee.

The 1972 White Paper[53] proposed an extension of the teaching force equal by 1981 to a 10 per cent rise over 1971 figures, in order to maintain standards. As a basis for planning the assumption might reasonably be that standards will decline if the figures are not met. However, with a decline in pupil numbers and the resultant reduction of teachers in training, the number of teachers in all schools had, by January 1980, fallen by 3,000 over a period of six months, to 467, 564. This produced a ratio of pupils to teachers in the region of 20:1. Ratios in the private sector are much more favourable being on average about 13:1, figures which show the private sector to be about twenty years ahead of the maintained sector in this regard. Indeed many classrooms in state schools, at both primary and secondary level, contained more than thirty pupils at the turn of the decade.

Against this background, local authority employed teachers are often said to comprise a comparatively insecure, poorly respected and poorly paid profession.

TABLE 4 *Qualified teachers in maintained schools* [54]

January 1981 (England)	
Nursery schools	1,597
Primary schools	171,444
Secondary schools	221,570
Total (including those in divided service)	402,514
Total for England and Wales	430,031

As new professions grew up during the nineteenth century, a typical pattern emerged of small occupational groups which exercised strict control over admission, insisted on high standards of qualifications, and established codes of professional behaviour for the safeguarding of clients' interests. Membership carried prestige in society, and usually commanded a high salary. In view of the crucial role which our society attributes to education in terms of the personal development and future happiness of individuals, as well as its connection with economic expansion and technological progress, it might be thought strange that teachers have never, in the main, enjoyed commensurate status.

The origins of the teaching profession, especially its religious context, have lent it a vocational quality, a job to be done for altruistic reasons, rather than for reward. Such an ideal could hardly expect to command a wide following. Non-productive work could not deploy large finances, and so it could offer a social ladder only to members of the lower working class. This was most noticeable in boys' elementary schools, which constituted a self-perpetuating system, whereas teaching the poor was one of the few occupations deemed suitable for a middle-class woman of that period.

In addition the teacher associations have a reputation for being frequently concerned with salary and pension demands, as well as other aspects of public spending, to such a degree that any quest for status and professional standing may be damaged by their insistence upon the right to more money rather than insistence upon a quality of performance which will draw to public attention their merits. The more typical strategy of professional organisations has been to seek strong representation on all bodies which employ their members, or determine their pay and conditions of service.

As education is a service which must be provided continuously for the whole child population the teaching body will always be too large and varied to achieve the exclusiveness of a 'learned' profession. The teachers' organisations have successfully pressed for the extension of teacher training to a three-year course, parallel to the length of training in some established professions, and the creation of an Honours Bachelor of Education course in the colleges concerned with initial training, with the ultimate object of making teaching an all-graduate profession.[55] However, developments of this scope have little significance relative to the total background and output of higher education.

Selection and opportunity

The Education Act, 1944, was under discussion in a climate which suggested the strong intention to organise a new school system that would avoid early differentiation. In fact there emerged little that was new; selective schooling beyond eleven was retained and three kinds of secondary school were suggested: the former grammar school, unchanged, became the post-1944 grammar school; the secondary modern school was the senior elementary school renamed; and the technical schools were the junior technical schools upgraded. This reality was not obscured by the hope expressed in the Act that all forms of schooling would enjoy parity of status. The grammar schools were the avenues to university, and enjoyed commensurate esteem, though expansion in higher education soon meant that more people were involved. Against this background educational argument to justify the tripartite system used notions of secondary modern or grammar school 'types of mind'—mental characteristics conveniently corresponding to provisions aimed at the needs of these presumed categories of child.

The Act urged that secondary school provision should be made in accordance with pupils' different ages, abilities and aptitudes. In the face of challenge the view of types of mind corresponding to types of school was replaced by grades of ability matching the schools. Justification of selection by test at 11 became a priority.

After the Act the 11-plus examination came under scrutiny and claims of objectivity on behalf of the test—that it was not so much competitive as allocative according to ability grade—necessitated close evaluation of the accuracy of 'intelligence'. As time went by and some secondary modern school pupils were clearly achieving academic levels not predicted for them the voices of sociologists, psychologists and educationalists raised against the 11-plus selection procedure came to be heard more clearly.

A growing understanding of the principles of psychological measurement revealed that IQ tests did not measure some absolute ability, but rather that 'intelligence' was, at least, partly an acquired quality which was profoundly influenced by such social factors as home conditions, size of family, educational experience and parental aspirations. Consequently, it was seen to be educationally wrong to decide the academic future of a child on the basis of such a criterion at the early age of 11. Moreover, the critical point of the scale which determined selection for grammar school was dependent on such extraneous factors as the number of grammar school places available in a particular local education authority and the size of a particular year group in that area. Also it was known that the existing system resulted in a considerable number of wrong allocations, and once the children were segregated in different schools it became very difficult to detect and correct such an error. Thus, for a mixture of reasons both ideological and educational, administrators had been moving towards the idea of a unified system of secondary education where a wide selection of subjects could be taught within one school, and where each individual would be educated in a range of subjects and to a level suited to his ability and aptitudes without anyone being labelled as a failure by virtue of a dubious system of selection.

In addition, for very much the same reasons, the systems of streaming in schools were criticised since any form of differentiation implemented might cause restrictive limits to be placed on a child's potential for development.

Power was added to the zeal for reform by publication in the 1950s and early 1960s of sociological studies[56] relating selection processes in education to our society stratified by social class. These researchers documented the continuing relationship between family social class and children's opportunities in the supposedly socially impartial education system. It was shown that working-class children were under-represented in grammar schools or among any higher ability groups.

Secondary modern school children, supposedly less intelligent, were predominantly from working-class families, and the grammar schools, and more so the independent schools, were strongly middle-class in intake. Thus the position in the pre-war fee-paying days still obtained in spite of 'objective' allocation. Statements were clearly made that all the intelligence test did was to reflect an academic view of what intelligence ought to be, i.e. the ability to perform the mental gymnastics necessary to absorb traditional learning presented on formal school lines. Once selection had thus been stripped of its pretensions the way became open for comprehensive reorganisation.

As plans and legislation for comprehensive reorganisation proceeded with some rapidity it was inevitable that some people felt that a doctrinaire programme was being rushed through without regard to parents' wishes or to the quality of education provided, particularly where the plans involved the merging of grammar schools which had enjoyed a long tradition of academic excellence.

Consequently the discussions came more and more into the political arena, and in time new sociological evidence suggested that not only was eleven-plus selection unsatisfactory, but also that the working-class child suffers cumulative disadvantages at every stage of his schooling, and that social barriers to educability are quite as important as the barriers to opportunity. Clearly, given the disadvantages under which large numbers of children labour, competition for educational advantage becomes meaningless. Moreover, since education provides the key to the individual's life-chances, fundamental questions of social justice are involved. However, these barriers cannot be removed simply by legislation and the need for social reform is clearly indicated.

Much of the more recent discussion about social class and educational opportunity has been centred on the 1967 Plowden Report, *Children and their Primary Schools*, which painted a clear picture of the vicious circle which existed in depressed areas, where education was inevitably seen as a brief prelude to work rather than as an avenue to further opportunity.

The proposals for education priority areas selected on the basis of eight criteria of need—the proportion of unskilled and semi-skilled workers in the area, size of families, proportion receiving state benefits, overcrowding and sharing of houses, truancy, handicapped pupils in ordinary schools, incomplete families and children unable to speak English—suggested that serious deprivation affects one child in ten, and the Report urged that these areas should receive more financial aid.

The criteria listed are not primarily educational ones, but could be taken as evidence of the need for a wide range of social services. This helps to underline the present policy of viewing education in the wider social context of the community in which the school is set. So too does the complementary proposal from Plowden which consists of a complete programme for involving parents more intimately with schools so as to combat the lack of parental aspiration prevailing in these areas, often believed to be the most important of the external social factors influencing achievement.[57]

A follow-up study of the Plowden sample four years after the original research found that all the expected relationships between the child's home and school achievement had come to pass.[58]

To offset the handicap of social background the Educational Priority Areas were set up. Modes of treatment were not precisely specified, though better teachers with extra allowances, links between teachers' colleges and educational priority areas and development of nursery provision, extension of school and social work contact, and the implementation of the community school concepts, were all regarded as essential ingredients.

The organisation of the education priority areas scheme was envisaged in two stages. The initial stage, adding some £11 m to the expenditure on maintained primary schools, ran until 1971, introducing special measures aimed at combating the social evils described, and including an evaluative research project to judge the effects of different innovations. The second stage was intended as a long-term project designed to continue or extend schemes which were discovered to be successful during the experimental stage.

The action research programme into the education priority areas was completed in March 1972 at a cost to the DES of nearly £100,000 and to the Social Science Research Council of almost £75,000.

Work in the five designated areas tried to identify which aspects of the working class culture stimulate educational under-achievement, and how this culture might be changed to remove the disadvantages. Critics of the programme reject the whole concept of cultural deprivation, pointing out that it is impossible for a child to be deprived of its own culture. Others claim that the proposals embodied in the Plowden Report and the EPA work are faced with a number of obstacles. Acland identifies some of these.[59] He argues that under-achievement is such a widespread phenomenon that isolating certain localities for positive discrimination will only touch a minority; also that even the Plowden research evidence shows how tenuous is the link between school variables and attainment, concluding that to focus resources in chosen schools will have little effect. Acland suggests too that although parental attitudes may well be the most powerful influence in children's school progress these attitudes are themselves rooted in material circumstances and cannot simply be abstracted and changed without parallel treatment of the environmental situation. To accomplish this and the kind of intensive supportive work with parents which would undoubtedly be required, costs well in excess of those envisaged by the Plowden Committee would be involved.

It seems, for the time being at least, that different levels of education will continue to recruit from different sections of the social structure. These groups of children will then be further differentiated by educational experience for different levels of occupation of unemployment. The persistent questions remain to be answered: do we have equality of opportunity in education; does our system, or should it, facilitate an harmonious distribution of the workforce which responds to economic needs, or does education in England and Wales constitute a process of socialisation imposed by a dominant group in order to preserve the existing stratified social *status quo*?

Future legislation is sure to take account of these and other considerations as educational provision continues to be an area of major political debate in the 1980s.

Further reading

In addition to published works referred to in the notes the following are suggested as further reading:

W. H. G. ARMYTAGE, *Four Hundred Years of English Education*, Cambridge University Press, 1964.

A. W. BACON, *Public Accountability and the Schooling System*, Harper & Row, 1978.

H. C. BARNARD, *A History of English Education from 1970*, University of London Press, 1963.

C. BENN and B. SIMON, *Half Way There*, McGraw-Hill, 1970.

M. BLAUG (ed.), *Economics of Education*, I, Penguin, 1968, and *Economics of Education*, II, Penguin, 1969.

H. C. DENT, *The Educational System of England and Wales*, University of London Press, 1963.

M. HYNDMAN, *Schools and Schooling in England and Wales*, Harper & Row, 1978.

F. H. PEDLEY, *The Educational System in England and Wales*, Pergamon, 1964.

K. RICHMOND, *The Literature of Education: A Critical Bibliography, 1945–70*, Methuen, 1972.

A series of government publications have examined different sectors of the educational system, and made recommendations, for example:

15 to 18 (Crowther Report), HMSO, 1959, vol. I, 'Report'; vol. II, 'surveys'.

Half Our Future (Newsom Report), HMSO, 1963. This dealt with the education between the ages of 13 and 16 of pupils of average or less than average ability.

Higher Education (Robbins Report), with five separate appendices, Cmnd 2154, HMSO, 1963.

Public Schools Commission First Report (Newsom Report), with a one-volume appendix, HMSO, 1968, with independent boarding schools and how they might be integrated into the state system.

Public Schools Commission Second Report (Donnison Report), HMSO, 1970, with a one-volume appendix, and a further volume on Scotland, prepared by a separate committee under the chairmanship of T. Ewan Faulkner. This second report concerned itself with independent day schools and direct grant grammar schools. Direct grant grammar schools were not included in the Commission's terms of reference until October 1967.

The Demand for and Supply of Teachers 1963–1986, HMSO, 1965. The ninth report of the National Advisory Council on the Training and Supply of Teachers, this deals with the staffing of maintained schools.

Report of the Committee of Inquiry into the Pay of Non-University Teachers (Houghton Report) Cmnd 5848, HMSO, 1974.

Helping New Teachers: The Induction Year, Reports on Education No. 84. HMSO, 1976.
16 and 18 Year Olds: Attitudes to Education, Reports on Education No. 86, HMSO, 1976.
Educational Priority, vols 1–4, HMSO.
Trends in Education (Journal, 4 publications each year) HMSO.

3 The employment services

Ken Roberts

Employment itself is sometimes provided as a social service. Some jobs would not exist purely as a consequence of hirers and sellers of labour pursuing their private interests through the market. Officially-titled job creation schemes are only the tip of an iceberg. Many 'ordinary' jobs are preserved only with the aid of state subsidies, as in British Rail and the British Steel Corporation, because, amongst other reasons, governments recognise the damage that unemployment can inflict on individuals and communities.

This chapter, however, is not primarily concerned with job creation exercises, with employment as a social service, nor with broader economic policies aimed at generating full employment. Nor shall we deal with the social services ranging through canteens, recreation centres, health insurance and housing sometimes provided as part of the 'compensation package', though it is worth noting that these provisions often act as substitutes for statutory services. We shall be concerned with services that, in most cases, do not directly create jobs except in the relevant services themselves, but assist employers and workers to create and locate the kinds of jobs through which they can achieve their own varied purposes.

The administration of Britain's employment services is the responsibility, ultimately, of the Department of Employment, formerly the Department of Employment and Productivity, and before that the Ministry of Labour, which was initially created in 1917 as an inducement to the Labour Party to join the national government, and took over some responsibilities, including the labour exchanges, from the Board of Trade. As happened in many spheres of social administration, the employment services subsequently grew haphazardly, different provisions being introduced at various times to meet needs as they became apparent. During the 1970s, however, the services were streamlined. Some are still directly provided by the

Department of Employment, but a greater number have been 'hived off', in the case of the Careers Service to Local Education Authorities, but mainly to recently created Quangos (quasi-autonomous non-governmental organisations), namely, the Advisory, Conciliation and Arbitration Service (ACAS) and the Manpower Services Commission (MSC). The latter's staff of over 20,000 now operate through three main divisions—the Employment Services Division (ESD), the Training Services Division (TSD), and the Special Programmes Division (SPD).

Since the 1970s the SPD has attracted considerable attention, its creation being a response to the exceptional (by post-war standards) level of unemployment, but employment services are not intended solely for the unemployed. They exist to help everyone, and are used by virtually all citizens at some time or another. Apart from the special programmes, the services fall into two main groups. First there are those that benefit the population in general: the placement and advisory services, the training services, employment protection measures and the industrial relations services. Second there are services that address the problems of particular sections of the workforce—beginning workers, the disabled, women, ethnic minorities, and the ageing. Most of these services rarely excite the imaginations of either politicians or the public at large and therefore escape the spotlight of controversy. Nevertheless, the contribution the employment services can make to the efficiency of the economy in general, and to the well-being of individual workers is often considerable. If not applause, their achievements deserve critical attention.

Unemployment and the Special Programmes Division

Unemployment remains unpleasant in the 1980s. Scroungers leading lives of luxury on social security are figments of uninformed imaginations. Joblessness is not a lucrative status. If there are individuals who are better off not working, this is testimony to their normally low wages and large families rather than the generosity of the Welfare State. There are strong pressures forcing the unemployed towards work. The desire to escape poverty is reinforced by often harsh and apparently arbitrary treatment at Supplementary Benefit Offices. Unemployment shakes individuals' confidence in their own abilities—even their personal identities. Under the attendant anxieties, standards for an 'acceptable' job quickly decline.[1] The long-term unemployed are rarely work-shy; they are mostly individuals suffering multiple disadvantages from amongst age, physical disablement, mental handicap, lack of qualifications and skill.[2]

In 1965 the Redundancy Payments Act was generally welcomed as promising to remove the pain from job-loss, and introducing flexibility into the labour market, yet today redundancy remains as fearsome a prospect as ever. Only around a third of all employees declared redundant meet the length of service requirements entitling them to redundancy pay,[3] and payments that are made rarely amount to small fortunes. Some workers are more or less permanently sub-employed, meaning that they have to endure repeated spells of unemployment. This condition is usually not due to personal inadequacy, but to the fact that jobs in marginal firms and industries are inherently insecure, and an unstable work history impedes individuals leaping from the 'secondary' to the 'primary' labour market.[4] All the relevant studies show that redundancy generally leads to a fall in earnings, status and skill,[5] changes that can inflict psychological in addition to financial damage.[6] When older, longer-serving workers are tempted by apparently generous redundancy payments, they risk sentences of permanent unemployment, the status of being burdens on the community, in addition to personal and family problems.[7]

The age-specific unemployment rates in Table 6 show that the youngest and oldest members of the workforce have suffered particularly harshly. Tens of thousands of young people have lingered out-of-school and out-of-work as firms have reduced recruitment and many older displaced workers have found re-absorption impossible. Female unemployment rates must be treated cautiously. It has been estimated that up to 200,000 married women remain unregistered, usually because they are not entitled to social security benefit and do not believe the employment service will offer suitable vacancies.[8] But the high unemployment rate amongst teenage girls shows that the days when women's work was plentiful have passed.

TABLE 5 *Unemployment rates for different age groups, January 1977*

	Males	*Females*
16–17	12.8	14.1
18–19	11.1	9.9
20–24	10.1	7.0
25–29	7.3	4.4
30–39	6.3	2.2
40–49	5.1	1.7
50–59	5.1	2.2
60 and over	9.5	0.2

In the face of mounting unemployment, special 'temporary' Job Creation Projects were first introduced in 1975, and from the beginning out-of-school youth was identified as a main target group. This remains the case in the now complex battery of schemes orchestrated by the Special Programmes Division of the MSC. The schemes have fallen into three main categories. First there are those that subsidise regular employment. By 1981 the Temporary Short-time Working Compensation Scheme, which encourages employers to adopt short-time working instead of redundancies by supplementing employees' earnings, was the sole survivor of such measures, but accounted for the majority of the individuals being assisted by the entire programme. The second group of schemes create jobs or training places, doing work that would not otherwise be undertaken, though it is acknowledged that some 'substitution' occurs. The Community Enterprise Programme (formerly the Special Temporary Employment Programme) finances projects of benefit to the community. Training for Skills is intended to benefit mainly beginning workers by offering grants to encourage employers to take on apprentices and other long-term trainees additional to their normal recruitment. The Youth Opportunities Programme (YOP) and Community Industry cater exclusively for young people, and are fully described later in this chapter. Job Release is a third type of scheme; it differs from the others in that it aims to transfer joblessness from young people to another section of the population, by encouraging early retirement.

Table 6 shows that in April 1981 these schemes accounted for 963,100 places, but the net reduction in registered unemployment was considerably smaller. When help is available to support training or jobs, some firms will avail themselves even if they would have hired labour in any event. The numbers being saved from unemployment, therefore, were significant but not immense when set against the two and a half million registered. Should the special measures have been expanded? Here we confront debates about the extent of 'real' unemployment, that is, the residue when individuals between jobs for

TABLE 6 *Special employment and training measures, April 1981*

Temporary short-time working compensation scheme	711,600
Community Enterprise Programme	13,500
Training for skills	28,500
Youth Opportunities Programme	145,000
Community Industry	6,200
Job Release scheme	58,300
	963,100

short periods, the virtually unemployable, and any not genuinely seeking work are subtracted from the total. Equally important, we face the problem that creating jobs benefiting both the wider community and the individuals directly concerned that fall outside the normal scope of private industry, central and local government is far from easy. An additional difficulty is that no one really wants to create a large reservoir of low-paid jobs which use labour inefficiently, and whose output is insufficiently valued to attract private enterprise or the public services. Special programmes have never been regarded as adequate substitutes for regular jobs. The services in question, therefore, were not created with long-term aims, but to alleviate unemployment until general economic recovery aided by the normal employment services eradicated the need for 'temporary' measures. But whether the measures will prove temporary is far from certain. Britain seems unlikely to sustain the rate of economic growth, around 6 per cent per year, considered necessary if, given the predicted growth of the labour force until the year 2000, registered unemployment is to be brought and kept beneath a million. In the absence of radical initiatives to stimulate the economy or reduce the supply of labour, the SPD could become a permanent branch of the employment services.

The Employment Services Division

The ESD offers a range of services to advise individuals, to assist their placement in employment, and simultaneously to help firms meet their labour requirements. These services further several complementary objectives: they promote the full use of manpower by bringing potential employers and employees into contact, they help to distribute labour throughout the economy in an efficient manner, and assist workers to find jobs consistent with their abilities and interests. The provision of these services, mainly through a network of over 900 employment exchanges, has a history dating back to the 1909 Labour Exchanges Act, but during the 1970s the organisation of the services and, equally important, their public image, were transformed.

Social security benefit payment has been separated from the employment exchange service, and in 1973 the first new-style Jobcentre was opened in Reading. There are now several hundred throughout the country and their numbers are increasing rapidly. These centres operate from bright 'high street' premises that link the job-seeker to two tiers of service. The first tier is offered in self-service areas where vacancies are openly displayed. Job-seekers can request further details of any vacancy at the counter, then personally approach the employer or have an appointment made by the Centre staff. The second tier is a 'back-room' advisory service to which job-seekers are referred for more general information about employment opportunities and advice on their own prospects. During 1977, in areas with Jobcentres, 42 per cent of all vacancies were notified and 26 per cent were filled by the ESD, compared with 30 and 20 per cent respectively in areas offering only the older-style employment exchange facilities. Jobcentres fill two-thirds of all vacancies placed on their books, and place 28 per cent of all registrants.

This latter figure is not as alarmingly low as it might initially appear. The unemployed must register with the ESD to be eligible for social security benefits, and the Jobcentres' clients, therefore, inevitably include the hard-to-place long-term unemployed. More to the point, the Jobcentres enjoy no monopoly in their local labour markets. Apart from private employment exchanges, individuals can respond to press adverts and seek jobs on their own initiative. The 'grapevine' is an important source of job introductions. It is cheap, and is used extensively by all grades of worker.[9] The ESD has no aspiration to place everyone. The intention is to supplement other job-finding methods, for the grapevines to which individuals are attached, although useful, can furnish only imperfect knowledge.[10] The Jobcentre is a relatively expensive method of placement, but, it is estimated, if in their absence the individuals currently placed took only a day longer on average to find work, the value of the earnings and production lost would exceed the costs of the service.

Employers' interests are not neglected by the ESD which recognises that it can only assist job-seekers if its service is valued by employers, and vice versa. Indeed, the ESD has made great efforts to market its services to industry. A labour market intelligence service enables officers to advise employers who often, it has been found, aggravate their own recruitment problems by demanding unrealistic standards from applicants in terms of age, level of skill and qualification.[11]

In addition to the above basic services that are increasingly delivered through Jobcentres backed by regional offices, the ESD offers a range of specialist facilities. Special registers are maintained in appropriate locations covering particular types of employment including nursing and catering, but the best known is probably Professional and Executive Recruitment (PER) which now operates through 39 special bureaux. Refurbished offices convey an up-to-date executive image, 'consultants' advise employers, and a computerised service provides almost instant national coverage of every vacancy and applicant. Since 1973 a charge of between 5 and 8 per cent of the annual salary involved has been levied on employers using this service which, by 1977, was showing a profit. The needs of employees, however, are given equal consideration to the extent of organising 'self-presentation courses' to teach applicants the best approach to prospective employers.

The ESD is prepared to mount special operations to deal with large-scale redundancies. Teams of officers visit construction sites where work is ending and other factories where redundancies have been declared. An Employment Transfer Scheme offers financial assistance for travel and accommodation away from home in search of work. From its growing range of services it is becoming increasingly possible for the ESD to assemble packages including guidance, information about job opportunities and re-training, and assistance with geographical mobility to meet the various special needs that can arise in particular areas. The reasons why the ESD has buried the dole-queue image cut deeper than the separation of social security payment from the employment services. There has been a real movement away from relying on the traditional, standard employment exchange service throughout the country, and towards creating a range of services matching the needs of various employers and different sections of the workforce.

As already mentioned, the ESD has no monopoly in the employment exchange business. It operates in a highly competitive market. In 1978, 5,548 private exchanges were operating under licence, and in addition numerous professional bodies, which can gain exemption from the licensing procedures, offer employment exchange services to their members. The 1973 Employment Agencies Act requires exchanges catering for the general public to become licensed through regional Department of Employment offices and, in addition to paying a fee, licensed agencies must comply with certain conditions. These include the prohibition of charges to job-seekers, and safeguards to ensure that individuals recruited to work overseas are offered outward and return travel. By 1974, 24 agencies had been prosecuted. The private agencies do not oppose the licensing system, but resent competition from the state-financed ESD. They have condemned the Jobcentres as 'public waste'—overstaffed, using unnecessarily expensive sites, and spending as much as ten times the cost per placement through private agencies.[12] But there is an opposing point of view presented by Brian Showler,[13] that calls for even tighter control of the private agencies and compulsory notification of all vacancies to the public service in order to reduce the latter's unit costs together with its dependence on employers' goodwill, thereby leaving the public service better-placed to pursue social objectives such as placing the disabled, older workers and other disadvantaged groups. The MSC, however, is not urging compulsory notification which, it believes, would simply generate unproductive paperwork.

Vocational training and the Training Services Division

Vocational training is a third major group of services provided through its own division of the MSC. Traditionally British industry has left training to individual firms and professions, with the state playing no more than a marginal role. During the last 20 years, however, the state's involvement has slowly increased both as an actual trainer, and as the supervisor of training provided elsewhere. The existence of the Training Services Division is the administrative response to this growing involvement. It is now recognised that the effectiveness of the economy is affected by the quality of labour the working population can supply, that appropriate training opportunities can mitigate problems associated with redundancy, and that young people's life-chances can hinge upon the opportunities available to acquire occupational skills. Yet whilst its involvement in education has been long-standing, it is only since the 1950s that the state has even attempted to exert a major influence over on-the-job training.

Collectively the services directly provided by the TSD are known as TOPS (Training Opportunities Scheme) and their mainstay is the Skillcentre course. Like the rehabilitation centres for the disabled (described below), the Skillcentres have their origins in facilities provided to cater for the wounded and re-settle ex-servicemen following the two world wars after which, then called Government Training Centres, they turned to their contemporary function of offering training to workers who wished to acquire occupational skills. By 1962, however, there were still only 13 centres with a total of 2,500 places. Their contribution to training a labour force totalling over 20 million was hardly significant. But by 1978 the number of Skillcentres had quadrupled and TOPS was handling 100,000 trainees per year. Trainees are eligible for grants during their periods of training which normally last between 6 and 12 months. Training has been mainly in manual skills, but the scheme is gradually being widened to cover white-collar, technical and management jobs. A minority amongst the trainees are already skilled workers who seek re-training following a contraction in demand for their existing skills. These trainees are often among their courses' 'high fliers' and rarely encounter difficulty in obtaining subsequent employment, but it proves difficult to attract existing skilled workers onto the courses. They consider themselves already skilled, and expect any further training to be on-the-job at their employers' expense.[14] Many of these men also hesitate before the loss of adult status that can appear involved in becoming a 'learner' once more. Other trainees are formerly non-skilled workers, some unemployed, who are seeking to enhance their status. Could greater numbers from among the unemployed benefit from the courses? The problem is to identify individuals who are both willing and suitable. The prospect of a 'course' involving assessment frightens many adults whose only previous experience of education was a failure.[15]

In their early years the Skillcentres encountered some resistance to 'dilution' from craft unions, but trainees are now generally accepted throughout industry. This is no longer the main problem. Three months following their courses in 1977 only 65 per cent of trainees were in employment and only 51 per cent were using the skills they had acquired, a situation due mainly to the difficulties involved in tailoring courses to industry's changing requirements. Training is an activity where the 'right' provision never remains appropriate for more than a short period. It is difficult to predict when redundancies will hit particular trades and regions. Unforeseen technological trends throw some individuals out of work and create shortfalls in other skills. Regional fluctuations in the level of economic activity create further problems, as do changes in the numbers of school-leavers entering the labour market. Firms encounter difficulty in adjusting to this turbulence, and so do the Skillcentres. As in other enterprises, their staffs and equipment are always in danger of becoming outdated.

To increase their own adaptability, the Skillcentres have recently been pioneering activities to supplement their standard courses. They now offer courses to equip instructors to train employees throughout industry, and special courses, for which a charge is made, to meet the needs of particular firms. In addition, under the TOPS framework, grants are offered to expand training in development areas and for older workers, and college-based courses are offered in regions where industry-based training is judged inadequate.

It is necessary to bear in mind that direct responsibility for training is still principally in industry's own hands, and that TOPS is intended only to plug the gaps. Until 1964 government intervention in training within industry amounted to no more than exhortation. Employers, possibly subject to the agreement of the relevant trade unions and professional associations, trained however many workers by whatever methods they thought fit in whatever skills they considered appropriate. Numerous criticisms were made of this laissez-faire system. It was alleged that firms often found it cheaper to poach than train and that consequently not enough school-leavers received training to satisfy the economy's need for skilled manpower, that the range and quality of training was often unsatisfactory, that there was no test of either the trainer's or trainee's competence, and that the imposition of rigid age and time limits, such as 5 years to be served before age 21 for craft apprenticeships, was socially unjust and economically wasteful.

The first decisive step beyond government exhortation was taken with the 1964 Industrial Training Act. Following this measure the Department of Employment established a Central Training Council beneath which separate Industrial Training Boards (ITBs), each dealing with its own industry, were created. The job of each board was and remains ensuring that sufficient training of a satisfactory standard is provided to meet its industry's needs, and in their early years the boards' main device towards this objective was a system of grants and levies. The boards imposed levies on firms belonging to their industries, used the proceeds to cover their own administrative expenses, and distributed the remainder in the form of grants to finance training. Standards could be laid down that firms' training programmes had to meet to qualify for grants; the engagement of training instructors, the provision of day release and an introduction to a stipulated range of skills could all be demanded. In addition the boards were able to establish their own training centres, appoint special training advisors, take the initiative in setting up group courses by several firms, and draw up syllabuses for use in training programmes. However, the main instrument used by the boards was the levy-grant system, through which it was intended to stimulate each industry to provide the right amount and quality of training. Following the passage of the 1964 Act the new system was introduced enthusiastically and heralded as a 'revolution in industrial training'.[16]

It proved a revolution that quickly turned sour. The financial competence of the ITBs became suspect as some ran into debt by paying more out in grants than they recouped in levies. Within industry there arose charges of 'red tape' as the boards declared criteria to be fulfilled to obtain grants, and firms obligingly played a 'training game' by appointing instructors, patronising conferences, and arranging for as many recruits as possible to be designated as trainees. Sceptics began to query whether the 'training industry' that had arisen was really enhancing the quality of training experienced by learners, and the call was raised to let the people on the spot arrange training at their own properly-informed discretion.

Since 1972 the boards' levies have been generally restricted to 1 per cent of their firms' payrolls. The ITBs continue in existence, but now concentrate on information and advisory work, whilst the TSD, with its broader responsibilities, dispenses grants on a more selective basis, acts as the general co-ordinator, and makes arrangements to complement training in industry.

No one claims that the current training position is faultless, but there now exists a varied set of procedures for influencing and constantly appraising the entire system. TOPS makes a growing contribution to the country's pool of skilled manpower, and the

Skillcentres are playing an increasingly active role in identifying skills in short supply, arranging relevant courses, and seeking the necessary trainees by methods that include television advertising. The strength of the current situation is that the TSD, through its own provisions together with its oversight of the ITBs now offers an administrative apparatus capable of monitoring training arrangements as a whole, and has developed diverse ways of intervening which allow flexible responses to forever changing labour market conditions.

Employment protection

There is a somewhat old-fashioned view that insists on regarding employment as an arrangement based on a free contract between each individual employer and employee, and suggestions that the terms of their relationship be subjected to external constraint can still be relied upon to provoke forecasts of economic collapse and social decay. The free contract view of employment, however, has possessed little resemblance to reality in Britain at any time during the twentieth century. To begin with, a variety of organised groups, namely trade unions and professional associations, intervene in the employment relationship, and the state has long been involved in the regulation of employment, partly to ensure that these other organisations conduct their affairs in the public interest. Governments have sometimes sought to strengthen, at others to undermine trade union power, and the state has been equally involved in the development of professional associations mainly, in the past, by encouraging their formation with a view to promoting high standards of practice. In addition, Britain has a long history of 'protective' legislation in which the state has directly stipulated the conditions under which employment can be practised. Since the nineteenth century, numerous Factory Acts have accumulated on the statute book aimed at ensuring, amongst other things, that conditions of work should be neither unhealthy nor dangerous, and restricting the uses to which certain categories of labour, especially that of women, children and young people can be put.

This brand of legislation is not mainly of historical interest. In recent years it has been up-dated and extended giving workers a host of additional 'rights'. The 1963 Contracts of Employment Act, modified in 1972, stipulates that every employee must receive a written copy of his terms and conditions of employment, and amongst its additional provisions lays down minimum periods of notice to be given before dismissal. The 1965 Redundancy Payments Act secures financial compensation for employees, the amount depending on length of service. But the greatest advances in employees' rights have occurred as a result of the 1974 Trade Unions and Labour Relations Act, and the Employment Protection Act of 1975, whose provisions were subjected to minor amendments in the Employment Act of 1980. The former measure was principally a repeal of the 1971 Industrial Relations Act, but the rights this latter statute accorded to employees in exchange for their new legal responsibilities, including the right to belong to a trade union and protection against unfair dismissal, were affirmed. The 1975 Act not only confirmed the worker's right to belong to a trade union, but removed his right not to belong, thereby legalising the compulsory closed shop and allowing workers to be dismissed without redress if they refused to become union members. In addition, the Act has given trade unions themselves a battery of new rights. They can now demand recognition and have their claims investigated by ACAS (see the following section). Companies have a responsibility to furnish trade unions with information for collective bargaining purposes, and to consult the unions in advance in the event of redundancies. Section 11 of the Act allows employees in any firm to demand parity with the 'general level of terms and conditions' for their type of work as determined by the Central Arbitration Committee, and in the early years of the Act's operation this 'loophole' was much-used as a means of forcing employers to break government pay guidelines. Individual employees now have a legal right to time off with pay for trade union and public duties, and to look for new jobs once redundancies are pending. The 1975 Act also requires employers to guarantee pay except when lay-offs are due to industrial disputes within the employing organisation, protects women against dismissal due to pregnancy and gives them the right to return to work. Perhaps most controversially, the Act has strengthened the employee's protection against unfair dismissal by offering more generous compensation and allowing re-instatement.

Claimants seeking redress for unfair dismissal now comprise the bulk of cases dealt with by Industrial Tribunals. These bodies, chaired by lawyers who are flanked by trade union and employer representatives, were first established under the 1964 Industrial Training Act as 'courts of appeal' before which employers could challenge their assessed levies, but they have subsequently been given much wider responsibilities. They judge disputes about redundancy pay and claims under the Equal Pay, Sex Discrimination and Race Relations Acts that are discussed in later sections of this chapter. They also handle allegations of unfair dismissal, now running at around 35,000 a year out of the total of some 46,000 cases brought before the tribunals. Two-thirds of these cases are settled 'out of court' with assistance from the Conciliation Service (described below). Amongst cases reaching tribunal hearings, the verdicts from which can be challenged at an Employment Appeals Tribunal, there is no apparent tendency for the employee to be favoured. In 1977 only 30.8 per cent of complaints for unfair dismissal reaching tribunal hearings were upheld. Nevertheless, employers' organisations have launched vociferous attacks on this piece of protective legislation. They complain of the time consumed even by conciliated cases, and have alleged that instead of protecting employment the legislation has destroyed jobs by making firms reluctant to recruit. Other aspects of the 1975 Act have attracted similar criticism—of increasing the costs of employment thereby reducing the demand for labour, but protection against unfair dismissal has received particularly widespread condemnation. An independent survey of over 300 manufacturing plants suggests that the legislation has reduced sackings and made employers more selective, but has not actually inhibited recruitment.[17] However, this evidence has not won employers' favour for the statute.

The long-running historical concern for health and safety at work continues to this day, and with the recognition that technological changes can introduce new dangers the 1974 Health and Safety at Work Act has led to a variety of new provisions aimed at ensuring that illness and accidents caused by work are kept to a minimum. When fully implemented, this Act will require the designation of safety officers and the creation of committees to enhance health and safety in all workplaces. A Health and Safety Executive also operates under the Act, and in 1977 spent £8.5m on research, testing and scientific support services.

A further body of protective legislation involves the Wages Councils which operate under the 1959 Wages Councils Act and enforce minimum rates of pay in industries where trade unions have been weak and wages low. In 1978 there were 41 Wages Councils covering around 2,750,000 workers in 390,000 establishments. In addition to fixing minimum rates, the Councils are also intended to stimulate free collective bargaining thereby removing the need for statutory wage regulation. Councils that work themselves out of jobs are wound up by the Secretary of State, whilst new Councils are created when new pockets of low pay are brought to public attention. At the moment the plight of homeworkers is attracting widespread concern. In 1978 the majority were earning less than 40 pence per hour, and some less than 10 pence. The employees involved are mainly women who are confined to their homes by dependent children, elderly relatives, disability or lack of transport,[18] and the creation of a wages council to cover this section of the workforce is under active consideration.

However, the effectiveness of the Wages Council machinery itself is also under criticism. The Councils have been accused of emitting complex agreements without the means of adequate enforcement, with the result that regulations are often breached.[19] Minimum rates are enforced on 390,000 employers by only 150 Department of Employment inspectors whose work has become best-known for the numerous breaches of regulations they uncover. In 1978 the inspectors visited 31,762 establishments following which arrears were paid to the workers at 10,624. Spot-checks in Blackpool found that a half the employers investigated were underpaying and in Cheltenham a third. The worst offenders were retailers, especially book-stores, licensed premises and hairdressers. Only 16 employers were prosecuted. The inspectorate hesitates before taking offenders to court since it recognises that wage regulations can be complex and firms can default unintentionally, and because culprits are mostly willing to pay arrears and bring their pay levels up to the statutory minima. In the event of legal proceedings the courts rarely impose draconian penalties, so prosecution is reserved for recalcitrants who offend repeatedly. If penalties and prosecutions were increased, employers might be prompted to familiarise themselves and comply with Wages Council edicts. But even if this happened, would it solve the problem of low pay that the Councils were originally created to tackle? A further criticism of the Councils is that their prescribed rates are amongst the lowest in the land.

Some call for a national minimum wage enforced by statute, but never explain who is to pay the bill. If all other things could remain equal, no one would seek to preserve low pay. In an ideal world we would all like to abolish redundancy and guarantee secure, safe, well-paid jobs for all. The problem is that other things stubbornly refuse to remain equal. Hauling in the tail-end of low paid jobs would mean surrendering the differentials enjoyed in occupations currently offering average and above-average earnings.

Certain forms of job protection are cost-free, such as safeguarding individuals against arbitrary dismissal. Others can pay for themselves. If a healthy worker is a productive worker it makes sound economic sense to promote health and safety at work. But when healthier workers are no more productive than others, someone has to pay the price and protective legislation itself will not generate the necessary wealth. In an expanding economy protective legislation can help to distribute the gains; it can ensure that labour receives its share, and that the benefits from economic growth are distributed to all workers, even those without industrial muscle-power. Unhappily, for the greater part of the 1970s Britain was a no-growth economy. Unemployment rose, investment sagged and firms' profit margins were squeezed. In so far as some groups of workers benefited from the new protective legislation, therefore, it was largely at the expense of others, particularly the unemployed. In advancing employees' rights the 1974–9 Labour administrations acted from the best of motives, but left their successors the task of either generating the wealth to pay the price, or modifying the legislation in question.

Industrial relations: the Advisory, Conciliation and Arbitration Service

The notion of the nineteenth century as an age when Britain's industrial power was based on a pure *laissez-faire* economy will not stand rigorous scrutiny. Protective legislation began before the Victorian era. More fundamentally, the very idea of economic forces operating free from all political constraints is sociologically naive. It took state power to build notionally free commodity and labour markets, and to create what is now called free collective bargaining by releasing trade unions from previous restrictive legislation, and encouraging firms and industries to establish negotiating procedures. Trade unions have never enjoyed any natural rights—only those guaranteed in laws that have been repeatedly modified. Governments have always sought to influence the conduct of industrial relations. The latter have never been free from politics, and recent battles over trade union law are but the latest episodes in a long-running historical saga.

Since 1961 successive governments have attempted to regulate the growth of salaries and wages by means of persuasion, social contracts and voluntary norms, and more formally through the National Board for Prices and Incomes, the Pay Board and the Comparabilities Commission. The Industrial Relations Act of 1971 attempted to impose a new legal framework on bargaining relationships. It lasted less than four years. Following intense trade union opposition its major provisions were repealed in 1974.

In addition to laying a legal framework, encouraging industries to establish their own bargaining procedures, and from time to time seeking to influence directly the outcome of collective bargaining, governments have also developed facilities to help the parties involved to reach agreements when negotiations through normal established channels fail, and it is these facilities that comprise the industrial relations services. The services are now offered through an Advisory, Conciliation and Arbitration Service (ACAS), a Quango that operates under the 1975 Employment Protection Act and whose controlling body contains representatives from trade unions and employers' associations. The main reason for 'hiving off' the industrial relations services was that, with governments becoming increasingly involved in regulating wage and salary levels, doubts had spread as to the ability of Department of Employment officers to act independently. No one has doubted the independence of ACAS. Some employers have argued that the legislation governing ACAS's procedures is biased against their interests, but the service itself has remained above suspicion of ministerial intervention. It has steadfastly refused to enforce governments' income policies. It will draw trade unions' and employers' attention to government guidelines and norms, but will not interpret let alone enforce them.

ACAS exercises a wide range of responsibilities. It acts as a base for the Certification Officer who has taken over the task of maintaining a register of independent trade unions from the Chief Registrar of Friendly Societies. It conducts enquiries and issues legally enforceable recommendations following trade union claims for recognition, and it is these proceedings that have led to criticism from employers that the law requires ACAS to operate on the assumption that industrial relations are best handled via trade union organisation and recognition. Yet the Grunwick case has shown that a determined employer can resist not only ACAS but trade union power as well. ACAS has the power to appoint special courts of enquiry to investigate particular firms and disputes, and can also undertake the kind of longer-term investigations into the general problems affecting particular industries that were formerly conducted by the Commission for Industrial Relations. But the above responsibilities do not cover the mainstay of the ACAS workload. Its main activities are the provision of industrial relations services to individuals, firms and trade unions, and these services fall into the three main categories named in the agency's title.

First there are advisory services. ACAS offers general advice and information to firms on all problems relating to personnel management including how to make the most effective use of manpower, and how to establish workable systems of industrial relations at the factory level. This kind of advice to industry is intended to help prevent disputes reaching the point where other forms of intervention from ACAS become necessary.

Second there is the conciliation service. Regionally-based conciliation officers keep in close contact with trade unions and employers, and familiarise themselves with industry's problems. Consequently when a dispute occurs that the parties are unable to settle amongst themselves the conciliation officer should already possess sufficient background knowledge and suitable informal contacts to be able to act as a mediator. Conciliation is essentially an informal and voluntary procedure. Conciliators intervene only at the request, or at least with the tacit approval, of the parties to a dispute. The job involves meeting the parties either separately or together, measuring the areas of disagreement that exist, making suggestions and, if possible, finding a basis on which negotiations can be resumed. The informal atmosphere in which this service is provided makes it difficult to evaluate its success. However, during 1977 the service responded to 3,299 requests for conciliation and settlements were achieved in 74 per cent.

In addition to acting as intermediaries in industrial disputes, the ACAS conciliation officers are also responsible for attempting to conciliate all applications to Industrial Tribunals before a formal hearing is required. Two-thirds of the 46,000 annual applications to tribunals are settled 'out of court' with the assistance of the conciliation service. Handling grievances prior to tribunal hearings has now become the 'bread and butter' of the conciliation service's work.

Arbitration is the final service that ACAS offers. If conciliation is unsuccessful and at the request of the parties, arbitration, usually by a single person, but alternatively by a panel nominated by ACAS and acceptable to the parties can be offered as a means towards reaching a settlement. The Central Arbitration Committee (which has replaced the Industrial Court) provides for more formal hearings and, amongst its other responsibilities, hears cases claiming 'fair pay' brought under section 11 of the 1975 Employment Protection Act.

The Secretary of State retains some of his former powers including the right to appoint Committees and Courts of Enquiry to investigate the circumstances surrounding specific disputes, the object usually being to make the relevant facts and issues public, thereby prompting the parties to a settlement. The Court of Enquiry used to be the best-known of all the industrial relations services, such bodies being appointed to investigate disputes that were already attracting public interest and concern, but due to the effectiveness of ACAS these set-pieces have now become rare events.

Young people

In addition to services benefiting the entire population, special services cater for various groups who, at least in the services' absence, would be disadvantaged in the quest for employment. Young people are a group whose special needs have long been recognised. The precursor of the current Careers Service, the Juvenile Employment Service, originated with the Education (Choice of Employment) Act in 1910, a measure which followed closely the creation of a national system of labour exchanges in 1909. It was realised at that time that the young would require special provision because they were recruited into different jobs than those sought by unemployed adults, because they stood an above-average risk of unemployment and misemployment and, probably above all else, because they were considered to be in special need of advice and guidance.[20] These considerations remain as true today as ever. Hence the survival of a separate Careers Service, outside the ESD, which was given its present title, structure and responsibilities by the Employment and Training Act of 1973. In 1976 the Service employed 2,651 careers officers plus 2,163 support staff, and by 1978 they had been joined by 640 unemployment specialists, posts separately funded by the Department of Employment to assist the Careers Service in coping with youth unemployment.

The Careers Service is concerned with education as well as employment, and its organisation is designed to facilitate contact with both the education system and the remainder of the employment services. Overall supervision is through the Careers Service Branch of the Department of Employment, but the Careers Service has not been 'hived off' to the MSC because the Department, whilst issuing guidelines and offering support, does not directly manage the Service. Local Education Authorities operate the Careers Service thereby forging links with local schools and colleges and, it is intended, giving the Service sufficient freedom from central control to respond to local needs and conditions.

The Service's statutory responsibilities are to offer vocational information and advice to all young people in education (except at universities) and to assist them in finding their first jobs. Careers officers may advise and assist young people after their initial entry into employment if their clients return for help, but once in employment individuals are free to use the ESD services.

Whilst they are at school or college, the Careers Service attempts to provide young people with whatever job information and advice they require. Careers literature is distributed through schools and public libraries. Careers officers give talks to audiences of young people, individual interviews are held, visits to places of work and even work experience schemes may be arranged before young people leave school. In some schools systematic courses of careers work extending over a number of years have been developed through co-operation between careers officers, careers teachers and other staff, but these schools are still the exceptions. A government enquiry amongst 1,733 school-leavers in 1968-9 found that none of the schools covered had a full-time careers teacher, and only 4 out of 10 pupils had received formal careers lessons.[21] More recent studies have portrayed school-leavers harshly critical of their inadequate preparation for working life. A study of 307 young people at 93 Leicestershire firms records that only 20 per cent felt the last year at school had been a good preparation for work.[22] The young people voiced demands for more realistic advice, works visits and careers discussions. Youthaid's enquiry among 250 16-year-old leavers from schools in London, Northumberland and Newcastle-upon-Tyne in 1977 uncovered equally widespread requests for more concrete information about jobs, social security and how to handle interviews.[23]

To help beginning workers find appropriate jobs the Careers Service offers employment exchange facilities. Approximately a third of all school-leavers are recorded as 'placed', and in addition to these official placements careers officers offer a great deal of informal advice on when, where and how to apply for suitable opportunities. Surveys of user-opinion show that, in contrast to their preparation while at school, young people are favourably impressed by the quality of service offered by careers officers during the initial entry into employment.[24]

The work of the Careers Service cannot be judged in isolation. Its efforts to prepare young people for employment have to be considered alongside the schools', whilst in dealing with out-of-school youth the Careers Service is but one amongst a battery of employment services, many created during the unemployment of the 1970s. School-leavers suffered more than adult workers, partly because one of the sources of rising unemployment was the growth in size of the school-leaving age-group, the consequence of a rising birth-rate from 1955 to 1965. But in addition to this, in a tight labour market young people find themselves competing for jobs amongst older workers who, being judged the more responsible and mature, tend to win employers' favour.[25] Officially measured unemployment, which has typically recorded 8, 10 or 12 per cent of 16–18-year-olds registered, underestimates the numbers affected. The Youthaid study referred to earlier found that 53 per cent of the school-leavers were unemployed for some period, on average 10.4 weeks, during their first six months out of school.[26] Needless to say, the risks of unemployment are not evenly distributed. Early in 1977 the national unemployment rate for 16–18-year-olds was 8.8 per cent, but on Merseyside it was 12.4, and in Knowsley (which includes Kirkby) 37.1. By the mid-1970s, in the depressed regions, tens of thousands of school-leavers were stranded with slim prospects of employment, and within these regions certain categories of young people suffered particularly harshly, especially school-leavers without qualifications.[27]

The plight of the young unemployed was eased by Job Creation schemes after 1975, then following the report of a MSC working party, *Young People and Work*,[28] the special measures for out-of-school youth were co-ordinated in a Youth Opportunities Programme (YOP). This is administrated by the Special Programmes Division of the MSC through 28 area boards on which employers, trade unions and local authorities are represented. The aim of the programme is to break the grip of joblessness upon young people, and not merely by providing temporary alternatives to idleness. The intention is to assist young people who find themselves in Catch-22 situations, unable to get jobs without experience and basic skills, and unable to obtain skills and experience without jobs.

The main element of YOP is the Work Experience Programme (WEP) which provides training lasting up to twelve months, sometimes in specially mounted projects, but usually in regular places of employment. Shorter Work Preparation Courses, usually college-based, are also organised. Trainees are paid a standard allowance, £23.50 in 1981, when the overall programme was aiming to cater for over 400,000 young people a year, roughly a half of all school-leavers. The organisers aim to meet an 'Easter guarantee'—the offer of a job or YOP place to every school-leaver before the following Easter. Access to the programme is via the Careers Service or ESD.

YOP in general and WEP in particular have been remarkably successful, at least in terms of the speed with which the schemes were launched. In the programme's first year of operation 12,000 WEP schemes offering 43,000 places were approved. Press and television adverts were used to publicise the predicament of the young unemployed and to encourage sponsors. A further sign of success was that 80 per cent of the early trainees found jobs either during or shortly following their courses, helped by the gains in self-confidence and social skills acquired.[29] However, as overall levels of unemployment have risen, the proportion of trainees moving directly into real jobs has fallen sharply.

Outside YOP there is Community Industry, introduced in 1971, which caters at any time for approximately 5,000 young people who are not merely unemployed but 'at odds' in ways that make their employment prospects exceptionally poor. Community Industry projects have been established mainly in the inner-cities and are intended to contribute something of value in their communities. WEP aims to teach social and life skills, but Community Industry, whilst endeavouring to achieve a 'judicious mixture', aims specifically to recruit younsters whose outlook, social demeanour or time-keeping would probably make them unacceptable to WEP sponsors. Out of 1,257 young people who left Community Industry up to 1974, 200 were dismissed and only 637 were in regular employment shortly afterwards.[30] These vital statistics may appear disappointing compared with WEP, but given the nature of Community Industry's workforce its record is far from undistinguished.

Training opportunities are the final element in the web of services for young people. In general the TSD has steered clear of direct involvement in the vocational training of school-leavers. This field has been left to individual firms, advised and influenced by their ITBs. However, the MSC has offered special Industrial Training Grants to firms and ITBs to maintain the volume of training in line with the economy's future needs, and to ensure that young people who would normally obtain apprenticeships do not miss the chance due to depressed economic conditions at their time of school-leaving.

In the future the MSC's main involvement in training school-leavers may take a different direction and deal with young people who are ordinarily denied all training opportunities. A third of beginning workers receive no formal training, and two-thirds of these obtain no further education.[31] Between 1960 and 1967 the proportion of boys obtaining apprenticeships rose from 36 to 43 per cent, but subsequently there has been no increase. On economic and social grounds, and in the light of the future prospects of the individuals involved, concern has been repeatedly expressed at the large numbers receiving no vocational training whatsoever, and since 1976 the MSC has been experimenting with Gateway Courses offering Unified Vocational Preparation to these youngsters. A 1979 consultative paper declared, 'It is the government's aim to establish during the 1980s a universal scheme of education and training opportunities for young people.'[32] The intention is to offer Unified Vocational Preparation courses lasting approximately six months, with training on the job backed by educational components, to the third of beginning workers who currently never step on to any training ladders. The MSC's experiments have found employers unconvinced of the need, and many of the young people reluctant to participate in education, but during the 1980s this could nevertheless become a growth area for employment services aimed at beginning workers.

The disabled

People suffering from physical or mental handicap are clearly at a disadvantage in the competition for employment. Probably because their handicaps are so immediately apparent, the disabled are another disadvantaged group for whom special provision is long-standing, though until the Second World War this provision was minimal. During the First World War rehabilitation departments were created in some military hospitals, and some government rehabilitation centres were opened, but these facilities were not developed during the inter-war years. It was only in the Second World War that the government began to give systematic consideration to the problems of the disabled. This consideration was related to the wider attempts being made to plan a Welfare State for post-war Britain, to an awareness that many returning servicemen would need rehabilitation, and to the expectation that large-scale unemployment would never return and the economy would need all the available labour power. The outcome was the Disabled Persons (Employment) Act of 1944 which remains the basis for provision today having been subjected to minor modifications in 1958. Since

1976 all the employment services for the disabled have been administered by the ESD.

A register of disabled persons is maintained, and anyone who is for some reason handicapped in the quest for employment and likely to remain so for twelve months can register, provided the person is judged potentially employable. In 1977 there were 532,000 on the register, and largely as a result of the special services available, the vast majority were in employment.

The law insists that any firm employing more than 20 workers must engage at least 3 per cent from amongst the registered disabled. The aim of this 'quota system' is to ensure that some demand for labour is directed in the disabled's direction, and in addition it is hoped that the quota will play an educative role by accustoming both employers and other members of the labour force to accept handicapped persons in ordinary jobs. The intention has been to give the disabled opportunities to 'hold their own' and prove their worth in all sections of the economy.

The 1944 Act allows the Department of Employment to reserve occupations for disabled persons, but so far only two occupations, electric lift operator and car park attendant, have been designated. This is an effective way of ensuring that they are offered some jobs, but the emphasis has always been on integrating the disabled in 'ordinary' employment.

Disablement Resettlement Officers (DROs) are available to advise clients, assess individuals' needs, and liaise with hospitals and employers, while Employment Rehabilitation Centres (formerly known as Industrial Rehabilitation Units) allow individuals to tone up following illness or injury and process 14,000 clients per year. Courses at these centres are free, last up to twenty-six weeks, and maintenance allowances are paid to those taking part. Little training in actual vocational skills is given, but in suitable cases subsequent vocational training can be arranged at the Skillcentres catering for the general working population.

When placement in outside industry is impossible, as with the severely handicapped, sheltered employment can be offered. A government-subsidised company, Remploy, provides sheltered employment for around 8,000 persons in all parts of Britain. In sheltered (from economic forces) conditions, disabled persons are able to earn a wage, working on tasks and at speeds suited to their capacities. Other sheltered employment, in 1977–8 totalling 5,500 places, is supported in schemes run by voluntary organisations and local authorities. This type of provision recognises that even when employment is not an economic proposition, occupational activity can still be of therapeutic benefit, a principle that has also been applied in occupational centres for retired workers (see below). But sheltered employment for the disabled is only used when outside placement appears impossible. The emphasis in the services is to enable disabled persons to become integrated into the normal workforce, and whenever possible sheltered employment itself aims at rehabilitation rather than the maintenance of permanent enclaves.

Are the services for the disabled adequate? They are certainly not above criticism and the MSC is actively considering possible improvements. The rise in unemployment during the 1970s left the disabled particularly vulnerable. Unemployment among the registered disabled crept upwards, and in 1977 stood at 14 per cent, twice the overall level for the labour force. Only 45 per cent of all individuals who pass through Employment Rehabilitation Centres are in employment or training three months after their courses. Yet in 1977 only 37 per cent of employers were fulfilling the 3 per cent quota. Official action has been inhibited by the fact that in 1978 only 2 out of 30 central government departments, none of the regional health authorities and none of the nationalised industries were meeting their quota requirements. Rigid enforcement of the quota is impossible—there are not enough registered disabled persons to go round—but some critics have suggested that more vigorous enforcement is both possible and desirable.

Other critics have questioned the value of the quota system, claiming that although it may have performed an educative function in earlier years it has now become counter-productive. Numbers on the disablement register have been declining, partly due to the retirement of the war disabled, but mainly because over a half of those who would be accepted fail to register. The employment offered to the disabled in sheltered conditions and outside is usually of low status, and the earnings of disabled workers fall well short of the general level.[33] Handicapped individuals who decline to register are seeking to avoid the high risk of unemployment faced by registrants, and also the process of being channelled towards routine, low-paid jobs.

There have been suggestions that the quota system be complemented or replaced by cash subsidies to encourage employers to recruit disabled persons. But what would the implications be for the disabled's status and self-respect? And would cash subsidies have the intended effect? The MSC's Special Employment and Training Measures include a Job Introduction Scheme which subsidises job trials for the disabled, but by February 1979 only 181 individuals had benefited. In a harsh economic climate it is inevitably difficult to enhance the disabled's employment prospects. It may be unrealistic to expect official measures to do more than 'hold the line' and ensure that the disabled's disadvantages do not multiply. In 1977 14 per cent of the registered disabled were unemployed, but 86 per cent were in jobs. The present employment services for the disabled can claim some credit for assisting so many to hold jobs, in most cases in outside industry.

Women

For working-class women employment outside the home has been normal ever since the industrial revolution. It has never been regarded as a right or privilege, but simply as a financial necessity. Nevertheless, the twentieth century has seen first the working woman, and more recently the working wife and mother gaining general social acceptance. In 1951, 40 per cent of married women worked, but by 1971 the proportion had risen to 64 per cent with little variation between social classes. Career women still face scepticism from some employers and colleagues, together with occasional disapproval from children's teachers and doctors. They face the strain of the double shift—paid employment followed by housework. Some remain nagged by doubts as to their children's welfare. Husbands who try to ease the strain may be punished by their own 'greedy occupations'.[34] But women and men are now searching for new balances within marriage.[35] The myth of motherhood, the idea that mothering is natural for women and essential for children, is being shattered. Alongside these changes, the case for a new deal for working women has been acknowledged in legislation.

Even when doing similar work, it has been customary for women to be paid less than men, whilst covert discrimination has restricted women to the less skilled and lower-paid jobs. Amongst school-leavers approximately 80 per cent of girls not continuing full-time education have entered jobs involving no systematic training, their recruitment to skilled manual occupations has been rare, and those professions in which women are numerous tend to be associated with the feminine role. Few training schemes have been suited to the needs of married women contemplating a return to work, whilst facilities to support the wife and mother in her domestic role so as to make a prolonged interruption of her career unnecessary have been equally exceptional. The net effect of these barriers has been to relegate most women to second-class jobs, and also to leave the female sex under-employed. Surveys of married women reveal a latent demand for employment which remains hidden because, not being eligible for social security benefits and doubting whether the employment exchanges will offer anything suitable, up to 200,000 fail to register and therefore do not swell the unemployment figures.[36]

Two statutes aim to remedy women's disadvantages. The 1970 Equal Pay Act entitles women to equal pay for the same or broadly similar work, whilst the 1975 Sex Discrimination Act, amongst other provisions, outlaws sex discrimination in hiring and promotion. The 1975 Act has also created the Equal Opportunities Commission (EOC) which monitors the relevant legislation, educates the public, and assists individuals who believe they have been denied their rights. But the EOC itself reports that progress towards sex equality in employment has been modest. In 1978 women were still earning less than two-thirds the male average, and the trend towards equal pay had halted. Women remained concentrated in less prestigious sectors of the workforce, and not only in manufacturing industry. A quarter of all university graduates are women, but in 1976 they comprised less than 10 per cent of lecturers and only 60 out of 3,303 professors. The EOC has complained of a lack of training and promotion opportunities for women. It has noted shop floor and trade union resistance to the principle of sex equality. It has also observed how some employers make strenuous efforts to resist granting equal pay. Popular strategies include creating different job titles and bestowing generous differentials for heavy and dirty work. The EOC recommends rescinding all special protection for women, as regards hours of work, for example, in order to reduce employers' excuses for contravening the spirit of recent legislation.

Feminists have directed some of their anger towards the EOC itself. The Commission has been criticised for an apparent lack of activity, but a problem with the Equal Pay and Sex Discrimination Acts is that individual cases of discrimination are notoriously difficult to prove. How does a woman who is not offered a job or passed over for promotion prove that gender was a relevant factor? How are women to know whether their work is sufficiently similar to men's to justify equal pay? Women who feel they have been denied their rights can complain to the Industrial Tribunals. In 1978 there were only 343 applications under the Equal Pay Act and 171 (including 14 by men) under the Sex Discrimination statute. The majority of these cases were conciliated prior to hearings. Of the 67 sex discrimination cases that reached a hearing, 53 were dismissed, whilst out of 80 applications for equal pay only 24 were upheld.

Its critics would like the EOC to play a more aggressive role, investigating entire industries and companies, and vigorously supporting applications to the tribunals. But is it realistic to treat the complete eradication of gender discrimination in employment as anything but a very long-term exercise? It will surely require at least a generation of 'liberated' women to enter similar occupations to men and to pursue equally successful careers, and at the moment not all women seek this liberation. Few openly oppose the *principle* of equal pay and treatment in job selection, but as in other areas of employment legislation, it is difficult to attract volunteers to bear the cost. Sex equality in employment would benefit the growing numbers of one-parent families that are mostly headed by women. The main short-term losers would not be men in general, but those households which contain a third of all married women, with a solitary male wage or salary earner. Experience in alleviating the disadvantages of other groups, including ethnic minorities, suggests that the law is less than all-powerful when faced with ingrained attitudes and widely vested interests.

Ethnic minorities

The presence of ethnic minorities in Britain is not novel. Immigrants have been entering the country since the nineteenth century and before. However, the upsurge of black immigration during the 1950s made the presence of minorities unusually visible, and by the early 1960s it was evident that these newcomers were being clustered in less skilled and prestigious jobs, this being one aspect of an emergent race relations problem. Newcomers to any society will not normally possess the skills and qualifications required for entry to prestigious occupations and, in addition to this, they rarely escape a degree of prejudice and discrimination. Earlier waves of immigrants into Britain including the Irish and Jews initially entered at the foot of the social scale before beginning the process of assimilation, and the treatment of white immigrant workers in other western European countries today broadly parallels the reception of black immigrants in Britain.[37] Instant assimilation was never feasible, but official policy has aimed at alleviating immigrants' disadvantages, and ensuring that their colour does not lead to these disadvantages being perpetuated through the generations.

Discrimination in employment on grounds of colour, race, and ethnic or national origin has been unlawful since 1968, but the current position is defined by the 1976 Race Relations Act. In addition to outlawing discrimination in employment and several other spheres, this Act has also created the Commission for Racial Equality (CRE) which has replaced and assumed the functions of the former Community Relations Commission and Race Relations Board. Apart from monitoring the legislation and assisting individuals who believe they have been discriminated against, the CRE also plays an educative role. It draws up codes of practice, promotes research, offers advice and thereby hopes to shape public opinion and behaviour.

In addition to the 1976 Act, a battery of further measures aim to reduce the disadvantages of ethnic minorities. Amongst recent immigrants, language is often a problem, and there is provision for special language classes in schools and further education, whilst language training in places of employment can be funded by the

MSC. The training of all teachers and careers officers now covers race relations. The Department of Employment offers a Race Relations Employment Advisory Service to industry. Training schemes and special measures available for the general population are intended to be of particular assistance to especially disadvantaged groups.

On the surface the situation gives grounds for optimism, Following the 1968 statute that first prohibited race discrimination in employment, early comment from the Department of Employment claimed that the Act was operating in a satisfactory manner and hinted at widespread changes in personnel practices. In the year covered by the 1971–2 report of the Race Relations Board, 464 complaints of discrimination in employment were received, but following investigation discrimination was proved in only 5 per cent, and all these cases were reported as having been successfully conciliated. Up to 1978, during the 1976 Race Relations Act's first year of operation, there were only 146 applications for redress to Industrial Tribunals, and at the end of the proceedings a mere 5 cases were upheld. Is racial discrimination as rare as these figures suggest?

Sceptics claim that existing measures are simply not working, and that the modest volume of complaints proves only that ethnic minorities have lost confidence in statutory bodies. There is persuasive evidence that racial discrimination in employment remains widespread. Situational tests mounted by *Political and Economic Planning* in 1974 found that as many as 46 per cent of coloured applicants for unskilled jobs were discriminated against.[38] There was less discrimination in other types of work, and its overall extent was less than recorded by comparable research in 1967, but unless the situation has changed radically since 1974 the inescapable conclusion must be that the trickle of cases reaching the Industrial Tribunals is misleading.

Perhaps most disappointing of all, investigations among black school-leavers find that even those born and educated in Britain are less successful than their white counterparts. Studies of white and Asian school-leavers, matched for qualifications and levels of aspiration, in Leicester and Walsall in 1975, report that the Asians were far less successful in the job market.[39] A 1977 study of 284 West Indian and 266 white school-leavers in Lewisham found that during the November-February following school-leaving, unemployment ran at 10 per cent among the whites and 29 per cent among the blacks.[40] All the relevant research indicates that unemployment among black minorities runs at two to three times the general level. The Lewisham blacks had only slightly lower educational attainments than the white sample and were equally energetic in seeking work, but laboured under a number of disadvantages. Later generations may not face the same language problems and may have superior paper qualifications to the initial waves of immigrants, but the latter's handicaps are nevertheless liable to be handed down. Black communities in Britain tend to be clustered in inner-city areas, faced with all the handicaps associated with poverty and poor housing. Add racial discrimination and it becomes easy to see why black school-leavers, despite their frequently high aspirations, are relatively unsuccessful in the search for skilled work, and often any jobs at all.

To further compound the situation, there is evidence that some black youngsters fail to use the very employment services intended to alleviate their difficulties. A 1974 report from the Community Relations Commission, based on interviews with several hundred black and white 18–25-year-olds contacted in different parts of the country, found that, 'Approximately half the young unemployed black people were not registered at careers offices or employment exchanges, apparently because they did not see registration as a means of getting a job . . . . The careers advice available to young black people is inadequate; both the Careers Service and the employment exchange are distrusted by many of them.'[41]

The ageing

Like the young, ageing workers face special employment problems, but whereas youth unemployment has attracted government concern and special measures, the problems of older workers have been almost totally neglected. Indeed, rather than assisting the ageing to remain in employment, the net effect of social policies has been to encourage their removal. The terms on which retirement pensions are available discourage men aged 65 and women over 60 from continuing in employment, and the special measures introduced to combat youth unemployment include a Job Release Scheme that offers incentives for those approaching retirement age to vacate their jobs.

There is little dissent from the principle that the ageing should be permitted to continue in employment for as long as they wish to do so and can contribute to the economy. Upon retirement the incomes of old people are often severely reduced, which even if not involving a subsistence existence can isolate the retired from the patterns of life to which they have been accustomed and that are normal in their communities. In addition, men in particular can suffer psychologically upon losing their roles as wage-earners, and society loses the value of the labour power of people who retire—a serious problem when the proportion of elderly people in the population is rising. All these are widely acknowledged reasons why the ageing should be assisted to remain in employment for as long as possible, such assistance being no substitute but complementary to adequate services for those who must retire. Nevertheless, there are strong pressures rooted in contemporary industry, and substantially reinforced by social policy, that conspire to exclude ageing individuals from the labour force.

The proportion of men aged over 65 who remain economically active has been declining for over half a century; from 59 per cent in 1921 to 31 per cent in 1951 and 19 per cent in 1971. Among women aged over 60 the employment rate has risen, but from a very low take-off point to only 12 per cent in 1971. Surveys[42] have shown that deteriorating capacity is one factor in most decisions to retire, but they also show that a fifth of retired men aged 65–70 would prefer to be employed.[43] The unemployment rate for individuals approaching retirement age is well above average. A survey of the registered unemployed in June 1973 found that 23 per cent were in the 60–64 age group, and such persons tended to remain unemployed for longer periods than younger workers.[44]

Some of the employment problems associated with ageing are rooted in the brute facts of human nature. Ageing is a gradual process. As people grow older their physical and mental capacities gradually decline, and accommodating the organisation of work to this process can be difficult. As jobs are mechanised it becomes difficult to adjust the pace of work to the capacities of ageing employees. Many 'light' staff jobs such as personnel work are now professionalised, and older workers can no longer be transferred to these positions. When light work is available the claims of the ageing have to be balanced against those of other groups, including the disabled. This applies with particular force in times of high unemployment. The accelerating pace of technological change has been transforming the mature skills and experience of the older worker from an asset into a handicap. When older workers are declared redundant they find it extremely difficult to discover new jobs. Yet when redundancies are necessary the fact that the compensation to which individuals are entitled increases with length of service has led to a general abandonment of the 'last in—first out' principle. It is frequently the older workers who find themselves on the scrapheap.[45] The claims of different age groups have to be balanced, and premature retirement often appears less harsh than unemployment among individuals in the child-rearing phase, or at the outset of their careers.

In an ageing society there is invariably pressure from young people to have senior posts vacated to facilitate their own advancement. Few firms enforce rigid retirement ages, but when the pressures described above are combined with the fact that state pensions, and often occupational pensions as well, become available at a determined age, it becomes easy to understand how many ageing workers are eased into retirement before it is really necessary for them to give up work completely.

The ageing comprise the one clearly disadvantaged section of the workforce whose difficulties have not stimulated any major policy initiatives during the last decade. From time to time the Department of Employment has exhorted firms to retain older workers but, as already argued, the net effect of social policies has been to decrease the likelihood of older people continuing in employment. Some local authorities and voluntary societies maintain occupational centres which retired people can attend. Here the ageing can work at their own pace under economically sheltered conditions, but are paid far less than would be considered acceptable in industry. These centres recognise the therapeutic value of occupational activity, but are really no substitute for proper services to assist the ageing who wish to remain in employment.

It is difficult to prescribe forms of intervention that would solve the employment problems of the ageing. Experience with other disadvantaged groups shows that we have yet to devise a fool-proof formula. The results of race relations and sex discrimination legislation indicate that bestowing a formal right to equal treatment may fail to grapple with the crux of the problem. Requiring employers to engage a quota of disadvantaged persons, as has been the practice with the disabled, can have the side-effect of labelling and setting apart the group concerned with unfortunate secondary consequences. Effective solutions to the employment problems of some disadvantaged groups may be contingent on broader changes in the attitudes and circumstances in which their disadvantages are rooted, and upon a buoyant economy.

Conclusion: in defence of Quangos

Quango-bashing has become a national pastime. The very use of the term evokes images of jobs-for-the-boys, patronage, and power without accountability. No doubt the criticisms contain some substance, but there is a positive case for Quangos that is well-illustrated by the employment services.

First they enable particular services to be insulated from other policies that governments are pursuing, which is impossible in normal departments headed by ministers who are bound by collective Cabinet responsibility. This is vitally important for the conciliation and arbitration services offered by ACAS; their credibility depends on their agency's independence.

Second, and equally important, Quangos are able to research, formulate and publicise their own policy proposals without commitment, and sometimes in the face of opposition from the government departments to which they ultimately report. This freedom has been of fundamental importance in allowing the MSC to inject a vitality that has enabled Britain's employment services to innovate in response to the needs of the population in general, and its disadvantaged sectors in particular, during the changing and frequently depressed economic conditions since the 1960s.

Further reading

Comprehensive and up-to-date information about all the employment services is published monthly in the *Department of Employment Gazette*, HMSO.

For more detailed information about the various employment services, and the problems of different groups, see:

Commission for Racial Equality, *Looking for Work*, 1978.

W. W. DANIEL, *Whatever Happened to the Workers in Woolwich?*, Political and Economic Planning, 1972.

F. FIELD, *Unequal Shares: the Disabled and Employment*, Low Pay Unit Paper No. 20, 1978.

K. HALL and I. MILLER, *Re-training and Tradition*, Allen & Unwin, 1975.

S. MUKHERJEE, *Through no Fault of their Own*, Macdonald, 1973.

R. and R. N. RAPOPORT (eds), *Working Couples*, Routledge & Kegan Paul, 1978.

B. SHOWLER, *The Public Employment Service*, Longman, 1976.

Youthaid, *Study of the Transition from School to Working Life*, 1979.

4 Income and need

Anthony Forder and Robert Stevens

In our society the primary sources of income are payments in return for labour and the use of wealth. For the majority of the population most of their income comes from employment either directly or indirectly through dependence on a wage earner. However it must be stressed that, for many, this income is not adequate to meet needs. A second source of personal income derives from ownership of land or capital. Most of this income is concentrated in the hands of a few wealthy people,[1] although a proportion of it goes to others including those who earn low incomes or who are unable to work such as the handicapped or elderly. These are the sources of income that are regarded as 'normal' in a capitalist economic market. This chapter is concerned with the issue of how to meet the needs of those people who are not adequately catered for by this system as it operates at present. This includes groups such as low earners, single-parent families, the unemployed, the elderly and handicapped people. But before going any further it is perhaps best to expand on the concepts of need, poverty and the adequacy of income.

In considering the adequacy of income, the concept of a 'poverty line' has proved a useful tool. The poverty line is a level of income per person or family below which they should not be allowed to fall. The original concept was developed by Rowntree[2] who devised an income scale that represented the minimum incomes on which families of different sizes could subsist while maintaining their physical health. Rowntree in his first survey was concerned to convince a sceptical country that poverty was a real problem, and chose a standard so exacting that no one could deny his conclusions. In a later survey[3] he used a rather more generous standard, which was used as the basis of Beveridge's calculations for an appropriate scale of benefits for the post-war social security scheme.[4]

One of the criticisms of Rowntree's concept of poverty line based on 'objective' criteria of need is that it takes no account of actual patterns of expenditure and the social pressures that influence these. Townsend,[5] for example, showed that families living on incomes equivalent to Beveridge's scale spent on average less on food than Beveridge considered that they needed. So the scale was in fact inadequate to ensure the maintenance of the physical standards at which it aimed. Many priorities in expenditure are determined by social conventions, the need for social interaction, and the pressures exerted by state services for higher standards of child care. Such standards are strongly influenced by changes in the general level of earnings, so a poverty line should be related to average income in some way. This approach to defining standards has been called 'comparative need'.[6]

As we have noted, and despite their weaknesses, Beveridge based his calculations for an appropriate scale of benefits for the post-war social security scheme on Rowntree's findings. Later scales, including the current supplementary benefit and national insurance scales, although increasing with general increases in earnings and expenditure have by no means taken full account of the particular circumstances of people living on low incomes. For example, poor people spend a much higher proportion of their income on fuel than others,[7] yet benefit levels have only increased in relation to the *general* level of expenditure on fuel, not to the increased expenditure incurred by poor families. Consequently many such families have suffered severe hardship since the 1973 fuel crisis.[8] Nevertheless the scale rates are still used in research and as an official criterion of the adequacy of income. The justification for the use of these rates can only be that they provide an absolute minimal base line. In other words, if people are living below the supplementary benefit level there can be *no doubt* that their needs are not being met. It should therefore be stressed that there are many whose income is equivalent to, or above, the supplementary benefit scale rates, but is still not adequate to meet their needs.

One of the most recent analyses of the extent of poverty in Britain was undertaken by the Royal Commission on the Distribution of Income and Wealth.[9] Relating family income to supplementary benefit levels the Commission found that:

> in 1975 4½ million people lived on annual incomes at or below the long term supplementary benefit rate and another 4½ million were below an income level equal to 120% of S. B. A further 5 million were below 140% of S. B. Taking these three groups together, we nearly have 14 million people or 26 per cent of the population, living below 140 per cent of SB.[10]

The Royal Commission's report was typical in that it demonstrated that the majority of those living on the lowest incomes were either elderly or members of single-parent families. Of the total number of people living at or below the long-term supplementary benefit level 44 per cent were elderly and 15 per cent were members of single-parent families.[11] The elderly also formed a significant proportion of those living just above the supplementary benefit level.[12] A further important finding of the commission was that a significant number of families may have had a member in full-time work yet have had an income little above the long-term supplementary benefit level.

Finally, much evidence supports the view that while there may have been a reduction in the extent of poverty in the immediate post-war years the proportion of those living in poverty is now steadily increasing. For example Townsend and Abel Smith estimated that in 1953 7.8 per cent of the population lived in poverty but by 1960 this figure had increased to 14.2 per cent.[13] Comparison between different studies is often difficult because of the different criteria used to define poverty; nevertheless recent studies indicate that anything between 20 and 30 per cent of the population are now living in poverty.[14] Indeed it has been argued that the proportion of poor people and the conditions in which they live are now similar to the depression years of the 1930s.[15] The higher incidence of poverty may be at least partly accounted for by the increased proportion of those unemployed since the mid-1960s.[16]

Few analyses forecast a significant reduction in these figures and many argue that the introduction of new technologies such as micro-processing will lead to their rapid escalation. Other groups containing a high proportion of poor people that are increasing in size are the mentally and physically handicapped. Three broad approaches to the reduction of poverty have been put forward—increasing the national income, redistributing income and redistributing wealth. Each of these is considered in turn.

Potential solutions to the problem of poverty

The increase of national income

The argument of many people, including members of the present government, is that only by increasing national income, that is, by producing more goods more efficiently, in order that these goods can be sold abroad and compete with imports in the home market, can we eventually solve the problem of poverty. This argument postulates that greater industrial effectiveness will reduce poverty, first by the increased employment which will be brought about by industrial growth and subsequently by the creation of reserves of wealth, a portion of which can, in the future, be used to ameliorate the conditions of those who continue to live in poverty. A number of criticisms can be made of this argument. First, the use of available resources to create incentives and hence foster industrial growth, at least in the short term, must result in the increased incidence of poverty, as resources are denied to the welfare sector. Second, there is no guarantee that industrial growth will actually lead to increased employment. This is because this growth may be based on the use of sophisticated machinery in the production of goods, rather than human labour. Finally, income created in the future may simply not be used to meet the needs of the poor. For example, the USA is a wealthier country than Britain yet poverty is more extensive in the United States than it is here.[17]

Income redistribution

In a capitalist society such as Britain welfare spending is financed primarily through income redistribution. Income can be redistributed in a number of different ways to take greater account of need. First income can be redistributed between individuals. Webb and Sieve[18] have distinguished two types of such redistribution, 'contingency' and 'income'. Contingency redistribution is designed to meet specific needs regardless of the relative incomes of those who lose or gain. This is the aim of 'universal' social services like the National Health Service as well as insurance schemes undertaken through the economic market. In contrast 'income' redistribution is more directly associated with income levels, and may be described as either 'horizontal' or 'vertical'. In horizontal redistribution the transfers of income take place between groups with the same income levels but different circumstances, as with earnings-related benefits and tax allowances for economically dependent adults. Vertical redistribution takes place between different income groups and is positive if it takes place from richer to poorer, and negative if it is from poorer to richer. The latter is, of course, rarely a deliberate aim of policy. It is one effect of a free educational system whose selection procedures favour those with higher incomes. It was also the effect of a housing policy that controlled or subsidised rents and mortgages for a large proportion of the population but ignored the problems of those in furnished accommodation who were often particularly deprived.[19]

Another way of looking at vertical income transfers is to consider what proportion they represent of the incomes of the rich and poor. Taxes have traditionally been evaluated in this way. Progressive taxes represent a higher proportion of the income of the rich than of the poor; regressive taxes, like a poll tax or tax per head of the population, represent a higher proportion of the income of the poor than of the rich; proportionate taxes have an equal incidence throughout the income range. Benefits can be considered in a similar way. It is important to note, however, that a 'progressive' distribution of benefits, though favouring the poor proportionately, may still result in the rich gaining higher absolute benefits than the poor.

Second, income can be redistributed over the life of the individual. To some extent this can be undertaken by individuals for themselves through personal savings. These can be reinforced by insurance through the economic market to meet contingencies like sickness, unemployment or a long life after retirement that are unpredictable for individuals but predictable for larger populations. Alternatively, provision can be made as part of the conditions of employment through sick leave and superannuation schemes. But some people have too low an income to cover all these eventualities without leaving themselves in continuous poverty. For others the cost of insurance may be particularly high because for them the risks of sickness, unemployment or death are very high. Some contingencies like having children or marital breakdown are uninsurable because the outcome is at least partly within the control of the people concerned. Such needs can only be met through state intervention.

Redistribution over the life-span implies a redistribution of income over time. This is possible in monetary terms but rarely in terms of actual consumption goods. Services that are not used when they are on offer are completely lost. Most consumption goods deteriorate over time and in any case involve costs of storage, so the goods and services on which savings are spent after a long period of time mainly come out of current production. In real terms, redistribution over the life-span involves one of two systems. The goods and services that would be unused as a result of current savings may be used in such a way that future production is increased, that is to say they are invested. Alternatively, they may be used by other people today in return for an undertaking to supply goods of similar value when they are needed by the saver. In a simple society parents maintain their children and those too old to work in the expectation that their children will maintain them in their old age. In an industrial society more complex arrangements are required, and these are known as 'pay-as-you-go' systems.

It is commonly assumed that the post-war social services have made a substantial contribution to the reduction of inequality by transferring resources from the rich to the poor. Surprisingly, the evidence available[20] suggests that the post-war social services make about the same contribution to greater equality as the pre-war services did. In other words most of the benefits of the post-war welfare state are not financed by the vertical redistribution of income from the rich to the poor but by horizontal distribution between groups with the same levels of income or by 'life span' redistribution. There are three prime reasons for this pattern of redistribution. First, those in power in Britain have consistently assumed that the imposition of increased taxes on those with higher incomes, to finance benefits for the poor (progressive income redistribution), would result in a serious loss of incentive amongst those who produce goods and deliver services. For example, it is argued that if taxed more heavily, key industrialists would emigrate and that people would refuse to work overtime. Second, certainly since the early 1950s, politicians have been reluctant to incur the unpopularity which such action would produce. Finally, those with higher incomes have been better placed than the poor to defend their incomes against increased taxation, both by political action and by devising tax avoidance schemes. Thus the limited extent of income redistribution has been a key factor in preventing the needs of the more vulnerable groups in society from being met.

Redistribution of wealth

Before going further it may be helpful to make a distinction between income and wealth and to put arguments about the latter into perspective. Wealth in real terms can be conveniently defined as property or resources already in existence. Income in real terms is the current production of goods and services in some specified period of time.

Wealth is important in three ways. First, it produces income. Second, it enables income to be transferred from one period of time to another. For example, investment of income this year can be used to produce a flow of income in future years. Third, in some forms, for example in the ownership of a business employing people, it may give direct power over other people's lives. For the purposes of this chapter the important issue is income production.

Because wealth is valued in terms of money in the same way as income there is a tendency for people to see the redistribution of wealth as a convenient way of solving the problem of poverty. However, wealth itself can only be realised at the price of reducing income, as one can see when one looks at the example quoted above. Thus from one perspective, for the purposes of solving income poverty the important factor is the redistribution of the income from wealth. The possibilities of using a redistribution of *individuals'* income from wealth to solve the problem of poverty are less than is usually thought. For example, in 1978 about 70 per cent of gross personal income before tax came from employment, about 10 per cent from self-employment and about 10 per cent from state cash benefits. This left about 10 per cent of personal income coming from profits and rent.[21] Some of this goes to pensioners and the remainder is taxed, often heavily. Therefore the amount of income from this source available for redistribution, while substantial in absolute terms, is clearly not enough to solve the problem of poverty as a whole. Nevertheless, a more equal distribution of wealth would make for greater equality of income and therefore make some contribution to the reduction of poverty, as well as reducing inequalities of power. For this reason some countries have instituted a tax on wealth. Such a tax was proposed by the Labour Party in its manifesto for the election in 1974 and a Green Paper was produced in August 1974.[22] However, no attempt was made to implement this during the period the party was in power.

Finally in this connection the issue of the socialisation of the means of production should be raised. Marxists and many Socialists argue that the problem of poverty cannot be effectively tackled until the means of production—the plant, machinery, land and raw materials—are owned and controlled by the state on behalf of the whole population.[23] They believe that the goal of maximising profitability can often conflict with the goal of meeting the social and economic needs of members of society. For example, profits may be 'exported' and invested in countries where labour is cheap thereby leaving unemployment and hardship in the area where those profits were created. Similarly, it is argued that resources are wasted in the development of sophisticated but unnecessary luxury goods, the sale of which brings high profits, rather than in the development of socially useful goods such as low-cost housing or transport systems. They would point to areas such as Merseyside, the north-east of England, the west of Scotland and Northern Ireland as examples of the occurrence of widespread unemployment and deprivation resulting from the lack of state control over the utilisation of profits.

Four methods of income maintenance

There are four broad approaches to income maintenance, each with its own limitations and advantages; income supplementation, compensation, earnings substitution, and proportionate compensation.

Income supplementation

Income supplementation means raising income as close as possible to a specific standard or poverty line. It involves an assessment of current income, or 'means test', and the payment of a sum that is approximately the difference between that income and the standard, or the remission of a charge which would reduce income below that standard. Typical examples are the supplementary benefits scheme discussed below, and the provision of free school meals to children of low-income families.

There are two major disadvantages to income supplementation schemes. The first is the effect on incentives to earn and to save. There may be little point in working if the result of this is a reduction in benefits which leaves income exactly the same. Similarly, there is little point in saving for old age or sickness if the extra comforts that the savings are intended to provide are lost through reduced benefits or pension. This is sometimes compared with the effect of 100 per cent rate of income tax, and referred to as an 'imputed marginal tax rate' of 100 per cent.[24] To counteract the disincentive effect some flexibility may be introduced into the system. Some income and some savings up to a specified maximum may be completely disregarded. Alternatively, or additionally, only a proportion of certain income may be deducted from the benefit.

The second disadvantage of income supplementation is the reluctance of people to accept the feeling of humiliation that may be associated with an investigation of means.[25] This feeling of humiliation may be created by the manner of the investigation, which is sometimes deliberately designed to counteract the disincentive effect mentioned above.

Compensation

Compensation attempts to relate income more effectively to need by benefits designed to compensate specific conditions or handicaps, without considering the financial position of the recipient. Typical examples are the widow's pension and the industrial disability pension under the National Insurance scheme, and child benefit. The advantage of compensation systems is that they avoid means tests and have no disincentive effect (except perhaps to discourage private insurance). Their most serious disadvantage is that unless the condition is highly correlated with low income, they tend to be an expensive way of dealing with poverty, since the benefit tends to go to many who are not poor. There may also be problems in defining the precise criteria of eligibility, and particularly the criteria for ending eligibility. For example, a widow ceases to be eligible for a pension on remarriage. In order not to penalise marriage as such, the same condition is applied to co-habitation.[26] But co-habitation is difficult to define, and unlike a legal spouse, a co-habitee has no legal responsibility to maintain his partner.

Earnings substitution

This is designed to meet the financial needs of those who would normally expect to maintain themselves by their earnings but are unable to do so because of lack of employment, sickness, disability or retirement. It is frequently a special form of compensation for which the condition is lack of employment. Unearned income is not considered, but because of the nature of the condition of eligibility incentives to work can be a major problem unlike other forms of compensation. Earnings substitution may also be in the form of income supplementation, as with supplementary benefits which cannot be paid to those in full-time work.

Proportionate compensation

Proportionate compensation is an earnings-related compensation system in which the benefits increase in direct proportion to the normal income of the recipient. Earnings-related national insurance benefits, many occupational superannuation schemes, and many tax allowances come into this category. They are a form of horizontal income redistribution whose main purpose is to spread income more evenly over the life-cycle.

The major systems for income maintenance

It was in 1955 that Titmuss in an important paper drew attention to what he called 'the three divisions of welfare', the three parallel systems of relating income and need through the state social security provisions, fiscal allowances and occupational benefits.[27] These different systems developed initially independently of one another, sometimes on conflicting principles, although two were state systems and the third subject to state support. It has only been in recent years that serious efforts have been made to integrate the three.

Fiscal allowances

The most important fiscal allowances are those for income tax. The first allowances for dependants were introduced by the same Liberal government that introduced so many other social reforms before the First World War. This was no coincidence. The reforms cost money; taxation had to be increased and it was easier politically to do this if allowance was made for particular responsibilities. It also fitted in with a general concern about the responsibility of the 'haves' for the 'have-nots'. The first such allowance permitted a stated amount of income to be free of tax for each child although child tax allowances have now been phased out. Since then allowances have been introduced to cover wives and a wide variety of special needs and responsibilities. They include allowances for other dependent relatives; for the housekeeper of a widower; for a person looking after the children of a taxpayer with a single-handed responsibility for their care; for elderly taxpayers with low incomes, for blind persons, and for widows.[28]

Another reason for granting income tax relief has been that the same income should not be taken into account twice for tax purposes. This seems logical when applied to pensions and pension contributions. If pension schemes are regarded as being a method of transferring income over the life-span of the individual, it is reasonable that the income should only be taxed at one point, and that the one where it is in fact used. It is also logical that if there is a direct transfer of income between two people without any service being performed, as when an elderly parent is paid an allowance by her son, then this should only be treated as taxable income for one of them. If the income is transferred to a person or institution which pays no income tax or pays at a lower rate, there is an advantage to be gained. To limit the possibility of abuse, the income must be transferred under a 'covenant' of a minimum of four years' duration. Since registered charitable institutions pay no tax on income, this has been a useful means of increasing the income of such bodies. The same means have sometimes been used or abused to reduce the taxation on a family's income. Much less logical is the decision that the same principles apply to income paid as interest in return for a loan. Under this arrangement interest paid on mortgage loans and bank loans has been excused income tax, because income tax is paid by the recipient.[29] Interest on hire purchase agreements has never been subject to a similar allowance.

Income tax allowances are a form of contingency redistribution on a horizontal basis with a regressive incidence. The higher a person's income, the higher the tax he pays both absolutely and as a proportion of his income, so the greater the relief he can receive for any specific contingency. Where taxes are not progressive, it is much easier to give reliefs that benefit those who have most need. In Britain the most important fiscal allowance outside the income tax system is the rebate of rates instituted by the Rating Act, 1966. Rates, which provide an important part of the finance for local authorities, are based not on income, but on the value of the housing occupied. It is a tax on householders and bears particularly hard on those with low incomes but better housing.[30] Rate rebates, by lessening the burden on low-income households, are designed to enable local authorities to increase their revenue without penalising the poor.

Occupational benefits

The provision of assistance to employees in time of need, particularly in sickness and old age, has a long history.[31] Its origins often lay in a sense of obligation fostered by the acceptance of a paternalistic relationship between employer and employee. The arrangement was usually informal. With the development of a more formal relationship between employer and employee with increased industrialisation, this assistance has either been abandoned or put on a more formal footing through occupational benefit schemes. In the later case the advantage for the employee is obvious, but the employer may also use these benefits as a means of attracting new workers and creating a stable work force. Naturally there has been a tendency for employers to develop schemes of this kind first for those employees whose services they most value. Salaried workers and skilled workers have been most favoured.[32]

Essentially occupational benefits are a method of redistributing income more evenly over the life-cycle with an insurance element for contingency redistribution. Because of the more favourable terms obtained by those with a better bargaining position, they are regressive in their incidence. Despite this they have been supplemented by fiscal allowances which have increased their regressive nature.

The state social security system

The state social security system has evolved from the original proposals made in the Beveridge Report published in November 1942.[33] Beveridge's aim was to provide a comprehensive plan to secure that all members of the community would be free at all times from want. To achieve this he recommended three schemes of benefit: social insurance payable on a contractual basis; social assistance payable on a test of need; and children's allowances payable to all without contract or test of need. These proposals were largely implemented by July 1948, but subsequent developments have given the system a quite different orientation from that envisaged by Beveridge.

Beveridge's central proposal was for a universal and comprehensive 'scheme of social insurance against interruption and destruction of earning power and for special expenditure arising at birth, marriage or death'.[34] This was instituted as 'national insurance' under the National Insurance and National Insurance (Industrial Injuries) Acts.

Initially contributions, subsidised by the state, were paid at a flat rate that varied in amount for the three classes of contributor: the employed (Class 1), the self-employed (Class 2), and the non-employed (Class 3). In return flat-rate benefits were payable to those who satisfied certain minimum contribution requirements. The benefits varied for the different classes so that, for instance, only

Class 1 contributors could claim unemployment benefit, and Classes 1 and 2 sickness benefit. Married women who worked had to pay a contribution to cover industrial injuries but could elect to pay the full contribution to entitle them to full benefits, including maternity allowance. Contributors who did not meet the minimum requirements were paid a proportionately lower benefit. Those in receipt of benefits were 'credited' with contributions so that future benefits were not prejudiced.

Essentially the Beveridge scheme was an earnings substitution scheme, redistributing income over the life-span of individuals and families. Contributions were regressive and benefits progressive, but the net effect only involved vertical redistribution in so far as the contingencies the scheme was designed to meet, like sickness and unemployment, were more frequent among those with low incomes or costs were met from general taxation. As the costs of the scheme increased in the early years governments became reluctant to accept responsibility for the increasing share of the costs that Beveridge had recommended,[35] and in 1952 the state contribution was fixed at 18 per cent. The regressive effect of the flat-rate contribution made it difficult to increase the income of the insurance fund without causing great hardship to low earners. So in 1959 the government introduced an additional graduated contribution at the rate of 4.5 per cent of all income between certain limits.[36] In return contributors would receive an additional earnings-related pension, but less than the economic value of the total contributions. This scheme was related to occupational pensions by allowing employers who provided adequate schemes with rights protected on change of employment to contract out of the scheme, but only on payment of a higher flat-rate contribution. In 1966 the Labour government extended this principle by introducing earnings-related contributions and benefits to cover the first six months of loss of earnings from other causes.[37] The aim of this measure, however, was not to balance the budget but to ease the problems of short-term loss of earnings, and to increase the mobility of labour. These earnings-related benefits were abolished in 1982 although contributions continued to be earnings-related.

The Social Security Act 1975 and the Social Security (Pensions) Act 1975 aimed to rationalise this system by a new scheme of contribution, through changes in retirement pensions and by the consolidation of the industrial injuries scheme. Beveridge's three classes of contributor were replaced by four classes of contribution. *Class 1* contributions paid in respect of employed earners now comprise two types of contribution: 'contracted in' contributions which will enable the contributor to draw an earnings-related pension and 'contracted out' contributions which are paid when the contributor belongs to an occupational pension scheme. Thus 'contracted out' payments entitle the contributor to a flat-rate pension. Contributions comprise a proportion of earnings between certain limits, the limits are changed annually but at present (1982–3) the lower earnings limit is set at £17.50 and the upper earnings limit is £120 per week. Contributions are as follows:

Contracted-in

Employee:	8.75 per cent of all earnings up to the upper earnings limit
Employer:	13.70 per cent of all earnings up to the upper earnings limit

Contracted-out

Employee:	8.75 per cent of all earnings up to the lower earnings limit PLUS 6.25 per cent of all earnings between the lower and upper earnings limits
Employer:	13.7 per cent of all earnings up to the lower earnings limit PLUS 9.2 per cent of all earnings between the lower and upper earnings limits.[38]

Women married since May 1977 or married women entering the scheme since that date are required to pay the full contribution, they cannot elect to pay at the reduced rate which used to be available to married women. However, women who were paying the reduced rate prior to May 1977 may elect to continue to do so. They pay only 3.2 per cent of all earnings up to the upper earnings limit but their employers' contributions are the same as for other employees. Class 2 contributions are paid by the self-employed at a flate rate of £3.75 per week but supplemented by Class 4 contributions—a levy of 6 per cent of annual profits or gains between £3,450 and £11,000. Class 3 contributions to keep a non-employed contributor in benefit are paid at a flat rate of £3.65.

Payment of Class 1 contributions entitles the contributor to all benefits available under the Social Security Scheme. Payment of Class 2 contributions and Class 4 contributions entitles the contributor to all benefits except unemployment benefit. Payment of Class 3 contributions only entitles the contributor to certain specific benefits, including widow's benefits and retirement pensions.

Under Beveridge's proposals social insurance was to be supported by children's allowances payable at or very close to subsistence level irrespective of the income of the parents and whether they were in employment or not. This 'was essential to ensure that low-paid workers with families to support would not be living below subsistence level when employed, or, when not working, receive more in insurance benefits than their normal wage.'[39] These allowances were instituted under the Family Allowances Acts, the new name indicating that they were intended for the benefit of the family as a whole and not to meet the specific needs of the individual children on whose behalf they were paid. They were a universal compensatory payment providing a progressive benefit. The 1975 Child Benefit Act which came into force in April 1977 superseded the Family Allowance Scheme. The act had several important elements including: payment of Child Benefit for all children in the family including the first child, the abolition of the element of family allowances whereby parents of apprentices and children attending higher education courses were entitled to benefit, and a special increase in allowance for the first child in single-parent families. The new Child Benefit was untaxed but child tax allowances were phased out over a three-year period after 1977. Finally it should be noted that neither the Family Allowance payments nor the Child Benefit payments ever actually reached the subsistence levels which Beveridge had proposed.

Beveridge's proposals for social assistance were designed to provide a net for those whose needs were not met or not fully met through social insurance. Beveridge expected these to be a small minority, mainly of people who had failed to meet the contribution requirements for insurance benefits. The largest number, diminishing over the years, would be those not entitled to the full retirement pension because they had not contributed for a sufficient length of time.[40] This was instituted under the title of 'National Assistance',[41] changed to 'Supplementary Benefits' in 1966.[42] Payable on a test of means to those who are not in full-time employment, it brings income up to a scale calculated according to the number and age of child dependants. A rent allowance which normally covers the whole rent paid by a family, or the interest on a mortgage for an owner-occupier is also available to Supplementary Benefits claimants, but after legislation in the 1981–2 parliamentary session this will be administered by the local authority. Supplementary benefits, like family allowances, are wholly financed by central government out of general taxation. Until 1980 the scheme was administered by the Supplementary Benefits Commission, a body with less independence than its predecessor, the National Assistance Board. Existing within the Department of Health and Social Security (DHSS), it had a full-time paid chairman, who was not a civil servant, and seven part-time members. It was serviced by officials of the Department and operated under regulations made by the responsible Minister. However, the Supplementary Benefits Commission was abolished in 1980 (see below).

It was the intention of the Social Security Act 1966, which introduced supplementary benefits and the Supplementary Benefits Act 1976 which consolidated legislation pertaining to supplementary benefits, to make them an entitlement in a way that had not been true of National Assistance. These benefits, however, have two intrinsic characteristics which mean that they can never have the security of National Insurance benefits. First, they are subject to a means test. Second, there is some element of flexibility in their administration, although this has been substantially reduced by the 1980 Social Security Act (see below). Such flexibility requires administrative discretion, which may be misused. In order to achieve consistency the Ministry has collected all the legal rules in a loose-leaf book entitled *The Law relating to Supplementary Benefits and Family Income Supplement*.

This difference between the two systems is also reflected in the different appeals procedures. For national insurance benefits the procedures are basically those of the courts, with a legally qualified chairman. Decisions are based on precedents, and further levels of appeal lie to the National Insurance Commissioners, who are experienced barristers, and on points of law to the civil courts. Important decisions of these bodies are published.[43] In contrast the supplementary benefits tribunals have no legal chairman and hold sittings in private (to protect the interests of appellants).[44]

However, the differences of principle between the national insurance and supplementary benefits systems have also made another objective of the Ministry of Social Security Act difficult, namely the amalgamation of the two administrations so that enquiries and applications that related to both could be dealt with at a single point of contact. There have been some amalgamations of offices, but it has not proved possible to train staff of the calibre that the Ministry can recruit in the rudiments, let alone the complexities, of both systems.[45]

Beveridge's aim had been that national insurance plus family allowances should normally be higher than the national assistance scale, including the rent allowance. This has never been the case for the majority of those receiving insurance benefits. The difference between the basic insurance scales for single people and married couples and the national assistance and supplementary benefit scales has never been sufficient to cover the rent of those who are householders. As we have seen, family allowances were instituted at a level below Beveridge's calculation of a subsistence minimum, and unlike other benefits initially were not increased with changes in the cost of living. Although the new Child Benefits which replaced family allowances have been increased, in terms of the amount paid, fairly regularly, when combined with unemployment or sickness benefits for dependent children the amount paid is still less than the supplementary benefit scales for children, which are also age-related. The result has been that national assistance and then supplementary benefit have been from the beginning mainly a method of supplementing inadequate national insurance benefits. A further problem has arisen in the past decade as unemployment has grown. Unemployment benefit is only paid for a maximum period of one year and then only to individuals who have made the appropriate contributions. Thus the scheme does not provide assistance to those who have been unemployed for long periods or for unemployed school-leavers. Payments to these groups are made through the supplementary benefits system. The final critical problem facing the supplementary benefits system is that the scale rates, the basic weekly payments for food, clothing, etc., in many cases are inadequate to meet the costs of these items.[46] The cumulative result of these three problems is that the supplementary benefits system is ineffective in meeting many of the demands made upon it.

The Social Security Act 1980

The Social Security Act of 1980 extensively amended the Supplementary Benefits Act of 1976. The act was introduced partly in order to implement a number of the changes which had been recommended by the DHSS team which produced the Supplementary Benefits Review in 1978 and partly in order to implement Conservative Party policy on Social Security. The first major change introduced by the Act was the abolition of the Supplementary Benefits Commission. Its advisory functions are now performed by the Social Security Advisory Committee, a new body established under the 1980 Act. But all of the regulative and discretionary functions previously exercised by the SBC are now performed by full time DHSS officials known as Benefit Officers.

Probably the most important changes created by the new Act related to discretionary payments. First, under the old system it was technically possible for claimants to request single payments for virtually any item which they required provided that that claim was 'reasonable in the circumstances'. Officials then had a fairly wide degree of discretion in deciding whether or not to meet the particular claim and if it were not met the claimant was free to appeal to a Supplementary Benefit Appeals Tribunal. These single needs payments, Exceptional Needs Payments as they were then known, played a vital role within the system as they enabled many claimants to obtain items, especially items of clothing, which they could not afford given the inadequate basic rates of benefit. However the 1980 Act introduced a drastic reduction in the flexibility of this system. It empowered the DHSS to lay down regulations which have extensively limited and defined the items for which single payments of this type can be made, the circumstances in which claims can be made, and the amount of money which can be made available for the purchase of particular items. For example, clothing grants, which previously could be made to any Supplementary Benefit claimant can now only be obtained in specific circumstances such as illness, pregnancy, handicap, attendance or accidental loss or damage. Similar types of limitation also now apply to Urgent Needs Payments which are made, for example, for visits to close relatives who are dangerously ill. In many cases Urgent Needs Payments now have to be repaid.

The discretionary elements of the system were also virtually eliminated in relation to certain regular weekly payments. These could previously be made over and above the basic rates and could cover any item of regular expenditure although most usually they were used to cover extra heating, dietary or laundry costs faced by claimants. Under the new Act these Exceptional Circumstances Additions were abolished and replaced by Additional Weekly Requirements. Payments under the new system can only be made for fuel, dietary, attendance and laundry needs and again conditions under which they can be claimed and the amount of money made available are rigidly specified.

The new Act has also given greater freedom to the DHSS to withdraw benefit from people who refuse to take jobs in circumstances where they would earn less than they can receive on Supplementary Benefit and there is already some evidence that these powers are being enforced rigorously by DHSS officials.

A further aspect of the Act has been a change in the way in which savings are treated. People whose savings amount to more than £2,000 now have no right to claim Supplementary Benefit. Savings of under £2,000 are ignored when calculating entitlement to basic benefit. However, if a claimant's savings are greater than £300 their rights to claim for single payments are drastically limited.

Finally, changes were made to the Supplementary Benefit scale rates. Long-term rates which can be claimed by the sick, the elderly and single parents are now paid at the same rate as National Insurance benefits. It should be stressed, however, that the government ignored pressures to abolish the short-term scale rate which, for couples, is almost £10 less than the long-term rate and which unemployed people are forced to live on, however long the term of their unemployment. The Act also resulted in the reduction in the number of different rates for children. There were previously five different scale rates, the amounts payable increasing with the child's age. There are now only three rates (Table 7).

Most aspects of the 1980 Social Security Act have been widely

TABLE 7 *Supplementary Benefit Scale Rates, November 1981–November 1982*

	Basic rate £	*Long-term rate* £
Husband and wife	37.75	47.35
Single householder	23.25	29.60
Any other person aged 18 or over	18.60	23.65
16–17	14.30	18.15
11–15	11.90	11.90
0–10	7.90	7.90

criticised. The Act has to a limited degree simplified the system but many measures have been seen as punitive and likely to result in the greater impoverishment of claimants. Particularly damaging, even in the short term, have been the failure to raise benefits for the long-term unemployed, and the drastic reduction of claimants' rights to seek discretionary payments.

Meeting specific needs

Retirement pensioners

The provision of adequate financial support for those who have retired from work on the grounds of age has proved a particularly intractable problem in Britain. The numbers of retired people, though large, are not as large as the numbers of children,[47] and on average their period of dependency is shorter than that of children. But unlike children they are not regarded as the responsibility of particular members of the economically active population, while from the point of view of society as a whole the support of the retired population cannot be seen as an investment like the support and education of children. There is therefore a general expectation that people will provide for their own retirement by contributions made during their working life. Yet there are both practical and psychological obstacles to this. The practical difficulties relate to those with low earnings or without earnings, and to the effects of inflation on the value of contributions paid before retirement and the value of the pension after retirement. The psychological obstacles stem from the tendency of most people to discount the future, that is to say to give more weight to current needs and desires than to future deprivations. This tendency is likely to be more marked among the poor, whose current needs are particularly pressing. The problem is further complicated by the fact that women live longer than men. Yet women in our society generally spend a shorter period of their lives in employment, because of family responsibilities and an earlier retirement age, and also generally have far lower earnings than men.

The inadequacies of the state insurance scheme in meeting these needs effectively has been discussed earlier. The growth of occupational superannuation schemes might have been expected to compensate for these inadequacies. Surveys by the government actuary showed a steady increase in the numbers of workers covered by these schemes from 8 million in 1956 to 11 million in 1963 and 12 million in 1967.[48] However, even at that date they covered only slightly over 50 per cent of the employed population, and provision was much wider for non-manual than for manual workers, for men than for women. By 1971 the fourth survey showed a decline of 1 million in the numbers covered, partly caused by a reduction in the workforce but partly by a fall in the number of manual workers covered. Many of the schemes, and particularly those for manual workers, were also deficient in various respects. These deficiencies included lack of provision for preservation of rights on transfer of employment; a rate of pension well below 50 per cent of normal earnings; and no provision for augmentation of the pension after retirement to take account of inflation.

The first proposals for major changes were made by the Labour Party twenty years ago and were incorporated in the 'Crossman Plan' of 1963. This plan included a substantial vertical transfer through the weighting given to the benefits of those with low incomes, was on a pay-as-you-go basis and would have made massive inroads into the private pensions sector. The Bill[49] to introduce it foundered with the change of government in 1970.

The Conservative government of 1970–4, in accordance with its general philosophy, wished to strengthen the private occupational pensions system.[50] The Social Security Act, 1973, returned to Beveridge's concept of a flat-rate basic state pension, though financed by earnings-related contributions and reviewed annually to take into account the increased rate of inflation. Occupational pensions were to become compulsory, with minimum standards laid down under the Act for those employers who arranged their own schemes, and a funded state reserve scheme for others.

However, before the 1973 Act was implemented the 1974–9. Labour government altered a number of provisions in the 1975 Social Security Pensions Act which came into force in April 1979. This Act considerably increased the importance of the State Pensions Scheme although not to the extent of the Crossman Plan. First, the flat-rate basic state pension became the first component of a two-part scheme. The first component is much the same as the previous flat-rate pension. The second component which replaces the funded reserve scheme is based on the individual's contribution record. When the scheme is fully mature the second component will provide for payments to the individual based on a proportion of his income over his best twenty contribution years. Thus the scheme will not become fully operational until 1998. This scheme will be inflation-proofed in much the same way as the flat-rate state pension. Employers who provide a funded occupational pensions scheme can 'contract out' of the second component of the state scheme on behalf of their employees although the private scheme to which they contribute must meet fairly rigorous conditions before this is possible. The contribution liability of employees who are contracted out is reduced (see p. 103 above). As noted above, the conditions which must appertain before an individual can be contracted out of the earnings-related state pension scheme are much more rigorous than those under previous legislation. He must belong to an alternative occupational pensions scheme which must be recognised by the Occupational Pensions Board and provide its members with a pension which is as high as the second component which they would have received under the state scheme. Further, these schemes must make provision, in certain circumstances, for the widows of contributors.

The provisions for State Retirement Pensions under the 1975 Social Security Pensions Act provide for four categories of pension. Category A pensions are payable after the minimum age of 60 for women and 65 for men to those who have paid the requisite contributions during their working life. During the period of five years after reaching this age the insured person may elect not to retire and provided this period of non-retirement exceeds seven weeks the pension, when it is received, will be increased by 1 per cent for every seven weeks for which this continues. If he does elect to retire he can still earn up to £45 without having his pension reduced, but after that figure the basic pension will be reduced on a sliding scale although the earnings-related element of pensions will not be affected. Five years after the minimum age the insured person is regarded as having retired whether or not he ceases employment, and the pension is paid in full regardless of earnings. Finally, since April 1978 people over pensionable age have no longer been required to pay their employee's contributions although employers continue to be liable for their share of contributions.

Category B pensions are first payable to the wife of an insured person after he has retired. Second they are payable to widows on their late husbands' contribution records. If, however, the widow has been entitled to a widow's pension for more than ten years she will receive retirement pension at a reduced rate. Finally, since April 1979 category B pensions can be claimed by a widower on his late wife's contribution record. For a wife the pension is paid at a lower rate whereas widows and widowers receive the same amount as category A pensioners. Category C and category D pensions are non-contributory. Category C pensions are for people who were over pensionable age on 5 July 1948, or married to such people. They are also payable to women whose marriage terminated other than by their husbands' death (e.g. by divorce) and who were over pensionable age at the date of that termination. Category D pensions are payable to people over 80 who are not entitled to any of the above pensions or whose entitlement to the other pensions is less than the full amount of category D pension. These pensions are again payable at two rates, the lower for a married woman.

The 1975 Social Security Pensions Act instituted a bi-annual review of pensions raising the amount of flat-rate pension in line with prices or earnings, whichever was the higher. However, the Conservative government in 1980 revoked this aspect of the Act and hence stopped the system whereby pensions are automatically related to wages and prices.[51]

The retirement pension may be increased by a graduated pension for those who have paid the appropriate graduated contributions between 1959 and 1974. Unlike the basic pension, which is regularly reviewed and raised to meet changes in the cost of living and national average earnings, the graduated pension is fixed in cash terms, so that its value will have been severely cut by inflation.

The retirement pension may also be increased by a supplementary pension under a test of need if the total income of the retirement pensioner and his family does not reach the level where supplementary benefit would be available if housing costs are taken into account. Pensioners have also received an annual Christmas bonus of £10, first instituted under the Pensions and Family Income Supplement Payments Act, 1973 (discontinued in 1975).

Children

Child Benefit This is a universal benefit payable for all dependent children. Eligibility is governed by responsibility rather than relationship. Legitimate children, illegitimate children, stepchildren and even children unrelated to the claimant are all eligible, provided that the child is maintained wholly or mainly by the person making the claim. Where children are living away from their parents they can be included in the family provided the absence is temporary or the parents are paying the equivalent amount of Child Benefit towards the cost of the child's maintenance. An exception to this is made where a child is removed from a family by the order of a court or a local authority has assumed parental rights under the Children Act,

1948. In these cases no Child Benefit is payable—or insurance benefit for the child—even if the parents are paying the full cost of the child's maintenance. Child Benefit is paid until a child leaves school. The present rates are £5.25 for each child in the family. Single-parent families receive an additional £3.30 regardless of the total number of children living in the family.

Child Benefit is the property of the mother of the family and she normally signs the claim form, although either parent may draw the allowance. It is payable monthly at post offices or weekly by special request.

National Insurance For all benefits, additions for dependent children make up the Child Benefit to a standard figure. This is considerably lower for short-term benefits than for long-term benefits. The current rates are £0.80 and £7.70 respectively. In addition a Maternity Grant is paid on the birth of each child (£25), a Guardian's Allowance for a parentless orphan (without regard to contributions), and a Child's Special Allowance for the children of a divorced woman whose former husband has died, both at the higher rate, for such additions.

Supplementary benefits These include in their needs scale an allowance related to the age of the child, although it should be remembered that this allowance is automatically reduced by the amount of Child Benefit.

Family Income Supplement[52] This is a non-contributory benefit payable to families, where the breadwinner is in full-time employment and there are dependent children, if the family income falls short of a prescribed scale. The scale is normally revised annually and at present stands at £74.00 per week for a one-child family plus £8.00 for each additional child. It represents a simplified poverty standard that excludes an allowance for rent. Families are paid 50 per cent of the difference between their income from other sources and the scale up to a maximum of £18.50 for a one-child family plus £1.50 for each additional child. Income is based on the average of the five weeks preceding the claim, and the supplement is granted for one year without further investigation of means.[53] Recipients are automatically entitled to certain other benefits such as free welfare milk and foods and relief of prescription, optical and dental charges. The benefit tends to favour one-parent families since the scale is the same for them as for families with two parents.

Educational welfare provision Since 1906 local education authorities have been able to assist children whose education was likely to suffer as a result of poverty. The Education Act, 1944, extended their powers and duties in this respect. It became a duty for local education authorities to provide school meals and these are subsidised by central government. In May 1978 about 5 million pupils (62.3 per cent) were taking school meals of which 23.6 per cent were provided free for those in families with a low income.[54] However, in 1980 legislation was passed which removed the provision of free school meals as a statutory requirement on local authorities and there are now very wide variations between authorities in terms of their provision of this service.

Milk was also provided for all school children and the whole cost met by government until this was abolished in 1971, except for children in infants' and nursery schools. Some local education authorities defied the government by continuing to provide free milk through the rates. It can still be given to junior children who are certified as needing it for the maintenance of their health. Under the same Act local education authorities can make grants to assist with the provision of school uniforms. They can provide clothing for children so poorly clothed that they cannot benefit from their education, recovering the cost in whole or part from the parents. They can also provide educational maintenance grants for children staying on at school beyond the age for compulsory attendance; and, on a much more generous scale, for children going on to further and higher education. Local authorities determine for themselves the amount and frequency of the benefits and the income levels at which they are payable. As a result, different scales tend to operate for free school meals, school uniform grants and educational maintenance allowances; entitlement to one is no indication of entitlement to another, and separate applications may have to be made. Scales for maintenance allowances for students taking first degree courses are also laid down by the Department of Education and Science (DES). For other courses allowances are discretionary. The DES makes recommendations but local education authorities do not have to follow them.

Welfare provision for the under-fives Free milk and vitamin foods, once provided on a universal basis, are now only available to those receiving supplementary benefits, family income supplement or through a means test.

Unemployment

The main provision for the unemployed is through the Social Security Act, 1975, and supplementary benefits. Provisions under this Act are very similar in their effect to those they replace. Unemployment benefit is payable at the basic rate if in the previous contribution year (which is also the calendar year) Class 1 contributions have been paid or credited equivalent to 50 weeks at the minimum rate. No payment is made for the first three days of unemployment in any period. Unemployment benefit ceases after one year, but eligibility can be reviewed after paying thirteen contributions. The unemployed person can be disqualified from benefit for a period of six weeks if the unemployment is 'voluntary' or due to misconduct. Where for any reason a man's national insurance benefit is below the supplementary benefit scale, he is normally entitled to supplementary benefits. Strikers may not receive unemployment benefit or supplementary benefit for themselves, and the amount which they can claim for their families is automatically reduced by £13.

Redundancy payments are an additional benefit for some forced into a change of employment, whether or not they actually suffer a period of unemployment. Under the Redundancy Payments Act, 1965, payments must be made to employees dismissed after more than two years' service because of a change in the employer's circumstances or his requirements. The payments are made in a lump sum by employers and partially refunded from a Redundancy Payments Fund created by compulsory contributions on all insured employees. The payments are related to the age of the employee and to the length of his service with the employer. He receives half a week's pay for each year of service under the age of 22, a week's pay for each year between 22 and 40, and one and a half weeks' pay for each year of service over the age of 41. Appeals go first to a tribunal[55] and subsequently to the civil courts. This system has many weaknesses, not least that the capital sums received are an inadequate substitute for a higher regular income in the absence of an effective retraining system.[56]

Sickness, invalidity and maternity

For practical reasons provisions for sickness and unemployment must approximate very closely together. It would be regarded as manifestly unfair to treat the sick less generously than the unemployed. If they are treated more generously then there is an incentive for unemployed people to get themselves certified as sick. This is likely to result in the wrong use of medical services. At the same time it may be more difficult to get a person back to work if he is registered as sick rather than unemployed.[57]

Despite this there is some discrimination in favour of the sick. Sickness benefit, unlike unemployment benefit, is available to the self-employed (Class 2 contributors). After 168 days of sickness, the sick person is entitled to invalidity benefit at a similar rate to the basic sickness benefit (for which there is no time limit). In addition, a person who is more than five years from pensionable age when the invalidity begins can receive an invalidity allowance of modest proportions which is higher for those who are invalided at younger ages. Those who become incapacitated less than five years but more than thirteen weeks from retirement receive invalidity allowance in the form of an increment to their pension. Finally those who have been unable to work, because of sickness, for more than twenty-eight weeks but whose contribution does not entitle them to invalidity benefit become entitled to a non-contributory invalidity pension. However, this is paid at a considerably lower rate than invalidity benefit.

Under the 1975 Social Security Act every employed person (but not the self-employed) is insured for accidents and prescribed diseases contracted at work. Although this industrial injuries scheme is administered in tandem with the national insurance scheme, benefits payable are more generous than comparable national insurance benefits. Injury benefit is paid for the first six months of unemployment resulting from industrial injury or disease. It is a very similar benefit to sickness benefit, it has the same increases for dependants. However the basic flat-rate payment is higher than sickness benefit.

Disablement benefit is a complex and important benefit paid under the industrial injuries scheme. It is paid during any period after the accident or the date of contracting the disease apart from any period when injury benefit is being received. Disablement benefit may be paid *even if the individual is able to work*. The basic disablement benefit may be paid weekly or, in the case of smaller assessments, as a lump sum gratuity. However there are a number of increases which often form the most important parts of the disablement benefit. These include a special hardship allowance, payable when an individual's earnings potential is reduced because of the accident or disease, and an unemployability supplement, paid when the injury or disease incapacitates the individual completely from work.

Benefits for loss of earnings due to sickness are heavily biased in favour of those who are in any case better off. Payment during sickness by the employer tends to be more likely and to continue longer the higher the individual's status.[58]

Maternity benefit is a form of sickness benefit for employed women who pay the full rate of national insurance contributions. Its purpose is to make it easier for them to discontinue work before the confinement and for some weeks afterwards. It is treated as sickness benefit for calculating invalidity. Maternity grant is a cash grant payable on either the father's or the mother's insurance record, on the birth of a child. Under the Employment Protection Act which came into force in April 1977 an expectant mother is guaranteed six weeks' paid maternity leave if she has worked two years with the same employer. Maternity pay comprises nine-tenths of her full pay less flat-rate maternity allowance. Further, provided that she informs her employer before she leaves that she wishes to return, her post must be kept open for her until twenty-nine weeks after the birth of her child.

Disability

For physically and mentally disabled people income is often primarily determined by the circumstances in which the handicap is received. As we have seen, the industrial injuries scheme provides a comprehensive system of benefits for those whose disablement occurs in the course of employment. War pensions are payable on a similar but slightly more generous basis to the industrial injuries scheme.

Another group to which the state has given special consideration is the victims of crimes of violence. The present scheme was set up in 1964 as a result of a campaign inspired by Margery Fry, an important figure in the field of penal reform. It is administered by the Criminal Injuries Compensation Board, which was set up jointly by the Home Office and the Scottish Office. It provides compensation in cases where personal injury is directly attributable to a criminal offence or to attempting to arrest a suspected offender. The rate of compensation is based on awards made in the civil courts.[59]

If the disability occurs in other circumstances as a result of someone else's negligence compensation will be decided by the courts, but will depend on the wealth and income of the negligent person or his foresight in insuring against this eventuality. The driver of a vehicle is legally obliged to insure against third-party risks, but may disobey the law to the detriment of the victim. Legal proceedings are in any case often very prolonged and this causes much suffering to the disabled. A psychological condition known as 'compensation neurosis' in which physical symptoms are retained until the claim is settled often delays rehabilitation.[60]

An interesting development in 1973 was the provision by the government of £3 million to set up a fund to meet the special needs of families caring for children under the age of sixteen with very severe congenital handicaps.[61] Known as the Family Fund, it is administered on behalf of the government by the Joseph Rowntree Memorial Trust, an approach which involves an interesting innovation. It provides grants to the parents of such children who, because of their social and economic circumstances, are in need of help which the Trust considers should be provided. There is no means test, but the Trust is expected to form a judgment on the effect of the child on the circumstances of the family. The help is to relieve stress on the family while the child is at home and can be provided notwithstanding that it is within the power of other statutory services to provide it.

One of the central weaknesses of Beveridge's national insurance system was that many disabled people who were unable to work and hence acquire a contribution record never became eligible for insurance benefits. Until the early 1970s this group of people were largely dependent for their income on supplementary benefits. However, the 1970s saw the introduction of a number of non-contributory benefits which, though limited in scope and certainly not generous in terms of the amount paid to claimants, at least began to bring those who were disabled but who had not acquired their disablement through work within the scope of the national insurance system. The non-contributory invalidity pension which we have discussed above can be claimed by the disabled. It was introduced in the 1975 Social Security Act as was the Invalid Care Allowance which is a taxable cash benefit paid at the same rate as the NCIP. It is for people of working age who cannot work because they have to stay at home to care for a severely disabled relative. A widely voiced criticism of the Invalid Care Allowance is that it usually cannot be claimed by married women. A reform instituted in 1970 and incorporated in the Social Security Act is the provision of an attendance allowance for the severely disabled, physically or mentally, who require frequent attention 'in connection with bodily functions', or 'continual supervision in order to avoid substantial danger to himself or others' either by day or by night. If such attendance is required by both day and night the allowance is at a higher rate. The allowance is only payable when the disabled person has already been subject to attendance for a period of six months. The allowances are administered by an Attendance Allowance Board, the majority of whom must be medical practitioners. Finally, anybody who is over 5 and under pensionable age and is unable or virtually unable to walk because of physical disablement may be entitled to a mobility allowance.

Widows

For widows the Social Security Act follows the National Insurance Acts. It takes into account the problems of adjustment in the period immediately after widowhood by the payment of the widow's allowance for a period of six months at a rate which is higher than the basic unemployment and sickness benefits. At the end of this period what happens depends on the age and responsibilities of the widow. A widow under 40 without children receives no further benefit. A widow with a son or daughter under 19 living with her receives a Widowed Mother's Allowance at the standard benefit rate. A flat-rate addition is payable for each child who is dependent on her. Since it is assumed that older women may have difficulty in finding employment, a widow receives a pension on a sliding scale according to her age when her husband dies or the last child reaches nineteen. If this occurs when she is under 40 she receives no further pension. At 50 or over she gets the maximum rate. If a husband's death is due to industrial injury or disease his widow will also be entitled to industrial death benefit. These benefits provide some compensation for the low level of a woman's wages for the support of a family.

The needs of widows and orphaned children have also been covered by some occupational pension schemes. The nature of the provisions has been very varied, like their provisions for superannuation. They may involve a lump sum payment or a pension or a combination of the two. The cover may be additional to ordinary pension rights or a substitute for part of them. It may relate to the death of the employee before retirement or after. It may cover children or not. The Inland Revenue Department again sets limits to these schemes. The maximum provision in a scheme for widows' pensions on the death of the employee before retirement would be approximately equivalent to a lump sum of two years' salary and a pension of a quarter of the salary annually. For widow's benefits after the retirement of the employee, the Inland Revenue makes a limit in approved schemes of 50 per cent of the husband's pension. In some cases protection for the widow may involve a reduced pension for the employee. These limits, coupled with the reluctance of employees and employers to face the costs of adequate schemes, mean that for most widows employment is essential to avoid having to live on an income at or little above the supplementary benefits level. Under the Social Security Pensions Act, 1975, a 'recognised' superannuation scheme has to provide a widow's pension of at least half the minimum rate for the employee's pension.

Almost all widows' benefits including those under occupational schemes cease if the widow remarries or during any period in which she co-habits with a man. The husband or co-habitee is expected to assume full responsibility for her and her children. Supplementary benefits depend on his application and eligibility. Co-habitation presents particular difficulties. It is hard to define and even when proved provides the woman with no legal claim on the man for herself or for the children.

Unsupported wives and mothers

For wives divorced or separated from their husbands, and women with illegitimate children, the first question is one of legal responsibility. A man is legally responsible for the maintenance of his children, legitimate and illegitimate; he is also responsible for the maintenance of his wife, unless when they are separated he can show that she is responsible for the situation. The Magistrates' Courts can make maintenance orders for a wife and her legitimate children payable by the husband, and affiliation orders for illegitimate children payable by the putative father. There is now no maximum to the amount which can be ordered for a wife and her legitimate children.[62] But the courts have always been influenced by the fact that it is easier to make an order than to enforce payment. An order for a small amount that is likely to be paid regularly may therefore be better than one for a large amount which will be resented and not paid. Other responsibilities of the husband, such as his co-habitation with another woman with children dependent on him, will also be taken into consideration. However, despite the relatively low payments required by some court orders, many are not paid, or are paid irregularly, or only in part. The Maintenance Orders Act, 1958, attempted to deal with this by making it possible to 'attach' part of a man's wages for this purpose, i.e., making a court order stipulating that the employer should pay the amount of the order directly to the court. However, many orders are still not paid, since an attachment order lapses if the man changes his employment. Where the recipients of supplementary allowances have court orders or other agreements for the maintenance of themselves or their children, half the orders for divorced or separated wives, and one-third of the orders for mothers of illegitimate children, are paid irregularly or not at all.[63] The Commission have powers to bring proceedings to obtain maintenance and affiliation orders, and criminal proceedings for persistent neglect to maintain.

Where payment of a court order is not made regularly it is the practice of the DHSS to pay the woman supplementary benefits at a full rate and to obtain the woman's authority to collect from the court any money paid under the order. This ensures a regular income for the woman. The same problem of co-habitation applies here as for widows with the added difficulty that the whole allowance lacks the legal protection provided in the case of insurance benefits by the Commissioners and the courts.[64]

Single-parent families

Just as the income needs of disabled people are being considered as a whole, so it has come to be recognised that single-parent families have common problems, whether the absence of one parent is due to death, divorce or separation before or after marriage, and whether the parent caring for the children is a man or a woman.[65] A minor recognition of this occurred in the administration of family income supplement. For the first time, in calculating needs, the requirements of a single parent were regarded as the same as those for two parents, and this was accepted for motherless as well as fatherless families. The most important recognition of this principle came in the appointment of the Finer Committee on One-Parent Families.[66]

The Finer Committee was concerned with all the needs of one-parent families (which represent about 10 per cent of families with children at any one time), but considered that their most urgent need was financial assistance. It has proposed a guaranteed maintenance allowance sufficiently high to raise the income of 90 per cent of one-parent families above supplementary benefit level, and to give most such parents a genuine choice about undertaking full-time work. There would be a means-tested element in the allowance in that it would taper off to zero for those with incomes at about the level of average earnings. Until the allowance can be instituted, it proposed that more generous supplementary benefits should be paid to these families. However, although single parents who are not in full-time work are after two years assessed on the long-term supplementary benefit rate and although all single-parent families are entitled to an extra £3.30 Child Benefit for the first or only child, there is much evidence to indicate that single-parent families still comprise one of the poorest groups in society.

Housing

The cost of housing is one of the overheads of living which it is very difficult for individuals, and even more for families, to control. As a result, given relatively fixed incomes, the cost of housing has a direct effect on the availability of income for other needs. The importance of this is recognised in supplementary benefits by including an allowance that normally covers the whole of the rent, including rates, paid by a claimant. A reduced rent allowance may be paid if in the view of the Commission's officers the rent is unreasonably high. For houseowners only the rates and interest on a mortgage plus a small sum for running costs can be paid. It is not considered desirable that the Commission should make capital payments and thus contribute to the capital assets of claimants. This creates major problems for owner-occupiers with mortgages who are in receipt of supplementary benefits over a long period.

Other means of mitigating the problems associated with the cost of housing are discussed in the chapter on housing. They include rent and rate allowances under the Housing Finance Act, 1972, rent control and tax allowances on the interest on mortgages. It is important to note that the transmutation of housing subsidies into rent rebates under the Housing Finance Act clarified that the major objective was then seen as income maintenance through supplementation rather than the encouragement of local authority housing.

Conclusion

The period between the end of the Second World War in 1945 and Labour's Social Security Acts of 1975 saw a dramatic growth of the social security system and the introduction of a wide range of measures for income maintenance. As we have seen, this growth entailed the introduction of a significant number of contributory and non-contributory national insurance benefits, the expansion of the national assistance scheme (subsequently the supplementary benefits scheme), the introduction of rent and rate rebates and family income supplement and the establishment of free educational and health services for those in need.

Most analyses of the relationship between income and need until the mid-1970s focused on four areas. The first area was that of the relationship between the market economy and the welfare system. In particular writers such as Titmuss clearly demonstrated that particular needs, especially the needs of the poor, could not be met effectively within the context of a free economic market.

The second area of analysis was fundamentally *technical* and comprised an attempt to identify how needs could be most appropriately identified and efficiently met. For example, there was much debate about the best measures of poverty and the identification of those actually living in poverty, these debates relating to analyses of appropriate levels of benefit in relation to needs. More specifically attempts were made to identify the best methods of structuring the payment of benefits so that they could be clearly understood by claimants and ceased to be administratively cumbersome. Similarly studies were made of the take-up of benefits and researchers tried to identify the best methods of encouraging those in need to claim the benefits to which they were entitled.

A third area to be studied was that of the activities of political parties and political leaders in so far as they affected the welfare and social security systems. The conclusions drawn, justifiably, were that differences, certainly between the two main political parties, were differences of form rather than of substance and that there were really no major conflicts between the political parties over the issue of income maintenance during this period.

The final area of analysis focused on the relationship between public attitudes and expenditure on welfare provision. The conclusion frequently drawn was that given public attitudes of hostility towards the poor and towards social security expenditure, the possibility of increasing taxation to raise the levels of benefit of the poor was fairly limited. It is probably fair to say therefore that most of those interested in the area of the relationship between income and need assumed that the welfare benefits system which had evolved since the war, whilst not necessarily expanding to meet new needs and whilst not always being adequate to meet existing needs would at least remain intact and provide those without alternative incomes with an adequate income to subsist.

However, recent developments tend to lead one to question whether the welfare benefits system will in the future be capable of meeting even this basic goal. First, the dramatic price inflation of the 1970s, especially in the costs of basic commodities such as fuel and food, has produced significant new problems to be faced by those living on subsistence incomes. Second, much evidence indicates that the current Conservative government, far from expanding the present system of welfare benefits or even maintaining benefits in line with inflation, is effectively reducing those benefits. As we have seen, there have been significant reductions in the help given to those in need to help meet the costs of fuel, drastic reductions in the extent of supplementary benefit discretionary payments, the breaking of the statutory link between price and wage rises and pension payments. It is therefore fair to say that benefits, for many, are at a dangerously low level and if they are further reduced then cases of very severe physical hardship will occur. Second, the system of welfare benefits which in the post-war period has not been a topic of profound political debate and conflict is likely to become one.

Further reading

For the history of these services before 1939, Gilbert and de Schweinitz are useful supplements to the more general works listed at the end of chapter 1. George (1968) covers general development from Beveridge to 1968 very thoroughly, King a more specific area. Stevenson is a very good account of the work of the Supplementary Benefits Commission, avoiding the issues raised by the more radical critiques of the social security system in George (1973) and Jordan. Of these two George's work is the more scholarly, but Jordan's is full of interesting insights. Atkinson is still the clearest exposition and analysis of the various ways used and put forward for tackling the abolition of poverty defined in terms of supplementary benefit rates. Burns, Richardson and Rodgers provide useful analyses of the principles involved in different forms of provision, with international comparisons which are to varying degrees dated. Wynn provides the basis on which a rational system of family support might be constructed, with many fascinating tables and charts. The most topical and comprehensive study of poverty in the United Kingdom is the Townsend book. Finally, two useful and up-to-date guides for use in working out entitlements are those by Lister and Drabble *et al.*

JANET ALLBESON, *National Welfare Benefits Handbook*, Child Poverty Action Group, revised annually.

A. B. ATKINSON, *Poverty in Britain and the Reform of Social Security*, Cambridge University Press, 1969.

E. M. BURNS, *Social Security and Public Policy*, McGraw-Hill, 1956.

RICHARD DRABBLE, MARK ROWLAND and NICHOLAS WARREN, *Guide to Contributory Benefits and Child Benefit*, CPAG, 2nd edn, 1978.

VICTOR GEORGE, *Social Security: Beveridge and After*, Routledge & Kegan Paul, 1968.

VICTOR GEORGE, *Social Security and Society*, Routledge & Kegan Paul, 1973.

B. B. GILBERT, *The Evolution of National Insurance in Great Britain*, Michael Joseph, 1967.

BILL JORDAN, *Poor Parents: Social Policy and the Cycle of Deprivation*, Routledge & Kegan Paul, 1974.

SIR GEOFFREY S. KING, *The Ministry of Pensions and National Insurance*, Allen & Unwin, 1958.

J. H. RICHARDSON, *Economic and Financial Aspects of Social Security: An International Survey*, Allen & Unwin, 1960.

BARBARA N. RODGERS *et al.*, *Comparative Social Administration*, Allen & Unwin, 1968.

KARL DE SCHWEINITZ, *England's Road to Social Security*, University of Pennsylvania Press, 1943.

OLIVE STEVENSON, *Claimant or Client?*, Allen & Unwin, 1973.

PETER TOWNSEND, *Poverty in the United Kingdom: A Survey of Household Resources and Standards of Living*, Allen Lane, 1979.

MARGARET WYNN, *Family Policy*, Michael Joseph, 1970.

5 Housing

Kathleen Pickett

Among those commodities which may be considered basic to normal civilised life—food, clothing, fuel and housing—housing poses peculiar economic problems. The cost of buying a house is very high relative to annual earnings and so the great majority of people need to obtain a loan if they wish to possess a house of their own, or alternatively must be content to obtain one by paying rent to its owner. In either case, the cost is reduced to one which can be paid out of earnings. Nevertheless, such payments are affected by rising interest rates which could increase them to an unacceptable extent. To meet this threat, a number of devices are possible. At the building stage, the standard of housing may be reduced or a greater number of dwellings may be built on the same area—that is the density of housing is increased. After this stage, maintenance may be neglected or the density of population increased by overcrowding. All are a means of reducing the cost of housing per person as well as of increasing profits.

In addition, the long life which houses normally sustain means that only a small proportion of the existing stock are of recent construction. Old dwellings, of however high a standard when built, may well deteriorate into slums and so give rise to conditions which will lead to intervention by some form of authority. Yet housing is a comparative newcomer to the field of social services. The needs of the old, the sick and those in extreme poverty have been recognised by the charitable for many hundreds of years. It was only after the upheaval of the Industrial Revolution with its mass movement to the new factories, and the resulting overcrowded, insanitary and disease-ridden communities in the central urban areas, that society generally was forced into recognising that some control over housing conditions in those areas was essential. It was in this context, with the fear of epidemics spreading from such concentrations of squalor, that the first housing legislation was introduced in the second half of the nineteenth century.

Gradually, after the First World War, when the promise of 'homes fit for heroes' became a discredited and derisive catchphrase, good housing was recognised as a need for which society must accept some responsibility. This social approach to housing with its implication that economic considerations must, if necessary, take second place where need accompanies an inability to pay, at least in full, is now largely accepted. However, the extent and the form of aid is still very much a matter of controversy.

Where the public pays the price through tax or rates the cost of meeting such a need must inevitably be a matter for close scrutiny, especially when there are so many competing demands to be met and the cost is so high. No doubt this is why housing under the public sector has never yet achieved an adequate level and has been and is still supplemented to a significant extent by bodies largely independent of the government. Early examples of the private provision of housing may be seen in the tied cottages and, in a few cases, the model villages of the landed gentry. Similarly, many manufacturers made prosperous by the industrial development of the nineteenth century built tied houses for their workers close to the factory or mine, not a few of which are still occupied today. During this period also charitable trusts endowed by wealthy patrons began to provide dwellings for the working class at low rents. These trusts led to the formation of non-profit-making housing associations which play an important part in the provision of low-cost housing today.

As good housing became recognised as a right, it was also seen as one of a complex of amenities necessary to a satisfying environment. These include access to shops, schools and open space, and facilities for recreation and association conducive to the development of good relationships between fellow residents. Until the advent of comprehensive planning powers, such amenities were largely supplied, if at all, on an *ad hoc* basis and subject to the whims of individual developers. The failure of this system to meet growing expectations became more apparent during the inter-war years as urban sprawl encroached upon the surrounding countryside. Ribbon development, coastal shanty towns and a general lack of care for natural amenities led to the introduction of an increasing number of controls. Rudimentary powers of planning and conservation in urban areas had been available to local authorities, though not generally used, since the early inter-war years. These were later extended to rural areas, but the establishment of a Ministry of Town and Country Planning at the end of the Second World War marked the beginning of the system of controls over all forms of environmental development which we have today.

Closely associated with such changes has been a change in values and expectations. For the majority of people in this country economic improvements have provided opportunities available only to a favoured minority before the last war. The increasing proportion of home owners, in spite of high rises in the cost of houses and mortgages, reflects this change. Nevertheless, the improvement has not been universal and for a few it appears that the difficulty of establishing an adequate home environment may have increased, or perhaps their needs are more easily overlooked in the general preoccupation with new and enlarging experiences. Around those with few resources, the vicious circle of multiple deprivation appears to have become more firmly closed.

In examining housing as a social service, four separate strands must be followed: first, the construction of new houses at a cost or for a rent which can be afforded by those on low incomes; second, slum clearance and renewal; third, the improvement and updating of structurally sound houses which have fallen below current standards; and fourth, the care of the general environment which is implicit in the term 'planning'. At different periods, different strands have been in the ascendant, but ideally a strong housing policy requires equal weight to be given to each. In the first half of this chapter, a historical account of housing legislation under successive governments since the mid-nineteenth century indicates how the emphasis has changed between these aspects; in the second half a more general discussion of special problems illustrates the need for adequate support in each area.

Early housing policies and control

The Victorian period

The massive overcrowding of the nineteenth century has disappeared, but one legacy remains in the recognition of the need for controls in the housing field. During the first half of that century, as new factories proliferated in the developing industrial towns and cities, migrants from declining agricultural areas streamed in to find work and a more prosperous life in urban centres. To answer their need cheap houses for rent were rapidly constructed, and became a popular and rewarding form of investment, while in many older houses each room contained at least one family, perhaps of eight or nine people. Lawton[1] describes conditions in Liverpool at this time where, as in other cities, back-to-back houses were commonly built round courts which were entered from the street by narrow, badly lit alleys. Octavia Hill[2] vividly describes the state of such houses in London where hardened mud caked the kitchen stairs over which hung the 'foul smells which the heavy foggy air would not allow to rise'. In Liverpool in 1841, 20,000 residents lived in cellar dwellings often below water-level.

In all urban areas mortality rates rose astronomically; there was a high incidence of tuberculosis and a constant risk of epidemics of typhoid, cholera and other contagious diseases. Concern at these conditions and dangers grew and culminated in a study sponsored by the 1832 Poor Law Commission under its secretary Edwin Chadwick. This *Report of the Sanitary Conditions of the Labouring Population of Great Britain* was published in 1842 and was followed by a Royal Commission[3] which reported in 1844 and 1845.

The ensuing legislation in 1848[4] was largely an attempt to raise the standards of public health by establishing local Boards of Health to secure the supply of clean water and to improve sanitation. In 1868, however, the Artisans' and Labourers' Dwellings Act was passed, which although still primarily concerned with the health aspect, was the first measure to enable intervention in the housing situation. Under this Act, houses could be declared unfit for human habitation by the medical officer of health for the authority and their owners required to make improvements or to demolish at their own expense. Later nineteenth-century legislation increased the power of the local authority to clear areas of unfit housing and to rebuild under an improvement scheme. However, little use was made of these powers, for they were expensive and largely impractical because of a requirement to rehouse a number of people equivalent to those displaced. Nevertheless, the principle of slum clearance was established.

From 1851 local authorities were empowered[5] to build new dwellings for rent; but again few took advantage of this opportunity and the scale varied. Liverpool Corporation was one of the earliest, constructing a block of tenements, St Martin's Cottages (part still standing, modernised and occupied). But against the background of massive private enterprise absorbed in the creation of suburban areas, and the redevelopment of central areas for the new railway complex as well as for commercial undertakings, the efforts of the public sector at this time were insignificant in spite of the exacerbation of an already serious problem by wholesale demolition.

In the face of this neglect by authority, charity—a major force in the Victorian period—stepped in. In London, Octavia Hill persuaded Mr Ruskin to put forward £3,000 to buy cottage property which she renovated with the help of occupants needing employment. Her use of the housing situation to put into motion a whole series of improvements, including employment, leisure activities and education, although on a local scale, was an example of social service at its most effective. Her example was followed by others and led in time to the development of housing management as a professional service.

During the same period a number of charitable trusts of differing sizes were set up to provide low-rent housing for the 'working classes'. These were the forerunners of today's housing associations and some, such as the Bournville Village Trust and the Sutton Dwellings Trust, have remained active. Set up initially by private funds, the rents were used to provide more houses. In 1909 support was given by Parliament to these organisations by their recognition in the Housing, Town Planning, etc., Act as Public Utility Societies, which enabled them to obtain loans on special terms.

The same Act was the first to facilitate a move beyond the small-scale 'improvement scheme', which had so little success, by giving borough, urban and rural district councils powers to formulate planning schemes for new building. These would take into account amenities and layout as well as ensuring proper sanitary conditions—a continuing government preoccupation. Attempts to make these schemes compulsory failed; nevertheless, the effect was generally to raise the standard of housing design and layout. The end of the nineteenth century and the beginning of the twentieth century had seen a growing interest, fostered by a few outstanding individuals, in the improvement of the urban environment. Often marked by strongly anti-urban views, hardly surprising in the context of the times, men such as Ebenezer Howard dreamed of the creation of residential areas which would combine the best qualities of urban and rural life. The realisation of these dreams can be seen in the two Garden Cities of Letchworth and Welwyn, and Garden Villages such as Port Sunlight and Bournville. This idea of a total environment which would provide for outdoor recreation in areas of open space and for the intellectual life in access to libraries, art galleries and other cultural facilities has been firmly established in accepted planning practice since that time.

The inter-war years

During the First World War, house building and house repairs were at a standstill. At this point in time, the great majority of houses were rented from private landlords and only the very wealthy could afford to buy their own. Few municipal dwellings were available: the public utility societies were the main providers of low-rent housing. A high proportion of houses were multi-occupied and sharing between parents and their married children was usual.

At the end of the war the Coalition government realised that changes must be made and more houses become rapidly available. Although the association between housing and public health remained, in that both were the responsibility of the Ministry of Health and would remain so until after the Second World War, housing was established as a need in its own right for which the government must take responsibility. During the inter-war years, the periodic increase and decrease in house construction reflect the ability and will of successive governments to provide some form of support to builders in the public or private sector. The days of low-cost materials and labour, which allowed a good return to the property investor, had passed apart from a short period leading up to the Second World War.

Certainly in 1919, costs had risen too far for any large-scale development to be expected from the private sector or the unaided local authorities. To meet this difficulty, the Housing, Town Planning, etc., Act of 1919 empowered local authorities to use the product of a penny rate for new council housing of a standard fixed by the government, any difference in cost to be met by an Exchequer subsidy. A subsidy could also be claimed for slum clearance schemes, but in the event few such schemes were submitted—the shortage of housing was too acute to allow any loss of housing of however poor a standard. The scheme for a virtually open-ended Exchequer subsidy was soon abandoned when it was found to entail an average cost of £60 a house each year—a quite unacceptable amount by the standards of that time—and once more the number of house constructions fell sharply. As an alternative the decision was made to subsidise building for sale,[6] in the hope that private builders might be more ready to keep costs low, and that the movement to these houses would release older ones for rent and so relieve overcrowding. At the same time, rent control, introduced during the war, was removed from lettings when vacant possession was obtained in the expectation that this would lead to an increase in privately rented accommodation. None of these hopes was realised before the Labour government came into office in 1924.

Under the new government the 1924 Wheatley Act[7] introduced a programme for the construction of 2½ million houses during the next fifteen years. All building agencies were to co-operate—private, local authority and housing associations—with a fixed Exchequer subsidy of £9 a house to be paid annually for 40 years while the local authorities contributed £4 10s. toward each of their own. Rents were again fixed at approximately pre-war level, though decontrol on vacant possession remained for private lettings. By the end of the 1920s nearly half a million council houses had been built with a small amount of slum clearance. Nevertheless, problems all too familiar today remained: the improvement had barely affected those in greatest need, for whom council house rents were too high, and the slums grew rather than diminished. Of the two aspects of government concern at this time—construction for 'normal housing requirements' and slum clearance—the first had received the most support while the second had been largely inhibited by the cost of compensation and rehousing. Fresh measures were required if there was to be any serious attempt to shift the balance of advantage towards those at the lower end of the income scale, and in the 1930 Housing Act a new government introduced new procedures and new subsidies which provided a basis for a more effective approach to slum clearance and the provision of low-cost housing.

Under this Act, the balance between council housing and slum clearance changed, and for the first time clearance took priority. Criticisms had been made that council house rents were too high for all but the skilled worker. Studies of Becontree[8] and Watling[9] confirmed that there was a high turnover rate in these estates. Many new residents found that they were unable to meet the added expense, in particular the cost of the journey to work, and so returned to the city centre. After 1930, and even more when economies under the Housing (Financial Provisions) Act, 1933, led to the abolition of subsidies for 'general need' housing, the first aim was slum clearance and rehousing. Until the outbreak of war in 1939 this proceeded at a rate never reached before or since. Nevertheless, 'general need' subsidies returned in 1935 for the balance had swung too far.

The 1930 Act also replaced the old definition of 'unfit'—closely associated with protection from disease—by a new definition which took into account 'lack of air space or of ventilation, darkness, dampness, absence of adequate and readily accessible water supply or sanitary accommodation or of other conveniences and inadequate paving or drainage of courts, yards or passages'. Five years later[10] overcrowding became an offence.

Another change in the housing situation occurred after 1932 when, with a degree of economic recovery, the speculative builder was able to take advantage of a good market for cheap houses for sale and for the first time owner-occupation spread to lower income groups. Although the workmanship was often poor, these houses served a useful purpose at a time when council housing had become more difficult to obtain. At the same time there was renewed interest in property investment and smaller houses were bought for letting. The 1933 Rent Act also decontrolled houses of high rateable value entirely, allowed decontrol on vacant possession for those of moderate value but controlled rents on those of low value. Under these conditions, housing societies were also widening their scope and though still seeing their function as the provision of houses for the 'working class', they did not confine their attention to the poorest section. In 1935 the National Federation of Housing Societies was formed and given official recognition in the 1936 Housing Act.

The spate of building during the 1930s inevitably led to problems of control and preservation. Government and public were still not ready for any stringent measures and this was a time when freedom for the builder was almost complete. The 1932 Town and Country Planning Act reflects the rather grudging admission that while the urge to build and to renew must be given encouragement, some restraints were required and some attempt should be made to maintain minimum aesthetic standards. On the one hand, the Act drew attention to the need to preserve certain amenities such as areas of natural beauty and historic buildings, while on the other it insisted upon the availability of essential services such as roads and water supply before development commenced. A rather weak piece of legislation—it was essentially local in its application and inhibited by the acceptance of large claims for compensation—it nevertheless prepared the ground for the post-war period. Then, with the experience of five years of controls in all areas of life, associated perhaps with the successful termination of the conflict, the British people were ready for some curtailment of freedom in order to achieve an improvement in their environment.

By the time the Second World War commenced, when, as in 1914, all housing developments were quickly brought to an end, each of the four aspects of housing need were established in some degree. The 1930s had given an impetus to the construction of new houses, and to slum clearance and replacement, greater than at any previous period. Improvement and updating, however, was hardly considered in the public sector and little outside since the days of Octavia Hill and her associates. Planning, although in its infancy, had arrived and had many influential supporters. These would emerge after the war and take part in its development into a discipline in which architects and geographers would associate to found a profession whose power would extend at an unprecedented speed. Even before the end of the war, in 1943, a Ministry of Town and Country Planning was created and the Town and Country Planning (Interim Development) Act of that year imposed development control over all land not already subject to a local authority scheme. Three reports published at the beginning of the war had exposed a number of problems which required far-reaching powers for their solution: the Barlow Report, *Distribution of the Industrial Population*, the Uthwatt *Report of the Expert Committee on Compensation and Betterment*, and the Scott Report on *Land Utilisation*.[11]

In addition, the inter-war years had seen the use of two instruments of policy whose varied application provides evidence—not always to be taken into account—of their effectiveness in making housing available at a cost which can be met by households on low incomes. One of these was rent control, in force at the start of the period, relaxed in 1923, preserved only for 'working-class' houses after the 1933 Rent Act and, after relaxation in 1938, saved from a final abandonment by the outbreak of war.

The second was the use of subsidies to stimulate house construction. At first available for both municipal and private dwellings and, like rent control, seen as a temporary measure, they have survived in some form to the present day. Between 1933 and 1935 they were given only for local authority houses provided as replacements for demolished unfit dwellings but this restriction may well have prevented other council house construction. Both rent control and subsidies have played an important role in government housing policy in the post-Second World War years—some might say with at least as much effect on political events as on the supply of dwellings.

Post-war developments

The end of the Second World War, like the end of the First, saw problems of housing need compounded by years in which no domestic building had taken place. By 1945 this had been aggravated by the loss of many houses through enemy action. Once more, slum clearance was a luxury which must be postponed while all efforts were given to providing additional accommodation. During the immediate post-war years a considerable amount of legislation affected all aspects of housing provision and environmental control and the foundations were laid for many new developments in the ensuing years.

Although by the late 1970s there were rather more dwellings available than households requiring dwellings,[12] the surplus does not necessarily arise in the area where it is required. In addition it includes second homes—an increasing feature of rural and seaside areas, a necessary margin of vacancies to allow for mobility and a large number of dwellings of a physical or environmental standard well below that acceptable today.

The main areas concerned in meeting housing needs will be considered in turn although none can, in effect, be isolated from the influence of the others, or from those two instruments of policy, rent control and subsidies, with their continuing cycles of imposition and relaxation. The current situation here will also be discussed at the end of this section.

New housing

The 1948 Labour government gave priority to council housing while a strict system of licensing restricted all other developments. From

TABLE 8 *The tenure of dwellings in England and Wales, 1947, 1961, 1971 and 1979 (in percentages)*

Tenure	*1947*	*1961*	*1971*	*1979*
Owner-occupied	27	44	50	55
Local authority and New Towns	12	25	31	32
Privately rented, including housing associations	61	31	19	13

Source: *Annual Abstract of Statistics*, 1981, HMSO.

1948 to 1952, 80 per cent of post-war houses were built by local authorities with the help of an increased government subsidy, yet even so every authority had long waiting lists and systems of allocation were introduced which took into account family size, present accommodation, war service, and often most important of all, length of residence within the authority. Various types of selection schemes have remained, which will be considered in more detail below under 'council housing'.

After the advent of a Conservative government in 1951, restrictions in private building were relaxed and since that time the proportion of houses built for owner-occupation has increased remarkably, so that today more than half the dwellings in England and Wales are owner-occupied compared with a little over a quarter in 1947.

The increased proportion of owner-occupied and public sector dwellings (Table 8) since the war has accompanied and is in part a consequence of the fall in privately rented accommodation which has become progressively less worthwhile financially. During the later 1970s an additional factor was a reduced rate of building by local authorities and a substantial increase in new construction by housing associations (Table 9)

TABLE 9 *New construction: annual net loss and gain in the public sector (in thousands)*

	1951–60	*1971–75*	*1979*
Local authority	+ 169	+ 118	+ 78
New Towns	+ 9	+ 12	+ 9
Housing associations	+ 4	+ 10	+ 17
Government departments	+ 7	+ 2	+ 1
Total	+ 189	+ 142	+ 105

Source: *Social Trends* 11, 1981, Central Statistical Office.

Today owner-occupation is the goal of the great majority of households and is particularly strong among the younger age groups.[13] Home ownership now extends over a considerably wider portion of the population than in pre-war days with currently about equal numbers of manual and non-manual mortgage holders. A number of reasons may be suggested for this including the drop in private renting, the policy of economic rents for council houses and the increase in available income among manual workers. Nevertheless, there still remain many unable to raise sufficient capital for the deposit, too old to qualify for a mortgage or unwilling to take on the responsibility of ownership, and for these council houses or other types of rented accommodation are still required. Income clearly acts as a constraint to those looking for a house, but the proportion of income which a household is prepared to spend on its purchase or rent varies considerably and is a choice available to all except the poorest.

The private sector

Little control has been exercised over the standard of private building since subsidies were withdrawn from this sector. A minimum standard of construction is laid down through building bye-laws but frequent inspection is required to ensure its maintenance and this is not always feasible. In 1946 the National House Building Registration Council was set up, representing a variety of interests which include the Royal Institute of British Architects, the Building Societies Association, the Town Planning Institute, building operatives and local authorities. It operates as an independent certifying body which can be used by any builder.

Few people are able to buy a house outright, especially since the inflation of house prices which brought about massive increases in the 1970s. The majority obtain a mortgage loan through a building society, which will advance a proportion of the value which is placed by the society on the house; this will often be rather less than the price paid by the purchaser. Loans, for which the house acts as security, vary according to the age and condition of the property and may be as high as 90 per cent for a newly built house. Repayment is made over a number of years which is usually twenty-five but can extend to thirty-five at the time the mortgage is taken out. The interest is related to bank rate and when this increased to 17 per cent in November 1979 rose to its highest level ever of 15 per cent in December 1979. By January 1981 the rate had declined to 13 per cent for loans of less than £15,000 though higher for greater amounts. The increase in monthly repayments which uprating causes added to heavy initial down-payments as house price increase has led to difficulties for many, and especially for young house-owners buying their first home. Building societies will usually provide an option of increasing the period of repayment, but this has obvious drawbacks.

A number of devices have been considered to help first-time buyers. Some building societies have introduced low-start mortgages where lower repayments are made for the initial years and gradually increase in the expectation that the ability to pay will also increase. Equity sharing schemes are used by some housing associations and local authorities where both occupier and association or authority retain a small proportion of the equity of the dwelling. The occupier pays rent and has the option of purchasing any part of the remainder of the equity which is sold on moving away.

Many first-time buyers' first purchase is an older terraced house, but these are unpopular with building societies who lend less than a quarter of their funds on pre-1914 houses. In 1975 a support lending scheme was introduced to encourage the societies to lend more on these houses, but it has had little success. Under the 1980 Housing Act, local authorities and the Housing Corporation must guarantee loans from building societies to their tenants who opt to buy their house, and in so doing have a legal right to a mortgage.

Most local authorities also operate mortgage schemes[14] and are allowed to lend up to 100 per cent of their valuation repayable over thirty years with interest. Money available for this purpose is limited and authorities tend to operate selection procedures so as to provide such loans to applicants who cannot obtain a building society mortgage, usually because the house is too old or on too short a lease. Currently most local authority mortgages go to first-time buyers. Loans may also be obtained through insurance companies combined with endowment assurance or through a bank, but until recently the latter expected higher repayments over a shorter period than did building societies. However, in 1981 a number of banks introduced a scheme where, for regular depositors, loans were provided at a constant rate of interest equal to that of the building societies' lowest rate, so providing the cheapest mortgages available.

Building societies originated in the late eighteenth century when their members raised money to buy land on which to build their own houses; once this was done, the society was dissolved. During the nineteenth century the two functions of investing and house purchasing became distinct and since then the societies have raised money from the public which is lent at a higher rate of interest to the house purchaser. The rate of interest allowed to the private investor must compete with other forms of investment and to a great extent decides the rate paid on the mortgage loan. At times of very high bank rates, such as occurred in 1973 and 1979–80, building societies may find that their loans are outstripping their investment funds. This is met by a decrease in new mortgages and a rise in interest rates. In 1973 and 1979 the government temporarily delayed the increase, but it has been suggested that the societies should prevent such crises by building up 'stabilisation funds' which would buffer the mortgage payer against the more violent fluctuations.[15]

Tax allowances may be claimed for mortgage repayments, the amount of tax relief being related to the tax liability and, therefore, highest for those who have big loans for expensive houses—generally those in the higher income brackets. Until the government's option mortgage scheme was introduced in 1968, those with low tax liability because on small incomes were not able to obtain any tax relief. Under this scheme,[16] purchasers may opt for a subsidy rather than income tax relief, which effectively reduces the interest on their loan by 2 per cent unless the interest rate falls below 6 per cent—virtually this occurs only where an annuity mortgage at a fixed rate of interest has been taken out, an arrangement discontinued some years ago.

The high cost of housing is related to rising costs of materials, labour and building land, the latter in especially short supply in the larger towns and cities. In an attempt to gain control of the increase in value of development land as well as the way in which it is developed the Community Land Act[17] was introduced in 1975. Phase 1 of this Act and the accompanying Development Land Tax Act came into effect in 1976. The scheme was planned to take eight to ten years to implement fully and it was hoped that this gradual introduction would gain it greater success than two previous attempts at control of land, lost with a change in government. In its final phase all land to be developed for non-agricultural purposes would have passed into public ownership before development took place, and the large increases in value which occur when permission for development is expected would be eliminated. However, this Act went the way of the others and was repealed in 1981.

Council housing

The great majority of houses built by local authorities are for rent, although a few may be built directly for sale. All such housing qualifies for subsidies, whose operation will be examined in a later section.

At a time of continuing housing shortage, one problem is the 'mismatch' of dwellings and households. In some areas of pre-war council housing there may be considerable under-occupation[18] where families have grown up and the children have left. In many post-war estates the same problem will arise in the not too distant future, especially in the case of houses built in the 1950s, when the urgent need for housing led to fast construction and occupation by families whose age and composition fell within a narrow scope.[19] Often in such estates there is a demand for houses from second and third generation households who may have a long wait for a suitable tenancy.

Those who obtain council houses fall into four main categories: from the housing list, through demolition and slum clearance, by exchange or transfer, or for medical reasons. A smaller category includes key workers who may be needed for local industry or by the authority, for example as social workers. The housing list contains the names of people who have themselves applied for a council house and in areas where houses are in short supply may well be inflated by those who have found alternative accommodation, those who have moved away and those who have put their names down for more than one authority. In the larger cities there are usually more housing list applicants than tenancies available and in this case selection procedures of some kind must be applied by the local authorities.

There is a statutory duty under the 1957 Housing Act to give reasonable preference to persons occupying insanitary or overcrowded houses, who have large families or are living in unsatisfactory conditions of some kind. Following a recommendation of the housing management sub-committee, the Seebohm Report[20] urged a broader interpretation of their housing responsibilities on the part of local authorities and also suggested that more attention should be paid to those in greatest need, especially those at greatest risk of becoming homeless or grossly ill-housed. The particular difficulties faced by such people in obtaining a council house are that they tend to be mobile, and so may not fulfil the residential requirements, and often migrate to areas with a serious housing problem, such as the inner areas of cities, to find work. They may also, in spite of rebates, have difficulty in paying the rent regularly. While a shortage of council housing remains, their priority will inevitably remain low.

The 1975 Sex Discrimination Act and the 1976 Race Relations Act make it unlawful for a local authority to discriminate in the provision of housing on grounds of sex, marital status or race. Nevertheless, racial discrimination in the quality of housing allocated appears to occur. (See under 'Ethnic minorities'.)

Selection procedures vary considerably between local authorities. In most cases there is a points system, in others a personal decision by the local authority housing manager, or in the cases where there is a surplus of council housing, a simple date order based on application time. It has been pointed out[21] that subjective factors, such as the strain of living with in-laws, are not measurable and so tend to be ignored, and that it is physical rather than social needs which are assessed. Housing managers usually visit the home of applicants before allocating houses, and on this basis they are 'graded' as being likely to take good care of their new house or as potential risks. This may lead to neighbourhoods or whole estates winning a reputation for 'roughness'[22] and the newest council housing goes to those seen as the 'best' tenants.

Single parents, transients and the disabled still have little chance of a council house, but the expansion of housing associations during the late 1970s and their closer links with local authorities have allowed greater flexibility. Applicants who do not fit the accepted council tenant pattern now have more opportunity to obtain suitable accommodation, though still relatively disadvantaged.

Where people have been displaced from houses declared unfit for habitation and compulsorily acquired by the local authority, in most cases because they have been living in a slum clearance or redevelopment area, local authorities have a statutory obligation to rehouse owner-occupiers, tenants, sub-tenants or married children, though not individual lodgers. Where they have been moved out of technically fit property, even though sub-standard, some authorities will consider that owner-occupiers who have been paid the market value for their houses should find accommodation for themselves, although tenants will usually be rehoused. There appear to be substantial differences in policy here between authorities and there are certainly difficulties in areas of housing pressure where it sometimes occurs that houses will be bought or rented if clearance is likely, in order to qualify for a council house when this takes place.

The ease with which exchanges and transfers—the former to tenanted, the latter to vacant housing—can be made either within or between estates can vary a good deal from one area to another. Some authorities co-operate more readily than others although few yet operate local bureaux through which such changes can readily be made. Housing management sub-committees in successive years have seen the process as one way of redistributing tenants so as to minimise under-occupation though the policy at present is more to facilitate such exchanges than positively to encourage them through financial inducements. Transfers to other members of the family on the death of the tenant responsible for payment is also a process where no general procedure is followed. An adult son or daughter who has lived for many years with parents in a council house will have a strong case, but separated or deserted wives will often find themselves in difficulties.

Under the Housing Finance Act, 1972, local authorities were required to fix 'fair rents' for their tenants and rent rebates could be claimed by low-income households. Rebates were previously available only where local authorities chose to provide them, subject to a means test of variable stringency: the 1972 Act standardised the procedure. The 'fair rents' scheme was repealed and local authorities were once more able to fix their own rents after the Housing Rents and Subsidies Act 1975 but from 1980 the Secretary of State controlled rent increases through the use of cash limits. The rent rebate scheme has remained, and will be discussed below under 'Rent control and security of tenure'.

The 1980 Housing Act introduced the concept of 'secure tenancy' for local authority tenants as well as tenants of development corporations, the Housing Corporation, charitable housing trusts, the Commission for the New Towns and the Development Board of Rural Wales. Secure tenancies can only be brought to an end, except by mutual consent, through a court order for which good reason must be given such as arrears of rent. Suitable accommodation must be available for an evicted tenant when the court order takes effect.

A secure tenant can take in lodgers—a welcome concession for council tenants—but not sub-let without the landlord's consent. Landlords of secure tenants are required to notify them of any improvements or demolition to be carried out in time to allow them to make their views on these changes known.

Perhaps the most controversial right of a secure council tenant is the right to buy the dwelling occupied if occupation has been for at least three years. (This does not apply to charitable housing trust tenants.) The price is current market value less a discount ranging from 33 per cent for tenants of three to four years, to 50 per cent for long-term tenants. In the first instance the landlord makes the valuation, but if this is disputed, the tenant has a right to a valuation by the District Valuer, whose decision is binding on both landlord and tenant. In addition, a mortgage which includes the total cost of the transaction is guaranteed. Some part of the discount must be repaid if the dwelling is sold within five years.

Arguments concerning the merit or demerit of selling council houses have continued for some years, with the Conservative party strongly in favour and the Labour party slowly conceding some ground. Although previously strongly opposed to their sale under any circumstances, the Labour Government relaxed its attitude in 1974 and while revoking the general consent to sell given by a Conservative Government in 1972, it allowed sales subject to the local authority concerned showing that they had no unsatisfied demand in their area. No discount was allowed and re-sale was forbidden for five years. Under the policy introduced by the 1980 Housing Act, council house sales are expected to average 100,000 a year.[23]

The advantage of council house sales include the satisfaction of an increasing demand for home ownership, the reduction in government housing subsidies plus local authority borrowing and maintenance costs, so that theoretically money is released for more housing. Among the disadvantages are that in most cases it reduces the stock of housing available for those in need, that in general it is the better housing in the more attractive areas that is sold so leaving local authorities with a stock of deteriorating and unpopular accommodation and that the financial advantages disappear when mortgage relief and loss of rents are taken into account.[24] Evidence given to the all-party Environmental Committee confirmed these disadvantageous tendencies.[25]

Housing associations

Housing associations[26] were defined in the 1957 Housing Act as non-profit-making societies whose object is to construct, improve or manage houses. Before 1919 they were the chief providers of low-rent housing for the 'working classes', but as this role was taken over more and more by local authorities the associations diversified their interests. Today many cater for special needs, in particular for the elderly, but also for other groups such as the disabled, ex-prisoners, single parents and students. Others provide rented accommodation at economic rents for those with higher incomes. Others again are formed by groups who wish to build their own homes and dissolve when these are completed.

In 1964 the Housing Corporation was set up with powers to assist in the development of societies, make loans and acquire land. This was accompanied by a rapid growth of the 'new style' associations and, incidentally, to considerable expertise in the improvement of older houses. By 1974 dissatisfaction with wholesale demolition and re-development, which had been steadily growing among the public generally as well as—for mainly financial reasons—among central and local government resulted in a change of policy to an emphasis on improvement. Because the housing associations had considerable experience in this area, the 1974 Housing Act gave the Housing Corporation additional funds which could be drawn by registered housing associations in order to buy older houses for improvement as dwellings for single households, or in the case of larger houses, to convert into flats.

The housing associations involved were to work in co-operation with local authorities who might also contribute by loaning money for their work. In return the authorities were able to refer to them applicants who did not fulfil their own requirements, in certain circumstances to nominate tenants and, most important of all, to see an increase in housing stock with a minimum burden to the rates.

As a result of this policy their expansion was considerable until

1979, and during that period they continued to encourage co-operation for new building and to fulfil their role of providing housing for disadvantaged groups.

By the end of the decade criticism of the Housing Corporation's administration of funds was growing. Generally it was believed that housing associations worked to uneconomic standards and had not been sufficiently controlled by the Corporation. In 1980 the Conservative government reduced its grant to the Corporation by more than one third while increasing their borrowing requirements and planned to free voluntary housing associations from direct government control. The function of the Corporation would then largely be to determine expenditure and approve projects submitted by the associations. Priority would again be given to providing purpose-built housing for the elderly and disabled as well as inner-city improvement, so largely reverting to their pre-1974 activities.

Housing associations are generally able to operate a more flexible letting policy than local authorities, for they are not bound by the same obligations. Their tenants can claim rent and rate allowances on the same basis as tenants of other landlords and they are now 'secure' tenants, though without the right to buy if with a charitable housing trust.

Privately rented accommodation

The fast decline of privately-owned rented accommodation in post-war years has been a major factor in the growing scarcity of low-cost accommodation. Worthwhile profits may still be gained by building and letting high-quality flats at economic rents, in London or in retirement towns, but low-cost rented accommodation owned privately is often old and frequently in poor structural condition, lacking basic amenities or providing them only on a shared basis. More and more such housing is being sold off to local authorities or housing associations, either with sitting tenants, or when the tenant dies or moves away. In General Improvement Areas and Housing Action Areas, the local authority has power to compel improvements or compulsorily purchase and this again leads to a loss of private provision. Although few would deny the need for such action, the loss of privately rented accommodation has serious implications for groups such as recent immigrants and single people of all ages who have difficulty in obtaining any other type of housing.

Slum clearance

Slum clearance[27] was resumed in the 1950s, associated with redevelopment plans for many urban inner areas. The 1951 Census had revealed a high proportion of houses without basic amenities and further information was supplied by local authorities in 1954 providing an estimate of 845,000 slum dwellings out of a total of 13 million permanent houses. Unfortunately, standards of assessment based on a new definition of unfitness varied between authorities and it is generally believed that this figure was much too low. This definition took into account the state of repair, stability, freedom from damp, natural lighting, ventilation, water supply, drainage and facilities for food storage and cooking and is considered to be too narrow by current standards. The addition of internal layout to the criteria in the 1969 Housing Act was a small improvement.

A later survey[28] in 1964 estimated 1.8 million unfit dwellings and a further 6 million sub-standard. Shelter[29] has suggested that at present rates it could take at least twenty years simply to clear all unfit houses and it has also been estimated[30] that there is a need for a 1 per cent annual replacement rate (141,000 houses) if account is to be taken of the fact that slum clearance is not a finite problem and that as standards rise there will be an increased need for improvement. Optimistic predictions in the 1960s that the disappearance of slums was in sight were made without allowing for this factor as well as the continuing process of obsolescence.

The change of policy from redevelopment to improvement in the 1970s led to a sharp decline in clearance. This has been criticised by Community Development Project Workers[31] as largely an economy measure—they believe that council houses for all in need should be a first priority and that there are still too many sub-standard houses including some constructed post-war, which need to be replaced. A number of post-war multi-storey blocks and some low-rise dwellings have already been demolished while others have been offered for sale. Poor standards of construction on council estates and in New Towns have led to structural defects which have rendered them untenable.[32]

The proportion of sub-standard dwellings varies considerably from one area to another. In Belfast, for example, one third of all dwellings are claimed by Shelter[33] to be unfit: 25 per cent without internal sanitation compared with 11 per cent in Liverpool and 6 per cent in Birmingham. Similarly overcrowding occurs in nearly 4 per cent of Belfast dwellings compared with a little over 1 per cent in Liverpool.

Overcrowding is frequently an exacerbating factor in sub-standard property although it is not by any means confined to such dwellings. In 1957 statutory overcrowding was based on a standard which took into account the number of persons by sex and the number of 'habitable rooms'. In 1980 this was broadened to allow the local authority to decide if an 'excessive number of persons' not of one household are on the premises having regard to the room available. Clearly this may allow 'overcrowding' according to the earlier standard as long as all residents are of the same household.

Improvement

The continuing presence of slum areas in spite of efforts to clear them has led to an increasing interest in improvement which culminated in the policy introduced by the 1974 Housing Act. Until the Denington Report in 1968,[34] the cost of improvements required to bring older houses up to acceptable standards was considered to be too high for this work to be worth undertaking on any large scale. The 1969 Housing Act, however, gave local authorities the power to declare General Improvement Areas in which an effort would be made to upgrade the total environment.

Within General Improvement Areas,[35] local authorities were able to acquire land and buildings and to buy houses for improvement and conversion or demolition if this was necessary to the plan for the area as a whole. In addition, house-owners were to be encouraged to improve their houses by an increase in the grant available, and in the case of landlords, by allowing rents to be increased over a period after the tenancies had been certified as reaching the required state, this to include basic amenities (indoor WC, fixed bath, wash basin, hot and cold water, sink) installed and in good repair. In the process improved 'controlled' tenancies became 'regulated' tenancies and so qualified for 'fair' rents.[36]

Under the 1974 Housing Act, six categories of pre-1919 housing were defined: Clearance Areas, Housing Action Areas, General Improvement Areas, Priority Neighbourhoods, Full Grant Areas and non-priority areas. Housing Action Areas[37] are generally areas with a high proportion of old and privately rented property which falls below the standard of the General Improvement Area but in which it is considered that remedial action could upgrade to that level. They are mainly located in the inner suburban areas of large cities and would previously have been scheduled for clearance at some time. Social as well as physical deprivation is a basis for designation and within them, local authorities have powers to enforce the provision of standard amenities and repair work.

Priority Neighbourhoods were areas similar to Housing Action Areas but seen to be of a lower degree of urgency and whose treatment depends upon the availability of resources. Their designation was discontinued in 1980. Full Grant Areas are again areas with a need for improvement, but less great than those in the previous four categories.

Grants for improvement have been available since 1949, and fall into two basic categories: 'discretionary' grants, paid by local authorities to owners improving their homes to a certain standard, and 'standard' grants which can be claimed by right by owners who install basic amenities. In General Improvement Areas, the aim is to give a 'life' of at least thirty years to property and currently the normal grant amounts to 65 per cent of expenditure to a maximum of £5,500.[38] In Housing Action Areas the proportion rises to 75 per cent to a maximum of £8,500. Outside these areas the proportion falls to 50 per cent to a maximum of £5,500 while owner-occupiers are only entitled to claim a grant if the rateable value of their property falls below a specified amount. In all cases higher proportions will be allowed if hardship can be shown. An Intermediate Grant is also available to provide basic amenities and a Repair Grant for repairs only, in both cases where a home has a 'life' of at least 15 years.

The uptake of grants is variable, being relatively high in the north-west and north-east, but much lower in other areas such as London. Community Development Project workers have suggested[39] that the Housing Action Area policy has failed because owner-occupiers in such areas are generally unable to meet their own contribution towards improvement work and Shelter estimated that by 1979 only one in three had taken up available grants. In addition, where improvements are made, the results may not always be to the benefit of those in most need, especially in London where pressure for housing has become so great that high profits can be derived from the modernisation of old dwellings. Originally, where a grant had been used to improve property, full or part repayment had to be made where the home was sold less than five years later; though even then old property was bought up and improved as an investment, especially in London. However, the 1980 Housing Act abolished this repayment requirement.

Rent control and security of tenure

Security of tenure is closely associated with rent regulation, particularly at times of decontrol or permitted increases, and the two are therefore considered here together. Some form of security has been given to tenants since the war, though with greater effect for those in unfurnished than in furnished accommodation; much furnished accommodation consists of a single room in a house occupied by the owner who, it may be argued, should have the right to decide whether he should share his home or not.

In post-war years, the cycle of rent control and decontrol continued as governments changed although some form of regulation, at least for the lowest rented houses, has always remained. The year 1957 brought decontrol for all houses above a very low rateable value, though even here small increases were allowed where repairs had been carried out. It was hoped that decontrol would encourage more people to let their property and also induce a redistribution of tenants, in particular persuading those in under-occupied property to move into smaller accommodation—in the event, neither aim was achieved to any significant extent.[40]

The 1965 Rent Act gave security of tenure to all but those in the most expensive privately rented accommodation; such 'protected' tenancies could be those controlled under previous legislation or 'regulated' tenancies. 'Regulated' tenancies are generally private lettings of unfurnished dwellings of low rateable value. Landlords may apply to a Rent Officer to determine a fair rent for their tenancy which then becomes a 'registered rent'. Tenants may make a similar application if no agreement can be reached with the landlord. Appeals against the rent officer's decision can be taken to a Rent Tribunal and further appeal to the High Court is possible. The fair rent may not be reviewed in less than two years unless changes in the tenancy occur, for example, in the services provided or in the state of repair.

'Controlled' tenancies were those controlled under legislation prior to 1965—mainly small dwellings with very low rents. These became 'regulated' as the local authority certified that the dwelling reached a certain standard of repair, with all basic amenities. Remaining 'controlled' tenancies became 'regulated' tenancies in 1980.

In 'regulated' tenancies, protection is given to the tenant and a court order is required in order to evict, which may be allowed only for special reasons such as that the tenant refuses to leave at the end of a letting or after being given notice for non-payment of rent, or that the landlord wishes to re-occupy the dwelling.

The 1980 Housing Act introduced 'protected shorthold tenancies' which are tenancies granted for 1–5 years. The tenant is protected from eviction for the agreed term in the same way as are tenants of regulated tenancies. They cannot replace a protected longer-term tenancy but the aim is to encourage landlords to provide additional rented accommodation. Criticism of this arragement is that as longer-term tenancies fall vacant they may be replaced by the relative insecurity of the shorthold letting.

Furnished accommodation provided by a private landlord is not subject to rent control. However, in those properties where the rateable value falls below the same amount as that of 'regulated' tenancies, the landlord or tenant may request the local Rent Tribunal to determine a fair rent. Security of tenure is then awarded for a renewable period of six months in order to protect the tenant whose application for an assessed rent has succeeded. An application for increased rent after the determination has been made will only be allowed when conditions of the tenancy have changed. The Rent Act of 1974 brought many residential furnished tenancies into the full protection of the 1965 Rent Act. Where the landlord does not live on the premises, these become 'protected tenancies' under the same terms as unfurnished accommodation.

Under the 1972 Housing Finance Act, the concept of 'fair rents' was extended to local authority dwellings. Rents were assessed on the basis of age, size, condition and area as the amount which would be paid on the open market or, alternatively, the amount needed to pay off the cost of building and maintenance. In the majority of cases this resulted in a considerably higher rent, for the policy of most authorities was to subsidise, in effect, newer houses through the rents obtained on the older housing stock. Although higher rents were normally asked for newer dwellings, these were rarely 'economic rents', the difference being made up in part by rate support and in part through the rents of older houses which had already had their cost covered. Both means of reducing council rents were to be removed by the 1972 Act. The increases were to be spread over a number of years and a right to appeal was available through a new body, the Rent Scrutiny Board. In the event, only the first increase was put into effect and under the 1974 Labour government the Housing Rent and Subsidies Act 1975 restored the local authorities' freedom to fix rents as they felt appropriate to provide a working balance without regard to the concept of 'fair rents'.

Under the 1979 Conservative government council rents increased by more than 20 per cent by 1981 and seem likely to rise further. The mechanism used was that of cash limits—that is, the size of grant provided by the government was calculated to take into account a rent contribution to each local authority obtained by means of a rent increase of a size decided by the Secretary of State. Authorities seeking to keep rents below this level would receive a grant reduced by a corresponding amount.

The 1972 Housing Finance Act aimed to support those in greatest need through new rebates, while ensuring that those able to afford an economic rent should pay. Such a policy can only be effective, however, where rebates are taken up by all entitled to them and extend over a wide enough range of tenant incomes—such evidence as is available suggests that neither condition has been satisfied. The 1972 rent rebates for council tenants were standardised rather than left to the discretion of the local authority, and assessed by a formula which took into account the gross income of the tenant and the number of dependants. An entirely new departure was that an equivalent rent allowance could be claimed by private tenants paying a 'fair rent'. A substantial part of both rebates and allowances was contributed by the government, the rest from rates. Further support to the low-income householder, whether owner-occupier or tenant, was given in the Act by an extended rate rebate scheme.[41]

Rent rebates and allowances and rate rebate schemes have continued to operate with periodic increases. To take some account of the rent increases of 1980, proportionately higher levels were introduced for all three to raise them to their 1972 value—but not high enough to close the gap. Rent arrears have increased considerably over the last few years and under some circumstances rent is paid directly to the landlord as part of supplementary benefit. The power to evict is little used by local authorities as there is an obligation to rehouse.

One further aspect of security of tenure is the prevention of harassment by private sector landlords attempting to obtain vacant possession. Penalties were increased in 1965 and again by the Criminal Justice Act 1972 but in general they remain too low to provide effective deterrence.

Housing subsidies

No direct subsidies for private building have been given since the war although the tax allowance on mortgage payments and the option mortgage scheme are forms of subsidy to the owner-occupier. Until 1980 the average subsidy for a council dwelling was greater than average mortgage tax relief, though the gap steadily diminished, until by 1981 it had virtually closed. 1981–2 mortgage tax relief at an average of £335 per head will overtake the housing subsidy of £234 per dwelling.[42]

Houses built for sale either directly by or through the agency of a local authority may also have hidden subsidies. On cleared inner city land, new housing for sale has been put up with the object of meeting a demand for low-price dwellings in the area; this would not be possible if the full economic cost of the land was included in the price. In justification, houses of this kind are seen as relieving local authorities of the need to provide the equivalent in rented housing and so first priority is given to applicants from their waiting lists and council tenants.[43]

Subsidies for council houses have followed a similar course to rent control: curtailment following increase, and followed by restoration. One aim of the 1972 Housing Finance Act was to place the financing of council houses on a more stable footing. It was expected that 'fair rents' would provide increased revenue to the authorities and the Act therefore allowed for a withdrawal of subsidies over the following four or five years. Instead the government was to pay 75 per cent of any deficit incurred by the local authorities on house building and slum clearance up to a certain cost, while at the same time, if rent income provided a surplus, this would pass to the government.

During the year following the Act, many local authorities had great difficulty in keeping within the cost limit for subsidies, because of the rise in the price of materials and labour. Under the 1975 Act there was a return to the 'residual' method whereby a subsidy was provided by central government which could be supplemented by the local authority if they so desired.

The 1980 Housing Act introduced a new formula to determine the level of subsidy which took as its base each authority's housing expenditure for the preceding year and adjusted this according to the 'reckonable' additional expenditure on housing and 'reckonable' additional income—largely from the Housing Revenue account (rents being fixed by the government) and the general rate fund in the current year. The responsibility for the calculation of 'reckonable' expenditure and income rests largely with the Secretary of State in consultation with organisations 'appearing to him' representative of local authorities. It could in certain circumstances result in no subsidy being provided. This new development has given rise to considerable dissatisfaction, largely because it leaves little room for adjustment by the local authority and a greatly increased share of responsibility by the Secretary of State for decisions on the level of new construction by each authority. In the event, subsidies for council house building in 1981–2 are reduced by 45 per cent from the previous year's level. Authorities are no longer allowed to retain a surplus on their housing account—any profit must be transferred to the general rate fund and will be taken into account as part of the relevant authority's reckonable income.

Since their expansion in 1974, Housing Associations have been placed on a new footing with respect to subsidies. Previously, subsidies were received annually for each completed unit, but after 1974 this was replaced by a grant equal to approximately 75 per cent of the cost of each new dwelling or improvement. The remaining 25 per cent could be borrowed, usually from the local authority or Housing Corporation, and recovered in rent. There has been mounting criticism of housing associations for their apparent lack of control over finance and the high cost of some schemes, especially relating to improvement, which it has been suggested is due to this rather favourable financial arrangement. Greater accountability and reduced payments have been introduced, mainly again through cash limits.

Largely as a result of the reduction in subsidies, there was a 29 per cent drop in new construction in 1980 compared with 1979 and the lowest public sector figure for construction starts since 1945. Nearly half the urban authorities were forced to freeze or restrict severely their building or improvement plans.

Social trends

While on the wholly physical side the aim of adequate accommodation for all is in principle a relatively simple objective which may even be ultimately achieved, associated social needs are often more complex and certainly less constant. A new house, whether moved into from choice or from necessity, requires a readjustment to a new social situation by its occupants. Where choice has been exercised, there is likely to be a greater readiness to accept new standards—some would say to conform—than where the decision has come from some anonymous authority. Where there has been a move, for example, from the inner city slum to a peripheral housing estate, the new environment will be strange in many ways and the adjustment may be painful—a familiar street full of variety is lost to a suburban landscape peopled with strangers.

Since the Second World War, many thousands have undergone this experience as new housing estates and New Towns have been constructed. Planners and housing authorities, although aware of the problems entailed, have tended in the past either to see them as beyond their responsibility or as requiring facilities which were not available. However, a gradual move towards acceptance of the need for social planning to accompany physical planning does appear to be taking place and may be observed in the history of the post-war estates and New Towns which follows.

Housing estates

Land shortage resulting in high prices for building plots has ensured that the bulk of new residential development, whether private or public, takes the form of estates. During the 1950s and most of the 1960s, when pressure was at its greatest, massive council estates were rapidly constructed, many on the periphery of the cities from which the 'overspill' was to come. The motto often appeared to be 'any housing is better than no housing' and with depressing frequency the all too well documented errors of pre-war days were repeated: a lack of facilities, especially shops, long journeys to work by poorly serviced public transport, and no entertainment to keep the children occupied. These and other complaints, including higher rents than had previously been paid and high bills for heating, reflected especially the increased cost of a move to the new areas which largely nullified the benefits obtained. The series of community studies by sociologists, especially those of the Institute of Community Studies in Bethnal Green,[44] built up a stereotype of the council estate as a dreary, lonely place where people 'kept themselves to themselves' and where there was a general nostalgia for the warmth and life of the city.

Perhaps it was unfortunate that, among many problems, these studies ensured that the loss of close community life, however important, made most impact, so that the unsuccessful search for a formula which might recreate a situation basically arising as a protective device against poverty and deprivation obsessed the planners to the exclusion of those other factors which might have been more readily corrected.

A general characteristic of new council estates is the homogeneity of their age and household structure. Especially where an estate population is largely drawn from the housing list, intake families tend to be young, larger than average and with children of school age or less. Such households tend to be most vulnerable in the housing situation, especially where the father is unskilled and in casual work and receive priority under the points system of allocation (see p. 138). When rapid development has taken place, the population tends to fall within narrow age limits, the birth rate is initially high and a third or more will be less than fifteen years old. Such a structure brings both short- and long-term problems. In the short term, many places are required in schools, as well as clinics for infants and ante-natal care. Later the schools may well have places to spare, while there is a great need for youth employment and training facilities for school-leavers. As time goes on, houses become under-occupied as children leave home.

Estates on which some residents have obtained houses through redevelopment or exchange tend to have a broader age spread including a far higher proportion of elderly, as do those which have grown more steadily. The New Towns Committee, with such problems in mind, recommended that there should be gradual development after the initial stage so as to minimise population imbalance.

In 1967, a sub-committee of the Central Housing Advisory Committee[45] suggested that where families have been moved away from areas in which they have been established for many years, welfare services should give more support, and that more accommodation should be found for the elderly so that families might be reunited and a more balanced population develop. When large-scale development took place a social development plan should be prepared to co-ordinate the provision of facilities and officers appointed to give information and help to new arrivals. Although not universally put into practice, New Towns in particular have now adopted many of these recommendations.

High rise flats, introduced in the 1950s in the belief that industrialised building would be economical and speedy, have always been unpopular,[46] and many studies have demonstrated how inappropriate they are for young children and the elderly. The collapse of systems-built flats at Ronan Point in 1968, closely following the withdrawal of extra subsidy for buildings more than six storeys high,[47] brought an end to their construction in the public sector. Current policy is to limit their use as far as possible to adult households and to make improvements to structure and facilities. Nevertheless, faults of construction combined with vandalism have led to their abandonment and even demolition in some cases.

The development of massive suburban council estates has come to an end. Many factors have played a part here, including the switch to improvement in the inner city, New Town development and an increasing preference for owner-occupation where income permits.

New Towns

Post-war New Towns were seen by politicians and planners as providing an opportunity to put into concrete terms aims and ideals which had developed over many years. Their early prototypes were the Garden Cities of Letchworth and Welwyn, established at the start of the century: these were a product of deeply felt anti-urbanism which originated at a time of massive industrialisation and the rapid expansion of towns with accompanying dirt, squalor and disease. Largely the inspiration of Ebenezer Howard, and incorporating the idea of Robert Owen's industrial villages, the Garden Cities aimed to combine the advantages of urban and rural living, the first in their provision for industry and other sources of employment and the second in their generous allotment of open space: the objective, 'a Town designed for healthy living'. Their success, which was financial as well as social, encouraged those who, forty years later, believed that New Towns would help to contain expanding urban areas so that access to the countryside would remain within reach of their residents and at the same time provide enough accommodation to reduce the pressure on the cities. This was the practical aspect, but other aims spelled out by the Reith Committee[48] in its guidelines for New Towns reflect the spirit of the time—the widespread desire to maintain the co-operation and comradeship of wartime years. The towns were to be 'self-contained and balanced communities for work and living' and 'of diverse and balanced social composition', 'locating skilfully the sites for houses of all classes in the various neighbourhoods'. Although 'balance' was not defined it has been generally taken to mean that the age and occupational structure should reflect that of the country as a whole and it was considered of the utmost importance that there should be no resemblance to the one-class towns which had grown out of large-scale council estates before the war.[49]

To achieve self-containment, industries which can provide a wide range of occupations must be encouraged to move to the New Towns. The Development Corporations which initially manage New Towns[50] allocate most of their houses to those who have obtained local employment. In doing so, the achievement of 'balance' is prejudiced, for New Town industries rely largely on skilled workers and provide relatively few openings for the unskilled. For this reason New Towns do little to alleviate the urgent housing problems of the big cities—rather perhaps increasing the pressures which result in the concentration of low-income and immigrant families in the inner areas.

Again, within the New Towns 'social mix' has been an elusive target. The early 'Mark I' towns such as Crawley and Harlow used neighbourhood units to encourage the development of a community spirit. Each contained a population of 5,000 to 12,000, its own primary schools and local shops and a variety of housing which would hopefully produce a cross-section of income and social groups equivalent to that of the town as a whole. This imposed interaction, though well-meaning, achieved little success and neighbourhood units were criticised as prejudicing the development of the town as a unit. Mark II New Towns such as Cumbernauld and Skelmersdale were built at higher densities and concentrated facilities in central areas but were unpopular with residents and suffered from traffic congestion. The latest New Towns have been built on a linear principle while densities have once more been reduced. In most cases an already established area provides a base on to which New Town development is grafted: an arrangement which can pose problems of integration,[51] but overcomes some of the initial difficulties resulting from a lack of facilities.

An increasing proportion of New Town houses, rising to 50 per cent, are for sale; often such houses are situated on the periphery and invariably they are segregated. In addition, New Town tenants are 'secure' tenants for the first twelve months of their tenancy. Professional workers, though mainly employees rather than self-employed, have been attracted to the New Towns especially in the south-east, but there is a tendency for higher-income households to move outside and commute. Some New Towns such as Skelmersdale in Lancashire and Corby in Northamptonshire have not been able to maintain an adequate economic base and the loss of industries has led to high unemployment.

In 1976 a government decision was made to transfer resources from New Towns to inner urban areas. New Towns in the course of construction have been cut back and no more will be designated. Nevertheless the achievements of New Towns should not be underestimated, not least the opportunity they have given for architectural innovation and the development of new ideas in transportation systems.

Disadvantaged groups

Although standards of housing have been raised for most people since the war and although the figures today of households and dwellings are almost in balance, it seems that the gap between the most disadvantaged members of the population and the rest has widened. Three groups whose problems appear to grow rather than diminish are the homeless, ethnic minorities and gypsies or travellers, while housing for workers in rural areas shows little improvement.

The homeless

'Homeless' tends to be defined according to the interests of those making the definition. Central and local government explain their preference for restricting this term to those who are literally without a roof over their head, as a need to concentrate on the most pressing cases. Some voluntary organisations, on the other hand, include all those living in unsatisfactory conditions, so producing massive figures whose impact may set in motion some new form of alleviation. The number of applications to local authorities by homeless families in 1977 was 42,300 of which 31,800 were successful; in 1978 this increased to 53,000 housed, following the implementation of the Housing (Homeless Persons) Act 1977 and was 55,700 by the end of 1979. Shelter has suggested that the number of homeless has more than doubled between 1968 and 1978.[52] Variation in the size of the problem over the country is considerable, but London stands out as being in by far the worst position.[53] Large young families are in a particularly difficult situation and over the last few years there has been growing concern over homeless single people, many still in their 'teens, who move into London with little appreciation of the problems there. In December 1977 Shelter estimated that there were 100,000 single homeless.

The Housing (Homeless Persons) Act 1977 transferred responsibility for providing accommodation for the homeless from the social services to housing departments, and made it a statutory responsibility in relation to homeless families, battered wives and single parents, that it should be on a permanent basis. Nevertheless accommodated homeless are not 'secure' tenants for the first twelve months of their tenancy. In spite of the continuing fall in the number of places available in hostels for single people, both young and old, no priority has been given to this group.

Until the 1960s most of the homeless families applying to the local authority for help were placed in hostels where they lived communally. Dismal conditions, which often included the separation of wives from husbands and children from mothers, were expected to encourage those accommodated to move on quickly, and a time limit operated. Publicity in the mid-1960s from a number of directions, including the television play *Cathy Come Home*, led to some improvement culminating in the 1977 Act, but the position is still far from satisfactory as instances of families being split and the use of substandard accommodation continue to arise.[54]

The acute housing problems of the mid and late 1960s led to squatting.[55] Begun as a protest movement against the restrictive rules in local authority hostels, it developed into an action group placing homeless families in empty houses and using the law against forcible entry to prevent re-occupation. It has had some success with a number of local authorities who grant licences authorising temporary occupation, but the Criminal Justice Act of 1977 revised the law on entry to premises, and this can be used by unco-operative authorities wishing to evict. Squatting decreased between 1977 and 1979 but a deteriorating housing situation led to a new upsurge in that year.

Ethnic minorities

Where pressures are severe, groups which pose particular difficulties or who may appear to increase already critical problems will inevitably arouse hostility and sometimes conflict. The housing situation is one of shortage and high prices and many see the coloured immigrant as at least an exacerbating factor, even a cause. Immigrants certainly compete for low-cost rented accommodation, for many arrive with little money and unlikely to find any but the lowest-paid jobs available. Without residential qualifications they are not eligible for council housing and they tend to move to areas where shortages are greatest because these are the places where there are most opportunities for work.

The coloured immigrant also faces positive discrimination in the search. Given the money to consider buying a house, building societies are generally unwilling to advance mortgages and estate agents will ensure that the houses made available to them are in 'suitable' areas. Houses bought by immigrants tend, therefore, to be those in areas of decay and twilight zones, where poor structural conditions combined with short leases reduce the price, usually met by a short-term loan with a high interest rate. Many large old houses in 'zones in transition'[56] pass to immigrants in this way, their rooms let out to cover the cost and provide an income. In London, such houses tend to be in the inner 'stress' areas, centres of multiple deprivation which have a particularly adverse effect on any children.[57] Inevitably ethnic groups concentrate in such areas in all the big cities, coming together in part for mutual support but also because of the combination of pressures through which all but a privileged few are barred from the normal dispersion process which is a stage in the assimilation of the immigrant.

Ethnic minorities continue to be under-represented in local authority housing[58] although authorities strongly deny discrimination, which is forbidden under the 1976 Race Relations Act. Nevertheless, certain of the rules used to decide eligibility for a council house operate against the coloured immigrant, especially residential qualifications, as do also cultural factors which produce unconventional family patterns and fear or ignorance in approaching authority.

It has been shown in Bedford[59] that West Indian and Asian applicants for council housing were allocated significantly more pre-1945 housing than white applicants including Italians and East Europeans. This appeared in part to be a result of the immigrants sometimes stating a preference for inner area housing but also to indirect discrimination in assessing the suitability of applicants for better housing. In spite of continuing recommendations no reliable records are available which would indicate the extent to which council housing is provided for this group.

Travellers and gypsies

Almost alone in being unaffected by the shortage and cost of housing, accommodation problems have increased for this group as for others. Their numbers are difficult to assess, but an estimate of 30,000 has been made. Although the Caravan Sites Act of 1968 appeared to be to their advantage, for it required local authorities to provide 'adequate accommodation for gypsies residing in or resorting to their area', provision was made for exemption from this obligation for a variety of reasons and full advantage of this has been taken by many authorities. Exemption can be granted in cases of land shortage, and no more than fifteen caravans need be accommodated. Since 1972 loans to councils have been available for the purpose of providing sites and by 1978 a total of 2,687 sites had been provided. Nevertheless gypsies claim that the authorities have failed in their duty under the 1968 Act as three or four times the number of sites now available are needed. The Cripps Report of 1977 suggested that authorities should help travellers to buy or lease land themselves, but again the recommendation has not been taken up. In 1978 the Gipsy Council asked the Council of Europe in Strasbourg to study their case, alleging harassment and adverse discrimination.

Rural housing

The urban situation gains attention, for this is the environment in which more than 85 per cent of the population lives today. Nevertheless, parallel situations arise in rural areas, perhaps with even less chance of remedy because less publicised and so unlikely to arouse interest in reform. Here, as in the cities, the stock of rented accommodation is well below what is required. One recent reform has been the abolition of tied cottages by the Rent (Agriculture) Act of 1976, which gave similar security of tenure to agricultural workers as to those in privately rented accommodation. A tenant occupying a house under a contract of employment, however, is not a 'secure' tenant but if he leaves his employment and if the house is required for agricultural purposes, the owner must rehouse and may approach the local authority for help. But for other village residents problems remain. The price for which country cottages can be sold to the urban emigrant is proportionately even higher than for town properties, taking into account size and structural standards, but life in the countryside is the goal for many city dwellers and they are ready to pay for their dreams. Some move out and commute, others wait until retirement. A growing number buy a second home for weekends and holidays. Shelter has calculated that there are about 120,000 second homes, a high proportion of them in Wales. Villages expand as new development is increasingly permitted while older properties are transformed into homes with urban amenities. The sale of council houses is an added danger for the stock is low to start with and in rural and seaside areas there will be much to be gained financially by selling.

The 1980 Housing Act precludes council tenants who have bought their property and who live in designated rural areas in Wales and in national parks from selling it within 10 years without first offering it to the local authority from which it was purchased. Many believe, however, that this does not sufficiently protect all the areas in danger.

Too often urban migrants form segregated communities which contribute little to the area in which they live. The town remains the provider of employment, entertainment and shopping facilities—even the local school will often be rejected.[60] Weekenders will bring all they need for their short visits and their empty houses during the week cause added resentment: many appear to have little understanding of the countryside and its ways. The younger villagers must often move into the towns to find accommodation they can afford, while a minimum of local employment, except to builders, is provided by the newcomers. The resentment of Welsh nationalists against these developments has led to a spate of arson attacks against absent English owners of second homes.

So far little has been done to redress the balance which is so much to the advantage of the urbanite. In a few areas such as the Lleyn Peninsula housing associations have built or bought homes to let at low rentals to locals. The removal of tax allowances on mortgages for second homes appears to have had little impact. Local government reorganisation has brought some rural areas with a high proportion of commuters under the same authority as nearby towns and cities and so a greater contribution to the rates by residents in newer property. The 1981 Census shows that far from being reduced by higher rates and the rising cost of petrol, urban-rural migration has accelerated during the last decade, and that attempts to attract higher income residents back to the city has had little or no success.

Current developments

Within the last five years, many changes have occurred in the urban housing situation. Although some of these may seem sudden and dramatic, largely they are the latest stage in a process which began at the time of the Industrial Revolution with the expansion of urban areas. The accelerating movement outwards from the mid-nineteenth century onwards of those with the resources or qualifications to escape has gradually deprived the inner city of the greater proportion of its more affluent, more skilled and younger residents. Most of the post-war housing policies have encouraged this process: the demolition of inner area property and its replacement by office blocks and ring roads, the construction of peripheral council and private estates, and New Town development. But these are largely dependent upon an expanding economic base which will accept the cost of this dispersion in transport systems, new locations for industry and commerce and the extension of services.

By the late 1970s continuing economic improvement could no longer be expected. At the same time the pressure of an expanding population disappeared. Governments were unable nor saw the necessity to finance large-scale building programmes in addition to their other commitments. The transfer of resources from redevelopment to improvement, from suburbs and New Towns to the inner city areas and from the encouragement of public to private development may well be seen as more in tune with the preferences of the 1970s than the policies of the 1960s, but in addition they were a response to demographic and economic change.

Unfortunately, even the resources available in the 1970s have largely disappeared. Funds provided to inner cities for their regeneration have been too small and some say also misdirected. In the event only the weakest impact was made on a rapidly degenerating social and physical structure. The riots and looting in the summer of

1981 have been most reasonably attributed to a combination of factors and it seems probable that among them the increasing residential polarisation of housing and population between the inner and outer city played its part. The reversal of this trend will need an unprecedented redirection of resources.

Further reading

A comprehensive account of all aspects of housing is given by Mary E. Smith in *Guide to Housing*, The Housing Centre Trust, revised 2nd edn, 1977. A more critical discussion of housing policies is provided by F. Berry in *Housing: The Great British Failure*, Charles Knight, 1974.

Planning in its widest sense is examined in J. Cullingworth, *Problems of an Urban Society*, Allen & Unwin, 1972, in which volume 2, *The Social Content of Planning* is most useful for the housing aspect.

On the financial aspect, useful books are L. Needleman, *The Economics of Housing*, Staples Press, 1965, and Adela A. Nevitt, *Housing Taxation and Subsidies*, Nelson, 1966.

Many community studies of the transition from inner city to suburban council housing estates were written in the 1950s and early 1960s. The best known, M. Young and P. Wilmott, *Family and Kinship in East London*, Routledge & Kegan Paul, 1957, should still be read, though not uncritically; and from a different standpoint, H. Jennings, *Societies in the Making*, Routledge & Kegan Paul, 1962. Two books which trace the movement of residents from inner Liverpool to a housing estate outside the city boundary are C. Vereker *et al.*, *Urban Redevelopment and Social Change*, Liverpool University Press, 1961, and K. Pickett and D. Boulton, *Migration and Social Adjustment*, Liverpool University Press, 1974. The latter includes an account of a privately owned suburban estate.

On the problems of commuter villages see R. E. Pahl, *Whose City?*, 2nd edn, Penguin, 1975.

On London's housing problems see D. Donnison and D. Eversley (eds), *London: Urban Patterns, Problems and Policies,* Heinemann, 1973.

On New Towns see F. Schaffer, *The New Town Story*, Macgibbon & Kee, 1970.

On living in high rise flats see E. Gittus, *Flats, Families and the Under-5s*, Routledge & Kegan Paul, 1976.

On General Improvement Areas see J. Trevor Roberts, *General Improvement Areas*, Saxon House/Lexington Books, 1976.

On Council Housing see David Hoath, *Council Housing*, Sweet & Maxwell, 1978, and Stephen Merrett, *State Housing in Britain,* Routledge & Kegan Paul, 1979.

On Housing Associations see Andrew Thompson, *The Role of Housing Associations in Major Urban Areas, A Case Study of Merseyside Improved Houses*, Centre for Urban and Regional Studies, Birmingham, 1977.

Statistics of house construction, slum clearance, housing loans are provided for England and Wales down to local authority level by the Department of the Environment in *Local Housing Statistics, England and*

Wales, quarterly with similar volumes for Scotland and Northern Ireland.

A guide to sources of housing data is available in the Social Science Research Council publication S. M. Farthing, *Housing in Great Britain* and M. C. Fleming, *Housing in Northern Ireland*, vol. 3 of W. F. Maunder (ed.), *Reviews of United Kingdom Statistical Sources,* Heinemann, 1974.

Statistics of housing from a number of government sources, with a commentary, are published annually by the Central Statistical Office in *Social Trends*.

6 The health services

Olive Keidan

The first national Health Service Act in 1946[1] imposed a duty on the Minister of Health to promote the establishment of a 'comprehensive health service designed to secure improvement in the physical and mental health of the people'. The Act did not, however, attempt to define 'health'. The World Health Organisation suggested that it is 'a state of complete physical, mental and social well-being and not merely the absence of disease or infirmity'. In such an ideal state chronic boredom would possibly be the greatest menace. This brief statement, however, links together the three major factors that are involved and interdependent in any consideration of what we mean by 'health' and the lines along which efforts must be made to promote improvement.

It has long been recognised that ill-health makes for inefficient social functioning and it is therefore costly to the community in general. The more complex and urbanised the society, the more necessary it becomes to take account of the effects of illness and to try to mitigate these effects by preventive measures and treatment. Apart from the economic and social aspects of the health of the community, we have as a nation long expressed humanitarian concern for the sick and disabled; they have been respectable objects of charity for centuries. The early legislation relating to begging makes exception of the 'impotent' beggar,[2] and the boom in hospital building and endowment by philanthropists in the eighteenth and nineteenth centuries was an expression of this concern.

When we consider what kind of personal health service provisions should be made we find many complicating factors. The acceptable standards of physical and mental fitness vary between one individual and another, and between one community and another. Individual expectations of health are affected by differences in the age group, the sub-culture, educational level and social class, and people tend to seek advice and help when their health is not conforming to their own expectations. The decision when and where to seek help is affected by factors other than disease, including emotional and social attitudes to sickness, doctors and hospitals.[3] The responsibility for the first step in diagnosis and treatment is left to the individual, and his action may depend more on his personality and social circumstances than on a rational decision. The value of health education has been acknowledged fitfully and some areas of practice such as health visiting have long had some responsibility in this. Its importance was given recognition in 1968 when the Health Education Council was established by the government.

The value of preventive services relating to personal health, such as child welfare provisions, and pre-symptomatic examinations, depends not only on the quality and comprehensiveness of the service provided but also on the active participation of the people for whom they are provided, and on a sensible use by them of these services. To provide a service may not be enough, it may also be necessary to provide instruction on the use of the service and in some instances to take the service to the people most in need, but who may through apathy or ignorance not avail themselves of its benefits.

It has been increasingly recognised that the benefit derived from medical treatment can be lost because of adverse social and economic conditions, such as poor housing, unsuitable employment, poor standards of nutrition and personal care, and apathy.[4] For the patients affected by sub-standard conditions some of the expenditure on medical care is wasted unless there is improvement in their life situation. This depends to a large extent on services outside the health service.

The community's attitude to the health and sickness of the individual has undergone considerable changes over the centuries. Crisis situations such as the cholera outbreaks in the nineteenth century, and the alarm at the poor physique of so many of the volunteers for the Boer War, made the nation aware of the increasing interdependence of the people. The developments in social services in general, in preventive measures relating to health, and in the way provision of medical treatment is made for the individual reflect the assumption of greater responsibility by the state.

Rising standards of living and demographic changes cause changes in the patterns of disease and demand for health care. The health services have to adjust to these, but as the social services tend to lag behind the community's needs they inevitably exhibit tensions. To understand the anomalies and uneven provisions of the services today we need to look to the past to see the needs they were provided to meet and the subsequent adjustments to later demands. A proper historical perspective is necessary; for example it is a mistake to think of the hospitals of the nineteenth century as treating the 'sick', they were for the care of the 'poor-sick'. There was an intimate relationship between poverty and sickness, a two-way cause and effect.[5] Improvements in the care of the sick and in preventive measures are the result not only of technical and scientific developments, but also of the organisation of other social services, of changes in standards of living, in expectations of health and service, and the extension of professional training in many fields.

The main concern of this chapter is with the personal health services. However, these services have been dependent on the prior development of the environmental health services, which are discussed in the next section. New developments in environmental health, following the reorganisation of both local authorities and the health service, are also briefly mentioned.

Environmental services and public health

Reform of insanitary living and working conditions began mainly in the nineteenth century. The 1832 Poor Law Commission did not fail to notice the close connection between poverty and sickness. One of the problems facing sanitary reformers such as Edwin Chadwick in those early days was in establishing actively interested local health authorities and effective central control, two elements which persist today as essential to health service organisation. The General Board of Health set up in 1848 to try to effect these reforms lasted only ten years but the zeal of the reformers continued until the Local Government Board was established in 1871, having control over health and Poor Law provisions and creating stronger central and local administration.

Occupational health was not within its province and is still outside the scope of the NHS. Concurrent with the 1974 NHS reorganisation the Health and Safety at Work Commission was set up in the Department of Employment. The links between occupational health and the NHS were considered by the Royal Commission on the NHS.[6] Overlaps occur between the NHS and occupational health services in the care of sick and injured employees, but while further reorganisation is considered undesirable at present the possibilities of alternative structures are being discussed.

The medical officer of health which each local authority had to employ, full- or part-time, after 1872 was a sanitarian concerned largely with environmental conditions, and it was not until the twentieth century that personal health provisions began to be included in his province.

The Ministry of Health, established in 1919, took over the work of the Local Government Board which included all aspects of public health provision except for school health services and occupational health, and responsibilities relating to housing and the Poor Law. In 1929 the Local Government Act put the management of all public hospitals and environmental health services under one local authority health department, which also had duties under Factory Acts relating to the hygiene and sanitary provisions within work premises; under the Food and Drugs Act, relating to sampling and inspection; under the Housing Acts, and under the port sanitary regulations. By the beginning of the Second World War the public health duties of the local authorities were very wide, although there was a 'pronounced tendency for Medical Officers of Health to concentrate their attention on the personal health services, and to lose interest in the older subject of sanitation'.[7]

The achievements of the environmental health services have been taken for granted by the public—perhaps that is their greatest achievement—but new problems are having to be met.

In the discussions and plans for reorganisation of the NHS in 1974 allocation of responsibility for community health had to be made between it and the local authorities. Clearly the local authorities would be responsible for control of environmental sources of disease, while the NHS would be responsible for the protection of the individual by immunisation and treatment; but prevention of food poisoning and the spread of notifiable diseases would involve action from both. In discussing this overlap the Working Party on Collaboration between the National Health Service and Local Government[8] felt that prime responsibilities could not rest with the NHS as the public might find the exercise of control necessary to contain an outbreak of disease more acceptable from the elected body. On the other hand as the social services have been 'organised according to the main skills required to provide them'[9] it would be out of line with this policy if the local authorities appointed their own medical staff. Instead a duty to collaborate in areas of mutual concern has been imposed on both authorities by the National Health Service Re-organisation Act, 1974,[10] and arrangements have been made for specialists in community medicine, called community physicians, to be seconded to the local authority as 'proper officers',[11] in which role they will be directly accountable to the local authority.[12]

Some aspects of mental illness are increasingly regarded as matters of public as well as personal health. The 1977 Annual Report of the Chief Medical Officer at the DHSS calls for consideration of 'wider mental health issues . . . concern with psychosocial factors and man's reaction to his total environment justifies the consideration of the promotion of mental health in ways that go beyond the limits of health and social services.' Many environmental factors can be seen as potentially damaging to personal development and constitute new problems for public health policies. Prevention of mental disorder through such policies seems to call for action in the face of growing demand for treatment. Alcoholism is on the increase—the DHSS estimates that about half a million people are seriously affected. The Report on Child Health Services[13] estimated that one in every six mothers of young children suffers from a psychiatric disorder which is likely to have its origins in the social and environmental conditions of the family. Prevention of such disorders lies outside the scope of the personal health services, but they present an increasing burden to them.

A satisfactory environment is acknowledged as the basis for good physical and mental health, consequently the increasing pollution of land, sea and air is regarded as a serious problem. Control over the environment is exercised by several different central and local government departments, but a Standing Royal Commission on Environmental Pollution was appointed in 1970 to overview the whole situation.[14] Health hazards to local communities from noxious and dangerous industries are also a matter of concern, but again, responsibility for planning and control is divided between different departments. The public health problems of the technological era may be regarded as being as formidable as those of the industrial era.

Personal health services before the NHS

Personal health care before the advent of the NHS developed along two main lines—hospital and institutional care, and community care—both of which have evolved over many years, and continue to change to meet new needs and follow new trends.

Hospital and institutional care

Hospitals were founded partly for the destitute sick and the poor, and partly to protect the community from the spread of infection. They were rather dangerous places to be in until towards the end of the nineteenth century when developments in medical science and staffing changed their functioning and direction. Institutional care grew up along different lines, catering for different needs with no form of central or even local planning.[15]

Under the Poor Law the destitute sick were treated, or at least housed, in infirmary wards or separate infirmaries under the Boards of Guardians. Medical care was minimal and 'nursing' was done by the pauper inmates of the workhouse, although conditions improved with the gradual introduction of trained nurses. These institutions, for want of other provisions, also came to offer care to sick people who were not destitute[16] and many were ultimately taken over by the local authority health departments after the Local Government Act, 1929, and turned into municipal general hospitals. By this time qualified medical and nursing personnel were available to man them and the standard of many became very good.

The local health authorities had already established fever hospitals and sanatoria under public health provisions and could have established general hospitals had they wished, although few did. By the end of the 1930s there were about 1,750 local authority hospitals of all types.[17]

The special needs of the mentally disordered were recognised by legislation which in 1808 allowed for the provision of county asylums at public expense. Sedatives and narcotics replaced physical restraint in the management of behaviour problems associated with mental disorder which coupled with more humane attitudes led to improvements in care and treatment.[18] Two major concerns regarding the hospital care of the mentally disordered can be seen in policy debates of the nineteenth century. One related to the cost of hospitalisation. While the paupers and the rich were catered for the burgeoning middle classes were dependent on their family or the Poor Rate. It was this latter situation that led to a proposal in Parliament in 1880 that mental hospital care should be a national rather than a local burden, paid for out of taxes rather than rates.[19] This early 'National Mental Health Service' was rejected by Parliament and had to wait until the NHS Act of 1946 to come into being. The second matter of concern related to compulsory admission to and detention in asylums. The 1890 Lunacy Act dealt with these through very complicated procedures.[20] The Act also imposed duties on local officers to protect lunatics at large from neglect and ill treatment, and on local authorities to build asylums for persons of unsound mind, which included mental handicap, although admission was strictly controlled through the certification procedures. A new era began with the Mental Treatment Act, 1930, which encouraged people to seek early treatment by allowing for voluntary admissions to mental hospitals, and for public hospitals to have out-patient clinics.

In the 1944 White Paper the number of public hospitals for the mentally ill was put at 101, with 130,000 patients; but there were also about 12,500 persons of unsound mind in other local authority hospitals and public assistance institutions. The mentally subnormal numbered 37,000 in the 61 certified institutions and 9,500 in public assistance institutions.

The voluntary general hospitals, of which there were more than 1,000 in 1944, varied enormously in size, age and function. Some were endowed in medieval times, many were founded in the last 200 years. Some became great medical teaching centres, with splendid specialist and consultant services, others were tiny cottage hospitals using the services of the local general practitioners. Some were provided by trades unions for their members. They were financed by voluntary contributions from charities, endowments and later from patients' payments. The voluntary hospitals tended to treat acute conditions, sending the chronic sick to the public health hospitals or Poor Law infirmaries. The teaching hospitals, which were a small proportion of the voluntary hospitals, needed the patients as teaching material, and therefore admitted the interesting cases. The distribution of voluntary hospitals was very uneven, and, as the major hospitals attracted the services of the more outstanding doctors, distribution of the latter was uneven too.

From the beginning of the twentieth century there were growing problems relating to finance and co-ordination in the various hospital services. Some neighbouring voluntary hospitals united under one administration, in an effort to make more effective use of their funds and to cope with the rapid developments in medical science and the consequent need for investment in new buildings and equipment.

Illness amongst the well-to-do was treated at home, at spas, or in the doctor's house until hospitals became safer.[21] Private paying patients were admitted to teaching hospitals or to private clinics and nursing homes which were run for profit. These paying patients were the main source of income for the voluntary hospital consultant or 'honorary'. The reputation of the doctor in the paying sector of the community was often related to his work in the voluntary hospitals, and his standing as a consultant there. Many doctors thus had a curious role, being on one hand the paid medical attendant to an independent and sometimes 'fashion'-conscious group of people and on the other hand being the benefactor of a large number of poor, dependent patients. The doctor's appointment to a voluntary hospital and the patronage of eminent specialists would certainly improve his career prospects while satisfactory attendance on influential private patients would enhance his income. For the young hospital doctor starting a career the early days would be fraught with anxiety, but the prospects were very enticing.

Community care

The development of public, voluntary and private care in the home was haphazard, dealing with areas of need as they were identified.

Personal medical care in the community was given by doctors of a wide range of training and ability. In 1858 the Medical Act established the General Council of Medical Education and Registration which laid down minimum requirements for qualification and kept a register of practitioners. The qualified doctor was thus identified, but while the standards of training were supervised the standards of care given were often limited by the financial situation of his patients.

Under the Poor Law the destitute sick could be seen at home by the medical officers of the Board of Guardians, but the adherence to principles of deterrence and economy meant that the service often came too late or was inadequate.[22]

Out-patient advice and treatment was available to the needy who could present themselves at hospitals, charity clinics and public dispensaries without referral from family doctors. Again the adequacy of the care was limited, not only by the state of medical science, but by the need for economy and the ignorance of the consumers.[23] The essential prerequisite of the patient's responsibility to obtain treatment for his condition—which Beveridge saw as the 'duty' of the sick person—was health education, and some local authorities began to use health visitors to offer health advice to households where infectious disease had been notified.

The majority were cared for by general practitioners for a fee. Patients could choose the doctor and doctors were free to charge what they wished, but were obviously limited in the size of fee by the capacity of the people to pay. Many doctors in poor areas had difficulty in extracting even small payments. Some commissioned collectors who settled bills by weekly payments. Others used a flat rate—perhaps sixpence—for all consultations. The problem of payment, often at a time when income was reduced by sickness, put an unenviable burden of decision about priorities, diagnosis and prognosis on families. The wage-earner and children were often first in line for care, the housewife and aged took second place. The doctor's position was difficult in that it would be uneconomic for him to give more care or medicine than that for which the patient could pay. Some workers' Friendly Societies and Provident Clubs were formed to ensure that money would be available for members to cover medical costs when necessary.

If an employed person is unable to work because of illness, it is obviously economically desirable that he should be helped to return to work and self-sufficiency as quickly as possible. The evidence given to the Poor Law Commission, 1909, showed some of the dangers to the community and the individual of lack of early medical advice, often leading to prolonged sickness and destitution. A radical change, creating a precedent in state action, occurred when Lloyd George's National Health Insurance Act was placed on the statute book in 1911. This Act entitled insured persons not only to weekly payments to help maintain a minimum income level during sickness, but also to free doctoring from the doctor of their choice, provided he had agreed to participate in the scheme. The general practitioners who did participate, known as 'panel doctors', were paid on a per capita basis. This method of remuneration had been the doctors' own choice; they rejected the idea of a salary.[24]

At its inception the scheme covered about one-third of the population, but by the time the National Health Service Act came into force more than half were covered. The scheme did not provide hospital or specialist care, and made no medical provision for dependants. Nevertheless this spread of contact between the public and general practitioners encouraged the idea of the family doctor. It also ensured better and regular pay for many doctors. Although this was a compulsory national scheme the financial side was administered by 'Approved Societies'. These were either co-operative undertakings, organised by trades unions and friendly societies, or were private companies. The societies varied in their resources and some were able to give extra benefits such as help with dental care and spectacles. This method of administering health insurance proved to be cumbersome and costly.

As there was no way by which the Insurance Committee could oversee the individual GP's work a system was instituted whereby a patient could complain to the local committee if the doctor failed to carry out the work he was contracted to do. This complaints system was taken over by the Executive Councils after 1948, and the Family Practitioner Committee after 1973.[25]

At the other end of the economic scale the rich used the services of eminent or fashionable doctors. Although medical and surgical specialisms were growing in the teaching hospitals, these doctors were frequently used by their patients as general practitioners. Because their income came largely from private practice, the hospital specialists had to keep a careful eye on the paying patient. 'Keeping in' with the patient could be time-consuming and frustrating.

Dental care, except for extractions, was almost unknown among the working population. Routine school medical inspections, starting in 1907, revealed something of the extent of dental disease. Little was done to improve matters except in the school health service and the maternity and child welfare services, although popular indifference, shortage of trained staff and their uneven distribution combined to keep these services minimal. The debilitating effects of dental caries were not widely known and people with little money to spare would be moved to seek care only by toothache, and then would take the cheapest and easiest cure—extraction. There was little charitable provision for dental care apart from the teaching hospitals. Popular dental education and a positive attitude to dental care was sadly lacking even in 1946. By the time the National Health Service Act came into operation the number of people who needed dentures was much greater than had been expected.[26]

A home nursing service for the sick poor of Liverpool was started by William Rathbone in 1859. Although many local health authorities took over the functions of these district nurses there were still some in 1948 who left the task to voluntary nursing committees.

The development of maternity nursing and care was one of the striking achievements of local authorities. In spite of great advances in epidemiology during the nineteenth century maternal and infant mortality remained high. The first legislation in the personal health field was the Midwives Act of 1902, which laid down standards for training, maintained a register, and prohibited untrained women from practising. The qualified midwives remained private practitioners, or worked for voluntary nursing associations.[27] With the passing of the Midwives Act, 1936, local authorities had to ensure that an adequate number of midwives was available in their area, which gradually brought domiciliary midwifery under local authority control as a public service.

Concern about the declining birth rate focused attention on infant mortality.[28] Infants died because of their insanitary surroundings and the ignorance and poor health of their mothers. Attempts to improve this situation were first made in 1862 when the Manchester and Salford Sanitary Association employed women visitors, the forerunners of the health visitors, to advise mothers on the care of infants. The results so impressed the local authority that it gave financial support to the work. Other local authorities started different schemes with similar aims, which were considerably advanced by the compulsory notification of all births to the local health authority after 1915. In 1918 the Maternity and Child Welfare Act established the local authority services for expectant and nursing mothers and children under school age. At this time there were already 3,000 health visitors employed in local health authorities.

The provisions of this Act meant that the care of large numbers of mothers and infants was undertaken by local authority midwives, doctors and health visitors, working from infant welfare clinics. For the family able to pay, ante-natal and post-natal care and infant care were given by their general practitioner, helped by the private midwife and the nursery nurse. Thus there grew up two different systems of care for mothers and babies; and when hospitals began to offer the kind of specialised care that some people required, yet a third system was added, with pre-natal, post-natal and infant clinics attached to the maternity hospitals and wards.

The school health service developed as part of a two-sided attack on the poor physique of school children. The complementary service was the provision of school meals to undernourished children. These were accepted, in spite of considerable opposition to this intrusion into family responsibility, as functions of the education service. The

Education (Administrative Provisions) Act, 1907, compelled local education authorities to have the children in elementary school medically examined at least three times during the school career. Unfortunately, the bogey of undermining parental responsibility, and the fear of intruding into the sphere of the private doctor, prevented an equally strong line being taken with regard to the provision of facilities for treatment and this remained optional until 1918. The duties placed on local authorities by the Education Act, 1907, necessitated the creation of a Medical Branch at the Board of Education, and the first Chief Medical Officer was appointed in the same year. When the Ministry of Health was created in 1919 the Ministry of Health Act transferred all the powers and duties of the Board of Education concerned with medical inspection and treatment of children to the new ministry.

Developments in psychiatry and psychology between the wars focused attention on the problems of psychological disturbance in children. With help from the USA the Child Guidance Council was founded in this country in 1927 as a training and propaganda organisation. Clinics were started by voluntary or statutory bodies orientated either to psychiatry or educational psychology. The first local education authority child guidance clinic was opened in Birmingham in 1932. By 1939 there were 48 clinics in all, 17 of them wholly maintained and 5 partly maintained by local education authorities. The war indirectly stimulated further acceptance of the need for such clinics. By 1945 the total number of clinics was 79 and of these 63 were wholly or partly maintained by local education authorities. From their early days a characteristic feature of child guidance clinics has been their teamwork. The team is usually made up of a psychiatrist, a psychologist and a social worker.[29] The 'team' structure led to some difficulties in the 1974 reorganisation as the employment of the three main workers on the basis of their skills would be by three different authorities.

The Chief Medical Officer of the Ministry of Education in his report for 1939–45 discussed the provisions relating to the school health service contained in the Education Act, 1944. He made a strong case for the school health service to continue under the Ministry of Education as before. One of the most cogent reasons for having a health service administered by the education authority was that 'The presence of children in schools made it possible to arrange effectively for their inspection in school'.

The Education Act, 1944, anticipated the National Health Service Act by ending the charges to parents for treatment given to school children. The duty of the local education authority under the new Act was to ensure that comprehensive facilities for free medical treatment were available, either at clinics, or hospital out-patients' departments or as in-patients. The local education authorities were to pay for hospital treatment, and to make arrangements where necessary with general practitioners and private dentists for care of children.

The National Health Service—the beginning

Planning and advent

Between the wars the personal health services were subject to scrutiny and planning from two different points of view. First, from 1920 onwards several reports and studies considered the inadequacies of medical care for the general population and the need for a more orderly service.[30] Medical resources were unevenly distributed both geographically and by social class. The medical and hospital provisions were not integrated nor were they planned on an efficient scale. The various studies suggested that as sickness was costly to the community people should be encouraged to seek treatment early and that it should be available regardless of ability to pay.

Second, the growing threat of war focused attention on the need to plan for civilian and military casualties. Titmuss, in describing this says, 'the pattern of the hospital services at the end of the war is due as much—if not more—to the kind of war that was expected as to the kind of war that happened'.[31] The Emergency Medical Service was established under the Civil Defence Act, 1939, and put under the control of the Minister of Health, who had power to direct voluntary and local authority hospitals, assume responsibility for the civilian and military victims of the war, and organise a 'nationally planned and financed service based on regional groups of hospitals', which was administered alongside and in the same hospitals as the services for other patients. Inevitably, it became increasingly difficult as the war went on to keep the two services apart. From this experience of planning on a nationwide basis there was no question of a permanent return to the pre-war inadequacies.

The broad principles of the post-war policy for health were contained in Beveridge's Report *Social Insurance and Allied Services* published in 1942 in which the proposals for national insurance rested on the assumption that there would be comprehensive health and rehabilitation services for the prevention and cure of disease: 'Restoration of the sick person to health is a duty of the State and the sick person, prior to any other consideration.'[32] Beveridge agreed with the Medical Planning Committee[33] that medical administration should be separated from income maintenance and that access to medical care should not depend on insurance contributions.

The 1944 White Paper, *A National Health Service*, was generally acceptable in outline but problems arose regarding administration and finance. The three main parties involved with the government in the discussion—the local authorities, the voluntary hospitals and the medical profession—were divided over these issues. The doctors, many of whom had been employed by local authorities, or Poor Law Boards,[34] and had experienced the disadvantages of lay control over medical practice without perhaps appreciating the advantages, rejected the proposal that the local authorities grouped into Joint Boards, should administer the health services. The medical profession played a large part in determining the new structure of the health service, which left the local authorities with considerably reduced responsibilities for health.[35]

The question of pay split the medical profession. The hospital-based doctors accepted a salaried service, but it was rejected by the family doctors, and in the clashes between them and the Minister of Health, Aneurin Bevan, they threatened to boycott the service.[36] The financial scheme they settled for was much like the panel system set up in 1911, whereby the GPs received a capitation fee for each patient on their list, which had the disadvantage that it rewarded good and bad practice alike and offered little incentive for improvement. The assessment of income appropriate for hospital doctors, GPs and dentists on the basis of which salaries and fees were fixed was undertaken by three separate committees, all chaired by Sir William Spens.

The National Health Service Act, 1946, provided a broad plan for extending a comprehensive and free service of medical and ancillary care, advice and treatment to all. The intention of the Act was to uproot as little as possible. No one was to be compelled to participate either as consumer or practitioner. Private fee-paying practice was to be available.

The day appointed for the Act to come into operation was 5th July 1948, which gave less than two years to prepare detailed plans at the local level. In view of the number and variety of agencies involved—local authorities, central government departments, voluntary agencies and individual practitioners—and of buildings, from nineteenth-century workhouses to up-to-date clinics, as well as the complex financial problems, it is surprising that the structure that evolved was as orderly as it was. Not only was there a great diversity in services, staff and buildings but also in the people who were to use the new services, ranging from the co-operative and capable to the apathetic 'uncomplaining poor'.[37]

The tripartite system

The structure set up under the National Health Service Act, 1946, organised the health service in three separately and differently managed parts, joined administratively only at central government level. These were the Hospital and Specialist Service administered by Regional Hospital Boards and Boards of Governors; the General Medical, Dental, Pharmaceutical and Ophthalmic Services administered by Executive Councils to which the individual practitioners were contracted, and finally the community services provided by the County Councils and County Borough Councils. Liaison between the local health authorities, central government and other branches of the NHS was undertaken by the Regional Officers of the DHSS, an office started in the last war. The principal regional officer was required to take an overall view of health matters in his area, with regard not only to the activities of the local health authorities, the RHBs and Executive Councils but also the many interested voluntary agencies, and to collaborate with the Regional Officers of the Social Work Advisory Service of the Ministry of Health.

Some of the difficulties then existing can be imagined when the number of authorities is considered.[38] The 15 RHBs were responsible for the hospital service working through 330 Hospital Management Committees; 36 Boards of Governors, linked with the RHBs, administered the teaching hospitals associated with university medical schools. The Executive Councils, 134 altogether, geographically were fairly well matched with the 175 local authorities, but the GPs being independent contractors may have had patients from more than one Executive Council and local authority area. Where the patients' health problems were compounded by housing difficulties an even more confused situation arose in the counties, where the housing authority was at the urban and rural district level, while the welfare and health services were top-tier functions. For some patients such as the elderly and handicapped, health needs could only be met by care from all three sections of the health service, and the welfare services. No one had authority to draw on all the resources, although the GP was regarded as the co-ordinator.

The problems of such a cumbersome service were quick to emerge, but pressure for drastic change was resisted because, as the Guillebaud Committee,[39] appointed in 1953 to examine the cost of the NHS, pointed out, the structure was the consequence of historical developments and had a future with a new generation to whom many things 'which now appear difficult or impractical will be comparatively simple'. By the time the NHS was reorganised in 1974 it had become very much a part of our way of life. Sir George Godber, writing his last report as Chief Medical Officer to the DHSS in 1973, said, 'A majority of health professionals have done most if not all their professional work within the Health Service.' About one-third of the population have been born into the NHS, and many more will remember little if anything of the pre-1948 services. The new generation had emerged, but so had new problems.

The hope that the NHS would reduce demand for medical care by improving health was recognised as an illusion—'at least for the present'—by the Guillebaud Committee and although the aim of the 1946 Act was to provide a universal and comprehensive service this has proved to be an unrealistic goal. All developed countries have found that demand for health care outstrips resources. This was not apparent, however, in 1947 when the Minister urged the RHBs to show a 'lively sense of independent responsibility';[40] but the financial difficulties of the early years which suggested over-spending and extravagance led to a tightening of control and subsequent confusion in the RHBs about their role.[41] The Guillebaud Committee reported that the charge of excessive spending could not be substantiated; on the contrary it appeared that the portion of the total national resources allocated to the health service had fallen and that increased expenditure was due to rising prices and the post-war population boom. The sobering lesson was that health service expenditure, high as it seemed, was as yet inadequate to meet demand.

The structure of health and welfare services also contributed to the impression of inefficient use of resources. In the 1972 White Paper on Reorganisation the Secretary of State pointed out that there has never been any single authority empowered to provide a comprehensive service, planned rationally, in a given area, nor, it might be added, for any given consumer group.

Proposals for unification

The first proposals for a unified and co-ordinated health service came in 1962 with the publication of the Porritt Committee's *Review of the Medical Services in Great Britain*. This committee, representing the Royal Colleges and other medical organisations, suggested that all medical services in a given area should be under one authority. There was general acceptance of the idea of unification but the magnitude of the changes envisaged required careful consultation and discussion with all interested parties and could only be considered in relation to proposals for the reorganisation of local government and the personal social services.[42] Several documents developed the proposals for change and the major matters for consideration. The first Green Paper[43] presented for discussion purposes in 1968 stressed the need to co-ordinate the service in more than name, and said that its proposed area health boards should be 'more than a roof beneath which separate parts of the service . . . could lead distinct and largely unco-ordinated lives'. Finding an administrative unit that would be large enough to be efficient and economical in use of resources yet small enough to be in touch with local needs and interests proved difficult. The paper was criticised on both counts, as its proposed area health boards, numbering about fifty and designed to be directly responsible to the Minister, were too small to carry out planning of some health service activities; while at local level they seemed to be too big for the participation by staff and public in the everyday running of the service. This Green Paper did not rule out the possibility of the new local authorities being responsible for an integrated health service, not a universally popular idea, and the second Green Paper[44] in 1970 firmly vetoed this. It also dealt with criticisms regarding the size of the area authorities by proposing that new bodies called Regional Health Councils, which, while not directly controlling the area authorities, would carry out some health functions, mainly those of planning for larger populations, medical training, planning hospital and specialist services, deployment of senior staff and administration of the blood transfusion service. The area authorities would still have a direct relationship to the central department, and would cover the same geographical areas as the proposed new local authorities, being about 90 in number, while the central department would increase its activities by taking over from the RHBs their function with regard to major building schemes. The central department would also aim to have more effective control over spending. At the other end of the scale local participation was to be encouraged by the establishment of district committees which would supervise the services at local level, and channel public and professional opinion up to the area authorities.

The third paper, a Consultative Document, came out in May 1971 and introduced yet another element in reorganisation. This was an emphasis on management. The requirements of management efficiency called for a strengthening of the regional level, as the direct relationship of eighty to ninety area authorities with the central department would be cumbersome. The proposed Regional Health Authorities would have 'real management responsibility within the chain of command', and there would be 'maximum delegation downwards matched by accountability upwards'. Members of the new authorities, deliberately kept small, would have to be people skilled and experienced in management. Members with these qualities could best be secured by selection rather than election. The document therefore firmly separated the management structure and function from local participation and representation of local interests, the latter need to be met by Community Health Councils.

The Consultative Document also announced that the organisation of the DHSS was being reviewed by management consultants 'to ensure that it will be fully equipped to carry out its new functions'[45] which are to set national goals and monitor performance, both of the service and its management. An expert study group looked at management arrangements for the rest of the new structure,[46] publishing its report (the Rogers Report) as a Grey Book, *Management Arrangements for the Reorganised National Health Service*, in 1972, presenting very detailed proposals. Other Grey Books published in the same year included the (Hunter) *Report of the Working Party on Medical Administrators* which outlined the role of the Community Physician, the new medical administrator for the reorganised service, who although directly descended from the local authority MOH and the RHB's Administrative Medical Office, was expected to be more of a manager, being concerned with planning and evaluating the local service and establishing priorities within the context of national policies. Three Grey Books from the Working Party on Collaboration between the NHS and Local Government explored the relationship of the reorganised NHS and environmental health, the personal social services, school health services and ancillary services.

The final proposals for unification were presented in the White Paper of August 1972 and mainly embodied in the NHS Reorganisation Act, July 1973, with the appointed day fixed for the following April.

The proposals were criticised at the time by the Opposition as not being sufficiently democratic, but on being returned to power shortly before the appointed day the Labour Government did not impose any changes at that time. A brief document outlining their criticisms of the separation between the management of the service and participation by the people it is serving was published in June 1974,[47] with their proposals for increased local authority representation on the Area and Regional Health Authorities, and some changes in the rules relating to membership of the Community Health Councils.

For many months the new authorities worked alongside the old, new staff appointments being programmed to take place during the transitional period. The DHSS instituted a series of Circulars (HRC) in 1972 which were sent out to all bodies concerned with the old and new structures, to advise on developments, explain and inaugurate changes in functions and new procedures. Information bulletins were issued to staff to keep them in touch with developments and regions had their own newsletters, giving information on local happenings. Joint liaison committees of senior staff from the different sections of the health services were set up to guide the various bodies concerned with planning the changes.

In spite of these measures it became apparent that much confusion and uncertainty remained. Difficulties and frustrations resulted from the competitive allocation of administrative jobs within the new structure. The Royal Commission on the NHS[48] suggested that this, coupled with unrealistic expectations of the benefits of reorganisation—arising perhaps from the information programme itself—contributed in some measure to the lowering of morale evident in the service after 1974.

The 1974 structure

Chart 8 outlines the structure set up under the 1973 Act. The 1980–3 plans for modification of this will be referred to later.

The Secretary of State at the DHSS is answerable to Parliament for the NHS in England, and since 1969 the Secretary of State for Wales is similarly responsible for the NHS there, which is constituted as a single region. This accountability of the ministers and their permanent secretaries has been criticised by the Royal Commission on the NHS as being inappropriate for such a vast undertaking[49] where important members of staff are not civil servants and exercise considerable professional autonomy. However the government in its plans for the new structure[50] has rejected any alternative, stating firmly that accountability must stay with the Secretary of State.

Ever since the Ministry of Health was set up in 1919 there has been a Chief Medical Officer on the staff to serve the Minister. His report *On the State of the Public Health* is published annually, a useful source of information on health matters. Over the years he has been joined by other professional officers. An independent advisory body, the Central Health Services Council[51] was set up under the 1946 Act. It was able to offer advice and criticism over a wide range of health topics, but was axed in the government spending cuts in 1980, although its standing committees continue.

The DHSS has its own regional offices (not to be confused with Regional Health Authorities) each covering several RHAs, which liaise with social services and other bodies to advise both the Minister and the Regions.

The structure that emerged in 1974 under the DHSS has been severely criticised for its over-elaborate management arrangements, which are under the 1980 Act preparing for gradual reorganisation and simplification. It is useful to examine the system that will be replaced.

Accountable to the Secretary of State are the fourteen RHAs, responsible for preparing long-term strategic plans in line with national policies, allocating resources between the AHAs and monitoring their performance, appointing senior medical staff in all but the area authorities concerned with the university medical schools, and a variety of services which require regional organisation.

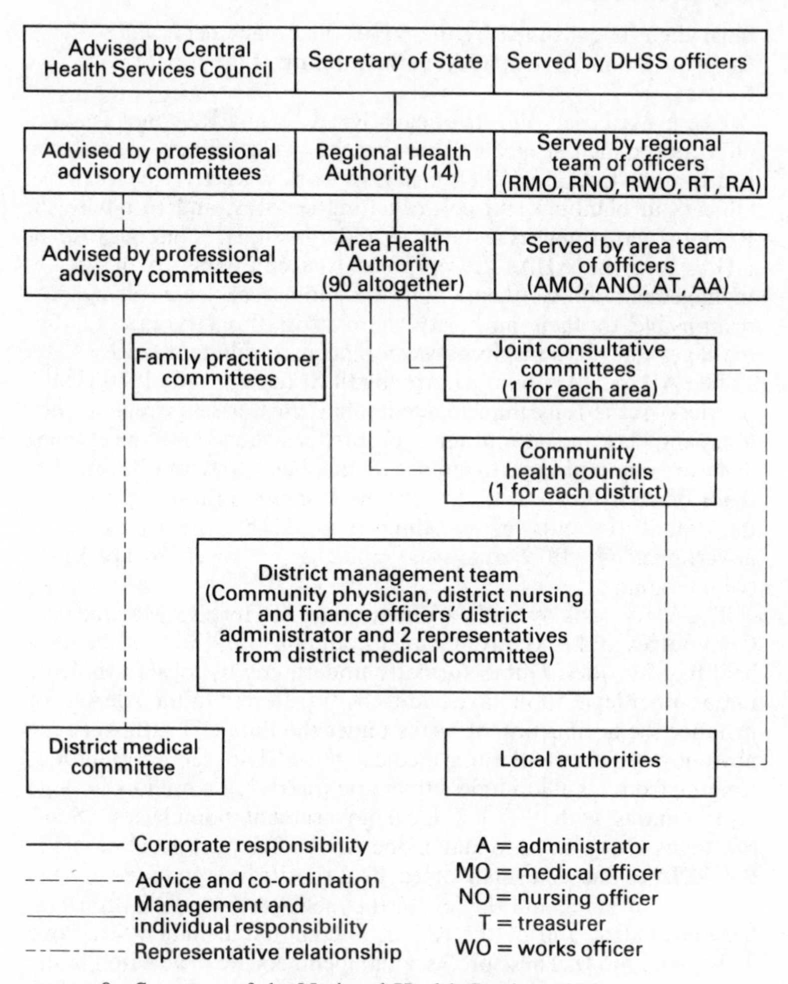

CHART 8 Structure of the National Health Service, 1974

The members of the RHAs are appointed by the Secretary of State, who has a duty to consult various bodies, and since the Labour government's proposals for increased democracy in the NHS were put into effect they must include about one-third local authority members, and representatives of the health professions. An innovation is the payment of chairmen, which recognises the heavy demands made on their time. The RHAs are advised by Regional Advisory Committees, representing the health services staff. These committees, provided that they are seen to be truly representative of their staff group or profession, are given statutory recognition and must then be consulted by the RHA. The machinery which allows for professional participation in the running of the service is referred to later.

The five salaried officers of each RHA form a Regional Team of Officers and include medical, nursing and works officers, an administrator and a treasurer. Their task is to work with the Area Teams of Officers in planning and co-ordinating services, and to advise the RHA on performances in the areas under its supervision. Because the RHAs and the AHAs are corporately accountable to the tier of management above them, and the individual team officers are responsible to their authority there is in this structure no line management relationship between officers at different levels.

The AHAs, 90 in number, are the third tier until the 1980 Health Services Act is fully implemented. They must assess needs in their area, and plan and administer a comprehensive service to meet them. They are required to carry out national policies, and may be removed from office if they fail to do so. One London authority refused to implement the cuts in spending required by the Conservative government in 1979 and was replaced by specially appointed commissioners.

The AHAs took over all the functions of the Hospital Management Committees and Executive Councils, and most of those of the local health authorities. Duties formerly undertaken by local authorities under other legislation have had to be transferred to the AHAs; for instance the notification of births under the Public Health Act 1936 must now be made to the area medical officer. They serve populations ranging from 1 million to less than one-quarter of a million, and are co-terminous with the new local government boundaries. (Some boroughs are grouped to match one AHA.) They are accountable to the RHAs. The chairman of each authority is appointed by the Secretary of State, and the rest of the members by local authorities, the universities, and by the RHAs, and should include at least one doctor and nurse. These professional members are in addition to the area advisory committees and the area officers.

The area team, made up of a medical officer, a nursing officer, treasurer and administrator, prepares plans for presentation to the region and, with local authority staff, for presentation to the Joint Consultative Committee, which is concerned with matters affecting both health and local authority services. Working through that committee they must ensure that medical services are provided for school health, public health and for the social services. They delegate executive responsibility to the District Management Teams, monitor their performance and co-ordinate their activities. Although the area officers are not managers of the district team, and both are responsible directly to the AHA, the status of the area officers is higher than that of the district officers.[52] The Central Health Services Council had reservations about this and recommend that the district community physician should be of equal status to the area and regional community physicians, in order to protect the quality of work at the 'level closest to the patient'.[53]

Each AHA with university medical and dental schools in its area is responsible for providing clinical teaching facilities, and is designated as a Teaching Authority, referred to in brief as AHA (T).

The functions of the former Executive Councils which were responsible for GPs, dentists, pharmacists and supplementary ophthalmic services have been taken over by Family Practitioner Committees,[54] one in each area, and just as the Executive Councils were responsible to the Secretary of State, so the AHAs in this matter are directly responsible to him and not to the RHAs. The FPCs have no management control over GPs, dentists, etc. who remain independent contractors as before.

The AHAs are also 'managers of hospitals' for the purposes of the Mental Health Act 1959, relating to discharge of patients. Three or more members of a committee or sub-committee of the AHA, not necessarily themselves members of the authority, have powers to discharge. Although the committee appointed for these purposes must have one or more AHA members on it, power to discharge can be exercised by three people who are not AHA members.

While most areas are divided into districts for the practical provision of services, nearly one-third of the smaller area health authorities are not further divided, and the structures and staffing of these differ from the rest.[55] There is only one team of officers performing the functions of both area and district teams, an arrangement that has come to be regarded as potentially more effective. Since 1974 some two-district areas have reverted to being single districts in the expectation that efficiency would be improved.[56]

The district forms 'the natural community for the planning and delivery of health care',[57] serving populations of about 250,000. It has a District General Hospital, or group of hospitals, although, because the siting of hospitals was in response to needs and local government boundaries of years gone by, the District General Hospital may not actually be in this district, or possibly not even within the AHA boundary. The natural patient 'flow' of the community is the basis on which districts have been identified, but no new boundaries preclude people using services they have grown accustomed to. Various management arrangements deal with problems of 'overlap'[58] which may also be concerned with the social work service available to the hospital, coming either from the local authority in which the hospital is sited, or from the local authority whose population is largely served by the hospital.

There is no district authority, no group of selected professional and lay people jointly responsible for the service. At district level the health service is fully integrated, and the local professional staff co-ordinate and plan all health care. There is a District Management Team composed of the district community physician, district nursing, finance and administrative officers, and two elected representatives from the district medical committee involving all the doctors working in the district, one a hospital consultant, the other a GP. Collectively and individually the team of six is responsible to the area health authority. All members of the team have equal status, there is no chief executive, and none may override the others. In order to ensure that there is no domination of any individual or group the team must come to a consensus decision on any matter that is not the prime concern of one member of the team. Any disagreements that cannot be resolved must be referred to the AHA. This management by consensus was felt to have advantages in that, although a relatively slow method of decision-making, it would command commitment by the whole team to its decisions, increase interprofessional understanding while maintaining professional autonomy.

The DMT was responsible for setting up Health Care Planning Teams, which focused on those categories of consumer who need a 'high level of interaction between hospital and community care'.[59] Since 1974 concern for meeting needs across social services as well as health boundaries has put greater emphasis on joint planning, and the Health Care Planning Teams were replaced in 1977 by Joint Care Planning Teams.

District organisation would, it was hoped, lead to an integrated service and an end to the domination of the hospital sector, which in 1979 still accounted for 70 per cent of NHS expenditure.

Dissatisfaction with the new structure was quick to emerge. Three tiers seemed cumbersome, delaying decisions and frustrating front-line workers, while the growth of administrative activity appeared to lead to duplication of effort, and to distance the service from those it served. The government's response to the growing criticism was a Royal Commission appointed in 1976, to consider how management and money might best be used in the interests of the two groups of people most affected—the patients and the staff.

The Royal Commission in its lengthy report in 1979 made over one hundred recommendations, covering the service given to patients, the NHS workers, relationships with local authorities, universities and the private sector, and the management and finance of the NHS. On this latter point the Royal Commission agreed with many critics that the NHS needed 'slimming' but warned that the abolition of a tier, which had assumed 'symbolic importance' could not be regarded as a panacea for all problems.

The consultative paper *Patients First* followed in the same year with proposals to simplify the management and structure of the NHS, in order to ensure, as its name implies, that the service is concerned first and foremost with the needs of the patient. Decisions about patient care must therefore be taken as far as possible at local level, to meet local need.

In August 1980 the Health Services Act was passed making provision for changes in local health administration, to be effected over two to three years. The new District Health Authorities which will replace both the AHAs and the DMTs will have features of both. Geographically they will be like the present districts, serving the smallest convenient area and many will follow the same boundaries. The principle of direct coterminosity of health authorities with local authorities which was a feature of the 1974 reorganisation will have to be abandoned although the duty to collaborate remains. The implications of this in retaining links between the two authorities are discussed in *Patients First*, and considerable flexibility will be allowed in the development of new arrangements. Some social services departments may be faced with an increased burden of administrative activity in having to liaise with two or more DHAs rather than one AHA.

Administratively the DHA will resemble the AHA. The chairman will be appointed by the Secretary of State and membership will include a hospital consultant, a GP, a nurse, a representative from both the university and trade unions, and others up to a total of sixteen. The team of officers will be like the DMT and will be collectively and individually responsible to the DHA. The Royal Commission observed that consensus management could interfere with the assumption of individual responsibility and both the DHA and the team members are advised in the DHSS circular on the new structure to clarify their mangement arrangements in order to avoid blurring of roles.

Directly accountable to the District Officers will be the new unit managers who will be in charge of the administrative units into which the work of the DHA will be divided. A large hospital, for instance, will constitute one unit, having chief officers each accountable to the District Officer of their respective discipline. Community services may form another unit, others may be arranged to deal with specific client groups, or to cover both a hospital and its community services.

In both district and unit management the function of the administor will be to act as co-ordinator for the group of officers. This does not imply that he will have the authority of a chief executive, but he will be responsible for interpreting policies to his team and others, and presenting reports to his authority—a difficult and delicate task.

Considerable flexibility is being allowed in the structuring of the new DHAs in order to respond to local needs and preferences. This can be compared with the original brief given to the Regional Hospital Boards in 1947, which asked for 'independent responsibility', but failed to predict the demand for health care, and the consequent need to determine priorities and control spending.

In February 1981 a handbook, *Care in Action*, addressed to the members of the new DHAs outlined the government's strategies and priorities. In it importance is laid on developing co-operation with the voluntary and private sectors in health and welfare services and it follows the *Priorities* documents in promoting joint planning across service boundaries to meet the needs of some groups of clients.

In considering the government's orientation to this changing structure it is worth reviewing the basic principles of the NHS, as outlined in the second Green Paper in 1970, and the objectives of the reorganisation process that is still going on.

Principles and objectives

The basic *principles* of the NHS which have 'stood the test of time' are that health care should be paid for out of taxes with the financial burden of sickness borne by the whole community, that there should be a service of uniformly high quality in all areas and for all people, that the doctor's clinical freedom must be protected, and that the family doctor team (the idea of a 'team' is a recent innovation) should be central to the service.

The *objectives* of reorganisation are to unite the health services, establish close links with local authority services, involve the professions and the public in the running of the service and ensure central control over finance through well-defined management structures.

As one of the objectives of reorganisation is government control over spending, and one of the cardinal principles of the NHS is clinical autonomy for medical practitioners (which involves decisions about allocation of health resources to patients), there have to be administrative arrangements whereby the conflict inherent in this situation can be resolved. Professional autonomy is respected by having all professional workers managed by members of their own profession, which also deals with the bogey of lay administration, while the objective of participation by the professionals in running the service offers another controlling mechanism in the management of resources at all levels.

At the operational level where the resources are allocated to the patients by the professionals there is representative machinery enabling them to be involved in planning. Differences in staff structure have had to be accommodated; for instance the nurses could be represented at district level by the District Nursing Officer as there is a clear hierarchical structure already operating,[60] but there is no such hierarchy for the doctors, GPs being under contract of service to the Family Practitioner Committees and the consultants under contract of employment to the RHAs. Some hospital consultants were grouped under the cogwheel system of joint planning,[61] but not all districts set these up. Participation in co-ordination and planning was extended to all doctors in 1974 by setting up District Medical Committees, to act as advisory and planning bodies. GPs and hospital doctors serve on these committees, and one GP and one hospital doctor from the committee join the District Management Team. Representatives are sent to a similar Medical Committee at area level. Evidence to the Royal Commission suggested that the multiplicity of advisory and representative committees is unnecessarily complex and wasteful of professional time and energy. As a matter of urgency a working group was set up under the CMO in 1980 to consider what was necessary for the changing structure, and has recommended that the District Medical Committees, which included both hospital doctors and GPs, should be replaced by two single-discipline committees, with cross-representation between the two. A GP and a consultant from these committees will be members of the DMT as before, and as the DHA will also have medical members, it is hoped that medical participation at district level will be ensured, with similar arrangements made for nurses and other staff. The working group will look at regional participation later.

Participation by the public has been divorced from the management structure. The lay members of the regional and area authorities are not directly representative of the public. New bodies, Community Health Councils,[62] have been set up for this purpose, one for each district. The original proposals in the White Paper were criticised in Parliament as giving so little power to the CHCs that they were likely to be toothless watchdogs. This situation was improved by making the RHAs responsible for appointments to the councils, not the AHAs as at first proposed, and by reducing the RHAs' share of nominations to the council to one-sixth. The local authorities nominate half and the voluntary agencies concerned with health matters in the district the remaining one-third of the members.[63] In order to keep criticism as objective as possible members of a CHC may not also be members of the regional and area authorities, nor may they be members of the teams of officers. The Labour government increased the strength of the CHCs in two ways, first, by making it mandatory for a spokesman from the District Management Team to attend meetings at the request of the CHC to answer questions; these meetings are open to the public and so present an opportunity for greater involvement and understanding by the consumers; second, by asking the RHAs to consult the CHCs regarding appointments to their area authority. An Association of CHCs was set up in 1977 to advise and assist the work of these bodies.

The Royal Commission found some confusion about the role of the CHCs, and widely differing opinions about their value and effectiveness. *Patients First* questioned the need for this separate consumer body when the DHAs, which will be more closely in touch with their users, are set up. The £4 million per annum spent on the CHCs might possibly be better applied, particularly as some CHCs felt that even at this level of funding they were too impoverished to be effective.

The objective of closely linking health and local authority services could probably be best attained by uniting them under one authority, but this has been rejected. Instead under the 1974 Act a duty to collaborate has been laid on both authorities as recommended by the Working Party on Collaboration,[64] through Joint Consultative Committees. As these were considered to be very important to the effective delivery of care by both health and local authorities it was suggested by the DHSS that the chairman of AHAs and local authority committees should be appointed to the Joint Consultative Committees and should be supported by their senior officers to consider specific areas of common concern, such as child care, mental health, and services for the elderly. New structures for co-operation were needed following the reorganisation of the NHS and other social services on the basis of skills rather than by category of consumer; staff were transferred from one authority to another, for example hospital social workers and home helps left the health service and joined the local authority social services, but they remain important workers in health care. The White Paper on Reorganisation emphasised that areas of common concern could not be left to emerge, but had to be identified and planned for. In the bleak economic climate of the late 1970s, the shortage of resources prompted the setting of priorities, and highlighted the persistent problems of those people whose needs crossed the service boundaries. A Consultative Document, *Priorities for Health and Personal Social Services in England* in 1976 outlined strategies for tackling some of the problems of waste, and lack of access to resources experienced by some groups of clients.

A circular in 1977 recommended that the Health Care Planning Teams set up in 1974 which focused on client groups should be replaced by joint care planning teams, composed of officers from the different services, working under the JCC. Joint financing of projects was introduced at this time, whereby NHS money and land could be used for local authority services, provided that these were ultimately of benefit to the NHS. As community care has been increasingly favoured the need for joint planning has grown. The portion of health expenditure allocated to personal social services is expected to increase from £54 million in 1980–1 to £58 million in 1982–3. This is however, a relatively small shift when the expenditure on the PSS in 1980–1 is about £1,450 million, while the NHS is £9,460 million.[65] National figures conceal the local variations in social services spending which have considerable effect on demand for NHS provision, and while the NHS formula for determining the allocation of money to Districts takes account of local variation in need, it takes no account of local authority provision.[66]

The principle of a *national* service in the sense of equality of access to health care was ruefully recognised in the second Green Paper as not yet established, although much had been done. Some areas and some groups still experience inadequate standards of care. Some of these inadequacies were revealed in the Department of the Environment White Paper *Policy for the Inner Cities*.[67] Poorer health standards continue in inner city areas with primary care services at a less than average level of provision. There are more single-handed GPs, fewer health centres and community nurses. The shortage of health workers is doubly significant in that the need for them is greater than in other areas. The report of the Black Committee in 1980, *Inequalities in Health* gives evidence of marked differences in health experiences and mortality rates between social classes.

Central government control over NHS finances has ensured that relatively deprived areas and groups are more favourably treated. The original NHS method of allocating resources to Regions and Hospital Boards was based on demand already satisfied rather than on any criterion of need. One year's spending was the basis of the next year's allocation. Capital spending on new projects brought an assured income later. Poorly endowed areas stayed poor, while the rich did well. The Resource Allocation Working Party was appointed in 1975 to devise a 'pattern of distribution responsive objectively, equitably and efficiently to relative need.'[68] The RAWP formula attempts to assemble local information on those characteristics of the population that reflect the need and potential demand for health care. On these data resources are allocated between the regions and districts, attempting to give 'equal opportunity of access to health care for people at equal risk'.

The hospital and specialist service

This was the greatest innovation of the National Health Service. The nationalisation of the hospitals secured a better distribution of staff and other resources, and the enlargement of the administrative areas beyond local authority boundaries made for a more efficient operational size. The fourteen Regional Hospital Boards (RHBs) based on the wartime Civil Defence regions, were responsible for hospital in-patient and out-patient provision, for domiciliary consultations, and for the appointment of senior medical staff. They had the task of planning the hospital service in their areas, deciding priorities and controlling finances. By employing the senior medical staff directly, they controlled the distribution of specialist services over the whole region. They allocated money to the Hospital Management Committees in their area. The hospitals, individually or in groups, were administered by these committees, who were responsible to the RHBs.

The members of the Boards and Committees were unpaid laymen appointed, in the case of the RHBs, by the Secretary of State and in the case of the HMCs by the Boards. The members were selected not elected, which led to some disquiet at a situation in which decisions about the disposal of large sums of public money were made by non-representative bodies.

The special needs of the hospitals associated with universities in medical teaching, and the anxieties of the staff about standards of education in this new, untried structure, were acknowledge by having them administered by Boards of Governors directly responsible to the Secretary of State. Since 1948 the fears of the universities that their voice would not be heard have been allayed. The Todd Report on Medical Education[69] in 1968 recommended that the teaching hospitals should come under the RHBs.

The 1960s were a period of optimism and plenty. The Chief Medical Officer of the Ministry in his annual report for 1966 looked back to the 1950s as an era of reorganisation of the 1948 inheritance,[70] and to the 1960s as an era of planning. The money available to the hospital service for the first five or six years was spent on patching and improving existing hospitals, but after 1955 it was possible to start thinking about major schemes of development. This presented a need for planning on a scale unknown before. In 1962 the Hospital Plan for England and Wales was published, to be reviewed and carried forward annually. It proposed that a District General Hospital should serve a population of 100,000 to 150,000 people providing all types of hospital and specialist services that did not require a substantially larger catchment area,[71] an idea that was basic in the reorganisation plans of 1974.

With each region undertaking its own building programme, progress was patchy, slow and increasingly expensive. Standard designs, 'Best Buy' hospitals and 'Harness' Units were devised, but even these in the economic stringency of the 1970s were considered to require too great a capital outlay. A new low-cost design was offered—the Nucleus Hospital—which while being a satisfactory District General Hospital of 300 beds can be added to in later building programmes.[72] It has had to be accepted that many of the old hospitals have a useful life still. The Royal Commission on the NHS reported that only about one-third of current hospital accommodation has been built since 1948, and another one-third was originally put up in the nineteenth century, when buildings were intended to last. This contrasts with the modern principle of a short life and early replacement which accommodates to rapid advances in medical care, and changes in demand.

The cottage hospital has also returned to favour. In the 'Priorities' Consultative Document 1976, the Secretary of State recommended the use of community hospitals, perhaps adapting existing small units, for patients not needing the facilities of a DGH, many of whom would be elderly.

The 1970 Green Paper reported that although the distribution of hospital resources remained uneven, much has been achieved. Specialist services are within reach of all. The fact that variations still persist in the availability of hospital care can be partly accounted for by the way in which hospitals were funded initially with the allocation of money based on previous spending, allowing resources of manpower and plant to draw revenue with them. New hospitals brought extra revenue for running costs to the RHBs. This system of payment was phased out with the introduction of the RAWP formula and the RHBs were required to find the running costs for any new projects from their overall budget.

The 1962 Hospital Plan also introduced for the first time a national policy on the level of hospital services to be made available. A target of 3.3 beds per 1,000 of the population was proposed, which represented an overall reduction in hospital provision. 'Over-bedded' regions like Liverpool which had nearly 6 beds per 1,000 had an inheritance of large numbers of hospital beds, with consultant attitudes to their use somewhat different from less well endowed regions. Waiting days in bed before and after treatment were a common and expensive feature of hospital practice, although this also suggests that health provision was used to meet social need. In spite of the high bed level the Liverpool Region population suffered from earlier mortality and longer and more frequent periods of sickness than prevailed elsewhere, and was described as the deadliest and sickest place in the country.

The national targets failed to take account of those variations in local need which reflect the constitution of the population, and have been replaced by the RAWP formula referred to earlier which takes account of population size, make-up and morbidity (using standardised mortality rates to give a guide to morbidity). The prevalence of mental disorder, however, cannot be deduced from mortality statistics and until more quantifiable information is available on those factors which influence the pattern of mental disorder the most reliable indicator is marital status, as it is evident that married people make less use of psychiatric services.

While the number of hospital beds has declined in line with policy, more people than ever have received in-patient treatment. This has been made possible by a more efficient use of beds and an increasing liaison with community services. A record figure of $5\frac{1}{2}$ million patients was reached in 1977.

Allocation of resources and the involvement of hospital staff in management have been the subject of several reports since 1948.[73] The report of the Salmon Committee[74] on senior nursing staff structure proposed new patterns of administration with preparation for management at all levels and clear lines of accountability. The doctor's managerial function was considered initially by the Advisory Committee for Management Efficiency in the National Health Service, and subsequently by a joint working party of consultants and Ministry staff.[75] The difficulties discussed in the working party (called 'Cogwheel') arose from the continuation in the 1948 structure of a long-standing system whereby most hospital consultants had equal clinical and administrative status. The control exercised by the RHBs, by whom the consultants were appointed after 1948, was indirect and limited largely to the allocation of resources. Apart from a few departments such as radiology there were no hierarchical structures as there were in nursing. It became increasingly clear that while the medical staff, because of their clinical autonomy, had control over, and responsibility for, the allocation of resources to their patients, there was little overall co-ordination of their individual activities. If the resulting inefficiency and waste were to be remedied and at the same time clinical autonomy protected, the doctors must be involved much more closely in administrative and management affairs.[76]

In the Cogwheel system specialists in the same area of practice, such as surgery, together discuss their clinical arrangements, while the chairmen of the specialist groups form a committee to plan the administration of clinical matters as distinct from the administration of the hospital. In this way the medical staff can be involved in assessing priorities. The Hospital Advisory Committee in 1972 reported that diehard attitudes undermined positive planning for the whole service. They noted that in some areas 'hostility to geriatrics may mean that proposals put forward by the Geriatrician may be automatically outvoted.'[77]

Hospital services for the mentally disordered

In 1948 the RHBs had the unenviable inheritance of large institutions for mentally disordered patients, many of whom were no more in need of medical care than the rest of the population. The National Health Service Act integrated these hospitals with all others in one administrative framework, while the 1962 Hospital Plan included services for the mentally ill in the District General Hospital

The Hospital Plan also proposed a reduction in the number of beds for the mentally ill and subnormal. In his report for 1968 the Chief Medical Officer said that the District General Hospitals would totally replace the old mental hospitals, assuming that community services and geriatric services provided full support. The RHBs in December 1971[78] were advised to plan for psychiatric units to replace the old hospitals, but the plans did not refer to the elderly who constituted nearly half of the inmates of the condemned hospitals. They were dealt with in a circular to the RHBs in 1972[79] which analysed and advised on the varying needs of old people. The enthusiasm for change in the care of the mentally disordered which urged the closing of the large institutions had by then been tempered by the realisation that these hospitals represent a valuable source of sheltered accommodation,[80] and that community care was not yet at the standard required. The Royal Commission on the NHS reported that by 1979 only one large hospital for the mentally ill had been closed, but not abandoned as it now caters for the mentally handicapped. New hospital provision for mental illness has been only one-third of that for acute conditions, partly because of the intention to reduce the beds but partly because in the scramble for money certain groups of patients were inadequately represented. While services for acute illness, including some mental illnesses, were favoured, long-stay patients were poorly served. In 1969 the RHBs were asked to review their services for these patients and make a more generous allocation of money, while the Secretary of State earmarked £3 million for improving services for the mentally handicapped. In 1970 the new government took this protection further and allocated a further £93 million over four years for all groups of chronic sick and handicapped who appeared to suffer the added handicap of being less eligible to their own RHBs than other patients.[81] The Royal Commission in 1979 noted that £44 million had been allocated for capital expenditure on mental disorder and geriatric services between 1971–5 with 'little noticeable effect'.

There have been dramatic changes in admissions to mental hospitals since 1948. The number of residents reached its peak in 1945 at 3.5 per thousand of the population. A century-long upward trend was reversed and by 1971 the hospital population had fallen to 2.25 per thousand.[82] The major change has been in the short-stay and younger section of the population. The 1977 DHSS Annual Report noted a continuing decline in in-patient provision and a shift to community care, as recommended in the White Papers *Better Services for the Mentally Ill*, 1975, and *Better Services for the Mentally Handicapped*, 1971. The strategies developed for making these changes are outlined earlier in the section referring to joint planning and in the chapter on Personal Social Services.

Although in-patient provision has been reduced the number of admissions and readmissions has been steadily rising. The admission rate nearly trebled between 1949 and 1971, and it has been estimated that the lifetime chances of admission to mental hospital now are one in six for women and one in nine for men.[83] The pattern of mental illness and psychiatric provision has approached more nearly the pattern for physical illness. Wards in District General Hospitals, outpatient facilities and day hospitals have expanded, partly a reaction to, and partly a cause of, changes in treatment and legislation. The Mental Health Act of 1959[84] replaced all previous legislation. It was made possible by new drugs which modify disturbed behaviour and by new attitudes to mental illness.

The Act uses the general term 'mental disorder' to describe all conditions of mental illness and deficiency, psychopathic states and 'any other disorder or disability of the mind'. As far as possible mental disorder is treated on an informal basis. Compulsory admission to hospital is used only where necessary to protect the patient or others, for which a formal request for admission must be made either by the patient's nearest relative or a mental welfare officer from the local authority Personal Social Services Department. There must also be a medical recommendation. Over 90 per cent of the admissions to hospital are on an informal basis—a dramatic reversal of the situation following the 1890 Lunacy Act.

A patient can be detained in hospital for observation for up to twenty-eight days on the recommendation of two doctors, or in a case of urgency for seventy-two hours on the recommendation of one doctor. Detention for treatment up to one year can also be ordered. Appeal against detention can be made to the local Mental Health Tribunal which has legal, psychiatric and lay members, and can order discharge.

The Act itself came under scrutiny by an Inter-departmental Committee which issued a consultative document in 1976.[85] The main matters of concern were the working of the law on compulsory detention and treatment, and the methods of dealing with complaints and exercising external supervision of the care of hospital patients.

A White Paper based on the consultative document outlined the government's proposals in September 1978.[86] The 'general philosophy is based on the need to strengthen the rights and safeguard the liberties of the mentally disordered, while retaining a proper regard for the rights and safety of the general public and of staff'–a difficult balance to strike, and particularly difficult in relation to the problem of mentally abnormal offenders. Mental illness and criminal behaviour are not mutually exclusive. Although psychiatric units have been established in some prisons a 'flood' of such patients was reported in 1969.[87] The needs of such people are particularly at variance with the new concept of the mental hospital as a therapeutic community in close contact with its environment, and since 1969 there has been a steady decline in their numbers, due, the White Paper suggests, to reluctance on the part of hospitals to admit offenders. This has led to some antagonism between the courts who see the need for psychiatric treatment for some offenders, and the hospital staff who are unable to offer secure accommodation, and may not wish to have the patient's length of stay determined on legal rather than medical grounds. The Butler Committee on Mentally Abnormal Offenders[88] recommended that regional secure units should be set up, something half-way between the high security of the Special Hospitals[89] and the open door of mental hospitals, but staffing problems have hindered development.

The least satisfactory part of the mental health hospital provision seems to have been for the mentally handicapped and the psychogeriatric patients. As noted, the Hospital Advisory Service was set up following disclosures of ill-treatment at some of the large institutions.[90] Patients detained for their own protection have been left unprotected from the rigours of life in understaffed, badly managed institutions.[91]

The Royal Commission on the NHS said, 'It is an accident of history that the NHS has had such a large responsibility for the mentally handicapped' (6.45), and added 'whether or not it is carrying too extensive a responsibility, the NHS is, in certain places at least, failing badly to fulfil its obligations'. The co-ordination of health, welfare and education services is desirable, but so also is co-operation between different disciplines involved in the care of the mentally handicapped. The Jay Report[92] went further and advocated an integration of nursing and residential social work skills in training for staff.

A National Development Group for the mentally handicapped was set up in 1976 to advise the DHSS, and a Development Team to advise authorities. They took over the work of the Hospital (now Health) Advisory Service with regard to mental handicap. In the same year the priorities document recommended increased spending on training centres and local authority homes. In order to achieve the level of community provision recommended in the White Paper, *Better Services*, for 1990 about 2,400 training centre places and 1,000 residential places will have to be added each year.

Elderly people form between 20 and 25 per cent of admissions to psychiatric hospitals. Those suffering from treatable mental illness have to be distinguished from those suffering from dementia. The former need the psychiatric services available to the general population, the latter are an increasing special case.

In 1977 it was estimated that the 85 plus age group would grow faster than any other age group taking 1976 as a base line,[93] and it is within this group that the mental infirmity associated with old age is likely to occur. Many of these people are in the old long-stay mental hospitals, but their needs cross service and specialism boundaries. Projects for joint planning within the NHS and between the NHS and local authority services emphasise the special needs of this client group.

Rehabilitation and disability

Rehabilitation, one of Beveridge's main reasons for advocating a National Health Service has been very slow to develop. The emphasis has been on traumas rather than disease. The hospital service has provided the artificial limb and appliance service, and has had responsibility for the vehicle service. Much discussion has centred on the value and safety of the three-wheeler car. Since 1976 Mobility Allowances have been made available to disabled people of school or working age, to replace the three-wheeler. Lady Sharp in her report, 1974,[94] was emphatic that social as well as physical needs should be taken into account when considering eligibility for a vehicle or allowance.

Responsibility for aids and adaptations has been borne by both the NHS and the local authorities, which has led to confusion. On the NHS side the hospital doctor has the power to prescribe aids for his patient but has little contact with the patient in his home setting, while the GP who will know more of the patient's social situation, has limited power to order the aids he sees are necessary.[95]

New efforts at rehabilitation of patients disabled through progressive diseases such as rheumatism can be seen in the appointment of consultants with specific responsibility for this.

Community services and primary care

Until reorganisation the community and domiciliary services were the concern of local health authorities and the Executive Councils.[96] The latter were the direct descendants of committees set up under the

1911 Health Insurance Act to administer the general practitioner service for insured workers. They are now called Family Practitioner Committees and with these general practitioners, dentists, pharmacists and opticians are independent contractors. Their funding comes directly from the DHSS and not out of the health authority's budget.

Reorganisation has made few changes in their practice. As the Staff Advisory Committee[97] said in 1972, 'we confidently expect that the great majority of staff will be doing the same job after the appointed day in the same place they are doing it today.'

The general practitioners

General practitioners were very unevenly distributed over the country in 1948. The Medical Practices Committee, set up to remedy this, identified areas that were under-doctored and for these 'designated' areas there were positive financial inducements to practise. In the over-doctored areas permission to practise would normally be refused. The ratio of doctors to patients has varied, partly because the number of doctors going into general practice has not been constant. As hospital work and opportunities overseas expanded in the late 1950s so the number of GPs declined. Projections about need in the Willink Report of 1957, based on incorrect assessments of the future size and shape of the population, contributed to the decline in numbers training in the early 1960s. By the mid-1960s the average GP's list of patients was nearly at the maximum permitted, 3,500, and in designated areas had risen over it. The numbers of designated areas had also increased. Rudolf Klein notes that it was in this period that the number of complaints by patients against their GPs reached its peak, and suggests that the bitterness resulting from their demoralisation and discontent spread over to the patients.[98]

More positive measures were taken to improve distribution of GPs in 1966 when the Review Body of Doctors' and Dentists' Remuneration[99] recommended additional allowances for practice in designated areas. At this point the distribution of medical manpower took an upward turn. The increase in general practitioners has continued, with increasing representation of overseas doctors, and women doctors. The under-doctored areas showed improvement in list size, being an average of 2,715 in 1977, a drop of nearly 1,000 in 10 years.

Payment of the general practitioners has presented difficulties. The negotiations before 1948 rejected payment by salary and agreed to capitation fees from a central pool into which the Treasury paid enough money to cover an estimated appropriate income for all the doctors and an allowance for practice expenses. The pool money was distributed through the Executive Councils.[100] The GPs were on the whole offered better pay than they had been able to command before, but the method of payment tended to reward good and bad alike. In 1966 a new system of remuneration was recommended by the review body which 'reflected more closely the individual doctor's services for his patients and his practice expenses'[101] based on negotiations on the *Charter for the Family Doctor Service* published by the British Medical Association in 1965. The new system included an annual basic practice allowance, not called a salary, but not related to the size of the doctor's list, special allowances for seniority, group practice and post-graduate training, inducement payments and initial practice allowances to doctors going to designated areas, and assistance towards the cost of ancillary workers and provision and improvement of premises.

Squabbles about pay have perhaps reflected some of the less easily identified troubles in general practice. The 1946 Act foresaw general practitioners working in health centres which were planned as the focal point for community services, to end the isolation of GPs and integrate their work with that of domiciliary nurses and the social services. They were also to be used by the hospital service for out-patient clinics, thus improving contact between the personnel in community care and those in hospital. Financial and administrative problems hindered their development. GPs feared a loss of independence and found in the few centres that were operative that the comparatively high rents reduced their own income when this was based solely on *per capita* payments. Ten years after the appointed day only ten had been opened. Other avenues of co-operation were explored, such as attachment of health visitors to general practices and, as the general practitioners were responding to encouragement from the Ministry to group themselves, the health centres did not seem so essential. From 1966 when the GPs' method of remuneration was altered to give allowances for premises, and more money was available for capital projects in local authorities, there was a renewal of interest in health centres: 2 were opened in 1965, 8 in 1966, and by 1977 17 per cent of all GPs were practising from 731 health centres, with 200 more in the pipeline. Since reorganisation the control of health centres has passed to health authorities with the DHSS earmarking money for their building.

Until 1976 when the NHS (Vocational Training) Act was passed any preparation for work as a GP was done on a voluntary basis, although government support for this was forthcoming from 1968.[102]

This early lack of interest in training for general practice reflected the profession's attitude to it, in spite of the declaration by the Cohen

Committee that 'the general practitioner must hold the key position in the Health Service'.[103] The Annis Gillie Report[104] suggested that his work had three aspects. He is the patient's first line of defence in times of illness—from birth to death. He acts as intermediary between hospital and patient, referring where necessary and arranging after-care. He can best mobilise and co-ordinate the health and welfare services in the interests of the individual in the community and of the community in relation to the individual. The committee recommended changes in the medical curriculum to give doctors awareness of the community as well as the individual, specific training for work in general practice, and opportunities for the general practitioner to maintain professional competence by part-time work in hospitals and continuing educational activities. They estimated that 90 per cent of all medical episodes were handled from start to finish by the GP.

The Todd Report[105] on medical education forecast great changes in the structure of general practice but said that there was 'a continuing need for a first-line preventive, diagnostic and therapeutic service which can deal in general terms with the total medical needs of the patient and when necessary guide him towards specialist services'. The developments since 1976 move towards general practice becoming a specialism in its own right, led by a vigorous Royal College of General Practitioners. The new regulations requiring future GPs to undertake a three-year post-graduate training programme will be operative from 1981.

In line with the plans for an integrated health service the GP is increasingly regarded as part of a primary health care team, working closely with community nurses (formerly district nurses, employed by local health authorities), health visitors (similarly employed) and, in some areas, social workers (employed by local authority personal social services departments). However, while the nursing services of the primary health care team can be costed for resources planning purposes GP services cannot. Patient demand and the autonomous professional response to it make detailed economic planning difficult. Rationing of health care at this level is not really possible. Furthermore it is a principle of the NHS that people should be able to choose their family doctor, which is another obstacle in the way of tidy administration. The element of choice for the patient is now somewhat curtailed by grouping of doctors and the use of deputising services, which can result in a patient rarely seeing the doctor of his choice.

General practitioners have also continued to certify incapacity for work, which started under the National Health Insurance legislation in 1911, and which may affect the way in which the doctor is regarded by some of his patients—more as a necessary contact in the procurement of payment than as the 'first line of defence in illness'. In emergency situations such as the 'flu epidemic or the withdrawal by the GPs of this service as a protest in 1970, certificates can be issued by local social security offices. The use of self-certification for all short periods of illness is advocated.

The general dental services

These services began with the severe handicap of too few dentists, which has persisted. Even today less than half the population can get regular dental care. The geographical distribution of dentists has been very unsatisfactory.

A study in 1967[106] found that there was a clear association between social class and the proportion of dentists in a population and a study of adult dental health in 1968[107] showed that the dental health of a population correlated with the ratio of dentists to that population. The Royal Commission in 1979 found the picture much the same.

Dentists have not been subject to the same restrictions as doctors in regard to the setting up of practice, but such restrictions would not be reasonable when even in the best-served areas the proportion of dentists remained below that enjoyed in other European countries.

The method of remuneration did not encourage the best in dental practice. The Tattersall Committee's Report[108] criticised the system, in which the Review Body on Doctors' and Dentists' Remuneration recommends an 'average' income for dentists; and the Dental Rates Study Group devised a scale of fees for items of service which would give the average dentist doing an average number of items of service this average income. If more than half the dentists worked faster than the 'average' last calculated they momentarily put up their individual salaries, but in due course a readjustment had to be made by lowering the scale of fees. The Tattersall Committee complained that this system put a premium on speed and took no account of quality.

In 1969 the principle of seniority payments to dentists was accepted, and those aged between 55 and 70 were allocated an extra £200 p.a. By 1977 the average income was £8,829 p.a. exclusive of practice expenses.

At the inception of the National Health Service the whole range of dental care including dentures was free, but from 1952 charges have been made except for certain categories, such as pregnant and nursing mothers and young people.

Preventive measures in dental health are desirable in view of the persistent shortfall in dentists and ancillary staff. These measures must largely be found in health education and water fluoridation.

The pharmaceutical services

The pharmaceutical services provide drugs under the National Health Service, and in 1948 everyone using the general practitioner service was entitled to free medicines. As the demand for drugs seemed excessive, and extra finance was required, a basic charge for each prescription was imposed in 1952. Pensioners and people on assistance could claim this back, but the system was cumbersome and many either did not claim the refund or did not have prescriptions made up. The prescriptions for that year dropped by 5 per cent. Since 1952 charges have been imposed and removed, and finally imposed again in 1968 on the basis of a payment for each item prescribed. A number of categories were exempted from the charges in an attempt to simplify procedures for needy patients.

The average cost of prescriptions has gone up from 15p in 1949 to 147p in 1977 and the number dispensed has risen from 200 million in 1949 to 296 million in 1977, costing £554 million.

Many pharmacists are independent shopkeepers, relying on their retail trade for a large part of their income. The Pharmaceutical Services Negotiating Committee, reporting to the Royal Commission, said that for some pharmacists NHS prescribing was unprofitable.

The distribution of pharmacists is not subject to any control, which has led to some difficulties, particularly in rural areas. The pharmacist is a useful source of advice and help in the community. His dispensing skills are less and less needed as pharmaceutical firms supply prepacked drugs, but his expertise should not be wasted.

The cost and the safety of drugs are matters of concern to the government. The Sainsbury Committee of Enquiry into the Pharmaceutical Industry reported in 1967 and suggested that the bill of the National Health Service for drugs had been inflated by excessive prices. The prices are now fixed by an agreement between the DHSS and the pharmaceutical industry. On the safety of drugs the Medicines Act, 1968, controls the marketing and trial of new drugs. New regulations in 1978 ensured that accurate and full information on drugs is contained in advertising directed at doctors and dentists.

The general ophthalmic service

Supplementing the hospital ophthalmic service are the ophthalmic medical practitioners, ophthalmic opticians (who may prescribe as well as dispense glasses) and dispensing opticians.

The status of the non-medical opticians has improved since the Opticians Act, 1958, set up a General Optical Council and required both ophthalmic and dispensing opticians to be registered. The council has the duty of supervising training and executing disciplinary functions.

The ophthalmic service is one of the few sections of the NHS where demand seems to be decreasing although costs continue to rise.

Community nurses

Local health authorities were the pioneers in community nursing, health visiting and domiciliary midwifery services, but since 1974 these have been managed by health authorities. Some of the previous duplication of work and inflexibility is reduced by having all nurses, whether hospital-based or in the community, under one administration, where they are grouped into health care groups each under a Divisional Nursing Officer. Midwifery services in hospital and at home are now joined together, which suits the modern situation of fewer births and a high level of hospital confinements with a very short in-patient period. Psychiatric nursing is similarly able to meet new treatment objectives by a flexible hospital/community nursing service.

Nurses have been quick to grasp the importance of clear administrative structures and training for management. The recommendations of the Salmon and Mayston Committees[109] on senior structures were largely implemented.

The pace of modern medicine and the tremendous surge in medical science and technology has made great changes in the nurse's role, although as the Royal College of Nursing in its evidence to the Royal Commission said, 'Nursing is basically a simple craft'. It is difficult therefore to ensure that the 'simple craft' that is at the heart of nursing is not crowded out by the new demands. The Briggs Committee[110] which examined the role, training and deployment of nurses saw the caring role of the nurse as a basis for training of all entrants. At present different programmes are arranged for the State Registered Nurse who has a three-year studentship, and the State Enrolled Nurse who takes a shorter, more practical course. As with the GPs there are now proposals to make post-registration training mandatory on all those who want to become district, or community, nurses. Health visitors have had such compulsory training for many years.

Domiciliary nurses work in primary care terms, doing bedside nursing and carrying out treatment in the home. With the new emphasis on community care the demands on this service will increase.

Health visitors are also nurses, working in primary care, but their main task is, as before, educational and advisory. They have been involved in community health for a century, but with a gradually changing function. The health education role has remained constant but the areas of ignorance that they deal with have changed. In 1909 they were concerned with infectious illness as well as maternal guidance, which centred to a large extent on teaching mothers how to prevent infectious disease in their babies and homes, and they supervised patients discharged from public hospitals. With improvements in public hygiene they became more closely identified with the maternity and child welfare services, giving advice on child-rearing. Increasing affluence and the universality of the National Health Service brought a need for a new community role for the 6,000 trained women in the field. Examination of this role by the Jameson Committee,[111] reporting in 1956, presented difficulties of definition. The health visitor's role was described as health educator and social adviser but it was not easy to limit these functions. The report suggested that 'she must take account of the unit—the family—of which the individual forms a part, and not only of physical but psychological and social factors'—an immense task. While mothers still need advice on the physical care of their children, there is no longer a clear distinction between physical and mental hygiene and advice on developmental problems is increasingly needed.

Work with old people has increased. Each year more than half a million elderly people are in touch with health visitors.

The Younghusband Report of 1959[112] recommended close links between the training of health visitors and the new two-year courses for social workers in health and welfare. The Health Visiting and Social Work (Training) Act 1962 established two training councils linked by a common chairman. The Seebohm Report of 1968, however, recommended that all social work training should be under one central body and distinct from health visitor training. Under the Local Authority Social Service Act 1970 separate establishments were set up. The Seebohm Committee was strongly opposed to the notion that health visitors 'might further become all-purpose social workers for general practice'.[113] In effect there is considerable overlap in the roles and the more that social and psychological factors affect health the more difficult it is to define them. Some of the problems of definition may be solved by the increasing practice of attaching social workers to the Primary Care Team.

Complaints machinery

Complaints machinery has been discussed in each document concerning reorganisation. The Porritt Committee saw no reason to change the systems already in practice and assumed that the small number of complaints against doctors indicated the public's satisfaction with the service. The alternative explanation is that the machinery, heavily weighted in favour of the doctor, is difficult to work and requires great persistence on the part of the complainant.[114] Doctors must be protected from irrational or malicious attacks, and sickness and death can arouse strong emotions of guilt and hostility. Complaints against GPs are channelled through the FPCs and are only concerned with breaches of contract not with the quality of professional practice. In the hospital service complaints have been dealt with 'almost entirely internally'[115] but with no further or more impartial appeal except to courts of law where appropriate. Statutory enquiries occasionally look into serious complaints.

The pressing need for some other body led to the appointment of a Health Service Commissioner (who was also the Parliamentary Commissioner for Administration) in 1973—Section 11 of the Reorganisation Act deals at some length with his office and duties—and a committee[116] was set up in 1971 to advise on hospital complaints proceedures and suggest a code of practice. However because of professional anxieties it has taken ten years for a national scheme to emerge for the hospitals. Complainants will have in future an internal hearing which will endeavour to make clear what occurred and where possible prevent any similar occurrence in the future.

Private practice

Private beds were always available in NHS hospitals, although the number has declined since 1949, and the take-up has been little more than 50 per cent. In 1977 there were less than 3,000 beds compared with more than 300,000 NHS beds.

Consultants could work part-time for the NHS and could admit their private patients, who paid for treatment and maintenance in the hospital.

The advantages and disadvantages of a private sector in the National Health Service have been debated almost continuously since the service was in embryo and refer particularly to the hospital service. On one side there is a belief that the consumer should be allowed choice. D. S. Lees suggests that 'medical care is a personal consumption good, not markedly different from the generality of goods bought by consumers'. It is also argued that a private sector brings in much-needed resources, to the ultimate benefit of all users. Certainly consultants can supplement their incomes at no extra expense to the taxpayers. On the other side Titmuss and other contributors to the Fabian literature believed that a two-class service would operate. The redistributive effect might be horizontal rather than vertical and there might even be a loss of resources from the free sector to the paying sector. In a comprehensive service, used by almost all the population, the standards of care would be of concern to all.[117]

In 1975 the government announced that paybeds would be phased out. Legislation was introduced in 1976 which set up the Health Services Board to effect this and to monitor developments in the private sector.

Opposition to the proposals led to the unusual situation of consultants taking industrial action, but agreement was reached before the legislation was effective. Equally militant were the two unions representing ancillary workers and including nurses, NUPE and COHSE, which were opposed to private practice and argue that their members who participate in the care of private patients as part of their NHS contract have a right to have their views heard.[118] The most profound complaint is that scarce resources are not being fairly distributed and private patients use public resources out of turn.[119] The new Health Services Board has proposed that there should be common waiting lists for NHS and private patients,[120] until such time as the proposed separation of the public and private sectors came into effect.

The Conservative government reversed this process in the 1980 Act by abolishing the Health Services Board and halting the phasing out of private beds in NHS hospitals. The principle of fair shares was retained, however, with common waiting lists being used for the seriously ill and for specialised diagnostic services and treatment.

The government called for a 'partnership' between the public and private sectors arguing that many people use both, and that private money will swell the NHS coffers.[121] However of the total spent on health care only about 3 per cent is within the private sector and this includes long-term nursing home care, by far the largest part of private provision. Partnership could also include contractual use of private facilities by the NHS, perhaps to reduce long waiting lists, or to use equipment which because of shortage of capital is not available in the local NHS hospital.

Privacy is valued by some people, but can be purchased in many hospitals for a relatively small sum. Modern hospitals are now designed to avoid the noisy, large wards which may be the main cause of complaint.[122] It is not however possible to book an amenity bed nor to ensure admission at a convenient time. For these two reasons people, encouraged by their employers, may choose to join a private insurance scheme. These schemes, through which most of the private care is financed, have increased both their membership, from about 50,000 in 1949 to over 1 million in 1978,[123] and the provision of private hospitals and nursing homes. Group membership has shown a particular increase, accounting for more than 80 per cent of subscribers, while individual membership has fallen off.

Private practice continued in the family practitioner setting, but, unlike the hospital service, it does not seem to the patient to be an attractive alternative. The British Medical Association in the period of grave dissatisfaction with the National Health Service in 1965 planned a private insurance scheme which included an annual payment, plus item of service payments. The scheme lasted only three years, getting limited support from practitioners and little from patients. Other private schemes have made little impact on the main body of users.

Private institutions are still the concern of the DHSS. They must register with health authorities[124] and are inspected and approved by them. The Royal Commission reported that 75 per cent of the private institutions performing surgery were run by religious orders or charitable bodies, while many of the medical beds provided are used by the elderly, chronic sick and convalescent.

The Royal Commission was of the opinion that the private sector was 'too small to make significant impact on the NHS'. Nevertheless they felt that if people were using the private sector in order to meet some 'reasonable requirement' about timing or privacy the NHS should make more effort to accommodate them.

The possibility that deficiencies in the NHS will lead to an increased development of medical care services as a profit-making activity with good potential for investment could be a matter for concern. The potential for exploitation is considerable, for which the government must take ultimate responsibility.[125]

Staffing and management

The NHS is the largest employer in the country. Of its 1 million workers doctors make up less than 7 per cent, while nearly 50 per cent are nurses. The management and administration of such an organisation is obviously a major task and 12 per cent of the employees are thus engaged. New attitudes to conflicts and disputes are emerging, with increased militancy in all groups of employees. COHSE has been in existence for 70 years but has only recently become a name familiar to all because of its conflicts with the DHSS on behalf of its 200,000 members. Junior hospital doctors and consultants have been engaged in industrial action either in the furtherance of their claims for better pay and conditions, or the promotion of their views on organisation and policy matters. At the same time democracy has been extended in the management structures since 1974. It has also found its way into the General Medical Council, which, founded in 1858, has supervised training requirements, kept a register of qualified practitioners, and been the 'regulator' of the medical profession. Following the recommendations of the Merrison

Committee[126] the GMC is to be composed of elected as well as appointed members and will have wider powers over medical training. Part of its new duties will be the registration of doctors from the EEC, as free movement of doctors between member countries is now permitted.

'Everybody's business'

'The time has come for a re-appraisal of the possibilities inherent in prevention.'[127]

Prevention of illness, care and after-care was a broadly based power given to the local authorities under the 1946 Act and continued in the 1977 Act. These powers and duties include residential and day care, aids and equipment and home help and laundry services for the sick, convalescent and handicapped; and a comprehensive mental welfare service. All of these services are focused on people already in touch with health services and clearly joint planning with the NHS is economically and socially desirable. But these services can be regarded as more ameliorative than preventive. The recognition that some of the demands on the NHS can be reduced by changes in personal behaviour is timely in the present economic climate. The comparison between the sums spent on curative services and on preventative services prompted the publication in 1976 of a Consultative Document, *Prevention and Health: Everybody's Business*, followed by a White Paper *Prevention and Health* in 1977. Three main areas where action is required are outlined. The first is in the amelioration of the processes of ageing; the second is in promoting healthier personal habits, in particular with regard to over-indulgence in food, drink and tobacco, coupled with under-indulgence in exercise; the third is in regard to environmental hazards. Campaigns to improve personal performance have been promoted, but the action planned as outlined in the White Paper is limited by lack of resources.

Issues of life and death

This chapter has so far been concerned with the control of death; in considering the control of life through family planning, abortion and euthanasia we come to more controversial issues.

Population policy—family planning and abortion

It has always been difficult for the state to influence patterns of fertility. While a woman may feel that the decision about her family size is a matter for herself and her spouse, the total community is obviously concerned about the size and 'shape' of the population. Since the late eighteenth century we have swung between fears of over-population and under-population.[128]

When family planning was discussed by the Committee on Abortion[129] in 1939 the population appeared to be still in danger of decline, consequently the committee recommended that birth control advice should be restricted to those women whose health was at risk. In a minority report one of the commissioners, Mrs Thurtle, said that as the wealthy could buy contraceptives the decision by the majority discriminated against and penalised the poor, who had 'visited upon them the shortcomings of their upper- and middle-class sisters'.

Before 1939 local authorities were empowered to give advice to married women who were medically at risk, but few did.[130] The major work was undertaken by the Family Planning Association (a voluntary organisation that aimed to be a pressure group but found that it had to do the work as well).

Since the 1960s anxiety has again swung to fears of over-population, which, coupled with increasing concern for the quality of life of children, has led to a very different view of contraception and abortion. The 1967 National Health Service (Family Planning) Act enabled local authorities to give advice to all women regardless of medical need or marital status. Statutory provisions for family planning were directed at women until 1972 when local authorities were allowed to do vasectomies without charge as part of their service.

On the recommendation of the Select Committee on Science and Technology in 1971 a Population Panel was set up. In its first report, 1973,[131] it recommended that a comprehensive family planning service should be an integral part of the NHS.

The question of payment for family planning was debated throughout the passage of the National Health Service Reorganisation Bill. Early proposals had not escaped from the thinking of the 1930s, in that medical need was considered to be the main criterion for free advice and supplies, whereas much evidence pointed to the importance of meeting social needs. This was emphasised when the Lords, led in 'revolt' by Baroness Llewellyn Davies, demanded free family planning for all. The Conservative government eventually arranged for a family planning service available for all under the National Health Service with supplies on prescription. From July 1975 all family planning services were free. One difficulty to be dealt with was the problem of payment to GPs. Family planning advice other than on medical grounds did not fall within the terms of the GP's contract, and new arrangements had to be negotiated. By 1977 95 per cent of all GPs were participating in the service.

In 1975 the population was stationary, by 1976 a slight fall was reported, attributed to the continuing decline in the number of births and a rise in the number of deaths following the 'flu epidemic. In 1977 the birth rate reached its lowest level, 11.6 per 1,000, but the death rate also fell to 11.6 per 1,000, and the continuing slight decline in the population related to an excess of emigration over immigration.

The great availability of contraceptives, and in particular the pill, which is extremely reliable, may have led to the increase in the incidence of gonorrhoea occurring throughout the 1960s. In 1972 there was a slight decline in the number of new cases, which has persisted. There is, however, a threat of the spread of penicillin-resistant strains of gonococci. Only close monitoring by Public Health Services can prevent them becoming widespread.

Abortion describes the termination of a pregnancy up to twenty-eight weeks (sometimes it is used for termination in the first sixteen weeks, later termination being called miscarriage). It is a very significant factor in all industrial societies. Comparative figures are misleading as societies where abortion is legal will produce fairly accurate information, while in other countries this will be concealed.

From 1803 in this country abortion was a secular crime, but the Infant Life Protection Act, 1929, carried a therapeutic clause in that an abortion carried out in 'good faith' to save the life of the mother was not illegal. This led to confusion of interpretation and there was no case law until 1938 when a gynaecologist, Mr Bourne, notified the police of his intention to terminate the pregnancy of a fourteen-year-old victim of rape.

The committee set up in 1937 to enquire into the prevalence of abortion found that the law relating to abortion was being flouted by all classes of women.[132] They did not recommend any extension of grounds for legal abortion and suggested only a hesitant and limited extension of family planning. Mrs Thurtle in her minority report said that 'it is not possible to enforce a law affecting a large class of persons—in this case the women of the country—unless the law has the sanction of that class'.

After the Bourne case in 1938 the legal grounds for abortion were extended from threat to the life of the mother to threat to her physical and mental health. No provisions were made regarding the physical or mental state of the unborn child, nor the social situation of the family. At its conference on abortion in 1966 the Family Planning Association made a strong plea for the law to be clarified, which was done in the National Health Service (Abortion) Act, 1967. Abortion is permissible if it is to protect the life, or physical or mental health, of the women. On 'social' grounds a woman's pregnancy can be terminated if it presents a risk to the physical or mental health of her existing children. It is also permissible if the unborn child is considered at risk. Two doctors have to agree to the abortion and by an amending Act in 1970 one of them is required to be the doctor who performs or supervises the abortion.

Abortions can be performed only in National Health Service hospitals or places approved by the Department of Health. At the end of 1977 there were sixty approved nursing homes. Several of these nursing homes were run in conjunction with, or were used by, pregnancy advice bureaux. In 1977 a register of approved advice bureaux was started and nursing homes were prohibited from accepting patients from fee-charging bureaux unless they were approved. In the first year thirty-three were registered.

Anxiety about the way the Abortion Act was being implemented led to the setting up of a committee in 1971, under the chairmanship of Mrs Justice Lane, to review the working of the Act, but not the principle underlying it. In their balanced and sensible report of 1974,[133] the Committee were 'unanimous in supporting the act, and its provisions' and thought that the gains outweighed any disadvantages.

Abortion legislation is still under attack from two sides. The woman's 'right to choose' is put forward as an argument for abortion on demand without the present legal constraints; on the other side persistent attempts are made to impose greater constraints through amending legislation.

Euthanasia and decisions about death

Euthanasia, like abortion, is a topic that generates heat. The thought of continuing into extremely ripe old age holds terror for some. Fears of being maintained in life, to be a burden on others and incapacitated oneself, have led to demands for some policy on euthanasia. Several private member's Bills have been presented to Parliament, albeit with little hope of success. In 1975 the Incurable Patients' Bill was presented by Baroness Wootton, which proposed that incurable patients should be able to refuse life-prolonging procedures, and be entitled to 'full relief of pain'; that there should be no duty on anyone to interfere with such a patient's actions to relieve pain even if this led to loss of life; and that people should be able to file a declaration about not receiving treatment in the event of them becoming mentally incapable of making their wishes known if they became incurably ill. These proposals, although sympathetically received, still cause considerable anxiety about the desirability of venturing into such difficult territory. Discussion during a Lords debate on the National Health Service Reorganisation Bill revealed some of the public disquiet and the desire for death with dignity. It has been argued that better care of the dying would reduce demands for euthanasia. In his foreword to the 'Care of the Dying' Symposium Report in 1973,[134] Sir George Godber, then Chief Medical Officer to the DHSS, pointed out that the health services, in particular hospitals and their staff, were orientated towards cure, and that care of the dying was not approached either in training or in practice in an orderly and open way. More than half of all deaths take place in hospital now, and over two-thirds are elderly. Those who die at home often have a need for support and services through a terminal illness. Cartwright's study[135] reveals some of the deficiencies, in particular the lack of collaboration between hospital and community services.

Developments in medicine open prospects of care undreamed of a few years ago, such as kidney machines and 'spare-part' surgery. The cost of these treatments is infinitely greater than anything previously undertaken, and decisions have to be made about priorities and expenditure. The CMO reported in 1977 that less than half the need for treatment for renal failure was being met. Particularly worrying was the fact that out of 80–100 new child patients in need of treatment only 35 were being dealt with. As consumers come to perceive their needs so the demand for treatment increases. People will be less willing to accept discomforts and distress that were once considered an unavoidable and natural part of life. Decisions about life and death are being presented to doctors and patients in a way that was unknown a generation ago.

Conclusion

Towards the end of 1973 Sir George Godber, the Chief Medical Officer of the DHSS, retired after many years in the health service. In his last Annual Report, 1972, he wrote of the advances and achievements of the National Health Service over twenty-five years, and stated 'in time of need for myself or my family I would now rather take my chance at random in the British National Health Service than in any other service I know'; but in the turbulent years following 1972 new realities of limited resources, increasing staff militancy and problems of managing so vast an enterprise have led to concern over lowering of morale and to predictions of disaster. However, throughout the history of health care periods of rapid change always seem to produce their Jonahs, while the process of evolution goes on nevertheless, with adaptation to the changing and complex social and scientific framework within which the phenomena of sickness and health are understood.

Further reading

A great deal of literature is now available on health services. It is a vast topic with many facets. Life and health have value in economic and ethical terms;

the management of health care and the quality of resources and health professionals are of interest to most people at some time. A short reading list will inevitably miss out excellent papers and books.
DHSS publications include:

The Annual Report of the DHSS. Now discontinued.
The annual report of the Chief Medical Officer, *On the State of the Public Health*. (This has a useful reference section at the end of each chapter.)
The Annual Report of the Health Advisory Service.
Health Trends.
Current Literature on Health Services (a monthly abstract series).
Hospital Abstracts.

There are government publications on many special topics, e.g.:

The Committee of Enquiry into the Cost of the NHS (Guillebaud Report), Cmd 9663, HMSO, 1956.
Royal Commission on Medical Education (Todd Report), Cmnd 3569, HMSO, 1968.
Committee on the Working of the Abortion Act (Lane Report), Cmnd 5579, HMSO, 1974.
Fit for the Future – Report of the Committee on the Child Health Service (Court Report) Cmnd 6684, HMSO, 1976.
Royal Commission on the NHS (Merrison Report) Cmnd 7615, HMSO, 1979.

Other publications

The office of Health Economics—founded in 1962 by the Association of the British Pharmaceutical Industry—publishes pamphlets on a variety of topics.

On the development of the health services useful books are:

BMA, *Health Service Financing*, 1970. This has a long historical introduction.
BRIAN ABEL-SMITH, *The Hospitals 1800–1948*, Heinemann, 1964.
BRIAN ABEL-SMITH, *National Health Service. The First Thirty Years*, HMSO, 1978.
W. M. FRAZER, *A History of English Public Health 1934–1939*, Bailliere, Tindall & Cox, 1950.
RUTH HODGKINSON, *Origins of the National Health Service*, Wellcome Medical History Library, 1967. A history of the Poor Law Medical Services between 1834 and 1871.
KATHLEEN JONES, *A History of the Mental Health Services*, Routledge & Kegan Paul. 1972.

Studies of the National Health Service include:

BRIAN ABEL-SMITH, *Value for Money in Health Services*, Heinemann, 1976.

R. G. S. BROWN, *The Changing National Health Service*, Routledge & Kegan Paul, 1973.

H. ECKSTEIN, *The English Health Services*, Harvard University Press, 1958 (an analytical study of origins and achievements).

ELLIOT JAQUES (ed.), *Health Services*, Brunel Health Services Organisation Research Unit, 1978.

RUTH LEVITT, *The Reorganised Health Service*, Croom Helm, 1978.

A. MCLACHLAN (ed.), *Problems and Progress in Medical Care (there are several publications in this series by the Nuffield Provincial Hospitals Trust)*.

ROSEMARY STEVENS, *Medical Practice in Modern England: The Impact of Specialisation and State Medicine*, Yale University Press, 1966 (an account of the development of both medical practice and the National Health Service).

ARTHUR WILLCOCKS, *The Creation of the National Health Service*, Routledge & Kegan Paul, 1967.

7 The personal social services

Eileen Holgate and *Olive Keidan*

The development of services for people unable to meet all or some of their needs within the confines of their own family and intimate social setting has been haphazard, veering between anxiety about the consequences to society as a whole of aiding its dependent members, and thereby encouraging dependency in others, and the compassion aroused by contact with people who led wretched and impoverished lives. Protection of the weak from exploitation of many kinds, such as child labour, confinement of unwanted relatives in mad-houses, and baby-farming, has had to reconcile fears about the consequences of interfering with individual liberty with the need to help the helpless. The growth of personal social services has centred on certain groups which have been identified at different times as having special needs—such as orphans, juvenile delinquents (a different category altogether rather than a facet of the whole group of children in need!), the frail elderly, the mentally disordered, the physically handicapped, addicts, immigrants, the homeless—and on the gradual emergence of social work as a profession.

Both statutory and voluntary agencies have made contributions to the development of social work services. In the statutory services emphasis initially and inevitably lay in administering the law and fulfilling the duties and obligations laid on the local bodies. Nineteenth-century developments tended to be dominated on the one hand by thoughts of poverty, destitution and the Poor Law, and on the other hand by the growing individualisation of services and the positive approach found in public health. The Education Act of 1870 signalled a comparable involvement by the local boards of education with many families, while the century-long pursuit of protection of and care for the mentally disordered, whether rich or poor, had a similar impact on central government and local authority provision.

The services for those who were the concern of the Poor Law

authorities covered all their needs albeit at a low level of provision. Health care, education, shelter were all provided by one statutory authority, with Relieving Officers acting as 'fieldworkers' and co-ordinators. The development of separate and specialist provision for some groups of clients enlarged the scope of local authority services, and required some specialisation by the staff involved. Preparation for work in local authorities was primarily concerned with the orientation of the staff towards their role as paid servants of the corporation or board, and acquiring a knowledge of the law to be administered.[1]

It was in the voluntary agencies that the processes of casework and group work were identified and training for social work as we know it today began. Courses giving a theoretical background to the fieldwork training of the volunteers who comprised the bulk of the workforce were started by agencies such as settlements and the Charity Organisation Society. From these early beginnings grew the first university departments concerned with social work training in Liverpool and London.[2]

A wide range of voluntary agencies grew up alongside the statutory services.[3] Many of their activities prompted a fundamental review of statutory responsibility, followed by changes in provision. There was, for example, a slow development in the safeguarding of children in their own families from the founding of the National Society for the Prevention of Cruelty to Children (NSPCC) in 1889 to the Department of Health and Social Security (DHSS) Memorandum on the management of non-accidental injury to children in 1974. A recent similar development can be seen in the growing recognition by a few voluntary agencies of 'battered wives' as a group for which special provison should be made rather than as individuals suffering a personal misfortune. The process of interaction and reciprocal involvement seems to have speeded up. The first shelter for 'battered wives' was only opened in 1971.[4]

The relationship between voluntary and statutory services and their respective roles was debated throughout the latter part of the nineteenth century. The Charity Organisation Society attempted to make a rational allocation of functions between voluntary and statutory agencies, the former to work with the remediable cases, while the Poor Law dealt with residual problems. There was considerable resistance among voluntary societies to any extension of statutory provision beyond a bare minimum, but pressure was growing for the state to play a more positive role in welfare. The debate culminated in the division of opinion found among the members of the Poor Law Commission of 1905.[5] The First World War and following Depression damped down some of the passion that had characterised discussion, while the gradual extension of positive statutory provisions in income, health, education and employment services removed some of the basis for argument, and pointed the way to the Welfare State.

The statutory services

In 1948 the local authorities shed their duties as destitution authorities and looked forward to what the Minister of Health in his Annual Report for 1949 referred to as the 'promotion of welfare for all regardless of means'. It has not proved easy to shake off the association of statutory care with poverty; there is still a tendency to think of poverty as the core problem and to assume that people without financial worries are people without problems.

In the 1948 reorganisation local welfare authorities had duties and powers under the National Assistance Act to provide domiciliary and residential care for the physically handicapped, the elderly and the homeless. Apart from those staff concerned with the blind there were few trained workers available, and very little interest in training.[6] Much of this work was already being undertaken by voluntary agencies who continued to operate alongside the statutory services.

Under the National Health Service Act the local health authorities became responsible among other things for the community care of the mentally disordered. Relieving Officers and welfare workers from the voluntary agency concerned with mental deficiency, the Central Association for Mental Welfare, constituted the bulk of the fieldwork staff. Some preparation for the new work, albeit small, was given through the National Association for Mental Health.

The local authority education departments continued their care of children at risk educationally and emotionally through school health services and child-guidance clinics. The School Welfare Officers evolved from the School Attendance Officers, who were employed by the School Boards to try to ensure that the law regarding compulsory education was being observed. The Home Office had responsibility for the new local authority children's departments set up under the Children Act, 1948, to provide a service for children deprived of normal home life.

Medical and psychiatric social workers were employed by the new Regional Hospital Boards (RHBs). Although there were well established professional social work courses there were far too few trained workers in 1948 to meet demand.

The probation service, providing the trained social workers to serve the local courts, continued under the auspices of the Home Office.

The Home Office has been more vigorous than the Ministry of Health in promoting social work training. The Probation Training

Board was set up in the 1930s while courses to train social workers for the new child care service were established before the inception of the service, in 1947. It was not until the Younghusband Working Party reported in 1959[7] that social work training for the local authority health and welfare services was fully considered, and even then the training for residential workers remained sketchy.

In 1948 the central government departments concerned with personal social services were the Ministry of Health, which had oversight of the local authority health and welfare services, and of the hospital and specialist services, the Home Office, which had similar responsibility for the local authority children's departments and the probation service, and the Department of Education, which was responsible for the education services, including school health and welfare.

The problems that such divided responsibility can bring were recognised after 1948. Joint circulars from central government departments to the local authorities in the 1950s urged co-operation in order to deal more effectively with families whose needs lay across organisational boundaries. The movement towards consolidation of the personal social services grew from the realisation that the fragmentation that was inherent in the services could be avoided by focusing on the family rather than on 'needy' categories.

The first move towards a comprehensive family service came in 1960 when the Ingleby Committee,[8] concerned with child neglect and delinquency, concluded that the long-term solution would lie in reorganisation of the various services concerned with the family, and their combination into a unified family service. In 1965, in the White Paper *The Child, the Family and the Young Offender*, it was announced that the government intended to form a small committee to review the organisation of the local authority personal social services in England and Wales. This committee (Seebohm) was asked to consider what changes were desirable in order to secure an effective family service. On discussing its brief the committee decided to extend the definition of the family: 'We could only make sense of our task by considering also childless couples and individuals without any close relatives: in other words, everybody.'[9] The report was published in 1968 and came through as an authoritative, sobering document. A case for an organisational change was built on a close analysis of the state of affairs both inside and outside the local authorities. Lack of resources, including trained social workers, inadequate knowledge about the nature of the problems a service was intended to combat, and divided responsibility resulting from organisational fragmentation, led to inadequacies and could lead to muddled situations.[10] A strong case for a radical reorganisation had certainly been made.

The committee proposed that each local authority should have a statutory duty to set up a unified Social Services Department providing social work and ancillary services, with its own principal officer, preferably a social worker, serving a separate Social Services Committee. At central government level there should similarly be one department responsible both for the relationship between central government and the new departments and for the overall national planning of the personal social services, together with the intelligence and research services, which were badly needed. On the question of training for social work the Committee recommended that the divisions and specialisms that had characterised training should end and that the three existing bodies concerned with training should be amalgamated.[11] Although the brief had specifically excluded consideration of the probation service and the voluntary sector the committee found considerable agreement on the need to integrate all social work training including that for probation officers.

Because the very size of the new department might mean a monolithic structure, cumbersome and slow to respond to needs, and because it was vital that social work should communicate itself swiftly and smoothly to people, it was suggested in the report that most of the fieldwork should be undertaken by teams of about twelve professional staff responsible for areas of 50,000–100,000 population. In order to counter the accusation that people had experienced difficulty in understanding the personal social services and that the services had failed to reach them, the Committee laid emphasis on the need for the services to be community-based. Participation in the planning, organisation and provision of the services was the essence of a community-based social service and there was a new opportunity for voluntary organisations to make their contribution and for local authorities to mobilise these organisations, encouraging them with professional help and financial grants.[12]

The Seebohm Report was well received in social work circles although in local authority circles generally there was some opposition to the proposal of the Committee to impose one set pattern of departmental organisation. In Parliament the report was given a good reception, both Lords and Commons showing near unanimity in accepting the reasoning of the Committee for reorganisational change and the pattern for the future. The committee had urged swift implementation of the proposals, but the government was awaiting the results of other committees of enquiry whose findings and recommendations would affect plans for reorganising the personal social services. In the end, however, with a General Election pending, the Local Authority Social Services Bill implementing the report was hurried through its final stages and became law on 29 May 1970, the reorganised service being scheduled to start operating from 1 April 1971.

The Act itself was quite a brief one since not all the Seebohm proposals needed legislation for their implementation.[13] It required local authorities to set up a Social Services Committee and to appoint a Director of Social Services together with adequate staff. The functions of the committee were to consist of those which up to that time had been performed by the Welfare and Children's Committees plus some from the Health Committee. Support for the latter had come, since Seebohm had reported, from the second Green Paper on the reorganisation of the National Health Service,[14] in which it had been recommended that all social work should be undertaken by the new local authority Social Services Department.

Initially it was not made clear which central department would have 'overlord' responsibility. This doubt was later resolved when it emerged that child care responsibilities, hitherto belonging to the Home Secretary, would in future lie with the Secretary of State for Social Services, who was already responsible for health and welfare matters, but that the Secretary of State for Wales would have responsibility at central level for personal social services in Wales. The Home Secretary would, however, retain, for both England and Wales, his existing responsibilities relating to juvenile courts[15] because of his overriding responsibility for protecting the public and ensuring the rights and liberties of the individual.

Within the Department of Health and Social Security, a new division, the Local Authority Social Services Division, headed by a Deputy Secretary, was set up to undertake the new functions of the Secretary of State for Social Services. A Social Work Division of that Department with regional offices was established. Interestingly, in a service becoming generic, specialist interests were retained at regional level with concern for particular consumer groups.

A Personal Social Services Council as recommended by Seebohm[16] was set up in 1973 as an independent, non-statutory body, to advise the Secretary of State on policy issues and to promote development of the personal social services both statutory and voluntary, but in the bleak economic situation of 1979 the PSSC was one of the casualties, ceasing to exist in 1980.

With regard to training, the Seebohm recommendation that there should be one central body was implemented by the formation in 1971 of the Central Council for Education and Training in Social Work, an independent body with statutory authority to promote education and training in all fields of social work and to award qualifications. It succeeded the two previous training councils in the fields of health and welfare and the care of children and the training committee of the Advisory Council for Probation and After-care.[17] This generic approach to social work has had its critics, most notably in the field of mental health. The 1978 Review of the Mental Health

Act discusses the role of the mental welfare officer and comments on the 'widespread concern at the lack of specialist knowledge' on the part of the social workers who perform statutory duties, and expresses the hope that some degree of specialism will return.

At local level Social Service Departments, under Directors of Social Services, were established on 1 April 1971, to be responsible for the previously separate services for children—the physically disabled, the elderly, and the mentally ill. A range of other services were included,[18] all adding up to the basis of a comprehensive service to the family in the community. Although in Scotland the probation service became an integral part of the Social Work Departments following the Social Work (Scotland) Act, 1969, it was not included in the reorganisation in England and Wales. The dilemma facing education welfare officers as to whether to remain within the education service or to transfer to social services remained, and still remains, unresolved. Hospital social workers remained in the Health Service and were only transferred with much reluctance in April 1974.

Change inevitably poses a threat and brings anxiety. It was, therefore, with very mixed feelings that social workers from separate departments merged with each other and set about establishing a generic service. Whereas, particularly in children's departments, the social workers had constituted a high proportion of the personnel, they were joined by home helps, occupational therapists and an increasing number of other groups, which effectively highlighted the minority status of the social worker in the new departments (see Chart 1).[19]

Before any real consolidation could take place there was a further upheaval occasioned by the reorganisation of local authority boundaries on 1 April 1974. In the two-tier system of county and district levels, Social Services Departments in metropolitan county areas were placed at district level but otherwise remained at county level. Some local authorities were untouched by the change, others not only became part of larger areas but changed counties as well.

April 1974 also heralded the restructuring of the National Health Service. This latter change affected Social Services Departments by adding the statutory responsibility for providing social work support for the health service and a statutory responsibility to co-operate through joint consultative committees.[20] This partnership by statute aimed to change the balance of care between hospital and home, recognising that many people in hospital do not require skilled medical and nursing care, and would benefit considerably from living in the community. Pressure on health authorities and local authorities to plan together has increased, not least because of the irrefutable evidence that in all the social services 'demand will always outstrip capacity' and therefore priorities must be established, with effective planning.

In 1976 a consultative document, *Priorities for Health and Personal Services in England*, 'embodying a new major approach to planning', laid down the government's overall strategy for developing community-based services, with emphasis on particular client groups—the elderly, the handicapped and mentally disordered—and on services for children and their families. One year later *The Way Forward* continued the debate started in *Priorities*, outlining new procedures through which each local authority would make known annually to the DHSS its plans for social services developments in the next five years. The local authorities were critical of the failure to recognise 'the corporate element of local authority planning which covered a range of other services',[21] and of what appeared to be a health service orientation. The relatively favourable treatment of health services in the economic crisis seemed to reinforce this, but the plans were defended by the Minister of State in his evidence to the House of Commons Social Services Committee on the grounds that there is no alternative to the NHS whereas the personal social services provide only a small proportion of community care and the shortfall can be made up by voluntary, community and family care.

In 1976 a combined health and local authority circular introduced the joint planning of complementary health and local authority services, establishing the principle of joint funding whereby AHAs would have discretionary use of funds for social service projects dealing with priority groups, and allowing for NHS land and buildings to be used for Local Authority Social Service Departments (LASSD) purposes. The Hospital Advisory Service[22] was also changed in line with the new policies. Not only was the name changed to Health Advisory Service to signify the extension of its remit to community health services, but also the Social Work Service of the DHSS was drawn in to allow for a comprehensive review of services in any geographical area for a particular client group.

In the following year another circular strengthened the position of the Joint Consultative Committees set up under the NHS Reorganisation Act, 1973, by requiring them to set up Joint Care Planning Teams, composed of working officers from both services and others with specialist knowledge.

At central government level the two advisory bodies in health and personal social services[23] came together to consider co-ordination of their respective services. They established a joint committee to advise on services concerned with children and their families as had been recommended in the Court Report on Child Health Services.[24] A joint working party on collaboration reported in 1978 on the delivery of services at field level[25] and emphasised the importance of meeting client need rather than administrative convenience.

Although the Conservative government axed both these advisory bodies and imposed severe economic restrictions on local authorities the broad policy objectives still aim at joint planning and collaboration. These are outlined in *Care in Action*[26] which is primarily addressed to the members of the new District Health Authorities. Among other matters it brings forward for consideration the possibility of increasing co-operation with the private sector. While local authorities do make use of private facilities for their clients, usually the elderly, this latest document suggests that more could be done with other client groups.

However it should be remembered that the long-term objectives of a Social Services Department, according to Seebohm, should involve more than work with groups of clients and should provide a 'community-based and family-oriented service available to all, reaching beyond the discovery and rescue of social casualties and enabling the greatest possible number of individuals to act reciprocally, giving and receiving service for the well-being of the whole community'.[27] A worthy objective indeed.

Work of the Social Services Department

In order to see the range of responsibilities and to begin to appreciate the scale of work undertaken by the Social Services Department it is necessary to select some aspects for detailed study. A starting point for a family-oriented service seems to lead naturally to a focus on children for whom the family remains today, despite doubts expressed from time to time about its functional usefulness, an important social institution.

Children and families

The family today pays considerable regard to its child-rearing functions. Improved standards of living and the development of educational, health, social security and other social services have brought considerable refinement and changes to family life. Parents, however, still provide not only for their children's nurture but for the first few years of life act as the chief socialising agents, thereby greatly influencing the pattern of their lives. As was noted in the Court Report, *Fit for the Future*, 1976, 'the circumstances of birth and early life cast long shadows forward'. Currently the basic model is perhaps less likely to follow the typical family of mother, father and two children as portrayed in TV advertisements. New patterns of family living are increasingly acceptable, such as the one-parent family, created not just by circumstances but by choice, and more reconstituted families will emerge as the divorce and remarriage rates continue to rise. Not all families function equally well in performing

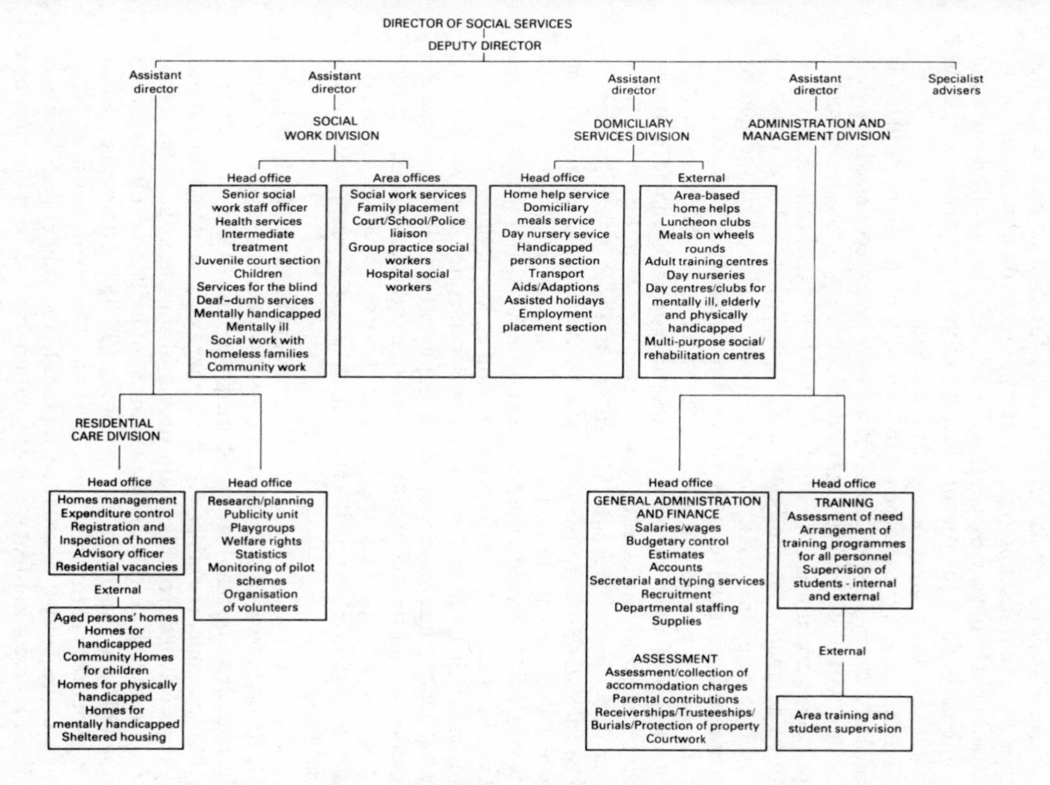

CHART 9 A model of a local authority Social Services Department

their child-rearing tasks. This may be because of personal factors or simply as a result of having to cope with inadequate housing or too little money. The failure of some families to care for and rear their children has become of increasing concern to society as a whole.

Like many other social services, those for children have developed in a piecemeal fashion, often erratic in execution and limited in the attainment of objectives. If a single word can describe the process it is 'pragmatism', the treatment of each problem as it arises and in the context of the requirements of the moment.

Although progressively over the course of time, and particularly in the last century, the needs of children were being recognised, it is only of late that a picture has emerged of services working on common principles and it was not until 1948 that the field of child care ceased to be dominated by the Poor Law.

Child care services in the 1940s were included in the general reappraisal of social services. At that time the care and supervision of children was allocated to different departments according to the legal definition of their functions. These departments included public assistance committees, education and health committees at local level and the Home Office and Ministries of Health and Education at central level. Not surprisingly there was a good deal of confusion over which department did what and for whom. The years of the Second World War produced a great number of children who required public care because of the disruption of family life and the increase in juvenile delinquency. The evacuation schemes, too, had shown up a great many child problems which might otherwise have remained hidden within the anonymity of the large industrial cities. A severe strain was placed on the local authorities' limited amount of accommodation for children, which in any case was already outdated.

In 1944 correspondence in *The Times*, initiated by Lady Allen of Hurtwood, drew attention to the generally poor situation of children in care, stressing that many orphaned, destitute or neglected children still lived under the chilly stigma of 'charity'. Too often they formed groups isolated from the main stream of life and education, few of them knowing the comfort and security of individual affection. As a result of Lady Allen's letter the Care of Children Committee was set up under the chairmanship of Miss (later Dame) Myra Curtis. Even before the Curtis Committee reported, the tragic case of Denis O'Neill forced its attention on the nation. He had been boarded out by his home local authority with foster parents in another county who neglected him to the point where he died.[28] The incident showed as nothing else could have done so vividly to what tragedy administrative muddle could lead. The report of the Curtis Committee in 1946[29] provided the blueprint for the Children Act,

1948, which placed a duty on local authorities to set up specialised Children's Committees under the central guidance of the Home Office. The Children's Departments established in 1948 were incorporated in 1971 into the newly constituted Social Services Departments.

Children in need of care

While every effort is made to prevent the breakdown of the family unit it is important to remember that not all parents are able to sustain a child-nurturing role. The child is now no longer seen as the 'chattel' of the parents; he is viewed as a person in his own right needing, in some circumstances, to be removed from his natural parents to permanent substitutes.

The estimated number of children in the care of local authorities in 1979 in England and Wales was more than 100,000, many of them received voluntarily into care as a result of temporary deprivation.[30] Full investigation of all requests for care is essential to discover what alternatives are available and also to identify families which may be at risk.[31] An increasing number of teenagers are the subject of care orders as a result of court action, a situation causing some concern because of the difficulty of finding placements for them other than in residential establishments which they have to leave at 18 often before they are mature enough to support themselves in the community.[32]

The 1948 Children Act underlined the requirement that each child in public care should be treated according to his own needs and abilities. While making it obligatory to rehabilitate a child with his relatives or friends if consistent with his welfare,[33] no legislation for preventive work was included, and this shortcoming became increasingly evident as difficulties were experienced in providing acceptable substitutes to the child for his own family, and social workers became frustrated by not being able to offer assistance to a growing number of families with problems which affected all areas of their life. The Ingleby Committee[34] had recommended that children's departments be given extended powers to promote the welfare of children and to work with families to prevent their breakdown under stress and consequent separation. There was widespread approval for Section I of the subsequent Children and Young Persons Act, 1963, giving the mandate for preventive work which became the special responsibility of local authority children's departments who developed ways of assisting families at risk. Some operated rent-guarantee schemes to prevent eviction, set up family advice centres, helped pay relatives' fares to look after children, and helped in a number of miscellaneous ways that would have been impossible before the Act.[35] This preventive work by Social Service Departments now continues, often in very imaginative ways, under the Child Care Act of 1980. Nevertheless, family breakdowns continue to occur and children[36] have to leave their own homes, temporarily or permanently. The Children Act, 1948, specified that where possible a child must be boarded out.[37] In practice, this was not always the best resource for a particular child and greater flexibility was provided by the Children and Young Persons Act, 1969.[38]

The Children Act, 1975, gave effect to the recommendations of the Departmental Committee on the Adoption of Children[39] and certain related matters arising from the report on the circumstances of the death of Maria Colwell.[40] It has since been followed by consolidating legislation, the Child Care Act, 1980.[41]

Central to recent legislation is the welfare principle giving 'first consideration to the need to safeguard and promote the welfare of the child throughout his childhood . . . and to ascertain the wishes and feelings of the child'.[42]

The 1975 Act, with its emphasis on substitute family care and its extension of the grounds on which the local authority could assume parental rights—an administrative decision of the local authority—over children who had been placed in care by their parents voluntarily, was criticised as being anti-parent. For example, the introduction of two new concepts in family placement,[43] custodianship and a defined placement period after which the foster parents including relatives could apply for custodianship and adoption without fear of these children being removed by the natural parents prior to a court hearing gave rise to the view that natural parents would hesitate to ask local authorities to care for their children in case they lost them altogether. But a government circular offering guidance on the time limits states that 'the welfare of the child is usually best served by parents exercising their rights and responsibilities in relation to the child' and it reminds local authorities that the new provisions make it even more important to undertake preventive work with families.

However, the fact that the interests of natural parents and their children may be in conflict, as demonstrated so vividly in the case of Maria Colwell, has been recognised in the provision for separate representation of children in certain court proceedings.[44]

The adoption section places a duty on every local authority to establish and maintain an adoption service as part of a comprehensive service for children; introduces a new procedure whereby parents are able to give early final agreement to adoption (freeing procedures) before an adoption order is made;[45] permits adopted people over the age of 18 access to their original birth records[46] and provides for the alternative of custodianship instead of adoption for relatives, foster parents and some step-parents. Although this adoption section has been consolidated with the Adoption Act 1976 at the time of writing this new Act had not yet been implemented.

Care in a family setting for children unable to live temporarily or permanently with their own parents continues to be more highly regarded than residential care. Adoption and fostering have hitherto been well recognised but distinct ways of securing family life but now the differences between the two are becoming blurred as older children with knowledge of, and ties with, their family of origin, traditionally fostered, are being placed in adoptive homes.[47] It is argued that adoption gives a child greater security because there is a legal commitment. But, as with marriage, the legal bond does not determine the quality of relationships and in this country there is no equivalent of divorce in adoption.

Adoption Until the Adoption Act, 1926, it was not possible for a parent to divest himself of his rights, liabilities and duties in relation to a child. Although what were known as *de facto* adoptions existed in practice these were not recognised in law and a parent could reclaim his child from the *de facto* adopters who had very few safeguards for contesting this. The *de facto* adoption process came into focus particularly during the First World War in connection with the widespread campaign to help Belgian orphans and it was largely as a result of this that England and Wales, lagging behind most other developed countries in this respect, passed the first adoption legislation which was designed to 'confer the privilege of parents upon the parentless'.[48] Today adoption is covered by the Adoption Act, 1958, and the Children Act, 1975,[49] which lay down in considerable detail substantive law and procedure designed to protect not only the child to be adopted but also the natural and adoptive parents. Adoption statistics used to reflect the social difficulties for women who gave birth to children outside marriage, the majority of adopters being childless couples adopting illegitimate babies. Now greater efforts are being made to enable the lone mother to keep her baby, society is more accepting of unmarried parenthood, the pill offers protection from unwanted pregnancies and abortion is more freely available.

With the shortage of babies for placement, statutory and voluntary agencies are widening their horizons. Children hitherto considered to be unadoptable because of being physically or mentally handicapped, of mixed race, or past infancy, are now successfully placed for adoption and today adoptive parents may be older and already have children of their own. The integration of an adopted child into a family does bring about problems which one would not expect to see in families in which the members are bound to each other by blood ties but there is evidence that in many families this artificial grafting process has resulted in happiness for adopted children and adoptive parents alike.[50]

Since the implementation in November 1976, of Section 26 of the Children Act, 1975, adopted people over the age of 18 have had the right of access to their original birth record. Previously a court order was necessary unless they happened to know their original name. People adopted before the implementation of the Children Act, 1975, are required to meet with an adoption counsellor before they receive any information, in order to ensure that they have considered the possible effects of any enquiries.

Foster care This is a generic term for a wide variety of situations ranging from temporary caretaking to quasi-adoption. Children can be placed privately by their parents with foster parents of the parents' own choosing, or by voluntary or statutory agencies. For children in long-term care the fostering options are open-ended, indefinite-term fostering, 'permanent' fostering, or fostering with a view to adoption, but foster care also includes day fostering and very short-term care. In most circumstances rehabilitation to the natural family is the aim. Foster parents currently have no legal rights in the child and social workers visit at varying intervals whether the child is privately fostered or placed by an agency. There is legislation covering private fostering and boarding out regulations provide the statutory framework for assessment of foster parents, placement of the children and visiting of the child in placement.

Currently about 40 per cent of children in the care of local authorities are in foster homes and there is again a move to place more children in a family setting. It is much cheaper to maintain a child in foster care than in residential care but the benefits are not seen only in relation to saving money for the local authorities but in giving a child the experience of family life.

The failure rate is estimated to be high, a factor which is often used as an argument against foster care, but there is growing evidence, particularly as the result of professional foster parents schemes, that, with careful assessment and support, it continues to be a valuable resource. Professional foster parents providing care for difficult, delinquent or disturbed adolescents undertake training for their task and are paid higher allowances than traditional foster parents.

Foster parents organised themselves into the National Foster Care Association in 1974 aiming to improve the quality of the service given to children throughout the country, to work for foster parents to have an effective share in policy-making on child care, and to demonstrate to the community and to professional agencies the value of the service provided by foster parents and to see this acknowledged by enhanced payments for all foster parents.

Child protection (*private fostering*) Local authorities have protective and supervisory functions for children who are privately placed in foster homes by their parents for a continuous period, which broadly speaking, places an obligation on people to notify the local authority of their intention to act as foster parents for periods of more than six days to children not related to them. The authority then has a duty to investigate the matter and in certain cases may prohibit the placement or allow it to go forward provided specified conditions are observed. Private homes must be visited regularly unless exempted by the local authority. In recent years there has been a substantial increase in the number of children privately placed, currently the number is estimated at about 9,000. This reflects to some extent the number of people from abroad who, unacquainted with conditions here, often have considerable difficulty in finding placements or assessing their suitability. Even though legislation attempted to clarify some of the difficulties which local authorities had experienced in administering the law, problems relating to such matters as the legal status of private foster parents and children remain. This is inevitable in an area where, as indeed in all areas of child care, there are conflicting interests to be borne in mind. First, it is now commonly accepted that the welfare of children, in this case those below the upper limit of the compulsory school age, should be protected. Second, the law should take account of the rights of a parent to place his child with a family through a private arrangement. Third, the law should not be so stringent as to make it impossible for a good neighbour or friend to act as voluntary host to a child as and when need arises. Compromise in the legislation has resulted in a set of complex, detailed duties, powers and prohibitions. Even with the legislation some private fostering arrangements are most unsatisfactory. Much greater control has been advocated as well as a more positive approach to supervision by statutory social work agencies.[51] There is provision in current legislation[52] for regulations to be made to tighten up procedures for this type of family placement.

When the custodianship section of the Children Act, 1975, is implemented, foster parents will be able to apply for an order giving them legal control over children they have fostered for at least one year. A successful application will mean that there will be no further supervision by a social work agency, a factor which may, or may not, be in the child's interests.

Day care Nearly 5 million married women go out to work, of whom about 1 million have children under 5. Surprisingly little has been done to help these working mothers. Where help is not forthcoming from amongst their own family circle they are sometimes forced to make unsatisfactory arrangements with private individuals.[53] Very few mothers can afford to have paid help in the home to look after a small child.

Officially sponsored or approved day care is provided by local authority day nurseries and nursery schools[54] and registered private nurseries, playgroups and child-minders. Local authority day nurseries existed before the Second World War but it was during the war years that they were greatly developed as part of government policy to free mothers for essential war work. After the war their number was allowed to fall on the grounds that in the interest of the health and development of the child no less than for the benefit of the mother the proper place for a child under two was with her at home. At the same time the intention was voiced of encouraging the growth of nursery schools for the 3 to 5s.[55] A few years later the Ministry of Health actively discouraged local authorities from providing day nursery places because of the public expense involved, particularly where the need arose solely from the mother's desire to supplement the family income by going out to work.

In a report compiled in 1967 on behalf of the National Society of Children's Nurseries (the Yudkin Report) it was pointed out that it was irrelevant to think of places in relation to the total pre-school population.[56] Some areas have far greater needs than others. But even in the highly industrial areas of the country where need might be expected at a high level, the provision of day nursery accommodation showed great variation. The acute shortage of places, even in areas where the population per thousand of the child population under 5 was relatively high, has meant that priority is given to special categories of families; unsupported mothers, those with poor health, or those with exceptionally deprived living conditions—leaving little if any room for others who may want day care. Existing nurseries usually have waiting lists despite the fact that graded charges are made to parents.

Yudkin's report, which followed closely on the Plowden Report, was very likely instrumental in rekindling interest in an area which had received little publicity since the war years. The provision of additional nursery places in selected areas was approved in the projects included in the Urban Programme which was announced by the government in July 1968. Initially thirty-four local authorities with areas of special social need were included in the programme, largely financed by the government, and subsequently enshrined in the Local Government (Social Needs) Act, 1969.

In the absence of local authority provisions, working mothers and others who must place their children during the day-time can make use of other recognised facilities, either with registered child-minders or in registered private day nurseries. Both methods are governed by the Nurseries and Child Minders Regulations Act, 1948, amended by Section 60 of the Health Services and Public Health Act, 1968. The child-minding laws, like private fostering, attempt to steer a course midway between trying not to discourage relatives, friends or neighbours from offering day care for a child and at the same time ensuring that, as far as possible, his health, welfare and safety is protected. Only people who take a child under 5, not related to them, for daily minding for reward are affected by the extensive powers to impose requirements or make prohibitions relating to the suitability of minders and premises. There is an increasing interest in child-minding and some local authorities are now prepared to provide equipment and arrange training for child-minders.[57] A National Childminding Association aims to improve standards generally and to have child-minding fully integrated into the whole child-care pattern as providing a valuable social service and offering an essential form of community care.

Private day nurseries are also covered by regulations. These nurseries are usually run on a commercial basis and, as the Yudkin Report suggested, are more likely to be utilised by middle-class families who see their value in terms of the educational advantages for their young children, than by working mothers. Some factories, notably in female-labour intensive areas such as parts of Lancashire, are also provided with nurseries but their numbers are small when compared to their potential use. A few hospitals and schools also have nurseries attached for the convenience of staff children, again a facility that could well be extended.

The development of play-groups for children of all ages has tended to confuse discussion of the need for adequate day minding facilities. Play-groups are intended to provide social and educational experience for children and by no means only for those considered deprived in some way. They do not normally cater for any one child on a daily basis. Day minding, on the other hand, must be available on a continuous basis for each child and is primarily intended to give relief to a hard-pressed parent or to enable her to follow employment.

A survey carried out in 1977[58] found the mothers of 64 per cent of all children under 5 would like day care facilities of various types for their children but only 32 per cent had them. A government circular on co-ordinating services for children under 5, issued in January 1978, recognised that facilities fell short of what was needed and urged local authorities to make maximum use of existing resources in the education, social services and health fields provided by both statutory and voluntary bodies. In September 1978 a further report[59] noted the persistent shortfall in government provision in this area, and it remains a weak contender for resources.

Court work

Where the State assumes an obligation to intervene between parents and their children the final arbiter is usually the court. The most common case continues to be that of the child aged 10 or over who has committed some act which, if committed by an adult, would have been liable to criminal prosecution. The state also has a right or duty to intervene where there is, for example, neglect or ill-treatment of a child, where he is in moral danger or lacks control. The juvenile court is the court most commonly used. A juvenile system, separate from the adult one, was established by legislation in 1908. During the Second World War it was suggested that the interests of both young offenders and society would be better served by abandoning legal and procedural considerations and concentrating on the welfare of the offender.[60] This line of thought was later examined by the Ingleby Committee but rejected by them in favour of further modifications of the juvenile court procedures. A Labour Party Committee under the chairmanship of Lord Longford took up the same theme and opted for abandoning the concept of criminal responsibility for children under 16 and concentrating instead on treating their criminality on welfare lines. In 1965 the Labour government published a White Paper on the subject under the title of *The Child, the Family and the Young Offender* based on the Longford Report. The radical proposal to abolish juvenile courts in favour of family councils run by the local authority children's departments produced considerable opposition. It was later modified in a further White Paper, *Children in Trouble*.[61] The Children and Young Persons Act, 1969, was based on this White Paper. Care proceedings are governed by the Children and Young Persons Acts, 1933 to 1969. Under these Acts, certain agents are authorised to bring children before a juvenile court, the police, the local authority social services and education departments and the National Society for the Prevention of Cruelty to Children. It is unusual to find a voluntary organisation like the NSPCC with such powers which it gained in 1889 and doubts are sometimes voiced about the appropriateness of the arrangement in view of the expansion of local authority responsibilities in this direction.

A child under the age of 14 years or a young person under 17[62] may be brought before a juvenile court under care proceedings. The grounds on which such action can be taken have been frequently modified over the years, but the law is quite specific about what the case must rest on. Court action can result in a parent losing custodial rights over the child and the child too may find his liberty restricted. So a balance must be preserved between the welfare of the child as the court sees it, and the rights of parents and of the child himself. Currently, the grounds for action are established by Section 1 of the

Children and Young Persons Act, 1969. They consist of a series of seven alternative conditions plus a requirement that the court must be satisfied that the juvenile is in need of care or control which he is unlikely to receive unless a specified order is made.

The specific conditions set out in the Children and Young Persons Act, 1969, section 1 (2) are that:

(a) The child's proper development is being avoidably prevented or neglected, or his health is being avoidably impaired or neglected, or he is being ill-treated;

(b) it is probable that the above condition will be satisfied in his case having regard to the fact that the court or another court has found that that condition is or was satisfied in the case of another child who is or was a member of the same household;

(bb) it is probable that the conditions set out in (a) above will be satisfied in his case, having regard to the fact that a person who has been convicted of an offence mentioned in the CYPA 1933, schedule I is or may become a member of the same household as the child;

(c) he is exposed to moral danger;

(d) he is beyond the control of his parents or guardian;

(e) he is of compulsory school age and is not receiving efficient full-time education suitable to his age, ability and aptitude; and

(f) he is guilty of an offence, excluding homicide.

If any of the grounds can be substantiated, it is still necessary to satisfy the court that it is not possible to bring about any improvement in the situation except through one of the orders it has the power to make. In effect, this means that the initiating agency must have taken steps to find out whether any action has been or could be taken to prevent the case from coming to court at all. Avoidance of compulsory action through the courts is an important theme in the legislation and has become an objective of social work support to families.

Because procedures require evidence that the parents are unlikely to provide adequate care or control unless an order is made, investigation by the local authority social services departments is a prerequisite of court action. This involves consultation and co-operation between the departments and the police, who are increasingly willing to consider the social needs of a child before deciding on prosecution.

Proceedings in a juvenile court are normally far less formal than in an adult court. Nevertheless, they are legal proceedings and this sometimes seems to conflict with the fact that, in deciding on the kind of treatment for the youngster before them, the magistrates must have regard to his welfare.[63]

When the juvenile court is satisfied that the case for care has been made out, it can make a limited number of orders. These fall into two categories. In the first type of order, the court decides that the child or young person may remain at home. The parent may be required to take proper care or exercise effective control, or a supervision order may be made with or without certain conditions, placing the child under the supervision of an officer of a local authority or a probation officer. The second type of order is a care order where the court in effect removes the child from home by assigning his care to the local authority. Special provision may also be made under the Mental Health Act, 1959.

Orders which allow children and young persons to remain at home are made for relatively short periods, for example the maximum period for a supervision order is three years. A requirement for Intermediate Treatment may be attached to a supervision order by a court. The term, not found in the Children and Young Persons Act, 1969, was used in the White Paper *Children in Trouble* to describe a form of treatment intended to enable a juvenile under supervision to come into contact with different environments, interests, and experiences in association with others of his own age 'intermediate' between measures which either leave him at home with his parents or remove him to the care of the local authority. The range of available facilities, both residential and non-residential, is set out in schemes proposed by Children's Regional Planning Committees.[64]

The concept of Intermediate Treatment is creative and imaginative, providing opportunities for individual and group activities, but uncertainty has arisen about who should benefit from it—young offenders, children at risk, or both groups.[65] A DHSS circular in 1977 provided the government's view of Intermediate Treatment as a preventive measure for children of all ages. For those not the subject of a supervision order with an IT requirement whose activities could be funded with money earmarked for IT purposes, there is financial help available under Section 1 of the Children and Young Persons Act, 1963 (now Section 1 of the Child Care Act, 1980).

It was intended, as a result of the Children and Young Persons Act,1969, that all children between the ages of 10 and 14 who committed offences would be the subject of care, not criminal proceedings and that, with certain new procedures, the prosecution of as many young people as possible under the age of 17 would be avoided. The Act has not been fully implemented so the procedures for young people have not become operative and children from the age of 10 still remain liable to prosecution for offences.

The 1969 Act, setting out as it did to integrate services for young people who commit offences more closely with those provided for children generally, transferred to social services departments a number of responsibilities in relation to young offenders, particularly supervision which had previously been the responsibility of the probation service, thereby substantially increasing the workload and leading to criticism from all quarters.[66]

More liberal measures for dealing with young offenders seem unlikely in the present climate of opinion. The Conservative government while giving support to the use of non-custodial sentences wherever possible, has also designated some detention centres to provide 'short, sharp shocks' for young people.

With the increased concern felt about children whose future may not be securely placed within their natural family the courts, under a range of family legislation such as the Matrimonial Causes Act, 1973, and the Children Act, 1975, have powers to make care and supervision orders.

A care order, under which the local authority is given parental rights, can last up to the time a young person reaches 18, or, in certain cases, 19. But the order can be revoked by the court before that time on the application of either the local authority, the child or young person himself, or his parent on his behalf.

The local authority to whose care the juvenile is committed has considerable power in deciding where and with whom the child may live, but the keynote of the care order is that it allows the local authority to treat the child in the same way as other children in its care. Like them he may be placed with foster parents or in residential accommodation. The care order also gives the local authority power to allow the child to return to his own home, the order itself remaining in force.

As a result of the 1969 Children and Young Persons Act, the approved school system was restructured and incorporated into a generic system of community homes which included all the residential establishments of the local authority together with some voluntary homes providing a range of specialised care according to the needs of children. The type and size of children's homes has undergone change. The large children's homes housing hundreds of children and institutional in character have now all disappeared and given way to an increasing number of smaller establishments, more often than not situated unobtrusively amongst other houses in residential areas. Everything is done to encourage a relaxed atmosphere, as opposed to the regimented and impersonal regimes which were in vogue not so many decades before. However, for some children the demands made by the open community home on their behaviour and co-operation may be more than they can cope with. For these more difficult children secure units have been set up. In order to help a small minority of children so damaged by their early experiences as to be beyond effective care in any local authority home, Youth Treatment Centres have been set up administered directly by the Secretary of State, DHSS.[67]

Prevention of child abuse

Child abuse, a term now used to describe physical, mental, emotional or sexual injury to children, is still mainly used in relation to physical abuse. Excessive punishment of children was not highlighted as a problem until the early 1960s when Professor C. H. Kempe in the USA coined the term 'battered child syndrome' to describe a clinical condition in young children who had received serious physical abuse at the hands of their parents or other caretakers. This emotive description succeeded in drawing attention to the problem but it was eventually discarded in favour of non-accidental injury (NAI) or child abuse which arouses a less punitive response towards the parents, many of whom need help and support.

In 1966 the British Paediatric Association produced the first memorandum of guidance on the subject in this country. The first government circular was issued in 1970 but it was the death in 1973 of 7-year-old Maria Colwell at the hands of her stepfather[68] that stimulated the government, spurred on by public opinion, to provide detailed guidance on diagnosis, care, prevention and local organisation for the management of cases of physical abuse. Area Review Committees were set up by local authorities and Area Health Authorities to determine policy and ensure an integrated approach; procedures for multi-disciplinary case conferences were established to deal with individual cases and 'At Risk' registers were introduced for actual and suspected cases of physical injury. These registers have been criticised because the criteria for registration and de-registration have not been clearly enough outlined and there is no requirement to inform parents of the inclusion of their child's name on the register.[69]

The Parliamentary Select Committee on Violence in the Family produced a report in 1977 on Violence to Children which was followed in 1978 by a White Paper, *Violence to Children*, calling for greater co-operation between the community and the professionals, early recognition of vulnerable families, more day care facilities, and education for parenthood in order to help reduce child abuse.

The National Society for the Prevention of Cruelty to Children has pioneered much of the work and research in this country in relation to child abuse, setting up Special Units in several areas and a National Advisory Centre in London to deal specifically with this problem. The government, recognising the value of the contribution made by the NSPCC, funds some of its work.

Children in long-stay hospitals

Since the Curtis Committee stated in 1946 that most of the problems presented by mentally and physically handicapped children were not within their terms of reference, children in long-stay hospitals, who also include the physically ill, have tended to be 'hidden' from the general public and often 'forgotten' by the professional carers—except those who actually look after them.[70]

A government circular in 1972 stressed the importance of maintaining links between children in hospital and their families in order to prevent abandonment. In 1974 it was suggested in the discussion paper *The Quality of Life of Long Stay Children in Hospital* that action be taken on behalf of the children, e.g. to provide better play facilities, unrestricted visiting, and involvement of social services departments and primary health care teams if home ties appeared to be weakening. Another government circular in 1978, still concerned with the maintenance of family links, urged health authorities and local authorities jointly to review the needs of children regularly and to establish procedures for effective liaison amongst the services involved.

There is growing support for the view that those children who do not require nursing and medical care should be returned to their own homes or placed in the community, preferably in foster homes, by the local authority.[71]

Understaffing and shortage of money may be partly responsible for the slow progress towards improving the quality of life for many children in long-stay hospitals, but the lack of public interest and concern must also be a contributory factor.

Adults with special needs

Adults with special needs were grouped together for Poor Law purposes as the aged and infirm. They have generally been exempt from the constraints imposed on the able-bodied who needed help, but most of the effort to do more than maintain them at a minimal level either by out-relief or in an institution came from charitable activity. New policies for these clients were outlined in the NHS Act, 1946, and the National Assistance Act, 1948. Under Part 3 of the latter act local authorities had duties and powers relating to the elderly, the handicapped and the homeless—all traditional clients of Parish Relief; while the NHS Act empowered local health authorities to provide services for the prevention of illness and the care and after-care of those suffering from illness or handicap. Schedule 8 of the NHS Act, 1977, gives details of the local authorities' functions following reorganisation which are still largely concerned with prevention, care and after-care through the provision of community services. The three main groups of clients for whom they have responsibility are still the elderly, the handicapped and the mentally disordered.

The elderly 'The increase in the number of elderly people represents one of the most significant social changes in Britain this century. One in seven of the population is now 65 or over.' The DHSS Annual Report for 1977 thus begins the chapter concerned with the elderly. On this significant change policy proposals for the elderly have increasingly emphasised the economic value of planning across service boundaries.

For centuries the elderly have been objects of charity and today we still assume that they will be willing recipients of the attention of young volunteers and will not suffer any stigmatisation thereby. Alms, almshouses, sheltered housing, parish and friendly visiting have a long and continuing history. The impact of old age in an industrial society, particularly on earning capacity, was realised largely through the work of Charles Booth, and the idea of a pension as of right grew from his promotion of this cause. The 1908 Old Age Pension Act established for the first time a specific age at which one could be officially elderly and not expected to earn a living. The inflexibility of this, endorsed by the 1926 Contributory Pension Scheme, may have done some disservice to those employed in heavy industry or rapidly changing industries who may not be able to continue in work until retirement age. They are neither pensioners nor disabled, but with the disadvantages of both.

Although the income needs of the elderly were established early their social needs were ignored. Beatrice Webb as a member of the Poor Law Commission in 1904 noted that money may not solve all the problems of the elderly. She suggested that local authorities should take some responsibility for the social care of those who were not being dealt with by the Poor Law but who were neglected and in need of care. No action was taken until the blitzes of the Second World War revealed the difficulties that some people struggled with. The hostels then set up for the homeless elderly became the pattern of post-war development.[72]

Another development that had significance for policies for the elderly was the abolition of the household means test in 1941, which relieved children of the duty to support parents with whom they lived and 'shifted the obligation to look after those who are old . . . from the family and from the household to the community as a whole'.[73] Geographical mobility, increasing affluence leading to young couples setting up separate households, working women and changes in the size and shape of families from few generations with large sibling groups, to four- and even five-generation families with much smaller sibling groups, have meant that some elderly people cannot be cared for by their families at all and others not without outside help. A new factor in this situation has been developments in medicine which can keep alive, and possibly heavily dependent, old people who would previously have died after a short illness, and this can put a great strain on the family. It seems from various studies[74] that the elderly have not on the whole been rejected by their families, but more flexible welfare provisions have had to grow from the rather rigid divisions of 1948 when the National Assistance Act ended the Poor Law. The tasks of the latter were reallocated between the National Assistance Board—dealing with financial assistance—and the local authorities who through welfare committees, or joint health and welfare committees,[75] had a duty to provide residential accommodation for all needing 'care and attention', while the new National Health Service provided hospital and medical care. Unfortunately the divisions met administrative rather than clients' needs. Difficulties arose when the clients did not conform to categories which put the sick into hospital and the fit into homes.[76] Clients not fit enough for admission to a home, needing more medical care and supervision than was provided and yet not really in need of hospital care, were shuffled uneasily between the two. 'Body swapping' between homes and hospital solved some of the problems but at the cost of the dignity of the client who, having become physically and financially dependent, lost all power to have any say in decisions about his future. Even with a good income the frail elderly were and still are at the mercy of those who care for them, although safeguards are provided through the duty placed on local authorities to register private homes. A demarcation line between health and welfare was provided by the Ministry in 1965 on the basis of the quantity and quality of nursing care needed.

The original hope that residences for the elderly should house no more than 35 people and should quickly replace the Poor Law buildings was dashed by increasing demand and restrictions on building. The review of the first ten years of the service in the Ministry's Annual Report for 1958 revealed that small homes had increased from 63 to 990 while the numbers of people in residential accommodation, mainly elderly and infirm, had almost doubled. Waiting lists and the development of domiciliary care led to a population in the homes that was more infirm and older. This increase in infirm residents required a higher staff ratio and some local authorities built larger units to make more efficient use of trained staff such as nurses and night staff, which added to the movement away from the idea of a 'home-like' home.

The main activity of local welfare authorities was concerned with the duty imposed on them under Part III of the National Assistance Act to provide residential accommodation. Under this Act they were also allowed to make agency arrangements with voluntary agencies providing accommodation or domiciliary welfare service. It was not until 1962 that the National Assistance (Amendment) Act gave local authorities powers to provide domiciliary services that would enable old people to continue to live in their own homes; but, while the legislation for children allowed local authority money to be spent on individual families to prevent children having to be received into care, no similar provision was made for adults; further, the Health Service and Public Health Act, 1968, specifically prohibits any payment to old people by local authorities.

In 1963 the local authority plans for health and welfare provision in the future were published.[77] The elderly were described as needing first and foremost a home of their own, support of various kinds to enable them to stay there, and residential accommodation when necessary. Only slowly have services to meet the needs of the elderly and their supporting families been provided. Laundry services, home helps, chiropody, meals on wheels, holiday relief and day care, clubs and recreational facilities have all been developed as ways of maintaining the elderly in their own homes, and have slowly broken down the rigidity imposed by the legislative restrictions of 1948.

The Seebohm Committee criticised the piecemeal provisions and lack of overall planning. They recognised that planning depends to a great extent on the identification of need, which is far from easy with such a heterogeneous group, and on the assessment of existing provisions, which again is not easy since the family, the community and other social services all make varying and interdependent contributions to the care of the elderly. Unlike childhood, old age does not begin and end within a specific period, so that families and public services cannot clearly foresee where their duties will begin and end.

Since 1971 the local authority Welfare Departments have become part of the Personal Social Services Departments. The demands on them will increase as the numbers of old people rise. In particular the growth in the 85-plus population places heavier burdens on them.[78] Already nearly half the personal social services' expenditure goes on old people. Surveys by Audrey Hunt[79] in 1976 of old people living at home and Amelia Harris[80] in 1971 of the handicapped and disabled, revealed the extent of the potential demand for social service resources. The Hunt survey of 6,500,000 elderly people at home found 30 per cent living alone, while the Harris survey found that of the 500,000 substantially handicapped women over 65, one-third lived alone.

The *Priorities* Consultative Document in 1976 assumed that the increasing demand would be met by increasing provision. For example, home helps are now serving more than half a million people, most of them elderly; *Priorities* suggested that the present ratio of 6 whole-time equivalents per 1,000 elderly population should be doubled but one year later this estimate was considered to be still too low in the Second Consultative Document. It was also proposed that meals services should more than double to over 1,500,000 per week, and places at day centres, where some old people take their meals, should also be substantially increased.

While the main emphasis in policy now is to maintain old people in the community there is still a need for greater provision of residential accommodation. In 1977 over 100,000 old people were in local authority homes and another 13,000 in voluntary homes were being rate-aided. Even the 1,500 in private homes make some demand on the local authority's resources as these homes must be registered with the authority and visited regularly. This level of provision is considered to fall below need, and it was proposed that accommodation should be increased from 18.5 places per 1,000 elderly to 25 places.

The need is undoubtedly there but the funding is not likely to be readily available, even if the joint planning of health and social services releases more for these projects. The Discussion Document, *A Happier Old Age*, in 1978 and the White Paper *Growing Older*, 1981, emphasised that the changing economic situation called for better use of voluntary and 'informal' resources. The nationwide 'Be a good neighbour' campaign, mounted in 1976 by the government, was intended to mobilise these 'informal' sources of help. The campaign drew on all sectors of society to form an Advisory Group to devise strategies for alerting the public to the needs of the elderly at home, and to get their participation in meeting local social needs.

Recreation and social contacts have always been largely the domain of voluntary agencies.[81] National organisations like Age Concern, and local groups, have promoted the welfare of elderly people in ways that are beyond the scope and capacity of local authorities. Current policies emphasise the importance of co-ordinating statutory and voluntary activities.

The local authorities' concern with the elderly must be flexible and must reach out to workers in other services, to voluntary agencies and to volunteers. Not all old people need help at all times and some not at any time. The problem is to put people in touch with services when the time comes. Often the deciding factor is an illness that reveals the slowly mounting difficulties the old person has had to face. Many ideas for crisis warning arrangements have been tried out and many ideas for avoiding illness and accidents have been proposed, but none is foolproof. In the care of the elderly, as with children, the local authorities are very vulnerable to criticism. In avoiding criticism there is the possibility that they will harass with the best intentions people who have begun to close in their lives and wish for no more than the bare minimum. Local authorities may have to have the courage to protect their clients from service as well as give it.

One consequence of the increase in very old people is the growing concern about mental disorder in old age. The incidence of senile dementia increases sharply with very old age. In his report for 1972 the Chief Medical Officer refers to the major policy document HM(72)71 which was issued concerning services for mental illness related to old age. The report distinguished between the needs of those whose illness (usually depressive) can respond to treatment and those who suffer from senile dementia, with deterioration of personality, impairment of memory and sometimes behaviour disorders. The latter need services based on co-operation between psychiatrists, geriatricians and the social services. The need to plan provision beyond medical care alone is recognised by the transfer at central government level of oversight of psychogeriatric services from the Mental Health Division to the Division for the Socially Handicapped, which is also responsible for the aged in general.

In cases where old people, or any others who are the concern of the Welfare Authority, are found to be living in insanitary conditions, neither receiving proper care and attention from others nor able to care for themselves, they can be compulsorily removed under Section 47 of the National Assistance Act. The local authority must apply to the court, with medical evidence, for authority to remove the person to a hospital or home for up to three months. Only after careful enquiry, bearing in mind the interests of the old person, and of others who might be suffering from the nuisance, will the medical, social and legal authorities take this step.

The local authority must also under Section 48 take responsibility in lieu of relatives and friends for care of the movable property of people in hospital or removed to homes and take steps to see that their own home is locked and all people who may be concerned notified—in fact to act as a responsible friend or relative.

Finally, under Section 50, if there are no relatives or friends to do so, local authorities can arrange for burial or cremation, and must respect the wishes of the deceased.

As with children, the local authority tries to fulfil, where necessary, the functions of the family for the elderly members of society.

The physically handicapped The physically handicapped fared better under the 1948 legislation than the elderly. One difficulty that occurs in discussing adults with special needs by categories, such as the elderly and the physically handicapped, is that the categories are by no means mutually exclusive. Blindness is now largely a handicap of old age, so are arthritis and rheumatism. However, provision for the physically handicapped was initially concerned with adults who would have been working and joining in community life if they had not suffered through some disabling accident, illness or congenital malfunctioning. Nearly half of these people are suffering from organic nervous diseases (such as epilepsy or multiple sclerosis), markedly different from the elderly disabled group where rheumatism and arthritis are much more common. As well as meeting the residential needs of this group local authorities had powers to make available domiciliary employment and recreational facilities, and had duties for the welfare of the blind deriving from the Blind Persons Acts of 1920 and 1938.

Definitions of physical handicap were approached warily. Blindness was perhaps the easiest category to establish, as educational needs can sift out children who cannot see well enough to read, while for adults the inability to perform work for which eyesight is essential was the definition used by the National Assistance Act. Hearing defects were divided into three categories—deafness with speech impairment, deafness without speech impairment (usually arising after language has been acquired) and 'hard of hearing'.

Other disabilities described in the 1948 legislation as the concern of local welfare authorities were 'substantial' and 'permanent' incapacity through illness, injury and congenital deficiency. These are referred to as General Classes. Diagnosis and assessment of a handicap is not easy. Amelia Harris, in considering definitions of impairment, disablement and handicap, refers to the confusion between 'disability' and 'handicap' which appear in common usage to be interchangeable; but not all disabilities leave people handicapped. She uses disablement to describe 'loss or reduction of functional ability' and handicap to describe 'the disadvantage or restriction of activity caused by disability'. Peter Townsend[82] considers another dimension, the individual's perception of his disability *vis-à-vis* his life situation may profoundly affect the extent to which he becomes or remains handicapped.

The DHSS figures do not tell the full story as there is no compulsion to register, nor is registration a prerequisite to obtaining welfare help. The Blind Register is probably the most complete. When the Personal Social Service Departments were set up in 1971 there were about 96,000 registered blind people (68,000 of them over 65), 34,000 registered partially sighted (21,000 of them over 65), 40,000 in the three deaf categories and 234,000 in the general classes. Since then there has been an increase in the number of blind people registered, and a decline in the deaf. The greatest change has been in the trebling of numbers in the general classes. This is not so much due to any major increase in the numbers of the disabled, but a response to new positive interest in their welfare.

Local authorities had powers under legislation in 1948 and 1962 to alter homes and provide fittings to improve independence at home but where a handicapped person was in need of greater care the provisions tended to be medically orientated. There were too few severely handicapped young people in many areas to justify expenditure on separate accommodation, and they have either 'grown up geriatric' or been rescued by voluntary agencies like the Cheshire Homes. The numbers are not large. Amelia Harris found in her study that only 20 per cent of the appreciably or severely handicapped were under 30. The *Consultative Paper Priorities for Health and Personal Social Services in England*, 1976, reported that there were 11,000 adults under 65 in residential homes, and 5,000 in long-stay hospital units, which included 1,000 in units for the younger disabled.

The situation of the handicapped at home began to improve with the passing of the Chronically Sick and Disabled Persons Act in 1970, and the subsequent appointment of a minister with specific responsibility for the disabled. Section 1 of the Act imposed a duty on local authorities to enquire into the numbers and needs of the disabled. The onus to make the first move appeared to have been transferred from the client to the local authority, but in a subsequent circular the local authorities were advised that they need not seek out *all* the disabled and that a sample survey would suffice. The intention is thus interpreted not in terms of identifying all individuals in need, but of planning for future services on the basis of more accurately estimated demand.[83]

This section of the Act came into operation in October 1971 after the new personal social services had been in operation for six months, and in some areas proved to be a great added strain to a service struggling to establish itself.

Local authorities were also given powers under the Act to install telephones and television sets but in practice provision has sometimes been held up by lack of resources. Since 1971 a decreasing number of telephones and TV sets have been provided per annum, but many more people have been given financial assistance with costs.

More positive policies for the handicapped developing in the late 1970s have been built around two important concepts. The first as expressed in *Priorities* is that the 'main aim of services for the physically handicapped is to enable them to lead as full and useful a life as possible' and, second that integration into the community rests on flexible and co-ordinated services. The Chief Medical Officer at the DHSS has stressed in his Annual Reports since 1977 that 'responsibility for meeting the physical, emotional, occupational, social and health care needs of disabled people falls on a wide range of statutory and voluntary agencies'.[84] In 1977, with help from the EEC, experimental Care Attendant Schemes were set up, which combined special housing with domiciliary support services. The Crossroads Care Attendant Scheme, a voluntary organisation with statutory support, gives aid to families caring for a disabled person at home. Joint funding by the DHSS and Local Authorities allows for the development of such schemes across service boundaries with the express object of maintaining the disabled in the community.

One of the most valuable contributions to this policy is contained in Section 4 of the 1970 Act, which makes it mandatory for public buildings to allow for access of disabled people. Pressure grew for the better implementation of this Section in 1977 when the Silver Jubilee Committee was set up. Pavement alterations and ramps make for easy movement and special toilet facilities are extensively provided.

The simple device of a figure in a wheelchair indicating facilities for the disabled is now ubiquitous. This is a very encouraging expression of the slowly growing recognition of the need of the handicapped to join in normal social activities. 1981 was declared to be the International Year of Disabled People by the United Nations. Government funding has been made available to statutory and voluntary co-ordinating committees, but little if anything can be expected in extra expenditure on services. One of the major concerns must be with prevention, particularly of perinatal handicaps. The Command Paper on Child Health Services, *Fit for the Future*, 1976, points out that 1 in 7 infants will be so impaired as to present problems when they reach school age.

Mobility of disabled people was the subject of a survey undertaken by Lady Sharp on behalf of the government. In her report, in 1974,[85] she suggested that the diffusion of responsibility between different bodies presented difficulties in making best use of resources including those of the disabled person himself. The DHSS is responsible for vehicle service, but some confusion exists about the criteria on which allocation of help rests. Originally a powered vehicle was to replace a lost limb, but there has been increasing pressure for non-driving disabled people to be helped, and the social as well as mobility needs of the disabled be considered. The Sharp Report concluded that while severe physical disability should not of itself be an entitlement to a car, 'all the circumstances of the household should be taken into account'.

Although responsibility for mobility rests with the DHSS the provision of such services has impact on the personal social services.

The mentally disordered Like the elderly and physically handicapped, the mentally disordered have need for a range of co-ordinated services, and like them they have suffered from a lack of public interest and shortage of resources in all sectors. In hospitals and in medical research mental illness and mental deficiency have been the poor relations,[86] while community resources have never met demand. The role of the local authorities has changed. Before 1948 they provided hospital and institutional care, long associated with the Poor Law, and although under the National Assistance Act of 1948 they retained responsibility for non-hospital residential care the hospitals for the mentally disordered passed into the control of the RHBs. The welfare element whereby shelter, asylum, supervision, basic nursing care and security were provided on a long-term basis was neglected in the re-interpretation of these institutions. It is evident that in the past many social problems have been alleviated by the availability of such asylum and that adequate substitutes have to be developed.[87] After 1948 local authorities were responsible for the community care of the mentally disordered.[88] They had powers under the 1946 NHS Act to provide 'prevention, care and after-care services' for illnesses which include mental disorders, and under the 1959 Act the power to provide this service for the mentally disordered became a duty. Also from 1948 the local health authorities had transferred to them the duties relating to certification and admission to hospital under the Lunacy Act of 1890 and under the Mental Treatment Act of 1930, and although the latter Act made voluntary admission to hospital possible there were still forms to complete and supervision to ensure that the voluntary patient was truly volitional. Other duties of the local authority concerned the ascertainment and supervision of the mentally handicapped in their area, admission to residential institutions and supervision of those discharged on licence, and the provision of occupation centres.

The new social work staff of the local health authorities in 1948 included former Relieving Officers who had been able to choose at this time which of their two main activities they would pursue: they could either work for the National Assistance Board, dealing with relief of financial distress, or they could work for the local health authority as Duly Authorised Officers dealing with the mentally disordered. Other recruits to the local health authorities included workers from voluntary agencies concerned with the mentally handicapped. The third kind of mental health worker, the Psychiatric Social Worker, who was expected to extend the activities of local health authorities from the crisis-orientated and legalistically based work to a casework service, did not materialise in sufficient numbers to make any impact. The Mackintosh Committee,[89] reporting in 1951, found that of over 300 professionally qualified practising psychiatric social workers only 8 were employed by local health authorities, and the Younghusband Committee[90] reporting eight years later found that the numbers had risen only to 26 full-time and 5 part-time workers. With the reorganisation of the local authority social services in 1971 specialism in the mental health field has given way to the generic case load, although social workers who carry out duties under the Mental Health Act still have to be designated as Mental Welfare Officers.

The out-moded legislation under which the mentally disordered were received for treatment, and the isolation of their care from the rest of health and welfare services was examined by the Royal Commission on the Law relating to Mental Illness and Mental Deficiency set up in 1954.[91] The subsequent Mental Health Act of 1959 brought together again for administrative purposes the mentally ill and those of subnormal intelligence, calling these conditions collectively 'mental disorder'. The term also includes psychopathic disorders. Section 4 of the Act classifies and describes the four main groups.

Mental subnormality represents two of these groups, the severely subnormal and the subnormal, the difference being determined by the degree of handicap suffered. For these people domiciliary and community care had been slow to develop. The range, causes and effects of mental subnormality were not sufficiently well established to allow for adequate provision to be made[92] and the social problems that appeared to cluster around subnormality in particular, coupled with the apparent high fertility rate of this group, aroused fears of national mental deterioration at the turn of the century. Efforts to deal with the problems of mental handicap fell into two main categories: for the severe subnormals—the idiots and imbeciles—there was need for institutional care other than in workhouses, lunatic asylums and prisons, and for the 'improvable' ones there was need for training and special educational facilities. Many voluntary agencies were founded in the nineteenth and twentieth centuries to offer in-patient care, training, after-care, supervision and family support.[93]

Legislation concerning services for the mentally handicapped as it developed split the duties and provisions between different agencies. Under the Poor Law Boards of Guardians dealt with pauper defectives, usually in the workhouse. Defectives could also be certified under the Lunacy Act, 1890, and sent to lunatic asylums. The Mental Deficiency Act, 1913, set up Mental Deficiency Committees of the local authorities to provide institutional care, supervision and guardianship, training and occupation, and in 1929 these committees also took responsibility for pauper defectives. The local education authorities had duties under the Education Acts to ascertain defectives in the area and to provide special classes and schools, but this did not extend to supervision of the special school leavers.[94] The quality of care provided varied greatly between one authority and another. Many delegated the work of community care to voluntary agencies which not only carried out the statutory supervision, but ran occupation centres and employed home teachers.

In the 1959 Act severe subnormality is described as arrested or incomplete development of the mind and it is assumed that such people will be unable to lead an independent life, or guard against exploitation. The 1970 Census of mentally handicapped patients in hospital found that about two-thirds were suffering from severe mental handicap. Physical and behavioural incapacities requiring medical and nursing care are often associated with this condition, but about a quarter of the hospital residents were not so incapacitated and could presumably have been accommodated in hostels within the community had facilities been available. The 1959 Act places a duty on local authorities to provide residential accommodation for those not needing hospital care, but it was not until the end of the 1960s that pressure for a change from hospital to community, as advocated by the Royal Commission of 1954, began to gather force. The Secretary of State for Health and Social Services allocated more money to local authorities for these needy groups (see also the chapter on the health services) and in the plans for the reorganisation of the National Health Services the hospitals for severely mentally handicapped patients were in the future to be smaller, and to serve one health area, thus promoting collaboration with local authority services and other health services. The hope that the isolation of the severely handicapped will end rests on this collaboration.

The white paper *Better Services for the Mentally Handicapped*, 1971, commented that local authorities had concentrated their limited efforts in the previous decade on residential homes and training centres, but comparatively little had been done to meet need. Out of the 174 local authorities in England and Wales in 1969, 28 had no residential places at all for children or adults, 69 had no places for children and 31 no places for adults—in all, 128 authorities with major deficiencies. The RHBs and the local authorities were asked in the same year to undertake joint planning exercises and by the time the 1972 Annual Report was published some success was noted.[95]

Further evidence of a more positive approach came in 1973 when the DHSS sponsored a programme of research into assessment and training at the Hester Adrian Research Centre in Manchester, and two years later a National Development Group for the Mentally Handicapped was appointed to advise the Minister on policies and services. A closely associated Development Team, set up in 1976, advises at local level on joint planning for comprehensive policies, and has taken over the task of the Health Advisory Service with regard to the mentally handicapped.

The 1976 *Priorities* Consultative Document reported progress on the general strategy outlined in the White Paper in the balance between community and hospital care. Residential places in 1974 were more than 50 per cent up on 1969, Adult Training Centre places were more than 30 per cent up while hospital places had decreased by 10 per cent. Even with these improvements there are still five times more mentally handicapped people in hospital than in local authority homes.

Apart from training and residential care local authorities are also required to provide support, including casework and welfare aids, for families who have handicapped members at home. 'Social workers should work with the family and with the staff of the residential home, the foster parent or landlady. They should also be in contact with other people as need arises.'[96] The Conservative government of 1979, while making cuts in the funding of local authority services, emphasised the importance of voluntary activity and self-help and it may be that any growth in family support services must come from the voluntary agencies.

Guardianship, under Section 6 of the 1959 Act, continues a provision that began with the 1913 legislation. It allows for a mentally ill or severely subnormal patient of any age who could live in the community, provided there was adequate protection and control, to be placed under the supervision of a guardian. Similarly people under 21 suffering from subnormality or a psychopathic disorder can be placed under the guardianship order. The local authority can act as guardian, and so can the parents of the patients. The advantage of a guardianship order is that it allows parents to exercise authority with support of the local authority that would normally not be appropriate for an adult and gives supervision to the handicapped person in the community. It is possible, for instance, to exercise control over the patient's place of residence and attendance at a training centre. The procedures applying to guardianship applications are as stringent as those for compulsory admission under Section 26 of the 1959 Act and require both medical and social services approval for presentation to court.

Subnormality is the second category described in the 1959 Act and refers to people whose condition includes subnormality of intelligence, and 'requires or is susceptible to medical treatment or other special care or training'. There is no clear demarcation line between these two categories, but an intelligence quotient of 50 'is commonly taken as a broad dividing line'[97] although it is accepted that it is not a precise measure and decisions about need for treatment and care must be based also on emotional stability, physical endowments, and the quality of support available in the family and community. At the upper end of the subnormal range there is again no clear dividing line and many people will lead ordinary lives even though they suffer from a mild degree of subnormality. The hospital census found that about one-third of the inmates had IQs above 50 and of these more than half had no disabilities that required hospital care. Their needs were social rather than medical and represented a shortfall in community provision.

Should severe subnormality and subnormality be included in the same legislative provisions as mental illness? This question is discussed in both the Consultative Document[98] and the White Paper reviewing the 1959 Act.[99] Inclusion suggests incorrectly that these are psychiatric conditions but in any case those sections of the 1959 Act now remaining in force that deal with compulsory powers in relation to psychiatric and behaviour disorders which may pose a threat to the patient or to others apply to any person regardless of his intellectual capacity. The White Paper is cautious and recommends retention of subnormality within the legislation, for the small number of patients for whom compulsion is necessary. One strong recommendation is that there should be formal recognition of the change of designation that has taken place in practice whereby the term 'mental subnormality' has been replaced by the term 'mental handicap'.

Psychopathic disorder refers to people who may or may not suffer from subnormality of intellect, but whose behaviour is abnormally aggressive or seriously irresponsible, and who require or would be susceptible to medical treatment. This category represents a tidying up of the mental deficiency legislation concerned with 'moral defectives'. The 1959 Act specifically excludes promiscuity or immoral conduct as being in themselves evidence of mental disorder. Defining these in anything other than personal and value-laden terms would be difficult. However, the Royal Commission discusses at length the problem of the psychopath: 'The difficulty is that what distinguishes psychopathic patients from ordinary citizens is their general behaviour, not loss of reason, or serious lack of intelligence'. Many psychopaths have therefore not been liable to treatment under the mental deficiency or the lunacy legislation and yet have been in need of protection themselves, or in need of a control broader than the criminal law would allow. The Royal Commission concluded that compulsory powers should be available to ensure training and supervision during adolescence and early adult life. Any guardianship order relating to a psychopath must be made before the age of 21 and be terminated at 25, by which time the patient should have shown either some adjustment to the demands of life, or that further training and supervision would have no effect.

The term 'psychopathic disorder' has also been criticised since it came into the legislation in 1959, but no acceptable alternative has been found, nor has there been general agreement on the use of this category. The Butler Committee Report,[100] the Consultative

Document and the two White Papers discuss the problem of legislating and providing services for these very difficult people who present 'considerable problems for social services departments'.

Mental illness is not defined in the Act, but is taken to refer to a disorder of mind in patients who have previously functioned normally. Mentally subnormal people may also develop mental illness. The range of mental illness is vast, extending from severe and very disabling schizophrenic breakdowns to a mild anxiety state in response to unusual stress. Equally extensive therefore must be the social service provisions, from residential care and sheltered occupation centres for the permanently mentally disabled to social work services in out-patient clinics and day hospitals and support of people at periods of particular stress, such as bereavement.

The White Paper *Better Services for the Mentally Ill* (1975) suggests that there has been a widening of the concept of mental illness from the purely clinical to an acceptance of the social and familial influences and consequences, and that this new approach should form the basis on which services are reorganised along interprofessional lines. The responsibilities of the local authorities include provision of day care and residential services, which should as far as possible be tailored to meet individual needs. The *Priorities* document stressed the importance of these services and proposed increasing expenditure for their development, as 'the most serious deficiencies in existing services ... are in local authority social services'. A real stimulus for improvement in these services can come from the transfer of resources from hospital to community as outlined in the Green Paper *Care in the Community*, July 1981. The paper suggests that about 15,000 mentally handicapped people and about 5,000 of the mentally ill currently in hospital could be more appropriately cared for in the community, and various ways of achieving the necessary transfer of resources are outlined.

The other major function of the LASSD with regard to this group of clients is in the provision of social workers who will support patients and their families, and take on the duties of Mental Welfare Officers under the 1959 Act, making application for compulsory admission to hospital if relatives are unwilling or unable to do so and he is satisfied that this is 'necessary or proper'. The 1978 White Paper suggests that the term 'Mental Welfare Officer' is now out-moded and should be replaced by 'Approved Social Worker'. The role of this social worker is by no means clear, and can perhaps be understood only in evolutionary terms.[101]

The proposed Approved Social Worker acting as a member of a specialist therapeutic team is a direct descendant of the Relieving Officer, the paid local authority officer, who, with changes in name and changes in law, has been statutorily involved for over 100 years with aspects of control and admission to hospital of the mentally disordered. The oversight of compulsory admission has never been a simple and single task. There have been other elements included in the statutory officer's duties which have usually combined together over time and have obscured the separate elements. As functions have changed with alterations in the orientation and intention of social services there has been a shifting of the officer's role rather than any basic reappraisal.

The Relieving Officer's early tasks under both the Poor Law and the Lunacy legislation involved him closely with the Justice of the Peace—the ubiquitous guardian of local law and order, including oversight of the dependent members of society. Certification of pauper lunatics for admission to the relatively more costly asylum rather than the workhouse was to guard the public purse, not to guard personal liberty. The use of certification by the JP for the latter purpose was introduced in the 1890 Lunacy Act, although distinction was still made between pauper and private lunatics on the basis of responsibility for their maintenance. Where the local authority was financially responsible, the local authority officer had the duty to apply for certification to the JP, but where relatives were responsible they had the duty not only to make application for certification but to visit at stated intervals. In 1948 the NHS Act ended distinctions between paying and non-paying patients, but the Lunacy Act continued to operate, and the Relieving Officers, re-named Duly Authorised Officers, worked now for the local health authority, retaining their close contact with JPs in the exercise of their duties. It was at this time that the Relieving Officer's duty to transport paupers unable to travel unaided to the institution might have been handed over to the new NHS ambulance service but for the fact that the RO also had a duty to hand over the patient to the receiving hospital as part of his continuing concern with order in the community. The task of transportation has remained inappropriately with social workers in spite of the development of psychiatric community nursing services.

The social background against which mental illness is defined and provided for has changed markedly from the concerns of 1890 with wrongful detention and financial responsibility, through the changes leading to the 1959 Act with redefinition of mental illness in medical terms (excluding the JP from the scene) to the modern broader view. The White Papers and the Consultative Document have drawn attention to the changing prospect in mental health. Several issues are controversial, in particular the powers of compulsion in admission, detention and treatment, and the role of the social worker needs redefinition.

Welfare rights

Ensuring the entitlement of the individual or family to financial benefits, services or exemptions from charges built into the complex system of the Welfare State is an aspect of work increasingly being undertaken by Social Services Departments. In order to inform the general public of benefits, the government advertises from time to time through the media. Such efforts in the short term are beneficial but claims drop radically when publicity is reduced and cost precludes prolonged national campaigns. Whilst ignorance of the right to claim is partly the reason for the low take-up rate, many people are still deterred because of a dislike of 'charity', the stigma of the means test, confusion about where to apply and anxiety about completing official forms.

Various voluntary organisations are active in the welfare rights field, but most local authorities accept this as their responsibility, thus confounding those who have criticised them for failing to make people more aware of their rights in order to save money. Since Manchester Social Services Department first appointed a Welfare Rights Officer in 1972[102] to investigate and develop ways of informing people at 'grass roots' level about their welfare benefits, a number of departments now have specialist workers. As it is so difficult, even for experts, to find their way through the administrative jungle of benefits and means-tested benefits, easier access to the legal profession through Citizens Advice Bureaux, Legal Advice Centres and Law Centres is a welcome development. Some consultations may be free or subsidised by the Government's Legal Aid Scheme.

To be effective welfare benefits must be used. As a positive aid to family functioning, there should be continued action at all levels to ensure that they become widely known.

Community work

Working with groups and communities is now considered an important aspect of social work. While the theory of community work evolved mainly in under-developed countries and the USA, there has been experimental work in this country from the 1950s.[103] The Home Office in 1969 promoted research projects in seven inner urban areas, which were predominantly experiments in community organisation.

The principal objective of community work has been described as being to help organisations and groups within the community (geographical community or community of interest) to identify their own needs and their own interests and to act together to influence policy and to obtain resources to meet those needs, and to develop the confidence and skill to achieve their own interests in a way that will lead to the improvement and greater fulfilment in life for themselves and for other members of the community.[104]

The Seebohm Committee emphasised the importance of a social services department being firmly based in the community it served and offering support not only to the social casualties but to the community as a whole.[105] The arrangement was seen as reciprocal with the community participating in the planning, organisation and provision of social services.

Although there has been a significant growth of community work in the 1970s it has been uneven, particularly in the social services departments where it would seem to be a marginal rather than a central activity.[106] Some voluntary organisations have shown more commitment, perhaps because they have a greater freedom to innovate.[107] Harnessing the energies of a community and stimulating it to greater effort may help modify the tranquillising effect that universal provision of a variety of social services may have had on the individual's view of his role and responsibilities in society.

Research

The importance of research for social planning in order to evaluate the adequacy and appropriateness of services was emphasised by the Seebohm Committee.[108] A number of Social Services Departments have established research sections, aiming to increase the operational efficiency of the organisation and to assist in decisions on priorities and the allocation of resources, sometimes in co-operation with universities and polytechnics.[109] The Social Services Departments' research role is further developed by the Social Services Research group, comprising local authority researchers and other interested people, who meet regularly to discuss their work. Knowledge of particular research activities may not, however, be widely known, leading to a duplication of effort even though the Institute of Local Government Studies at Birmingham University runs a clearing house for local authority Social Services Departments research.

Probation and after-care

To describe the Probation and After-care Service as a benevolent, family service might seem almost contradictory when it is so closely aligned with the courts, yet a closer look at its tasks seems to support such a description. Its history goes back to the appearance of the Police Court Mission in 1876,[110] which provided voluntary workers to assist offenders appearing before the London courts. At the same time in the USA a system of probation was being developed.

In Great Britain, the Probation of Offenders Act, 1907, authorised the appointment of probation officers, describing their function thus: 'to advise, assist, befriend.' This somehow encapsulated the caring elements of a professional social work relationship and it was retained not only in the Criminal Justice Act, 1948, but also reappeared in the Children and Young Persons Act, 1969, which placed on local authority social workers the main responsibility for supervising juveniles.[111]

The general requirements of a probation order are that the probationer lead an honest and industrious life, be of good behaviour and keep the peace, and inform the probation officer of any change of employment and address. A strict time-limit of between six months and three years is imposed by the duration of the order into which special requirements may be written. There is no denying that the legal authority of the court is an aspect of a probation order and has become embedded in the probation officer's social work. The value of probation is that it offers help to the offender within the community. Whilst the probation officer has a great deal of autonomy in relation to an individual probationer for whom he is responsible by order of the court, he is also responsible to the community.

Work with the offender remains central to the probation service, and the service has gradually become involved in the after-care of people discharged from detention centres, borstals and prisons. Voluntary organisations had previously undertaken much of this work and continue to do a great deal. In October 1964 a Probation and After-care Department was formed in the Home Office, the central government department responsible for the service. As the main object of after-care is the reintegration of the offender into the community, participation of ordinary members of the community was accepted as a necessary part of the process and the probation officers began to recruit groups of volunteers to assist them in their task of rehabilitation. By 1966 probation officers were seconded for limited periods for welfare work in the prisons as part of an effective system of 'through care', a process which begins immediately an offender receives a prison sentence and extends to his return to the community. To work successfully this system requires close liaison between probation officers concerned with prisoners inside the prison and those concerned with his family outside prison.

The Criminal Justice Act, 1967, confirmed the transformation of the Probation Service into the Probation and After-care Service. It also added new duties connected with parole, a form of conditional release from prison offering the offender responsible supervision in the open as soon as it is commensurate with public interest. The final decision to grant parole licence lies with the Parole Board which works in close co-operation with the probation service. Following the 1970 Wootton report,[112] the Criminal Justice Act, 1972, legislated to attempt to reduce the number of prison sentences by providing alternative methods of sentence to the courts, supervision orders with suspended prison sentences, community service orders, probation day training centres and deferred sentences.

As a result of the Act, day training centres were set up in Liverpool, Sheffield, South Wales and London, offering therapeutic, practical and educational activities. Day training centres are not a cheap resource as compared with Community Service orders where the offender follows his own employment but carries out an unpaid community task for not less than 40 or more than 240 hours in a year. When tried out initially in five areas, Community Service orders were judged so successful that the provision was extended to all areas from 1975 and this is now the aspect of probation work which is increasing most rapidly.

Whatever his future duties, the probation officer already has a wide range of responsibilities including those in relation to social enquiry reports for courts and divorce court welfare duties, areas of work which are growing steadily.

Following the Children and Young Persons Act, 1969, the Probation Service feared that it would lose all its work with juvenile offenders to local authority social workers, but it continues to be responsible for supervising a number of youngsters, particularly over the age of 14. The service is also involved in some adoption work and in acting as guardian *ad litem* representing children in court proceedings under the Children Act, 1975.

The Probation and After-care Service retained its independent, specialist status despite the Seebohm Committee's concern about this in relation to a unified Social Services Department[113] and despite the example set by the Scottish reorganisation when it became absorbed into the generic Social Work Departments. One argument for remaining separate was that a service primarily for offenders must remain immune from the possible vagaries of local politics.

The probation officer, as a mediator between the offender and society, considers his client best served by an agency that, although managed locally, is funded and guided by the Home Office. Probation is a well established service, one which saw the value of volunteers, which experimented in group work before it became a fashionable method of social work, which continues to try new methods of social work intervention[114] and which is now determinedly moving in to the community. Whilst reflecting changes in society and questioning its role, probation emerges as a confident, progressive profession.

Voluntary agencies

In 1948 Lady Williams in her introduction to *Voluntary Social Services since 1918* asked, 'Have the voluntary services outlived their usefulness?' This question posed at the end of the Second World War expressed something of the great changes that had been taking place in society. Statutory provisions had largely eliminated the need for charity which had been the *raison d'être* of many voluntary agencies. With the expected reduction in the manifestation of poverty those agencies most concerned with the particular evils that seemed to be a consequence or a cause of poverty—disease, ignorance, crime, mental deficiency—were faced with a need to review or relinquish their activities.

The Central Association for Mental Welfare, for example, handed over its functions to the new local authority mental health departments with a sense of satisfaction in this culmination of its pioneering work. The National Association for Mental Health, however, handed over its fieldwork activities in mental after-care, but continued its important work in teaching, propaganda and in the co-ordination of promotion of services for the mentally disordered.

The National Council of Voluntary Organisations continued and extended its function. Today it promotes co-operation between different agencies at local level through local councils of social service; and at national level amongst agencies pursuing similar objectives in different localities. It also offers advice and specialist help in setting up and running voluntary organisations through personal contact and a wide range of publications.

The variety of voluntary agencies, some well supported by public money, makes anything more than a broad description difficult. They include national organisations with very specific functions, local organisations with general welfare aims, self-help groups, community activities and many more variations on similar themes. Their workers may be paid professionally qualified staff, or untrained volunteers. It is, however, possible to examine the work of a few of these agencies which exemplify some of the current trends in the voluntary sector and in social work in voluntary agencies.

The professionalisation of some voluntary organisations has made it increasingly difficult to draw clear lines of demarcation between the statutory and voluntary field. The Family Service Unit is an example of this, developing from a small agency, which during the Second World War started experimental preventive work with families in a way that was much criticised because it was so personal and intense, to a fully professional service staffed by trained social workers, providing broadly based social work services for disadvantaged families. The majority of referrals are from local authorities who support the work of the FSU with substantial grants.

Dr Barnardo's, another fully professional voluntary social work service, differs from the Family Service Unit by virtue of the fact that it receives little financial help from national or local government and is almost wholly dependent on voluntary contributions, but on the other hand from the range of activities undertaken it might appear that its work is indistinguishable from that of local authority Social Services Departments. Now moving rapidly away from its traditional residential care image into a pioneering and socially orientated one, it has developed into a widespread organisation, particularly in the densely populated areas, providing a full family service with the focus on children deprived of a caring, stable family environment. It offers a comprehensive family care service working on the principle that a child should be helped, if possible, in the context of its own family using whatever method of social work intervention is appropriate. Play schemes, babysitters, day-centres, holidays, are examples of services provided. For children who require placement away from their own homes there are still the Dr Barnardo's residential establishments for physically handicapped, emotionally disturbed and educationally subnormal children, although increasing attention is being given to foster care and adoption for these children. As with the Family Service Units, the relationship with the local authority is regarded as mutually advantageous.

The National Marriage Guidance Council was established as a voluntary organisation with volunteer counsellors in the late 1930s in response to the growing concern about the rising divorce rate.[115] It first received a government grant in 1948 and now receives about two-thirds of its income from the government. The work the counsellors undertake is seen by the Marriage Guidance Council as overlapping the sphere of medicine, social work, education and pastoral care. Its own image is of a 'grass roots' organisation dependent on tapping good-will locally to provide voluntary counsellors for the well-being of the community. Some workers trained as counsellors by the Marriage Guidance Council are attached to health teams and social services departments. The organisation also has paid, professional workers at local, regional and national levels.

While voluntary agencies are free to innovate and experiment, or to work with clients who may be unacceptable to the city fathers as worthy of public aid (an example might be vagrants) those agencies that rely heavily on statutory funds may find that they have to accept the constraints of oversight and accountability.[116]

Voluntary agencies have perhaps felt threatened from time to time since 1948 but they are currently being wooed by the Conservative government as it proceeds to cut public spending. The Secretary of

State for the Department of Health and Social Security in a speech in 1979 said that 'they represent those most valuable elements in a free, open and plural society—diversity and independence'.

Volunteers

Reference has already been made to the contribution of volunteers in both statutory and voluntary agencies and it is interesting to note that with the increase in the number of needs which the community recognises as having to be met by welfare services the wheel has gone full circle in relation to who gives the help. The volunteer of the nineteenth and early twentieth centuries, whilst not wholly disappearing, gave way to the qualified professional social worker, who in his turn has begun to accept the volunteer back again.

In June 1966, the National Council of Social Service and the National Institute for Social Work Training, recognising the urgent need to examine the contribution made by volunteers to the work of voluntary and statutory agencies, set up a committee under the chairmanship of Miss Geraldine Aves to enquire into the role of voluntary workers in the social services in England and in Wales.[117] The Committee reported positively on volunteers, seeing them as resources and the voluntary nature of their engagement as an expression of participation and practical democracy. They seemed to have special gifts to offer—gifts of time, permanence, independence of outlook. It is an interesting commentary on the present state of social work that volunteers, rather than professional social workers, are seen as having time and offering continuity. The latter used to pride themselves on these aspects of their work.

Demands on social services are such that professional workers are constantly under pressure. The contribution of volunteers is valuable as long as they are not regarded as a substitute for professional staff in order to maintain a service more cheaply.[118] Keen amateurs offer an extension and enrichment of the services, as demonstrated, for example, in hospitals and in the probation service which have recruited, organised and supported voluntary workers for several years. The need to have an organiser responsible for the co-ordination of volunteer effort within the agency has been highlighted in various projects.[119]

The Aves Report recommendation that a focal point for all aspects of the work of volunteers should be established resulted in the setting up of the Volunteer Centre in 1973, funded by central government and the voluntary sector.

A fairly recent arrival in the voluntary sector is the 'conscripted volunteer', for example, the probationer undertaking community work as part of his 'treatment'. Therapy is for the giver as well as the receiver and clearly underlines one of the most important aspects of voluntary effort.

Self-help groups

The most striking development in voluntary effort in recent years has been the emergence of self-help groups. Self-help was, of course, a great virtue in nineteenth-century England and was possibly most evident in Friendly Societies and Mutual Benefit Societies. Whilst the older voluntary organisations, such as Barnardo's, are regrouping and finding new roles, there are today lively new groups attempting to meet their own needs.

One such group is Gingerbread, the eye-catching name for an association of one-parent families set up in 1970 with its national headquarters in London, and an increasing number of local branches. Members are divorced, separated, widowed, unmarried, prison spouses or parents whose partners are seriously disabled, and a substantial number of men is included. The local groups aim to provide a warm, friendly atmosphere, to help combat the loneliness and isolation which confront so many one-parent families and also to act as a pressure group for provision of better services for one-parent families and their children. That it met a need was dramatically demonstrated by the rise in membership from 5 to 5,000 in its first four years.

Pressure group activity combined with the satisfactions of social contact and sharing has been demonstrated by the Disablement Income Group, while the National Society for Mentally Handicapped Children (largely the work of parents of such children) has moved from a self-help situation to be an employer of paid professional staff, moving into the vacuum unexpectedly created when the Central Association for Mental Welfare handed over its functions to the local authorities in 1948.

The value of self-help is recognised and forms an important part of community work in local authority and in voluntary agency activity.

The churches as providers of social services

In the latter part of the nineteenth century and the early years of the twentieth, the churches and individual Christian philanthropists played a large part in the development and provision of personal social services. Today the basic unit of the Anglican and the Roman Catholic Church remains the parish, and the parochial system gives the parishioner 'the inalienable right to be cared for by the parson of the parish',[120] but the vast increase in population and the steady decline in the number of clergymen makes this care impossible, while the decline in church affiliation might also make it unacceptable to many members of the community. It would be difficult to decide who constitutes the flock today and what the difference is between pastoral care and social work. Pastoral care, the caring activity of the church, is caring for the 'whole person', but social work, the caring activity of the state, also offers care to the 'whole person'. Is the priest, therefore, faced with a loss of congregation, redefining his role today by undertaking social work in the community? A note in the Aves Report, 'we are aware that religious bodies of all denominations are increasingly finding themselves challenged to define what might be their special contribution to meeting human needs of all kinds whether at national or local level', might sound like a comment on an institution which has lost its way. Instead a vigorous ecumenical movement is gaining ground. At local level group ministries are being established in some areas with a single church serving all denominations and the clergy actively involving themselves together in the community.

The British Council of Churches is the central co-ordinating body and as such can act on behalf of all churches on issues of importance. An example is the Community and Race Relations Unit, acting for the improvement of relationships between the majority of the population and racial minorities.

The Roman Catholic Church supports regional welfare agencies throughout the country. They are mainly concerned with the care of children but in some areas, e.g. Liverpool, there has been an extension into other spheres of social work. The Church has a long history of effort for the single homeless and offers a housing advice service as well. A Social Welfare Commission was established in 1968 as a consultative and advisory body for matters relating to social welfare and social policy.

An outstanding figure in the work of the Church of England was Josephine Butler whose concern for the situation of women led to the development of moral welfare work which eventually became the direct responsibility of the Church. Statutory social services as they developed began to cover much of the work pioneered by the Church but there was no specific provision for unmarried parents and their children. Moral welfare work continued, therefore, to be staffed and financed by the Church of England in all the dioceses of the country. Many social services departments have now taken over responsibility for unsupported parents and any associated adoption work, although in a declining number of dioceses the Church continues, by mutual agreement, to do this work, grant-aided by the local authority. Increasingly dioceses are establishing Boards of Social Responsibility serviced by advisers who are engaged in enabling the Church to respond in a relevant manner to the social needs of today.

The basic dilemma, however, remains regarding the special contribution the churches should make in personal social services. It is right that they should concern themselves with local, national and international affairs, it is right that they should be involved in services to groups and individuals. But if the aim of the Church is the promotion of man's spiritual, as well as his material, well-being, perhaps it should have its own distinct ways of proclaiming the relevance of its particular message to people in the modern world.

Industry as a provider of personal social services

Industry is not acknowledged as a purveyor of personal social services; nevertheless it is responsible in a fragmented and as yet largely undocumented way for some highly organised services.

The various Factory Acts safeguard the work force generally and trade unions, described in the Aves Report as 'the prime example of self-help organisations', assist particular sections mainly in relation to conditions and wages. A number of companies, recognising that personal problems at home or at work can affect performance and that boredom and frustration on the shop floor or strain and anxiety at management level may result in sickness and absenteeism, are appointing welfare officers to deal with the personal problems of the work force. The Post Office was a pioneer in this field, employing its first regional welfare advisers in 1947.[121]

Some companies offer subsidised nursery facilities in order to attract workers with young children. Occasionally provision is made for school children before and after school during term time as well as in holidays.[122] The compulsory provision of nurseries by large companies would help not only working mothers but also lone fathers who wished to continue in employment and to care for their children. The TUC now supports the idea of workplace nurseries, although it believes that it is the state's responsibility to provide a comprehensive and universal service for the care and education of children under school age.[123]

Where provision is not made perhaps industry could introduce meaningful flexitime to prevent the necessity for many very young children being taken to child-minders before parents and children are fully awake or having to be collected late in the day following an evening shift.[124] The Equal Pay and Opportunity Campaign Group is attempting to encourage all employers to take action to improve their provisions for working parents, both mothers and fathers, when they have to cope with domestic crises by highlighting agreements currently being made between progressive unions and managements.[125]

An increasing concern in the community for the elderly is reflected in industry, where attention has been turned to older and retired employees, pre-retirement courses being offered to the former and social clubs, day centres and pension schemes as well as home and hospital visiting by paid workers and volunteers being provided for the latter.

Since the 1944 Disabled Persons (Employment) Act, industry has had to offer employment to the handicapped. A useful partnership should be possible between local companies and social services organisations in order to promote further the well-being of the disadvantaged and to extend schemes for the employment not only of the handicapped but also of ex-prisoners and others with social problems. Industry does, of course, give routine tasks to hospital patients and others to be undertaken in sheltered workshops.[126]

Conclusion

We cannot be entirely satisfied with the social services, nor should we be. Every step taken to improve the quality of life and relieve burdens has a consequence in altered perceptions of one's own duties, responsibilities and rights. Thus the base from which social services spring changes. New methods of care replace old ones and are abandoned in turn. The old ways are re-examined in the light of new insights and assessments of need. There is an uneven progression which brings not only the anxieties always associated with change, but also its challenges and hopes.

Further reading

Because the literature on the personal social services is so extensive, it is only possible to give a brief supplement to the books already mentioned in the text.

On social services generally see chapter 1 of the *Report of the Committee on Local Authority and Allied Personal Social Services (Seebohm Report)*, Cmnd 3703, HMSO, 1968. *The Report of the Poor Law Commission*, 1909, gives very full information on services at the turn of the century.

The Open University has many useful and up to date publications.

The reader should take note of the many government reports in this field.

8 Law as a social service

Clive Davies

Law is often recognised as 'the oldest and richest of the social sciences', [1] but seldom as the oldest, most pervasive and richest of the social *services*. It is not readily viewed in this light, partly because 'it has always been there', in the Judaic-Christian tradition, God-given and eternal. And because, on the other hand, so many people (including such eminent thinkers as Plato and Marx[2]) regard law as inimical to mankind, a social *dis*service—or at best a necessary evil. Yet the provision by the state of a set of legal rules, means for their enforcement and a system of tribunals to determine disputes arising under them meets all the criteria of 'social service' suggested earlier in this book:[3] it results from collective action, is designed to meet social needs and is motivated by 'social' rather than narrowly economic considerations. Among the declared aims of law in contemporary Western societies, apart from the maintenance of a 'Welfare State', are the provision of social order, the maximising of individual liberty and the protection of the weak against the strong (including the citizen against the state)—'services' hardly to be sneezed at, however much taken for granted by those of us accustomed to living under 'the Rule of Law',[4] and even though, like other social services, unevenly and imperfectly provided.

Law, however, is more than merely one social institution among many. It is the fundamental social institution, the basis of all others. To a great extent, law *is* society. Does law shape society, or is it the other way about? Do most people refrain from murder, for example, because it is forbidden by law, or is murder forbidden by law because most people refrain from it? The answer to all these questions is yes: the relationships are reciprocal. While 'every legal system serves the purposes of its society',[5] and primitive, feudal, capitalist, socialist and Welfare State societies all evolve systems of law to suit their own requirements,[6] it is also true that legal systems, in turn, determine the structure and functioning of societies.

The close connection, even identity, of a society and its law might seem obvious but it is often overlooked. Thus one critic of English law thought that it could not 'by itself remove the major inequalities from society. They derive from differences in wealth, education and power.'[7] He failed to see that inequalities in wealth, education and power are not immutable differences like those in height, weight, beauty and intelligence that law must accept as inevitable, but socially created and legally supported differences, which law may seek to reduce or remove, as indeed it has been doing in diverse ways in Britain in this 'egalitarian' twentieth century.

There is much more to law, then, that the traditional image of bewigged counsel arguing nice points before robed judges, and it would be inadequate to confine a discussion of law as a social service to 'legal aid as a social service'. It is necessary to attempt to look at law and legal institutions in their wider aspect: at substantive law (the basic rules laid down by law) as well as adjective law (the ancillary rules providing for their implementation).

Law and justice, though closely connected in most people's minds,[8] are separate concepts. One difference, that law is found everywhere and justice nowhere, arises not only because justice represents perfection, unattainable in an imperfect world, but also because there is too little agreement among mankind as to where justice lies: it depends on one's ideology and where one happens to stand. Some people, for example, think socialism just: others think it theft. Justice is like the rainbow or the stuff that pipe-dreams are made of—agreeable to contemplate but profitless to pursue. A more practical quest is for the elimination or reduction of the more blatant and avoidable *in*justices, as they seem to us, in society.[9] Injustice under law may arise from three sources: the content, quality and adequacy (or lack of them) of the law itself; unequal knowledge and understanding of the law among those who are subject to it; and unequal access to the services of lawyers and the courts. They are discussed successively in the following sections.

Law and its reform

A society's law is the formal part of the set of rules by which its people live and are governed. Consensus and conflict theorists disagree whether law represents more closely the tacitly agreed wishes of society in general or the wishes of its ruling classes.[10] Current English law,[11] like most systems, is a mixture of both—there is undoubted consensus, for example, for the laws prohibiting murder, rape and theft, but not for the laws abolishing capital punishment, flogging and birching. Those of us who do not like the law are free in a Parliamentary democracy to try to change it, and can hardly fail to succeed if the consensus (or even a bare majority) is with us, given sufficient ability, determination, good organisation and time.[12] English law is nothing if not flexible.

For contemporary English law is the product of more than 1,000 years' continuous 'organic' growth. Earlier in this century Sir William Anson likened it to 'a house ... of rambling structure ... built by many hands ... convenient rather than symmetrical'.[13] There may be too strong a hint of affection, not to say complacency, in that description: Sir William probably gave little thought to the discomforts of those confined to the house's bleaker attics and more dismal basements, still less to those obliged to clean its chimneys and drains; his viewpoint was from the drawing-room. But rambling old houses have drawbacks as well as advantages even for those who own and control them, and another dispute is between those who think that the time has come to knock the old place down and replace it with a modern structure, and those who believe that it can be modified yet again to meet the strains of the late twentieth century as it has met, with relative success, those of previous times.

The law is to be found in *Acts of Parliament* (or statutes) and *case law* (or precedents, or judge-made law). Until the mid-nineteenth century, case law was the major part and statute law a mere appendage, but now 'more law is made by Parliament and Ministers of the Crown than by judges',[14] a consequence of the shift towards a more closely controlled society and the Welfare State. Confusingly for most laymen, case law is composed of two separate streams, *common law* and *equity*: common law, the older and still principal part, originally developed in early Norman times from the customary law of the Anglo-Saxons, while equity originated in the thirteenth century as a supplement to remedy the grosser defects of the common law; and has been revived, as 'new equity', from 1947,[15] notably by Lord Denning, who believes that judges still have a duty to shape law, as far as they have the power to do, to accord with 'ordinary right-thinking people's idea of what is right'. For centuries law and equity were administered in two separate systems of courts; the Judicature Acts, 1873–5, fused the two systems of courts, but retained the separateness of the two systems of law, so that a right or remedy today may still be either 'legal' or 'equitable', and thus subject to different rules.

Another division is between *private law*, governing the relationships of citizens among themselves (marriage and divorce, wills and intestacy, contract, tort and so on), and *public law*, governing the relationship between citizen and state (criminal law, constitutional law and administrative law). More familiar to most people is the division between *civil law*, which provides remedies for citizens injured or aggrieved by the actions of others, and *criminal law*, which provides punishment or other sanctions for actions treated as wrongs committed (primarily) against the state. The importance of this distinction is emphasised by the provision of, broadly speaking, separate sets of courts,[16] the greater degree of stigma attached to criminal behaviour and the different burdens of proof applying to civil and criminal proceedings—the plaintiff in a civil case need prove his case only 'on a preponderance of probabilities' but a criminal prosecution must be proved 'beyond reasonable doubt'.

The beginning of the nineteenth century, soon after the eminent jurist Sir William Blackstone had described English law as 'the best birthright and noblest inheritance of mankind',[17] was the period of the 'Waltham Black' code, when nearly 150 crimes (many petty) were punishable by death, when small children could be hanged for stealing, and when the ordinary Englishman had little contact with law except when he, or someone he knew, found himself in the dock on a criminal charge. Common people had little notion of having any rights at law, still less of pursuing them to court. Nineteenth-century law now seems openly to have served the interests of *laissez-faire* capitalism, particularly those of entrepreneurs. There was scant protection for employees, tenants or consumers, for the doctrine of freedom of contract meant that people must be bound by the terms of agreements 'voluntarily' entered—little allowance being made for the social realities of differences in the parties' knowledge, wealth and bargaining power. Workpeople were especially disfavoured: the common law doctrines of common employment (that a workman injured as a result of the negligence of a fellow-workman had no redress against his employer), of contributory negligence (that a person injured in an accident for which he was even partly responsible had no claim at all) and that 'a personal action dies with the person' (that a person's dependants had no claim in respect of an accident resulting in his death) all militated against the interests of working people at a time when industrial accidents maimed and killed with horrifying frequency. Few working men had the vote till quite late in the century, and, though the Combination Acts (which outlawed trade unions, while leaving employers free to combine) were largely repealed in 1824, their effects lingered on much later—the Tolpuddle Martyrs were tried in 1834. Those who could or would not work were subject to the 'deterrent' harshness of the Poor Law, described elsewhere in this book.[18] Female inferiority was a doctrine as firmly established as *laissez-faire*: women were without the vote and married women without the right to control their own property.

The past century has brought reforms in all these areas. Common employment, contributory negligence and 'personal actions die with the person' were abolished by statute in, respectively, 1948, 1945 and 1846–1934.[19] The rights of workpeople to form unions and strike were firmly established in 1871 and 1906.[20] Statutory attempts have also been made to secure minimal conditions of employment for certain classes of worker[21]—though such provisions can have only limited effect in a society where supply and demand and relative bargaining-power continue to dominate such issues. Attempts to protect tenants have been made by a long line of Landlord and Tenant and Housing Acts, discussed elsewhere,[22] and to protect consumers by a succession of Food and Drugs legislation, the Sale of Goods Act, 1893, and, most recently, the Fair Trading Act, 1973. The rigours of the Poor Law have been replaced by the relative generosity of Social Security.[23] Women achieved the right to vote on the same terms as men in 1929, the right to control their property after marriage in 1935 and the right to be treated generally as men's equals in 1975.[24] 'Law for the underprivileged' is beginning to develop as a new and separate branch of law, and gradually winning acceptance in the curricula of law students at universities and colleges.[25]

The most important socio-legal changes of the twentieth century, however, have been made by the great public law statutes creating our mixed-economy Welfare State society—the various nationalising Acts and the statutes providing for education, the health service and the other social services. Major statutory reforms in private law (realms more generally thought of as 'lawyers' law') include the simplification of land law by the property legislation of 1922–5, the introduction of legitimation and adoption in 1926,[26] the liberalisation of divorce law by the Acts of 1937 and 1969,[27] modernisation of the law of inheritance in 1925–38,[28] and the introduction of the citizen's right to sue the Crown in 1945:[29] 'Judicial legislation', too, has continued, by such relatively little-publicised steps as the introduction of legal abortions as early as 1939,[30] and the extension of tortious liability in negligence in 1932[31] and intimidation in 1964.[32] In criminal law the major development has been the attempt at a more humane attitude to young offenders in the Children and Young Persons Acts of 1933 and 1969, though another landmark in law reform was the Criminal Justice Act, 1948, which abolished flogging and birching and sought to lay the foundations for a more constructive post-war penal policy. These last reforms, especially the Act of 1969, have been increasingly attacked since the mid-1970s as 'too soft on criminals' and having manifestly failed to work (the 'crime rate'[33] rose some five-fold between 1948 and 1978), and the Conservative government elected in 1979 promised a return to sterner methods of crime control.

1965–75 was an unusually active decade in law reform: an unprecedented spate of books and pamphlets critical of the law (see Further Reading) in the mid-1960s, was followed by the passage of statutes, many of which brought in reforms suggested in the books.

Among the statutes were the Criminal Law Act, 1967, abolishing the ancient and anomalous distinction between felonies and misdemeanours; the Parliamentary Commissioner Act, 1967, establishing the British Ombudsman; the Sexual Offences Act, 1967, legalising most forms of homosexual activity; the Abortion Act, 1967, putting on a statutory footing the law given in the judgment of 1939; the Theft Act, 1968, rationalising and modernising the law relating to offences against property; the Children and Young Persons Act, 1969, transferring to social workers a greater share of the responsibility for the treatment of young offenders; the Divorce Reform Act, 1969, providing a completely new basis for the law of divorce; the Sex Discrimination Act, 1975, and the Race Relations Act, 1976; apart from important Acts introducing changes in the machinery and administration of the law, some of which are mentioned in Section 3, below. The 1980s seem likely to be, by contrast, a period of cautious retrenchment, not to say reaction, in the sphere of law reform.

For, while criticism of the law remains, quite rightly, strong, it is hard to judge which reforms should secure priority. Arguably the most urgent need for reform is in the mundane sphere of taxation law, for greater social equality and improved social services (if they are what society really wants) can be achieved only by taxation: yet (legal) 'tax avoidance' and (illegal) 'tax evasion'[34] are widespread, revenue law being viewed as a kind of game, in which taxpayers try to find loopholes in the law while Parliament tries to stop them. In a complex economy the task of devising a fair and effective system of taxation must be difficult, and it is not made easier by the employment of able and highly paid experts to thwart the intentions of Parliament, nor by the fluctuating tax policies of successive governments. Improvements, however, could be made, with will and application; a start might be made, possibly with more than symbolic value, by abolishing the judge-made rule that taxing statutes must be interpreted 'restrictively', that is in favour of the taxpayer[35]—and so against the interests of the beneficiaries of taxes (the old, the sick and people who cannot work).

Wider assent would doubtless be given to the need for clarification of the law. As Mr Justice Scarman has said,[36] law must be complex (because human behaviour is complex and there must be rules of law to cover its every aspect), but it need not be obscure. Law which can be found only in assorted statutes (enacted at the rate of nearly 100 a year) and cases (reported at the rate of over 1,000 a year), some of them centuries old, is highly obscure. In Sir Leslie's view, consolidating and codifying statutes should have high priority, and few would disagree, but Parliamentary time is not easily found.

The law relating to compensation for tort is a 'forensic lottery', in one writer's words,[37] in which a person is likely to receive compensation if he is injured by a car but not if injured by a bicycle (because motorists must be insured while cyclists need not), compensation depending, in any case, on the chance of reliable witnesses happening to be available. For years debate has continued about replacing the 'fault' or 'liability' basis of tort (that compensation should be payable only by someone who is negligent or in some other way at fault) by the 'insurance' idea (that every injured person should be entitled to compensation—from a central, presumably state-organised, pool of funds—irrespective of the tortfeasor's financial standing and degree of fault).[38] An obstacle to this reform is that 'fault' theory accords with most people's idea of what is morally right.

The issue of civil liberty leads to continuous controversy between libertarians, jealous to preserve and extend civil rights (the rights of the individual against the state and its agents the police), and the 'law and order' faction, who would curtail such rights in the interests of greater social order. The former school of thought is ably represented by the National Council for Civil Liberties (NCCL);[39] the latter has no such continuous sounding-board but is equally ably represented from time to time by eminent ex-policemen[40] and men of law[41] and may well constitute a 'silent majority'. The question arises most often in the sphere of criminal procedure and evidence, where the law is regularly castigated from opposite flanks as acquitting too many who are guilty[42] and convicting too many who are innocent.[43] Do such converse criticisms cancel each other out, suggesting that the present system is working reasonably well, or do they support each other in urging the need for radical reappraisal?

Criminal law in general, indeed, still marred by such anachronisms as the caging of a (presumptively innocent) defendant in a 'dock' in court, the power of magistrates to imprison without trial by refusal of bail[44] and of Crown Court judges to do so for contempt of court,[45] seems a ripe field for reform to its many critics. Both more subtly and more fundamentally, the substantive rules of criminal law are criticised for systematically discriminating against the poor, weak and uneducated by treating their typical forms of wrong-doing (assault, simple theft, burglary) as crimes, while dealing less harshly with the arguably equally anti-social misconduct (mental cruelty, excessive profiteering, environmental pollution) more typical of the educated, rich and powerful;[46] reform in this area, going to the roots of society as well as of criminal law, would present great difficulties both in drafting and subsequent enforcement, even if it commanded popular support (which is doubtful). All these issues are well illustrated in the sphere of juvenile crime: there is widespread tolerance for the errors of youth, but most crime is committed by juveniles, and all crime is at best an irritating nuisance, at worst a frightening menace; society's consequent ambivalence between the concept of juvenile offenders as 'children in trouble'[47] requiring help, and as 'little criminals' requiring punishment, is perennial.

The law is capable, in theory, of adding almost infinitely to the 'enlargement of rights' thought by Professor Titmuss[48] to be the hallmark of the Welfare State. The right to a dwelling, to a job and to privacy, for example, sound desirable, but all present problems. The first would require dispossession of the 'overhoused' to make room for the homeless, a course of action acceptable to few. The second could be realised in practice only by creating large numbers of state-provided jobs, which could be construed as a return to the workhouse or chain-gang solution, worse than the present system of enforced idleness on 'the dole'. So too, one man's right to privacy is a restriction on everyone else's right to knowledge. On all of these issues there is too much disagreement for the path ahead to be at all clear.

What can law reform do, within the existing social framework, to help the deprived and underprivileged in a general way? Much of the above is relevant, of course—especially the redistribution of wealth by more effective taxation and the right to a (reasonably paid) job and to shelter; but the law relating to the provision of education and health services is highly relevant too. Is law the best instrument for attacking discrimination against women, coloured people, ex-prisoners, ex-mental patients, gypsies and other travellers, the unintelligent and other disadvantaged groups? These, too, are questions about which society in general (like the 'experts') is uncomfortably divided and undecided.

Parliament, the prime agency of law reform, cannot easily act when the wishes of society are so far from clear: MPs, in any case, lack expertise, and Parliament is too preoccupied with other matters. Government departments attempt to keep under review the law affecting their own work, but they also are too preoccupied with day-to-day management to have much time for wider horizons and the more distant future. Accordingly *ad hoc* government committees and working parties are set up from time to time to examine and report on specific issues. In recent times, too, permanent committees have been established to keep the law under constant review: the (part-time) Law Revision Committee and Criminal Law Revision Committee, and the (permanent) Law Commission; the last-named body, whose establishment in 1965 was possibly the most far-reaching step in twentieth-century law reform,[49] has produced a ceaseless flow of working papers and reports, many of them resulting in legislation. The Commission's primary function, however, is the Augean Stable task of examining the tangled mass of existing law, clarifying it and enabling it to work more effectively, rather than to address itself to the large 'political' legal issues mentioned above.

Effective pressures for more controversial changes in the law, in fact, come principally from permanent and *ad hoc* interest and pressure groups[50] and occasionally from idiosyncratic individuals. Thus industry, the professions and the trade unions strive constantly to preserve and expand their rights and privileges at law: bodies like Justice, the Howard League, the NCCL, the NSPCC and the RSPCA work ceaselessly to advance their various aims; other bodies spring to life from time to time to meet particular situations, such as the construction of a new airport (the Cublington Residents' Association), a flood of pornography (Lord Longford, Mrs Whitehouse and the Festival of Light), or the abuse of legal process by drug manufacturers (the Thalidomide Parents' Association); while strongly-motivated individuals like A. P. Herbert (divorce law reform in the 1930s) and Raymond Blackburn (enforcement of the Gaming Acts in the 1960s) may sometimes achieve changes in the law if they are well placed, persistent, able and fortunate. If, as Eugen Ehrlich said, 'the centre of gravity of law is in the will of the people',[51] their will expresses itself in curiously roundabout ways.

Public legal knowledge

The legal maxim 'ignorance of the law excuses no man' has the corollary that everyone knows the law—an absurd proposition, for even lawyers are often ignorant of large areas of law outside their own specialisms. Every man cannot be his own lawyer any more than he can be his own doctor, because he lacks the necessary knowledge; but just as it is good for a man's physical and medical health to have a working knowledge of his principal bodily functions and the like, so is it good for his legal, social and political health to have a general understanding of the main principles of law.

Such a basic understanding is generally lacking. Englishmen down the ages, learning that solicitors' offices and law-courts are places best avoided, have viewed law with distaste and fear. But ignorance of law is a disadvantage in a complex and impersonal society where it may be encountered suddenly and unbidden. The legally ignorant are too much at the mercy of smart alecs, cheats, the unscrupulous, the powerful, the knowledgeable, users of small print and others who can exploit them. Laws against tenant harassment and unfair trading practice, for example, cannot help people who know nothing of them or the rights and remedies they give.

One of the virtues of the English legal system is often said to be the part played by ordinary people in its administration. Lay justices (JPs) are indeed regularly and fairly deeply involved, but they are only some 20,000 and far from representing all sections of society—though the basis of selection has broadened somewhat in recent decades. Jury service also involves lay people in the work of the courts, but the commitment is neither regular nor deep; the basis of their selection, too, has broadened considerably in recent years, by the removal of property qualifications and the reduction of the qualifying age to eighteen[52]—Lord Devlin's description of the jury as 'male, middle-class, middle-aged and middle-minded' is no longer accurate. Surprisingly few people avail themselves of the daily free entertainment offered in the courts: those who do usually find the experience impressive and instructive.

Schools provide little education in legal matters. A-level law, it is true, is offered at some secondary schools, but it is not a popular choice, and in any case academically-inclined sixth formers are a very small proportion of the school population. All that most school children learn about law is a few disconnected anecdotes, having little relevance to the child's own life. Emphasis is laid on the law's aggrandisement and mystique, so that it comes to be seen as distant and remote, to be treated with awe, reverence and fear rather than an ever-present influence in daily life that, in a Parliamentary democracy, is supposed to belong to ordinary people, to control and shape for their own use and benefit.

The report of the Royal Commission on Legal Services, 1979, supported the suggestion that legal education be introduced into schools.[53] The Law Society now provides teaching material on various aspects of law for school children, and increasing numbers of lawyers, particularly the young, are anxious to cultivate greater social awareness than the profession has traditionally been credited with, a spirit which might well find a mutually useful outlet in involvement with schools. Few school teachers feel equipped to teach law, and there is a dearth of non-academic books on law for school children. Legal education for children, like sex education thirty years ago, is virtually unexplored territory. Many would argue that it is neither desirable nor necessary and even its advocates tend to disagree about approach, method and subject-matter. One useful approach might be to begin with the child himself, exploring in the context of his own day-to-day life and relationships such socio-legal concepts as the nature of rules, rule-enforcement, the right-duty complex, and property. Such a method of study might lead to a much needed demystification of law, a better appreciation of what law can and cannot achieve and an understanding that rules of law can be made and unmade at will: law would be brought down to earth, to the level of everyday life, where it rightly belongs.[54]

Public legal education, however, is not a matter of widespread interest today, and may not become one. This is to be regretted, because a wider public knowledge of law might have two important consequences for society. At the individual level, a person can function better if he has a fairly clear idea of his rights and duties: he is less likely to become either a victim of injustice or a menace to others. At the more general social or political level, it seems important at a time when increasing numbers of people are for diverse reasons turning to violent and other extra-legal remedies for various kinds of real or imagined wrongs that there should be a wider understanding of the virtues as well as the limitations of our present system of government and the practicable alternatives available.

The services of lawyers and the courts

Lawyers

The 30,000 solicitors of England and Wales are the general practitioners of law in that it is they who deal first with members of the public. They are generally thought of as office-bound, and many do specialise in non-litigation work like conveyancing, but they have a right of audience in the lower courts (where some 98 per cent of cases are heard) and some do a great deal of advocacy. The 4,000-odd barristers (or counsel) are akin to consultants in that they may be approached only through a solicitor, though their training period is shorter and their examinations somewhat easier than those of the junior branch of the profession. Barristers have a sole right of audience in the superior courts (where they appear wigged and gowned) and they are traditionally thought of as advocates, though many specialise in paperwork and are seldom seen in court; in general it is from the Bar that judges are drawn. The division between the two branches, like so much else in English law, is less logical than time-honoured, and the argument for fusion is raised periodically, but it receives little support from solicitors and less from the Bar; there is little general public interest in the question.

Lawyers have traditionally served the interests of the well-to-do (though, in doing so, they may incidentally have served the interests of individual liberty for all) and still broadly do today, service of the large corporations and house-owners having succeeded that of the great landowners in earlier times. Legal education reflects this bias: much attention is given to land law, conveyancing, wills and intestacy, company law, trusts, taxation and the complexities of civil procedure in the superior courts, very little to branches of law that affect the poor, such as welfare law, furnished tenancies, industrial accidents, fair rent legislation or juvenile court and administrative tribunal procedure—though, as mentioned earlier, 'law for the underprivileged' is gradually beginning to gain acceptance in legal education. The bias is reflected, too, in the situation of solicitors' offices, which are many in the business quarters and middle-class residential areas but few in working-class districts. (Barristers' chambers are confined to the centres of the great cities, some three-quarters of them in London.)[55] Lawyers' fees, of course, are well beyond the means of ordinary people.

A rudimentary system of legal aid for the poor existed from medieval times in civil cases in the *in forma pauperis* procedure, and from the nineteenth century in the better-known dock brief.[56] The Poor Prisoners Defence Acts of 1903 and 1930 put criminal legal aid on a statutory footing, but very few defendants were represented down to 1945. The Rushcliffe Committee Report[57] of that year led to the passing of the Legal Aid and Advice Act, 1949,[58] still the principal Act. Applications for legal aid in civil cases are dealt with by local Legal Aid Committees of the Law Society, those in criminal cases by the court. People with very low incomes and capital receive free legal aid; the modestly well-to-do are ineligible; those between the two extremes may be granted legal aid but be required to make a contribution according to a sliding scale. The lawyer receives his normal fee for the work, less 10 per cent.[59]

Spending on legal aid grew from less than £1 million in 1945 to over £100 million in 1980–81, a large increase, even allowing for inflation, and a measure of expansion of the service. Some critics, indeed, consider it deplorable—especially the expenditure on criminal defences. On the other hand there is well-documented evidence of a large unmet need. The 1974 annual official *Report on Legal Aid and Advice*[60] succinctly summarised some of the deficiencies:

> We have little doubt that (a) there are many people whose legal rights are . . . at present going wholly by default; (b) some of these are unaware even that they possess such rights; others realize it but either do not know how to obtain help in enforcing them or lack the money or the ability, or both, to do so; (c) there is a severe overall shortage of solicitors in the country and . . . their geographical distribution is very ill-suited to serve the poorer and more disadvantaged sections of the community; (d) there are considerable areas of the law, notably those relating to housing, landlord and tenant matters and welfare benefits where expert advice and assistance is urgently needed but is often hard to come by.

Five years later the Royal Commission on Legal Services[61] reported: 'at present there are too many people whose rights, for want of legal advice and assistance, go by default'.

Recurring criticisms of the legal aid scheme are that the financial limits have always been too low, so that going to law is a luxury available to the very rich (who can afford it) and the very poor (who receive legal aid), but not to those between; that too high a proportion of expenditure is on divorce (87 per cent of certificates in civil cases in 1977–8);[62] that legal aid has never been made available for tribunals;[63] that too little money is available for criminal appeals—of the thousands of such appeals reaching the Court of Appeal each year, the majority are 'home-made', often semi-literate scrawls on prison notepaper. The Legal Advice and Assistance Act, 1972, which introduced 'new legal aid' (making it easier to get up to £25 worth of free legal advice) did nothing to meet these particular criticisms.

The deficiencies of officially-provided legal aid are mitigated by a number of supplements, some well established and some more recent: a systematic survey carried out in three London boroughs in 1968–70[64] found that, in addition to the (few) solicitors offering their services under the official scheme, legal aid and advice were being given by nine 'legal advice centres' (mainly nineteenth-century charitable foundations in the 'poor man's lawyer' tradition), local authority legal departments and rent officers, Citizens Advice Bureaux, Members of Parliament and political parties, local authority services, the probation service, the courts, the police, hospitals, social security officers, trade unions, newspapers and miscellaneous other individuals and organisations. Since 1970 'duty solicitor' schemes and 'neighbourhood law centres' have begun in London and other cities. Under duty solicitor schemes a rota of solicitors is arranged to provide free legal advice at court to people recently arrested and charged with crimes.[65] Law centres, a very different concept, are staffed by full-time salaried lawyers who offer a continuous service of advice in all legal matters to the people of particular underprivileged districts.[66] The scene is thus rapidly changing and somewhat confusing: one observer described it as 'like the police before Peel'—fragmentary, unsystematic and incomplete.

Among various proposals for further reform are the establishment of a 'public defender' responsible for advising everyone charged with crime, the extension of lay advocacy (and even 'self-advocacy'), the introduction of the 'contingent fee' system found in some states of the USA (whereby the lawyer acts for an indigent client on the basis that he receives no fee if the action is lost but a share of the proceeds if it is won) and, more wholesalely, the introduction of a 'National Legal Service' providing a universal and all-embracing service on the model of the National Health Service. None of these proposals found favour with the Royal Commission on Legal Services, 1979.[67] Perennial obstacles in the path of reform are the shortage of funds (reflecting the problem of priorities within all the social services, and in national expenditure generally) and the insufficiency of lawyers to supply legal advice to all who need it—though the number of barristers and solicitors has grown rapidly in recent decades. Another is the conflict between those who wish to see an expansion of legal aid and advice within the existing framework (retaining, in particular, the autonomy of the legal profession) and those who contend that a solution can be found only by creating a new salaried service responsible either to the state (the National Legal Service model) or to community action projects (the neighbourhood law centre model). Thus, although the will for change has never been stronger, the way forward is far from clear.

Courts and tribunals

The English court system,[68] like English law, is a bewildering mixture of old and new. The House of Lords, the Court of Appeal (Civil Division) and the High Court all have medieval origins, but the Court of Appeal (Criminal Division) was first established (as the Court of Criminal Appeal) in 1908. The new Crown Court, set up by the Courts Act, 1971, replaces the former courts of assize and quarter sessions, both dating from medieval times. County Courts were not established till 1846. Magistrates' courts (which deal with the great majority of criminal cases and have important civil jurisdiction too) have existed continuously since the fourteenth century. Experimental Small Claims Courts (intended to settle minor disputes cheaply, informally and quickly) first sat in Manchester and London in 1974.[69]

Administrative tribunals are largely twentieth-century innovations, concomitants of the Welfare State. There are now more than sixty different kinds of tribunal and they have evolved unsystematically, in response to different needs, so that they vary greatly not only in size, jurisdiction and composition but also in nature and function.[70] Some (like social security tribunals) were established because the ordinary courts were too expensive, formal and slow; others (like planning tribunals) because the courts lacked expertise, policy consciousness or doctrinal flexibility. In some cases (like the Transport Tribunal) there is only one tribunal based in London; in others (like general commissioners of income tax and social security tribunals) there are hundreds, distributed throughout the country. In terms of numbers of cases dealt with and the aggregate cash value of those cases, the most important tribunals are those dealing with such matters as income tax liabilities, social security benefits and rent control; but tribunals which adjudicate less frequently (like planning tribunals and the professional disciplinary committees) make decisions which profoundly affect the lives of the individuals concerned and are also highly relevant to a crucial social problem—the balance between social control and individual liberty. Some tribunals have 'judicial' powers, that is powers to determine the facts of disputes and to decide them according to law: others have 'quasi-judicial' powers, powers to decide cases according to the requirements of 'policy' rather than fixed rules of law. From some tribunals there is a full right of appeal to the courts, from some a right of appeal only on points of law, and from others no right of appeal, but a right of access to the courts by seeking a 'prerogative order' of certiorari, mandamus or prohibition; not surprisingly, the provisions for judicial review of tribunals has been described by one authority as 'cluttered . . . up with an incoherent, complex, inefficient and jumbled mass of rules'.[71] In 1957 the Franks Committee made detailed recommendations on the constitution and working of tribunals:[72] some led to reforms while others (such as the provision of legal aid for tribunals and their power to subpoena witnesses) have remained unimplemented.

The most common complaints about courts have changed little over the centuries: that they are dilatory and expensive, and often do injustice. A more recently emphasised criticism is that they are, for social and economic reasons, beyond the reach of ordinary people, so that legal rights are without remedies. More specifically, criticisms are made from time to time of the archaic dress and speech, the jury system, the conduct of prosecutions by the police (instead of an impartial public prosecutor), the use of unpaid and almost untrained lay magistrates, the social isolation of professional judges and the characteristically Anglo-Saxon adversary mode of trial—that is, the 'gladiatorial combat' model as opposed to the inquisitorial or 'truth-seeking-tribunal' model favoured in European countries; all of these, of course, have their defenders.

A simple remedy for many of the deficiencies would be a great increase in the number of courts, a solution that would take time (for judges cannot be produced overnight) as well as money (where once again the problem of priorities within the social services arises). The rationalisation of the Crown Court by the Courts Act, 1971,[73] has been almost universally welcomed, by consumers as well as lawyers. A similar restructuring and rationalisation of magistrates' courts and administrative tribunals is widely regarded as due.

A more radical change would be the re-arrangement of the courts' existing work-load to conform more closely to the demands of social benefit and justice. At present, for example, the division of work between the High Court and the County Courts is determined solely by the cash value of claims, and in practice the use made of the appellate courts is determined by the same test—and so, in many cases, by the wealth of the parties. So too, on the criminal side, although the broad rule is that cases go to the Crown Court or a magistrates' court according to the gravity of the offence charged, in a wide range of offences (including many motoring offences, also theft and kindred offences) the accused has a choice; the option for a Crown Court trial (with its greater thoroughness and better chance of acquittal) depends more on the ingenuity, advisedness, experience and wealth of the accused than on the objective importance of the case. The jurisdiction of administrative tribunals has been determined by historical accident; disputes arising in such areas as rents, industrial injuries and welfare rights often fall automatically to be decided by a tribunal—more cheaply, informally and expeditiously than in an ordinary court.

As these examples show, the English legal system often appears to offer two separate classes of adjudication—'Rolls-Royce' justice for the rich, powerful and well-connected, and 'mini' justice for lesser folk. Thus a business firm's multi-thousand-pound suit or a rich man's trial for drunken driving, though hardly of greater *social* consequence than an unemployed workman's claim for £5 a week or an uneducated youth's trial for burglary, will normally receive a much more careful and expert hearing. So blatant an operation of market-place principles ('you gets what you pays for') is arguably as inappropriate in the sphere of law as in education and medicine.

There is little general interest in such questions at present, however, and it may be that a system in which, as Lord Birkenhead cynically observed, 'the courts, like the Ritz Hotel, are open to all', is indeed generally acceptable to society at its present stage of development.

The path ahead

This brief and necessarily elliptical account of English law and its institutions has dwelt more on its weaknesses than on its virtues. That is not because its virtues are not recognised. It is not enough to say that it is the best system we have, and that, miraculously (if sometimes creakingly), it works—and works quite well compared with many of our other social institutions. It must also be said that its better aspects (particularly the incorruptibility of our judges, including 'the great unpaid', the lay magistrates) are admired and envied by the world—despite occasional 'scandals' like that about 'jury-vetting' in 1979.[74] It may even be, as its many admirers claim, 'the best in the world'. But it is certainly not, in Sybille Bedford's words, 'the best we can do', and it will never be that without ceaseless informed criticism.

Law offers a better reflection of society than any other social institution because as well as being fundamental and all-pervasive it is also highly exposed. Its present state of muddle and confusion reflects the uncertainties, ambivalences, conflicts and, perhaps most of all, apathy in late twentieth-century Britain about the kind of society its people want.

Further reading

Of the many excellent general introductory books about English law for the student and general reader, P. S. James, *Introduction to English Law*, 10th edn, Butterworth, 1979, and William Geldart, *Elements of English Law*, 8th edn, prepared by D. C. M. Yardley, Oxford University Press, 1975 (a shorter book), are among the most widely read.

Books about the English legal system (dealing principally with the machinery of the law, the court system and the development of the various branches of law) are likewise abundant and include A. Kiralfy, *The English Legal System*, 6th edn, Sweet & Maxwell, 1978, and G. R. Y. Radcliffe, *The English Legal System*, 6th edn, edited by G. J. Hand and D. J. Bentley, Butterworth, 1977. Two 'readers' or 'source-books', Geoffrey Wilson, *Cases and Materials on the English Legal System*, Sweet & Maxwell, 1973, and Michael Zander, *Cases and Materials on the English Legal System*, 3rd edn, Weidenfeld & Nicolson, 1980, are both collections of the raw materials of law-making.

The *Report of the Royal Commission on Legal Services*, 1979 (see note 53 below) offers a comprehensive and clearly-written account of its subject-matter. Though long, at 4 volumes (it cost £1.2 million to prepare), its separate chapters provide well-documented and succinctly summarised discussions of separate topics like law centres, legal aid, tribunals, etc. Nor is it as conservative and complacent as its liberal and radical critics declared it to be; it is frequently censorious of existing services, and makes many modestly radical suggestions for innovation. Michael Zander, *Legal Services for the Community*, Temple Smith, 1978, is much more strongly critical of the *status quo*.

Of special interest to social workers is Michael Zander, *Social Workers, their Clients and the Law*, 3rd edn. Sweet & Maxwell, 1981, a clear and comprehensive *vade mecum*; J. D. McClean, *The Legal Context of Social Work*, Butterworth, 2nd edn, 1980, is an alternative treatment of the same subject.

Two brilliantly perceptive accounts by a laywoman are Sybille Bedford's *The Faces of Justice*, Collins, 1961 (comparing English and foreign legal proceedings), and her *The Best We Can Do*, Collins, 1958 (about the trial of John Bodkin Adams). Ronald Rubinstein (another layman), *John Citizen and the Law*, 3rd edn, Penguin, 1952, is now unfortunately out of print.

The separate branches of English law (e.g. family law, divorce, criminal law, equity, tort, etc.) are admirably covered by a wide range of books too many to be catalogued here. In most branches the reader has a choice between introductory students' texts (often supplemented by books containing extracts of cases and statutes) and the larger, more comprehensive, practitioners' works: thus in criminal law, for example, he may choose between Rupert Cross and P. Asterley Jones, *Introduction to Criminal Law*, 9th edn, Butterworth, 1980, a simple introduction (supported by the same authors' *Cases and Statutes on Criminal Law*, 6th edn, Butterworth, 1977), J. C. Smith and B. Hogan, *Criminal Law*, 4th edn, Butterworth, 1978, a longer and more penetrating students' textbook, and J. F. Archbold, *Criminal Pleading, Evidence and Practice*, 40th edn, Sweet & Maxwell, 1979, 'the criminal practitioners' bible'.

More critical accounts of English law are given in Brian Abel-Smith and Robert Stevens, *Lawyers and the Courts*, Heinemann, 1967; the same authors' *In Search of Justice*, Allen Lane, 1968; Michael Zander, *Lawyers and the Public Interest*, Weidenfeld & Nicolson, 1968; and Lord Devlin and others (ed. by Michael Zander), *What's Wrong with the Law*?, BBC, 1970. John Parris, *Under my Wig*, Barker, 1961, offers a more personal, amusing and irreverent critique. Martin Mayer, *The Lawyers*, Dell, 1967, a popular critical paperback about law in the USA, is worth the British reader's attention if only because so many American legal issues and problems become those of Britain a decade or so later.

The more amorphous areas of jurisprudence, law in relation to society and the sociology of law, are dealt with in Dennis Lloyd, *The Idea of Law*, Penguin, 1977 (a very lucid layman's introduction to jurisprudence); W. Friedman, *Law in a Changing Society*, Penguin, 1972; Morris Ginsberg, *On Justice in Society*, Penguin, 1965; Alan Harding, *A Social History of English Law*, Penguin, 1966; Harry Street, *Freedom, the Individual and the Law*, 5th edn, Penguin, 1982; N. S. Timasheff, *An Introduction to the Sociology of Law*, Harvard University Press, 1939; and G. Gurvitch, *Sociology of Law*, Kegan Paul, 1947.

Some of the theoretical issues raised in this chapter are taken further in Pauline Morris, Richard White and Philip Lewis, *Social Needs and Legal Action*, Martin Robertson, 1973, and by Colin Campbell and Paul Wiles (eds), *Law and Society*, 1979, in the same publishers' 'Law in Society' series.

Latest editions of books should always be consulted when possible; in a period of rapidly changing law a book that is even a few years out of date can be very misleading.

9 Towards an evaluation of the Welfare State

Anthony Forder

The first chapter set the background to the development of the 'Welfare State' and to the descriptions of individual services presented in the following chapters. Those descriptions present a confusing picture partly as a result of the pursuit of different and sometimes contradictory objectives. Changes of policy, often following a change of government, reflect these contradictions.

The purpose of this chapter is to lay some foundations for an appraisal of the system as a whole. After an initial description of the basic compromises involved in the welfare state, the discussion will be presented as a series of arguments between social scientists of different persuasions, followed by an attempt to draw the arguments together and relate them to the services described.

In considering the theories of social scientists two points need to be noticed. First, these are not objective discussions about alternative explanations of agreed facts. The information available is at once so complex and so patchy that there is little agreement about what is true or significant. Explanations therefore tend to take the form of simplified 'models' of the relationship between what the theorists regard as the most significant elements. The selection of what is significant is profoundly influenced by the values of the social scientists involved. This is inevitable in an appraisal that involves views about what should be as well as what is.

The second point to notice is that what social scientists consider significant is influenced by their particular discipline. So economists focus on the distribution of resources, political scientists on the structure of government and the processes of decision-making and sociologists on more holistic approaches to the structure and processes of society. In each of the arguments being discussed we will be considering a continuum of views conventionally seen as being from 'right' to 'left' of the political spectrum, from reactionary or conservative to radical, but concentrating more on the extremes of the continuum.

In each argument the conservative pole will generally be presented from the point of view of disciplinary specialists and the radical pole by Marxism. Marx was a theorist who spanned a range of disciplines in a way that was more common in the nineteenth century when the boundaries of disciplines were being established than it is today. The breadth of his radical analysis is still one of the strengths of his theoretical system.

The 'welfare state'

Marshall has pointed out that at the beginning of the twentieth century the future of the country was seen in terms of a choice between a modified *laissez-faire* capitalism and socialism.[1] But in his view, by the middle of the century a third way had been found, a combination of capitalism with economic planning and universal social services, that became known as the 'Welfare State'. In a later article he enlarges on the nature of the compromise,[2] as a combination of three different systems for the allocation of power and resources, based on different and sometimes conflicting principles—the capitalist system, the welfare system and the democratic system.

A capitalist system is one based on private ownership of the means of production. Resources are distributed through the operation of an economic market. Power is based on the ownership of property and the possession of saleable skills.Capitalism emphasises the value of individual self-determination within a system in which self-interest is harnessed to the common good by using resources as an incentive to action. Resources are therefore distributed as rewards for contributions to the good of others who can pay for them. The competitive attitudes and the inequalities that result are accepted as a reasonable price to pay for individual autonomy.

In a welfare system resources are distributed on the basis of need rather than desert. The definition of need is partly a technical matter, for example in the prescription of medical treatment, and partly a matter of determining priorities between the needs of different individuals and groups. Thus power tends to fall into the hands of various experts including professionals and administrators. There is an emphasis on equality as a central value. Co-operation is stressed rather than competition, and the main incentive to action is an appeal to altruism and the common good rather than to self-interest as such.

Western democratic systems are a form of representative government, in which there is accountability to a popular electorate. It has sprung from the same ideals of individual freedom and responsibility as *laissez-faire* capitalism, and similarly stresses the right and ability of the individual to make rational choices in contrast to the paternalism of the welfare system. However, the use of a majority vote for decision-making makes possible collective action, affecting individual freedom and creating a bias against minority interests that are often the concern of welfare. Democratic values include a wide distribution of power; and accountability as well as responsiveness to the views of the populace. In this way they are opposed to the concentration of power without accountability which occurs under capitalism.

While there is no doubt about the compromises involved in a welfare state from the conflicts between these systems, there is considerable dispute about its nature. Is it a new form of society as Marshall suggested or does the basic capitalist structure remain much the same? Is the compromise a stable one or it is just a stage in a long-term transition to socialism? Is it a desirable state, and if undesirable what direction should changes take?

In examining these controversies, first consideration will be given to theories of the economic market. This argument has been primarily conducted by economists. Second, two contrasting sociological models for the examination of social processes in different societies will be presented—the functionalist or consensus model and the Marxist or conflict model. These models present alternative views of the role of governments and of the social services in societies in general and in welfare states in particular. Third, two models of political decision-making in Western democracies will be presented—the pluralist and the elitist models. These throw further light on the potential for change within welfare states. Following this theoretical presentation, four major issues in the welfare state will be briefly examined; limitations on the state provision of services, professional influence, poverty and social justice. Comment will be made on the relationship between the arguments in these topics and the theoretical positions previously discussed.

Theories of the economic market

From 1776 when Adam Smith published *The Wealth of Nations* until the present day, one strand of economic theory has held that in a free competitive economic market there will be a tendency for the economy to reach a natural equilibrium in which resources will be used with maximum efficiency. This doctrine is associated with the so-called 'classical' and 'neo-classical' schools of economics which for most of the 200-year period have dominated Western economic theory.

This doctrine, and the theories associated with it, was developed at a time when the dominant 'liberal' philosophy stressed an individualistic view of man. In this view people are seen as being individually motivated by the search for pleasure and the avoidance of pain, each person seeking to maximise his own satisfactions as measured by these criteria. Since the individual can know best what gives him satisfaction, he is seen as the best judge of his own welfare. Social welfare is seen as the sum total of individual satisfactions. Therefore the highest value that springs from this view of man is the freedom of the individual to make his own decisions provided he does no active harm to others. Thus there is a bias against state or other collectivist action that involves compulsion. These value assumptions are always operating implicitly or explicitly whenever economic theory is used to justify a competitive economic market as a means of distributing resources.

In its developed neo-classical form the theory is an exercise in logical analysis.[3] It assumes a free competitive economic market in which individuals pursue their own goals in exchanging goods and services for use in consumption and production. It also assumes that among the processes of exchange are the payment of wages to workers, of profit to the owners of capital and of rent to the owners of land. The analysis shows that in these circumstances a situation will ultimately be reached in which no further exchange of goods and services can take place that will make one person better off without making another worse off, while in production there will be a similarly efficient deployment of labour, capital and land. This situation, known as the 'Pareto optimum' after its first formulator, is seen as an ideal condition from the point of view of the maximisation of social welfare. The argument therefore runs that if a competitive economic market will produce at least an approximation to this ideal without state intervention, the role of the state in economic affairs should be limited accordingly. It should ensure that the market is indeed free and competitive; it should ensure that the basic needs of those who cannot provide for themselves are met; and it should provide certain 'public goods'. Public goods are goods and services which can only be efficiently provided through collective action because it is impossible or very difficult to prevent people who have not contributed from enjoying the benefits. Examples are military defence, the maintenance of law and order, and the provision of such things as sewers, roads and lighting. This view of government provision of services has been called 'residualist', since the state is only concerned with the residual services that the economic market cannot provide.

To Marx and the Marxists the liberal concept of freedom is too narrow. True liberty is seen as being incompatible with economic inequality. Poverty restricts the range of choice open to people. But even more important, the man with only his skills to sell is in a very poor position to bargain with the capitalist or landlord who owns the means of production. Since equality is incompatible with a capitalist market system, the ultimate aim must be the abolition of that system and its replacement by communal ownership of the means of production. Economic incentives and economic control have to be replaced by altruism and social responsibility. Starting from this point of view, neo-classical economic theory appears as a subtle and sophisticated attempt to provide 'scientific' support for social inequalities generally, and in particular the socially determined privileges of the owners of land and capital. Marx and Marxists believe that the change from a capitalist to a communist society is ultimately inevitable, although there may have to be a revolution first.

Most Western economists reject the Marxist analysis, but they also tend to have reservations about the extent to which neo-classical theory can justify a policy of non-intervention by the state.

The most widely accepted reservations about the ability of the competitive market economy to maintain an efficient equilibrium are enshrined in Keynes's general theory of employment, interest and money.[4] Keynes was concerned about cyclical unemployment and his theory shows how an unregulated market can attain equilibrium with massive unused resources of labour and capital. The theory therefore gives government a role in regulating the economy, stimulating demand and investment in depressive phases of the cycle and curbing them in the boom. However, the failure of governments to control inflation in the 1970s using the Keynesian model has resulted in the re-emergence of monetarist theories of the economy.[5] These fit more readily than Keynesian theory with neo-classical theory and similarly support a policy of non-intervention by the state except for the need to control the money-supply—admittedly a much more complex operation than appeared in the nineteenth century.

There are other economists who generally accept the neo-classical analysis, but consider that intervention by the state is justified in a much wider range of activities than is accepted by more orthodox neo-classical theorists. One justification for this is the existence of 'externalities'. Externalities are the costs and benefits to other people which are not taken into account by a person making a decision purely on the basis of his own interests. For example air and water pollution are cost externalities of many forms of domestic and industrial activity; unemployment is a cost externality of closing a factory. Neo-classical theory assumes that externalities are relatively unimportant. But clearly much of the provision made by social services and by government aid to industry is concerned with correcting externalities of the economic market and industrial system.

The inequalities created by a capitalist market economy also present problems to many economists who accept a neo-classical analysis. This relates to two basic inadequacies of the Pareto optimum. First of all the Pareto optimum is not a unique position, since it can be shown that there is a different Pareto optimum for every different distribution of income and wealth. Second, the Pareto optimum excludes consideration of all the many exchanges that could make some people better off and others worse off. Some of these exchanges will, at a common-sense level, certainly increase the total sum of individual satisfactions. An obvious example of this would be the transfer of, say, £5 from a very rich man to a very poor man. The gain to the latter will almost certainly be much greater than the loss felt by the former. So many economists accept that compulsory transfers between rich and poor can be justified on the grounds of efficiency as well as equity.

Just as there are numerous intermediate positions among those who accept the value of a competitive economic market in supporting individual freedom, so there are also many intermediate positions for those who believe that the inequalities of income and power of the capitalist system are unacceptable. One range of variations lies in the extent to which a competitive economic market is seen as having any function in the ideal system of production and distribution. Another range of differences concerns whether a socialist or communist state can be established by reform or only by revolution. On the whole socialists tend to support a reformist strategy and are more accepting of some private enterprise in the final state. Marxists are more likely to believe that revolution is both essential and inevitable, and to consider that the capitalist system must be completely abolished.

These different theories have fairly obvious implications for beliefs about the nature of the Welfare State and its future. Those who believe most firmly in the neo-classical theory of the economic market and its ideology, are opposed to the Welfare State, both in terms of management of the economy and the provision of social services. The role of the state should be limited to controlling monopolies (including professional monopolies), controlling the monetary supply to prevent inflation, and making provision at a basic minimum level for those who cannot provide for themselves. Their policy for the social services is to transfer them back to the economic market as far as possible, making provision for income redistribution where this is essential. The alternative is seen as a gradual extension of state intervention on 'the road to serfdom'.[6]

To those who accept both neo-classical analysis and the mixed economy, regulation of the economy and the provision of social services by the state are seen as necessary for the avoidance of a waste of resources and excessive poverty and hardship. But they are seen as being compatible with and probably necessary for survival of the most important aspects of the capitalist system. Pinker[7] sees their approach as being essentially a return to the mercantilist philosophy and theories that preceded Adam Smith and the rise of classical economic theory. Mercantilism was nationalist in outlook, being associated with the rise of the nation state, and saw no need to question the role of the state in advancing its own interests and the interests of its people by whatever interventions could be shown to be effective.

Socialists tend to regard the provisions of the Welfare State as stepping stones to a socialist society. In this they agree with the more extreme exponents of the capitalist market economy, but value the end positively as a road to true freedom. They see social services as fundamental to the objectives of society and therefore reject a residualist view.

Marxists tend to see attempts to manage the economy as relatively futile defences of a doomed capitalist system. They often have an ambivalent attitude to the social services, welcoming the amelioration of the conditions of the workers, but fearful that it is only prolonging the existence of the system they wish to abolish.

The consensus and conflict models of society

Sociologists have been engaged in a long-standing argument since the middle of the nineteenth century on the most appropriate paradigm for the examination of social processes. Nisbet[8] has suggested that sociological traditions can best be understood as part of a more general reaction against the extreme individualism of the philosophy of the enlightenment in the eighteenth century and *laissez-faire* liberalism of the nineteenth. This reaction took both a conservative and a radical form. The conservative reaction can be traced through Durkheim to the functionalist theory of Parsons. It emphasises social stability, community of interests and a consensus on values. The most radical reaction can be traced from Marx to present-day Marxism. It stresses the role of conflicting interests in the structure of society.

Marx saw the structure of society at any particular period of time as being determined primarily by the relationship of people to the means of production, through the appropriation of the surplus production above a basic subsistence minimum. In a primitive economy, tools are primitive, there is little surplus and there is a large measure of equality. In a feudal state land and labour are the primary means of production. Power lies in the hands of the owners of land, who appropriate the surplus production to maintain both their power and their privileges. There is therefore an essential conflict of interests between the land-owners and the serfs and peasants who labour on the land. In a capitalist society it is the ownership of land and capital, but particularly the latter that determines the location of power and privilege and the resultant conflict. While it may be possible for the dominant elite to retain their position by the use of coercion, it is more efficient to persuade people that the distribution of power and privilege is legitimate and justifiable and where this is not possible to buy off opposition by genuine but minimal concessions. To Marxists government is never neutral. If it is not synonymous with the dominant elite, it is always its servant.

In functionalist theory society is seen as a system, in which, like a biological organism, the parts with their separate functions all serve to maintain the system as a whole. This model focuses on the essential stability of most societies which is seen to rest on a broad consensus about the values to which appeal can be made for the resolution of conflict. Conflict is seen, not as an essential element of the structure of society, as in Marxism, but as an indication of the malfunctioning of the system. The implication is that most conflicts can be reconciled by an appeal to reason and to agreed values or by the recognition that there has been a real shift in the importance (and therefore in the power) of some element in the system. To functionalists government is just one of the elements, though an important one, in the system, and dedicated to the needs of the system as a whole.

To both the functionalist and the Marxist the developments of the Welfare State are functionally determined. Their function, as Mishra[9] has suggested, is one of integration in two different senses. The welfare and economic activities of the state improve the functioning of the system through the co-ordination of its parts, by for example, the stabilisation of production, the development of required skills and the maintenance of the health of the work force. This is system integration in Mishra's terminology. The developments also help to reduce alienation and to create a sense of unity by making people feel their individual needs are recognised and to some extent met. Mishra calls this social integration.

However, the context in which these two sets of theorists see these functions being performed, gives quite a different meaning to the institutions of the welfare state. To functionalists social integration involves recognition of a genuine community of interests, and the development of institutions for system integration is part of a long-term process of functional specialisation. But to Marxists the change is essentially an illusion. The structure of society remains a capitalist structure and there has been no essential change in the distribution of power and privilege. As a means of social integration welfare institutions merely help to disguise the basic conflict between the classes.

Functionalism is a theory in the positive tradition, that is to say it attempts to provide an objective and value-free account of social processes. However it gives implicit approval to the values of the supposed consensus and sees conflict as dysfunctional. Though the theory does not require that sides are taken in the conflict, it implicitly supports the *status quo*. Its proponents tend to evaluate positively the present situation as a reasonably good as well as an inevitable adaptation to the present situation, but are also conservative in the sense that they doubt the possibility of effective change except of a marginal kind. In contrast Marxism is pessimistic in its evaluation of the present and of the potential effects of marginal change, but optimistic about the long-term future since Marx foresaw the inevitability of an ultimate change to a socially just communist society.

Pluralist and elitist models of political decision-making

While the argument about consensus and conflict models of society has taken place between sociologists of different persuasions, and is of very long standing, the pluralist-elitist controversy is more recent, and has taken place between political scientists and political sociologists.[10] The pluralist model has been developed by political scientists from studies of decision-making in Western democracies mainly in the post-war period. The elitist model is essentially a critique of pluralism developed by radical political sociologists. Both accept the democratic values listed earlier. The difference between them lies in the extent to which they believe that Western capitalist democracies achieve these ideals.

The pluralist model hypothesises that in Western democracies power is widely distributed among different groups and organisations. The groups include political parties, trade unions, industrial and business firms, the civil service, central and local government, military organisations, professional organisations, the churches and countless voluntary organisations and pressure groups set up for specific purposes. Government policy is essentially a compromise between the interests of these different groups, none of which is so influential that it can control policy. If any one centre does grow too powerful, countervailing centres of power will grow up, as trade unions have grown up to counter the power of industrialists and employers. The distribution of political power is achieved through universal adult suffrage, which makes elite groups responsive to non-elite pressure and opens the way to popular influence. The distribution of economic power is achieved through a competitive market economy and a balance between the powers of employers and employees through trade union activity.

Support for the pluralist model has come mainly from studies of pressure-group activity in influencing decision-making. It is recognised that this takes place in the context of massive political inactivity among the majority of the population, except during national (but not local) elections. It is assumed that this inactivity is symptomatic of a broad consensus on the appropriateness of the decision-making process. In this context pluralism becomes a theory of competing elites rather than a theory of non-elitism.

The elitist model sees the wide distribution of power described by the pluralists as largely illusory. In this view the interconnections between the members of the most powerful elite groups ensure that power is accumulated in the hands of a relatively small ruling class. In this ruling class policy preferences are broadly agreed and determine political and economic decisions which are accepted by the people as a whole. This compliance is ensured by the socialisation of the general populace into an acceptance of the existing order through education and the media of mass communication.

The positive evidence for the elitist model comes mainly from studies of the origins and connections of those people who hold the most important positions in political, economic, administrative, military and religious organisations. Having shown the way in which these leaders come from a relatively narrow social stratum, it is assumed that their common interests ensure agreement about the primary need to protect the interests of private property and to subordinate policy to those interests.

The negative evidence for the elitist model comes from the changes that do not occur, the questions that are not asked, and the possible solutions that are never seriously considered. Hall *et al.*[11] introduce their case studies of policy changes at national level in Britain, with a very careful evaluation of the two models. They conclude that the pluralist model provides the most useful framework for examining changes that do take place, but the elitist model may provide a better explanation of the limits within which change is considered.

Limitations on the state provision of services

Having presented so briefly the various theoretical perspectives, it is useful to see their implications for issues which affect a number of services. The first of these is the extent of state intervention in the economy, the second concerns the place of the professions in the welfare state, and the third concerns the causes of poverty.

The arguments about state intervention in the economy relate to two separate issues—the provision of social services on the one hand,

and macro-economic measures concerned with the maintenance of economic stability and growth on the other. This section is primarily concerned with the former, but something must also be said about the latter.

It is clear that conflict between distribution through the economic market and through the welfare system is a crucial issue in determining the extent of the state social services. This issue is discussed in the chapter on income and need,[12] but is mentioned in one form or another in almost all the other chapters. In each area of need some compromise is struck between state and 'private' or market provision, and these compromises have remained remarkably stable over the greater part of the post-war period. Yet for different types of need the proportions provided through the state or through the market vary markedly.

For example, about 10 per cent of total personal income comes from state-administered benefits. This proportion has been quite stable over the whole period since 1948.[13] Rates of benefit have tended to rise under Labour governments, but never enough to change the proportion significantly. Of course a great deal more income comes from the state in the form of wages and salaries to its employees and pensions to former employees, but here the state operates either through the economic market or on a similar basis.

In contrast to this, about 97 per cent of health services are provided through the NHS and only about 3 per cent through private provision.[14] While the Labour Party would like to reduce that 3 per cent without actually outlawing it, the Conservatives defend it and hope for an extension, without actively supporting it. Private educational provision reveals a similar picture, though more difficult to quantify.

Between such extremes as these, housing presents a more complex picture. Over a very long period, going back at least to the end of the First World War, there has been a steady expansion in the public provision of housing to let, while within the private sector there has also been an expansion of home ownership, accompanied by an absolute as well as a relative decline in private tenancies.[15] The result is that provision is more equally divided between the public and private systems and the interests of two groups, home-owners and council tenants, have become politically important. There has also been much more variation between the policies of the two main political parties. Labour governments have tended to favour more public provision, with higher subsidies and more control over private landlords. Conservative governments have favoured a greater expansion of home ownership, less control of private landlords and less subsidy to council tenants except on a means test or to enable them to purchase their homes. The present government response has been particularly extreme in cutting the building programme as a way of reducing public expenditure and in requiring local authorities to raise rents to a level that in some cases will produce profits. Nevertheless neither party has yet made much difference to the general trends (although the present government may yet do so), and the Labour party never pursued the policy of municipalising the private rented sector or attacked the economic privileges of owner occupiers.

If one takes the democratic process seriously, then one has to account for this stability by an assumption that politicians are responding to the attitudes of the majority of the electors. There certainly seems to be substantial support for the present balance, at least in the negative sense that people are broadly against reduction of existing services or the increase in taxation required to meet an expansion. While minority groups may press for expansion or contraction of state services in particular areas of need, a majority can normally be found for the maintenance of the *status quo*. More fundamentally this balance is maintained in a situation in which the majority of British people have an individualistic outlook consonant with the principles of the economic market. They accept the importance of financial incentives and support wage differentials; they consider that individuals have a duty to maintain themselves and their dependents; they believe in self-help to such an extent that for example they may consider defrauding the social security system by working as well as drawing benefit is less reprehensible than living on social security;[16] avoidance of taxation even by illegal means is commonly seen as legitimate. They have an implicit belief in liberty in the liberal rather than the Marxist sense. A substantial minority see poverty as being due to personal failure.[17]

Such attitudes have clear implications for the limits of state provision of social services, but they may have different implications for state intervention in the macro-economy. The belief in the individual's responsibility to work is complemented by a belief in his right to work, so that the government is seen as having a major responsibility for maintaining high employment levels and even individual jobs.[18] It is also seen as responsible for ensuring the continuation of economic growth and controlling inflation, both required for the maintenance of economic incentives. It is here that the failure of successive governments has led to the most serious loss of confidence in the political and economic system as a whole.

This analysis gives support for the value-consensus postulated by functionalists and for the pluralist model of the political process. Marxists, however, would explain the same situation in quite different terms. The balance between the state and the market is set primarily by the needs of capitalists and capitalism. Where state provision of services is high, capitalist interests are at the least not challenged and at the best positively supported, as in the provision of universal education and health services and all those services that contribute to the maintenance of law and order. The apparent consensus is based on a 'false consciousness' on the part of the proletariat on where their true interests lie sustained by the ideological hegemony of the capitalist class. The problems associated with the management of the macro-economic system, which to non-Marxist economists are primarily technical matters awaiting solution, to Marxists are symptoms of the ultimate crisis of capitalism.

Professional influence

A second issue that occurs in several chapters is the extent to which professionally qualified workers control or should control the services provided and decide the needs that are to be met.

The term 'professional' is generally used rather loosely and in fact there is no agreed definition of what a profession is.[19] For the purposes of this discussion it is enough to treat the title of 'profession' as a status symbol that is given to or sought by occupations which wish to gain status and authority on the basis of the recognition of special skills and knowledge. Emphasising the importance of their expertise, they claim the right to make decisions within their field, and dispute the validity of criticisms from those without that expertise. They expect a wide measure of autonomy in the exercise of their responsibilities both in serving their clients and in developing new techniques. They do not expect to have to carry lay people, or even the body of their colleagues, with them to endorse the decisions that they make.

To attain this autonomy (or more precisely 'functional autonomy' since it is limited to decisions related to a specific function) professionals have used many methods.[20] Teachers have established the school and the classroom as territories in which the authority of the head teacher and the teacher respectively is paramount. It is very difficult for outsiders, whether administrators, politicians, government inspectors or parents to penetrate the barriers that deter intervention so as to influence curriculum, or teaching methods or disciplinary procedures.[21] Doctors have ensured that the structure of the NHS both protects clinical independence and makes the service as independent of political control as possible.[22] Lawyers have rejected a service based on salaried employment in favour of a system of payment by item of service, which limits external influences on the practitioner/client relationship, and leaves the lawyer as the dominant partner.[23] The general comments in the Introduction on the influence of professional objectives on the structure of the services should also be noted.[24]

There is no doubt that the numbers and influence of the members of occupations seeking professional status has increased enormously in states with welfare systems, whether capitalist or communist. The meaning attributed to such developments in a welfare capitalist state will depend largely on the theoretical or ideological standpoint taken by the analyst.

To *laissez-faire* economists professional power, whether exercised through a professional association or a government organisation, is a form of monopoly which distorts the free choice provided by a free economic market. On the one hand the economists advocate the removal of state-protected monopoly privileges like the legal support of the solicitor's monopoly of conveyancing in property sales, and the prevention of practices that restrict competition such as the rules of professional associations that forbid advertising.[25] On the other hand rather than provide free education and health services, they consider that the state should give people vouchers to pay for services which they could supplement from other income.[26] Thus competition would be stimulated.

The Marxist analysis is critical of the role of professions in capitalist states for very different reasons.[27] Professionals are seen primarily as agents of the state in the support of capitalism. The more sophisticated analyses recognise that this relationship is not a simple one. It is affected by the contract developed with the state at the time of the first emergence and recognition of the profession when the political and economic situation might have been quite different from the present situation. This accounts for some of the differences between, say, doctors and social workers. A profession's position will also be affected by the degree of importance attached to professional activities for the stability of the state and for the promotion of capitalism. So while the state needs both doctors and teachers to maintain and reproduce the labour force, what doctors do to patients is less dangerous to the state than what teachers can do to children. So doctors can safely be given clinical freedom but teachers must not engage in 'political indoctrination' except to give implicit support to the present system. Having created these centres of power the government must recognise that sometimes professionals will successfully oppose the policies that it puts forward, but in the main professionals can be expected to favour the system that supports their relatively privileged position.

To pluralists, and to some extent to socialists, professionals and their associations are additional and generally beneficial centres of influence that ensure that a wider range of factors is taken into account in decision-making. Halmos,[28] for example, has seen them as a 'third force' operating to humanise the relationships between labour and capital, employer and employee, the citizen and the state.

Theories of poverty

The existence of serious poverty on a large scale has been a matter of considerable concern at least since the last half of the nineteenth century. The continuance of such poverty within welfare states has been a matter of growing concern since the early 1960s. Numerous theories of the causation of poverty have been put forward which are related ideologically to the theories discussed earlier. These theories have implications for the changes in the social services required to reduce poverty.

In the nineteenth century poverty was seen as being primarily due to the moral failings and personal inadequacy of individuals. In 1977 an EEC opinion poll[29] on perceptions of poverty found that 43 per cent of the people interviewed in Britain held views of this kind. This was a much higher proportion than in other European countries. Luxemburg came next with 31 per cent holding such views. The implications of such theories are that most of the poor should be educated or punished out of their unproductive ways while assistance should be confined to a relatively small number of those who are physically or mentally incapable of supporting themselves. The nineteenth-century Poor Law was based on these principles.

Rowntree's study of York in 1899[30] gave much prominence to the cycle of poverty within the life of individuals. The major causes of poverty were seen as old age, having dependent children, low wages, unemployment and sickness. This theory is mentioned in chapter 4, and provided the basic rationale for Beveridge's proposals for social security. The social security system has however failed to abolish poverty. This is partly because Beveridge's scheme was never fully implemented, but partly also because of inadequacies in his analysis which will be evident from a consideration of chapter 4.[31]

The 'cycle of deprivation' theory of poverty is a more humane elaboration of the nineteenth-century doctrine of personal inadequacy. It is associated in this country with the name of the Conservative politician, Sir Keith Joseph.[32] Instead of blaming the individual for his own condition he sees the cause of individual poverty as lying in the passing-on of certain attitudes and characteristics through the family. These characteristics prevent people from taking advantage of the educational, cultural and other opportunities that would enable them to break out of their poverty. The implied solution is a family-based educational programme to break the cycle, in which teachers and social workers are likely to be most involved. Rutter and Rutter's[33] thorough examination of the evidence from many sources in this country suggests that such influences are nothing like as important as the theory suggests. They found that recruitment into the body of the poor and 'promotion' out of it was too common a phenomenon.

Often confused with the cycle of deprivation theory, but very different, is Oscar Lewis's theory of the culture of deprivation.[34] Lewis studied a slum community in Mexico. He found that people in the community had many of the attitudes, values and characteristics that Sir Keith Joseph attributed to his 'problem families'. In his experience, however, they were propagated not just by the families but the whole ethos of the community. In part these attitudes were a realistic response to the situation in which people found themselves. Living from day to day, for example, was a natural response to a situation where disaster was always round the corner. Political apathy was an appropriate response to constant failure to obtain improvement in their situation. But changing the situation would not be sufficient in itself, since the responses were too deeply ingrained to enable the members of the community to respond to new opportunities. This analysis implies the need for a comprehensive community development programme, in which a deliberate effort is made to stimulate an interest in development and to provide services and opportunities in response to the stimulated demands. Both the American and the British poverty programmes seem to have been influenced by this kind of analysis.[35]

Finally the continuance of poverty can be seen as due not to specific failure, whether of people or services, but as an inevitable consequence of the structure of society. In any society a concentration of power will tend to result in a concentration of privilege, and hence in the existence of poverty and deprivation. In a capitalist society relative deprivation is a necessary consequence of a competitive system in which incentive is maintained by a hierarchy of differentials: there must always be some group at the bottom of the pyramid. But this analysis contends that the extent of relative deprivation in a capitalist state is determined by the role of profits in maintaining a highly privileged class.

Ideologically the theories that focus on the individual and the family are essentially conservative, although Rowntree's evidence about the importance of low wages has radical implications. The theory that poverty is a consequence of the structure of society is favoured by Marxists and some socialists. The culture of deprivation theory is ambiguous, depending on the capacity of the system to respond. In this connection the history of the British poverty programme is significant. Bennington[36] has recorded how the views of the workers in these schemes tended to change over time. Starting from a consensus theory which expected improvement from improved communication between the poor and those who provided the services, the workers tended to shift to a 'pluralist' approach, involving the development of new centres of influence and the manipulation of power. When this in turn failed they concluded that the causes of poverty were rooted in the system, and that only a radical approach had any hope of success.

Theories of social justice

One of the major aims of some people in promoting the Welfare State is the advancement of social justice. The question therefore arises as to whether the concept of social justice can provide an over-riding principle against which different approaches to the Welfare State can be evaluated.

If justice is defined as rendering to each person what is his due, social justice is concerned with the distribution of benefits and burdens throughout a society as it results from the operation of its major institutions. Miller[37] proposes that there are three broad criteria on which systems of social justice can be based: on rights, on desert and on need. Runciman[38] puts these criteria into political terms, suggesting a conservative, a liberal and a socialist theory. In the conservative theory there is a social hierarchy governed by a stable system of interconnected rights and duties. Privileges are offset by responsibility to those below. The liberal theory also has a hierarchy, but based on merit. Privileges must be earned, and the key to justice lies in equality of opportunity in competition. The socialist theory, in Runciman's view, is one of complete equality, but it can probably be better expressed as 'From each according to his abilities, to each according to his needs'.[39]

Both Miller and Runciman regard these criteria or theories as fundamentally incompatible, and consider that there is no principle that can finally place them in an order of priority. Rawls,[40] however, believes that it is possible to devise a theory of social justice which transcends such a pluralist approach. He makes use of the concept of a social contract. To work out the principles of the contract it is necessary to imagine people working from a position in which they would be ignorant of how they themselves would be placed with regard to those morally neutral contingencies such as birth, family and personal capacity which might affect what people received under the system. Rawls considered that in these circumstances the following general principle would be agreed:[41]

> All social primary goods—liberty and opportunity, income and wealth, and the basis of self-respect—are to be distributed equally unless an unequal distribution of any or all of these goods is to the advantage of the least favoured.

From this general principle, Rawls developed two subsidiary principles:[42]

1 Each person is to have an equal right to the most extensive total system of equal basic liberties compatible with a similar system for all.
2 Social and economic inequalities are to be arranged so that they are both:
   (a) to the greatest benefit of the least advantaged... and
   (b) attached to offices and positions open to all under conditions of fair equality of opportunity.

These principles are put in order of priority, so that I must be met before 2, and 2(a) before 2(b).

It is important to note that Rawls is not advocating complete equality, or that the least advantaged receive more than others. It is consistent with these principles, for example, that there should be great inequalities provided only that this results in the least advantaged having a higher income than they would otherwise have had.

Runciman[43] makes use of Rawls's contractual paradigm, but is much more cautious than Rawls himself in elucidating principles. All he is prepared to conclude is that while it is impossible to forecast the actual weight that would be given to the different criteria of need and desert, it seems certain that the distribution of income would be very different from the present distribution, and there would be little room for inherited wealth.

Miller, however, is very critical of Rawls's paradigm as well as the conclusions that he draws from it.[44] Miller considers that different principles of social justice are connected with wider views of society. An emphasis on rights, for example, is logically and functionally connected with the acceptance of a hierarchical form of society, especially where, as in feudal society, relationships are seen in terms of personal loyalties; an emphasis on desert is related to the impersonal operation of an economic market; need will have primacy in a social commune. Rawls's original contractors are deprived of such a wide view of society. So, in Miller's opinion, it is not surprising that Rawls's principles of social justice turn out to be very close to a 'liberal' theory of social justice modified in a socialist direction. This can be seen in the emphasis on personal liberty as well as in the way Rawls applies the principles to the organisation of the economic system. It reflects both Rawls's personal views and the nature of the American society in which he lives. The implication of Miller's position is that political philosophy cannot solve the dilemma of choice between different principles of social justice on its own, but it can help to clarify the issues, to give consistency to judgment, and to choose the principles that relate most closely to a particular society and the direction which its members wish it to take.

Whether Rawls's paradigm is fully acceptable or not, it does provide a useful way of stimulating imagination. While his general principle is open to a wide range of interpretations, it could probably gain a wide measure of intellectual acceptance as it stands. Even in this form it provides some basis for a critique of the institutions of our society and of other socialist or communist societies.

Concluding summary

At the risk of further over-simplification of complex theories, and the varied positions that can be held by different supporters of a particular theory, it seems necessary to try to summarise the issues raised in this chapter.

It has been suggested earlier that one way of looking at theories of the Welfare State is to put them on a conservative-radical continuum. However it should be clear by now that this is too simple. On the one hand the relationship between the theories at the conservative end of the continuum is a complex one. On the other hand when one considers their implications for change and possibilities for the future, there are some unexpected agreements between theories at opposite ends of such a continuum.

It is in the attitudes expressed towards capitalism that the theories fit most easily into the right-left continuum, but it is here also that the complex relationship between neo-classical economic theory, pluralism and functionalism can be seen most readily. Each of these three theories sees a positive role for a capitalist system, but for different reasons which affect their interpretations of the welfare system. Neo-classical economists tend to see the capitalist system and the economic market as the most important defence of individual liberty against state tyranny as well as providing an efficient system. Extreme exponents therefore see the welfare state as a threat to both liberty and efficiency. Pluralists see capitalism as one of many ways of ensuring that power is widely shared, so that Dahl and Lindblom[45] include a modified neo-classical analysis in their exposition of pluralist theory. But equally they value the welfare system for the same reason, while its very development seems to provide evidence of the validity of their model. Functionalists attempt to avoid value judgments and accept both capitalism and the welfare system because they are there and have a role to play in the total system. Functionalists will tend to accept both neo-classical and pluralist analyses as valid accounts of processes within the system, with pluralism, in particular, providing a justification for their belief in the existence of a consensus on values.

In contrast to these theories socialism and Marxism view capitalism negatively, although socialists are more likely to accept that a capitalist market economy may have a limited place in the good society. Socialists tend to support the Welfare State as a step on the road to socialism, but Marxists tend to be ambivalent about it, as a prop for the capitalist system.

It is in looking to the future that lines cross more overtly. Functionalism and Marxism are essentially deterministic theories; that is to say they see people as having a very limited capacity to control the way in which society will develop, and indeed to be to a large extent moulded by the societies in which they live. In functionalism the tendency of the system towards equilibrium makes the control of gradual change almost impossible, while revolutionary change is completely unpredictable. Marxists generally see the decline of capitalism and its replacement by a communist society as inevitable although people can speed or delay the process. In the meanwhile the potential for gradual change is limited by the concentration of power in the hands of the capitalist elite.

As against this, neo-classical economists, pluralists and socialists lay emphasis on the ability of people to influence the future positively, and on the possibility which flows from this of being able to initiate gradual change. It is in the direction of desirable change that they disagree. Neo-classical economists want to move towards a more dominant place for the capitalist economic market; socialists want to move in the other direction, while pluralists are likely to favour a mixed economy.

It can be seen that the arguments between these different theorists concern what is, what is possible and what ought to be. Into this debate political philosophy makes its contribution to considering what ought to be. If one accepts Rawls's position, it is possible to evaluate the present against absolute principles of social justice. If one accepts Miller's view, conflicting principles have to be balanced in the context of a wider view of what society is and what it ought to be. In either case, it is not difficult to show that our society falls well short of any credible criterion of social justice one uses. If other societies are little better, we must still ourselves face that challenge.

Further reading

Like the first chapter, the issues discussed here are so broad that further reading is essential for a grasp of the issues involved.

Until the last decade, almost all the analysis of British social services was presented within a fairly limited framework. Much of the writing was primarily descriptive and what analysis there was, was of the short-term effect of specific measures and proposals. The main theoretical argument was carried on between writers like Titmuss, who took an implicitly socialist view, and the *laissez-faire* economists of the Institute of Economic Affairs. This argument is still relevant because it probably encompasses the main alternatives that are regarded by most politicians as politically viable. It was dealt with in rather more detail in the last three editions and has been omitted to make room for new perspectives.

It is essential to read some of Titmuss to understand much of what is written on social administration. *Essays on the Welfare State* has been particularly influential. *Social Policy: an Introduction* provides a short account of his approach in his last years. *The Gift Relationship* presents his case for the relevance of altruism to the provision of social services. Reisman's posthumous evaluation of Titmuss's work is particularly useful.

Pinker's work is an important part of the transition from an empirical approach to a more theoretical analysis. *Social Theory and Social Policy* examines the origins of social administration and its relationship to sociological and economic theory. *The Idea of Welfare* provides a theoretical justification for the mixed economy in the context of an examination of the limits of altruism. Forder and Jones *et al.* also have relevance here, providing a conceptual analysis which is useful for understanding the main issues at an empirical level.

In the 1970s the theoretical analysis has been carried a lot further, largely as a result of the introduction of a Marxist perspective. George and Wilding present a very useful analysis of the ideology (but not the theoretical content) of different economic perspectives on the role of the state in chapters 2 to 5.

Their examination of the consensus-conflict, pluralist-elitist arguments in chapter 1, and of the present situation should be treated with more caution. Mishra is much fairer on the consensus-conflict issue. Ginsburgh and Gough present the Marxist analysis in its clearest form. Hall, Land *et al.* provide a useful and fair summary of the pluralist-elitist argument in a social administration context in chapter 8, and Dowse and Hughes provide a more extended discussion of the same issues (chapter 5 supported by analysis in chapters 1 to 4). Pritchard and Taylor are excellent for the analysis from a radical point of view of the historical background to the present political situation, and for showing the differences between a socialist and a Marxist point of view. Holman provides a useful summary of theories of poverty, and Runciman deals effectively with the concept of relative deprivation with historical and current empirical evidence, as well as with the concept of social justice. Ginsburgh, Gough and Taylor-Gooby and Dale present Marxist perspectives on the welfare state.

ROBERT E. DOWSE and JOHN A. HUGHES, *Political Sociology*, John Wiley, 1972.

ANTHONY FORDER, *Concepts in Social Administration—a Framework for Analysis*, Routledge & Kegan Paul, 1974.

VIC GEORGE and PAUL WILDING, *Ideology and Social Welfare*, Routledge & Kegan Paul, 1976.

N. GINSBURGH, *Class, Capital and Social Policy*, Macmillan, 1979.

I. GOUGH, *Political Economy and the Welfare State*, Macmillan, 1979.

P. HALL, H. LAND, R. PARKER and A. WEBB, *Change, Choice and Conflict in Social Policy*, Heinemann, 1975.

ROBERT HOLMAN, *Poverty: Explanations of Social Deprivation*, Bedford Press, 1978.

INSTITUTE OF ECONOMIC AFFAIRS, *Towards a Welfare Society*, 1967.

K. JONES, J. BROWN and J. BRADSHAW, *Issues in Social Policy*, Routledge & Kegan Paul, 1978.

RAMESH MISHRA, *Society and Social Policy—Theoretical Perspectives on Welfare*, Macmillan, 1977.

ROBERT PINKER, *Social Theory and Social Policy*, Heinemann, 1971.

ROBERT PINKER, *The Idea of Welfare*, Heinemann, 1979.

C. PRITCHARD and R. TAYLOR, *Social Work: Reform or Revolution*, Routledge & Kegan Paul, 1978.

D. A. REISMAN, *Richard Titmuss: Welfare and Society*, Heinemann, 1977.

W. G. RUNCIMAN, *Relative Deprivation and Social Justice*, Routledge & Kegan Paul, 1966.

P. TAYLOR GOOBY and J. DALE, *Social Theory and Social Welfare*, Edward Arnold, 1981.

RICHARD TITMUSS, *Essays on 'The Welfare State'*, Allen & Unwin, 1958.

RICHARD TITMUSS, *Commitment to Welfare*, Allen & Unwin, 1968.

RICHARD TITMUSS, *The Gift Relationship*, Allen & Unwin, 1970.

RICHARD TITMUSS, *Social Policy: an Introduction*, Allen & Unwin, 1974.

Notes

Notes to Chapter 1

1 For a discussion of different definitions see Kathleen M. Slack, *Social Administration and the Citizen*, Michael Joseph, 1966, pp. 11–13.

2 For a discussion of theories accounting for the development of social services see John Carrier and Ian Kendall, 'Social policy and social change—explanations of the development of social policy', *Journal of Social Policy*, vol. 2, no. 3, 1973, and 'The development of welfare states: the production of plausible accounts', *op. cit*, vol. 6, no. 3, 1977. Also John Baker, 'Social conscience and social policy', *op. cit.*, vol. 8, no. 2, 1979. For a discussion of the process of problem-definition and different perspectives on the social services, see M. Fitzgerald, P. Halmos, G. Pearson and J. Warham, *Introduction to Welfare: Iron Fist and Velvet Glove*, Open University Course DE 206, Units 1–4, 1978.

3 For a discussion of the role of Benthamism and Christian humanitarianism in social reform in nineteenth-century England see J. Hart, 'Nineteenth century social reform: a Tory interpretation of history', *Past and Present*, 31, 1965, pp. 38–61; reprinted in W. D. Birrell, P. A. R. Hillyard, A. S. Murie and D. J. D. Roche (eds), *Social Administration: Readings in Applied Social Science*, Penguin, 1973.

4 Kathleen Heasman, *Evangelicals in Action: An Appraisal of their Social Work*, Bles, 1962.

5 I am indebted to the Librarian of the House of Commons for this information, and for a copy of the report by Mr Goldsworth Gurney of 4 August 1857, giving details of the final solution of the problem.

6 The classic account of the Poor Law is provided by Sidney and Beatrice Webb, *English Poor Law Policy*, Longmans, 1910, and *English Poor Law History 2: The Last Hundred Years*, Cassell, 1963 (reprint of 1927–9 edn). See also Further Reading at the end of this chapter.

7 Home Office, *Report of the Committee on the Care of Children*, Cmd 6922, HMSO, 1946, particularly paras 136–56.

8 Charles Booth, *Life and Labour of the People of London*, 2nd edn, 4 vols, Macmillan, 1882–97. B. Seebohm Rowntree, *Poverty: A Study of Town*

Life, Macmillan, 1901. Rowntree's study is short enough to read in an hour. Extracts from Booth's massive work can be found in H. W. P. Fautz (ed.), *Charles Booth on the City*, University of Chicago Press, 1967 and A. Fried and R. M. Elman (eds), *Charles Booth's London*, Hutchinson, 1969.

9 For an interesting discussion of the majority and minority reports, see Una Cormack, 'The Royal Commission on the Poor Laws 1905–9 and the Welfare State', Lock Memorial Lecture, 1953; published in A. V. S. Lockhead, ed., *A Reader in Social Administration*, Constable, 1968.

10 For a presentation of the evidence on the origins of this programme see J. R. Hay, *The Origins of the Liberal Welfare Reforms 1906–1914*, Macmillan, 1975, and the collection of original documents in J. R. Hay, *The Development of the British Welfare State 1880–1975*, Arnold, 1978, in which documents before 1919 are well represented.

11 *Social Insurance and Allied Services: Report by Sir W. Beveridge*, Cmd 6404, HMSO, 1942, para. 31.

12 Statistics of unemployment and inflation can be found in the *Annual Abstract of Statistics* and *Social Trends*, usually covering a ten-year period.

13 Reviews of social security benefits occurred irregularly in the 1950s and 1960s with intervals between reviews averaging about eighteen months. Under the Social Security Act, 1973, annual reviews became mandatory.

14 Attempts to influence prices and incomes up to 1967 are discussed in J. and A. M. Hackett, *The British Economy: Problems and Prospects*, Allen & Unwin, 1967, chapter 7. Policy from 1964–77 is discussed in various places in M. Stewart, *Politics and Economic Policy in the UK since 1964: The Jekyll and Hyde Years*, 2nd edn, Pergamon, 1978. This stresses how party attitudes changed from the position taken in opposition after a year or two of damaging policies in government. A summary of National Incomes Policies from January 1970 to July 1975 can be found in the Royal Commission on the Distribution of Income and Wealth, *Report No. 4: Second Report on the Standing Reference*, Cmnd 6626, HMSO, 1976, App. A.

15 *Op. cit.*, para 4.

16 Britain's contribution to the CAP was estimated at £1,552m for 1980 in November 1979. *The Times* Parliamentary Report, 29 November 1979.

17 The National Assistance Act, 1948, the National Insurance Act, 1946, the National Insurance (Industrial Injuries) Act, 1946, the Family Allowances Act, 1945.

18 Further discussion of the concept of the Welfare State can be found in Chapter 9.

19. See R. M. Titmuss, *Essays on 'The Welfare State'*, Allen & Unwin, 1958, pp. 208–9. See also Martin Rein, 'Social class and the health service', *New Society*, 20 November 1969.

20 See Guy Routh, *Occupation and Pay in Great Britain, 1906–60*, Cambridge University Press, 1965.

21 R. M. Titmuss, *Income Redistribution and Social Change*, Allen & Unwin, 1964. Studies by the Central Statistical Office on the incidence of taxation have shown that it is proportional over a wide income range.

Regressive indirect taxes and insurance contributions counteract the effects of a progressive income tax. The results of the studies were published in various issues of *Economic Trends* from 1962 onwards and are discussed in Adrian L. Webb and Jack E. B. Sieve, *Income Redistribution and the Welfare State*, Occasional Papers in Social Administration, no. 41, Bell, 1971. See also the reports of the Royal Commission on the Distribution of Income and Wealth, initial, second and fourth reports on its standing reference, Nos 1, 4 and 7 (Cmnd 6171, 6626 and 7595).

22 For a fuller discussion on the issues discussed in this section see Anthony Forder, *Concepts in Social Administration*, Routledge & Kegan Paul, 1974, chapters 6, 7 and 8.

23 J. A. G. Griffith, *Central Departments and Local Authorities*, Allen & Unwin, 1967, pp. 525–8. In addition Griffith found that each department had its own traditional attitude to its relationship with local authorities, which he classified as '*laissez-faire*', 'regulatory' and 'promotional' (p. 515 *et seq.*).

24 This issue is discussed and the evidence of the need for change presented in vol. 3 of the *Report of the Royal Commission on Local Government in England* (Redcliffe-Maud Report), Cmnd 4040, HMSO, 1960.

25 In 1965, of 172 counties, county boroughs and new London boroughs, 7 had populations of over 1,000,000, and 44 had less than 100,000. See J. A. G. Griffith, *op. cit.*, pp. 28–9, for a discussion of this.

26 See chapter 6, p. 174.

27 J. A. G. Griffith, *op. cit.*, pp. 528–9.

28 The absolute principle was modified by the Local Government (Financial Provisions) Act, 1963, Section 6, which empowered local authorities to incur expenditure up to the value of a penny rate for the benefit of the area or its inhabitants.

29 Redcliffe-Maud Report, *Vol. 1, 'Report'; vol. 2, 'Memorandum of Dissent'; vol. 3, 'Research appendices'*. Scottish Department, *Report of the Royal Commission on Local Government in Scotland* (Wheatley Report), Cmnd 4150, HMSO, 1969. Welsh Office, *The Reorganisation of Local Government in Wales*, Cmnd 3340, HMSO, 1967, and *Local Government Reorganisation in Glamorgan and Monmouthshire*, Cmnd 4310, HMSO, 1970.

30 *Report of the Royal Commission on the Constitution* (Kilbrandon Report), Cmnd 5460, HMSO, 1973, summarised and discussed in Edmund Ions. 'The prospects of regional government', in Kathleen Jones (ed.), *The Year Book of Social Policy in Britain 1973*, Routledge & Kegan Paul, 1974.

31 'Regional economic planning machinery', *Board of Trade Journal*, 17 June 1966.

32 Redcliffe-Maud Report, vol. 1, chapter 9; vol. 2, chapter 4; Wheatley Report, chapter 26.

33 Under the Local Government Act, 1963.

34 Ministry of Housing and Local Government, *Report of the Committee on the Management of Local Government* (Maud Report), HMSO, 1967.

35 *Ibid.*, p. xiii and paras 150–2.

36 Department of the Environment, *The New Local Authorities: Management and Structure*, HMSO, 1972.
37 Royston Greenwood, C. R. Hinings and Stewart Ranson, 'Inside the local authorities', in Kathleen Jones (ed.), *op. cit.*
38 See pp. 178–80.
39 The term 'Quango' is of American origin, and not wholly appropriate to the British situation since most British Quangos are clearly 'governmental'. The assault on quangos by the present government has been piecemeal. The first proposals came from the Department of the Environment and were surprisingly small-scale. The potential for saving when important functions have been transferred to other organisations may prove to be very small.
40 Beveridge Report, *op. cit.*, paras 44–7, 161–5.
41 Department of Health and Social Security, *The Future of the National Health Service*, HMSO, 1970, para 31.
42 Maud Report, vol. 1, paras 103 – 8.
43 Anthony Forder, *op. cit.*, pp. 53–4, 92–6; Olive Stevenson, 'Co-ordination reviewed', *Case Conference*, vol. 9, no. 8, February 1963, reprinted in Eileen Younghusband (ed.), *Social Work and Social Values*, Allen & Unwin, 1967.
44 Reference can be made to a study of professional education and identification by the Merseyside Interprofessional Working Party reported by A. Dufton, O. Keidan and G. White in 'Aspects of interprofessional training', *New Era*, 6 June 1971. It was found that in general the participants had only a sketchy knowledge of one another's training courses and the scope of their work activities.
45 Hence the joint financing arrangements described on p. 246.
46 See pp. 176–7.
47 *The Civil Service*, Cmnd 3638, HMSO, 1968.
48 See pp. 215–16. The Report accepted the recommendations of the Maud Report but for putting forward the case for requiring local authorities to set up a separate social service department. *Report of the Committee on Local Authority and Allied Personal Social Services*, Cmnd 3703, HMSO, 1968.
49 See p. 186.
50 For a full account see D. J. Harris, *Cases and Materials in International Law*, 2nd edn, Sweet & Maxwell, 1979, chapter 9.
51 For a fuller account see D. Lasok and J. W. Bridge, *Introduction to the Law and Institutions of the European Communities*, Butterworth, 1976.
52 The attempt to develop compensatory social policies is described in M. Shanks, *European Social Policy—Today and Tomorrow*, Pergamon, 1977. See also International Committee of the National Council of Social Service, 'The future of social policy in the European Communities', *Journal of Social Policy*, vol. 6, no. 3, July 1977.

Notes to Chapter 2

1 Today the churches no longer control the majority of schools in this country. Nevertheless the Education Act, 1944, made divine worship and

religious instruction compulsory in maintained schools where no other subject is statutorily compulsory.

2 At the end of the nineteenth century the Church of England was responsible for almost 12,000 schools, and 2 million children. The Roman Catholic Church and other voluntary groups educated another $\frac{1}{2}$ million. Local authority schools, though totalling far less, in fact themselves educated $2\frac{1}{2}$ million children.

3 These had developed a liberal curriculum. They normally took boys and girls from elementary schools at 12 or 13, and were regarded as a form of post-school training.

4 Cambridgeshire, 1924. A committee of churchmen and teachers drew up a syllabus for religious instruction in schools. In 1942 over 800 local authorities used this syllabus and both the Minister of Education, R. A. Butler, and the Prime Minister, Winston Churchill, gave it their approval.

5 For an expansion of this point see R. A. Butler, *The Art of the Possible*, Hamish Hamilton, 1971.

6 *Children and their Primary Schools* (Plowden Report), vols 1 and 2, HMSO, 1967. One of a series of contemplative and exploratory reports by Central Advisory Councils.

7 For example, J. W. B. Douglas, *The Home and the School*, MacGibbon & Kee, 1964; B. Bernstein, 'Social class and linguistic development' in A. H. Halsey, J. Floud and C. A. Anderson (eds), *Education, Economy and Society*, Free Press, 1961; J. Floud, A. H. Halsey and F. M. Martin (eds), *Social Class and Educational Opportunity*, Heinemann, 1956.

8 *Teacher Education and Training*, HMSO, 1972. Report of the James Committee, under the chairmanship of Lord James of Rusholme.

9 Cmnd 5174, HMSO, 1972.

10 This includes, in England and Wales, universities, primary and secondary schooling for which the DES is responsible, and education in Scotland except for the universities which are the responsibility of the Secretary of State for Scotland.

11 See especially DES, *Education and Science in 1972*, HMSO, 1973.

12 *Education and Science in 1976*, HMSO, 1977, p. 11.

13 The Order in Council, raising the minimum leaving age to 16 from 15 was made on 22 March 1972.

14 Pupils must remain at school until the end of the spring term of their sixteenth birthday for those born between 1 September and 31 January. Pupils born between 1 February and 31 August may leave on the Friday before the last Monday in May (since 1976), or until the end of the summer term for the remainder.

15 Voluntary post-school education may include universities, polytechnics, further education colleges, colleges of education, plus adult education and youth service. Financial aid applies to universities and college of education students and to many in further education establishments.

16 DES, *Annual Report 1980*, HMSO, 1981, p. 11.

17 Cmnd 5174, HMSO, 1972. Plans included a 90 per cent provision of school places for 4-year-olds and 50 per cent provision for 3-year-olds,

and they were expected to cater for all children whose parents wished for them to have nursery schooling.

18 Two new surveys were into parental involvement in nursery education, by the Thomas Coram Research Unit of the University of London, the second on the relationship between supply and demand of nursery education, by the Scottish Council for Research in Education, at a total cost for the two of over £130,000. Other surveys in the field are: *The Experience of Young Children at Home*, from January 1975 by the University of Keele at a cost of £34,000; *Developing Materials for Assessment and Evaluation*, from April 1975 by the National Foundation for Educational Research at a cost of £39,000; *The Aims, Role and Deployment of Staff in the Nursery*, from April 1975 by the National Foundation for Educational Research at a cost of £57,000; and *Play Exploration and Learning in the Pre-School Child*, from October 1975 by the University of Keele at a cost of £67,000.

19 See DES pamphlet *Towards the Middle School*, HMSO, 1970; also *ibid.*, *Launching Middle Schools*, HMSO, 1970.

20 Circular 10/65. This was a request document aimed at persuasion rather than legislation.

21 Schools not maintained by a local education authority, but in receipt of *per capita* grant from the DES, provided that 25 per cent of their entry was open to local authority pupils. By not taking up their quota of places, and thus diminishing financial support, local education authorities can put pressure on direct grant schools to accept maintained status.

22 For example, London, Anglesey, Bristol, Coventry.

23 J. Ford, *Social Class and the Comprehensive School*, Routledge & Kegan Paul, 1969.

24 *The Public Schools and the General Education System* (Fleming Report), HMSO, 1944.

25 First Report (Newsom Report), HMSO, 1968.

26 See *Education and Science in 1972*, p. 19.

27 Provision made by the Education Act, 1944.

28 BA courses are now available at many colleges, of ordinary or honours status, but do not include a professional studies component.

29 Universities in England and Wales: Oxford and Cambridge, systems of related autonomous college units, over 10,500 students in each university; London federation of colleges, 33,000 students; Durham and Newcastle, before 1963 one University of Durham, 3,000 and 6,000 students respectively; Wales, federation of colleges, 15,000 students; Manchester, Birmingham, Liverpool, Leeds, Sheffield and Bristol, nineteenth-century civic universities, 6,000 to 9,000 students each; Reading, Nottingham, Southampton, Hull, Exeter and Leicester, younger civic universities—pre-1939–3,000 to 6,000 students; Keele (1949), Sussex, York, East Anglia, Essex, Lancaster, Kent and Warwick, the new universities, 2,000–4,000 students; Aston, Bath, Bradford, Brunel, City, Loughborough, Salford and Surrey, former colleges of advanced technology, universities since 1965, 1,500 to 3,500 students.

30 University standard work available also at the University of Manchester

Institute of Science and Technology, the Manchester Business School, the Royal College of Art, the London Graduate School of Business Studies, the Cranfield Institute of Technology, and the independent University of Buckingham.

31 As amended by the Education (Miscellaneous Provisions) Act, 1953.

32 See *The School Health Service and Handicapped Pupils Regulations*, HMSO, 1953 and 1959.

33 *The School Health Service and Handicapped Pupils Regulations*, 1953

34 *Special Needs in Education,* 6 August 1978, Cmnd 7996, HMSO, 1980.

35 Report of the Working Party into *The Role and Training of Education Welfare Officers* (Ralph Report), HMSO, 1973. Membership appointed by invitation of the Local Government Training Board, to 'investigate the functions of education welfare officers in order to identify common elements and to advise the Board on the most appropriate training for them (including a system of examinations)'. A new system of examinations for social work qualifications for education welfare officers came into effect after the old scheme was phased out in spring 1975.

36 *Youth and Community Work in the 70s*, HMSO, 1969.

37 Secretary of State for Education in reply to a Commons question, 29 March 1971.

38 *The Youth Service and Similar Provision for Young People*, HMSO, 1968. A report for the DES on behalf of the Youth Service Development Council, by the Social Survey Division of the Office of Population Census and Surveys.

39 National Youth Bureau, 1980, 17–23 Albion Street, Leicester.

40 Two local authorities have 25 per cent of pupils in the immigrant category, five local authorities between 20 per cent and 25 per cent and six more between 15 per cent and 20 per cent. These concentrations are in urban localities.

41 DES, *Education in Schools: A Consultative Document*, HMSO, 1977. This paper is commented upon in the memorandum of the Commission for Racial Equality, *Schools and Ethnic Minorities*, CRE, Occasional Paper No. 3, February 1978. See also: Education Survey No. 13, *The Education of Immigrants*, HMSO, 1971; Education Survey No. 10, *Potential and Progress in a Second Culture*, HMSO, 1971; *Organisation in Multi-Racial Schools*, National Foundation for Educational Research, 1972. A report sponsored by the DES.

42 These points are made in the National Union of Students submission to the DES, *Towards a Multi-racial Society: Education and Deprivation of Black Youth*, 2 September 1977.

43 *Ibid.*, p. 3. DES figures for pupils in schools for the educationally subnormal show that 2.7 per cent of West Indian schoolchildren, 0.63 per cent of indigenous pupils and 0.4 per cent of Indian and Pakistani children attend such schools.

44 A. Little, 'Schools and race' in CRE/BBC TV, *Five Views of Multi-racial Britain*, CRE, 1978.

45 Plowden Report, Special Groups S. 155 and Appendix 12.

46 The Secretary of State must under Section 4 of the 1944 Act appoint these councils which replaced the Consultative Committees on Education. The Act specified that the councils would 'advise the Secretary of State upon such matters connected with educational theory and practice as they think fit and upon any questions referred to them by him' (section 4[1]). Reports include Plowden, 1967, and her Welsh counterpart Gittins, 1967, Crowther, 1959, and Newsom, 1963. Council membership is for a period of three years in the first instance, and does not really exclude anyone, although responsibility ultimately lies with the Secretary of State: 'Each council shall include persons who have had experience of educational institutions not forming part of that system.'

47 In England there are 470 HM Inspectors, nearly 50 in Wales. See the DES pamphlet *Her Majesty's Inspectorate Today and Tomorrow*, HMSO, 1975. One aspect of the work of the inspectorate is to inspect independent schools for DES recognition.

48 Previously 146 in England and 17 in Wales. The present 105 local education authorities comprise 39 new counties, 36 metropolitan districts, 8 Welsh counties, 20 existing outer London boroughs, the Inner London Education Authority, and the Isles of Scilly.

49 Education Act, 1944, First Schedule, Part II.

50 Subject to the Council for National Academic Awards approval of compatibility with university standards.

51 The University of London colleges are self-governed, overall finances being controlled by a Court including outside members, and the supreme executive body, the Senate. The University of Wales colleges are represented at Court, which is the chief governing and legislative body, Council being the executive body controlling finance; all academic matters are handled by the academic boards.

52 Determined by a means assessment of the student or his parents. Some of the Department's grants are available for first degree mature students.

53 *Education: A Framework for Expansion*, *loc. cit.*

54 *Statistical Bulletin*, September 1981, 14/18, DES.

55 Support was given to courses with an educational studies component leading to the B.Ed. degree and qualified teacher status. The B.Ed. award was introduced following the Robbins Report, 1963, and needed the sanction of the universities. After CNAA agreement to assist in validating such degrees, universities tended to follow suit.

56 See for example, J. W. B. Douglas, *The Home and the School*, MacGibbon & Kee, 1964; A. Little and J. Westergaard, 'The trend of class differentials in educational opportunity in England and Wales', *British Journal of Sociology*, vol. 15, 1964, pp. 301–16; the excellent summaries and references in O. Banks, *The Sociology of Education*, Batsford, 1968.

57 Discussed in A. H. Halsey (ed.), *Educational Priority*, vol. 1, HMSO. Project directed by A. H. Halsey of the Department of Social and Administrative Studies, University of Oxford.

58 J. M. Bynner, *Parents' Attitudes to Education*, HMSO, 1972.

59 H. Acland, 'What is a bad school?' *New Society*, 9.9.1971; H. Acland. 'Does parent involvement matter?' *New Society*, 16 September 1971.

Notes to Chapter 3

1 D. Marsden and E. Duff, *Workless*, Penguin, 1975.
2 M. J. Hill, *Men out of Work*, Cambridge University Press, 1973.
3 D. Marsden and E. Duff, *op. cit.*
4 G. M. Norris, 'Unemployment, subemployment and personal characteristics', *Sociological Review*, 26, 1978, pp. 89–108 and 327–47.
5 F. Herron, *Labour Market in Crisis*, Heinemann, 1975; W. W. Daniel, *Whatever Happened to the Workers in Woolwich*?, Political and Economic Planning, 1972.
6 S. Parker, 'The effects of redundancy', in G. Esland *et al.* (eds), *People and Work*, Holmes MacDougall, 1975.
7 S. Mukherjee, *Through No Fault of their Own*, Macdonald, 1973.
8 'The unregistered unemployed in Great Britain', *Department of Employment Gazette*, 84, 1976, pp. 1331–36.
9 See M. S. Granovetter, *Getting a Job*, Harvard University Press, 1974.
10 See B. Thomas and C. Madigan, 'Strategy and job choice after redundancy', *Sociological Review*, 22, 1974, pp. 83–102; R. Martin and R. H. Fryer, *Redundancy and Paternalist Capitalism*, Allen & Unwin, 1973.
11 'Vacancy study', *Department of Employment Gazette*, 82, 1974, pp. 222–23.
12 Federation of Personnel Services, *The Government Job-finding Service: a Case of Public Waste*, 1976.
13 B. Showler, *The Public Employment Service*, Longman, 1976.
14 K. Hall and I. Miller, *Re-training and Tradition*, Allen & Unwin, 1975.
15 E. Belbin and R. M. Belbin, *Problems in Adult Re-training*, Heinemann, 1972.
16 Lady Williams, 'The revolution in industrial training', *Sociological Review Monographs*, 13, 1969, pp. 89–103.
17 W. W. Daniel and E. Stilgoe, *The Impact of Employment Protection Laws*, Policy Studies Institute, 1978.
18 Low Pay Unit, *Seventy Years On*, 1976.
19 G. Palmer, 'Uncertain councils', *New Society*, 31 October 1974.
20 K. Roberts, *From School to Work*, David & Charles, 1972.
21 R. Thomas and D. Wetherell, *Looking Forward to Work*, HMSO, 1974.
22 T. Keil, *Becoming a Worker*, Leicester Committee for Education and Industry/Training Services Agency, 1978.
23 Youthaid, *Study of the Transition from School to Working Life*, 1979.
24 *Ibid.*
25 M. Colledge, G. Llewellyn and V. Ward, *Young People at Work*, Manpower Services Commission, 1977.
26 Youthaid, *op. cit.*
27 M. Colledge *et al.*, *op. cit.*
28 Manpower Services Commission, *Young People and Work*, 1977.
29 P. Bayly, *The Work Experience Programme*, Manpower Services Commission, 1978; S. Smith and R. Lasko, 'After the work experience programme', *Department of Employment Gazette*, 86, 1978, pp. 901–7.

30 E. Balmer, 'Community Industry: the first two years', *Careers Quarterly*, 26, 1974, pp. 17–20.
31 M. Colledge *et al., op. cit.*
32 Department of Education and Science, *A Better Start in Working Life*, 1979, p. 1.
33 F. Field, *Unequal Shares: the Disabled and Employment*, Low Pay Unit Paper No. 20, 1978.
34 R. and R. N. Rapoport (eds), *Working Couples*, Routledge & Kegan Paul, 1978.
35 R. and R. N. Rapoport, *Dual Career Families Re-examined,* Martin Robertson, 1976.
36 'The unregistered unemployed in Great Britain', *op. cit.*
37 S. Castles and G. Kosack, *Immigrant Workers and the Class Structure in Western Europe*, Oxford University Press, 1973.
38 N. McIntosh and D. Smith, *The Extent of Racial Discrimination*, Political and Economic Planning, 1974; D. S. Smith, *Racial Disadvantage in Britain*, Penguin, 1977.
39 D. Brooks and K. Singh, *Aspirations Versus Opportunity*, Commission for Racial Equality, 1977.
40 Commission for Racial Equality, *Looking for Work*, 1978.
41 Community Relations Commission, *Unemployment and Homelessness*, HMSO, 1974, p. 7.
42 Acton Society Trust, *Retirement*, 1960.
43 P. Lewis, 'Off the scrapheap', *New Society*, 6 February 1975.
44 'Characteristics of the unemployed: sample survey, June 1973', *Department of Employment Gazette*, 82, 1974, pp. 211–21.
45 S. Mukherjee, *op. cit.*

Notes to Chapter 4

1 See, for example, Royal Commission on the Distribution of Income and Wealth, Report No. 4, *Second Report on the Standing Conference*, Cmnd 6626, HMSO, 1976, chapter 3: The Distribution of Personal Wealth.
2 B. Seebohm Rowntree, *Poverty, A Study of Town Life*, Macmillan, 1901, chapter 4.
3 B. Seebohm Rowntree, *Poverty and Progress, A Second Survey of York*, Longmans, 1941.
4 Sir William Beveridge, *Social Insurance and Allied Services* (Beveridge Report), 1942, reprinted, Cmnd 6404, HMSO, 1974.
5 Peter Townsend, 'Measuring poverty', *British Journal of Sociology*, June 1954.
6 J. Bradshaw, 'The concept of social need', *New Society*, 496, 30 March 1972, pp. 640–3.
7 Alisdair Aird, 'Goods and services', in *Why the Poor Pay More*, ed. Francis Williams, Macmillan, 1977.
8 See, for example, Merseyside Right to Fuel Group, *Claimants who Stayed out in the Cold*, 1972.
9 R. Layard, D. Piachaud and M. Stewart, *The Causes of Poverty: A*

Background Paper to Report No. 6 of the Royal Commission on the Distribution of Income and Wealth, HMSO, 1978.

10 *Ibid.*

11 *Ibid.*

12 *Ibid.*

13 Brian Abel-Smith and Peter Townsend, *The Poor and the Poorest*, Occasional Papers in Social Administration No. 17, Bell, 1965.

14 See, for example, Peter Townsend, *Poverty in the United Kingdom: A Survey of Household Resources and Standards of Living*, Allen Lane, 1979.

15 See, for example, George Clark, *Whatever Happened to the Welfare State*, City Poverty Committee, 1974.

16 See page 8.

17 For an analysis of the extent of poverty in the USA, see Lester A. Sobel (ed.), *Welfare and the Poor*, Facts on File, New York, 1977.

18 Adrian L. Webb and Jack E. B. Sieve, *Income Redistribution and the Welfare State*, Occasional Papers in Social Administration No. 41, Bell, 1971.

19 See Adela Nevitt, *Housing, Taxation and Subsidies: A Study of Housing in the UK*, Nelson, 1966.

20 Figures are presented regularly in the *Annual Abstract of Statistics*, HMSO.

21 *Ibid.*

22 *Wealth Tax*, Cmnd 5704, HMSO, 1974.

23 See, for example, André Gorz, *A Strategy for Labor*, Beacon Press, Boston, 1967.

24 This approach is particularly associated with P. Kaim-Caudle. See his articles in *Social Services for All?*, Fabian Society, 1968, and *Lloyd's Bank Review*, April 1969. See also A. R. Prest, *Social Benefits and Tax Rates*, Research Monograph No. 22, Institute of Economic Affairs, 1970. There is very little evidence of the actual effects on incentives of any tax rates. See C. V. Brown and D. A. Dawson, *Personal Taxation, Incentives and Tax Reform*, PEP Broadsheet 506, 1969, for a discussion of the evidence.

25 See Sheila Kay, 'Problems of accepting means-tested benefits', in David Bull (ed.), *Family Poverty*, Duckworth, 1971.

26 DHSS, *Co-habitation: Report by the Supplementary Benefits Commission to the Secretary of State for Social Services*, HMSO, 1971. See also *The Co-habitation Rule: a Guide for Single, Separated, Divorced or Widowed Women Claiming Supplementary Benefit or National Insurance*, Poverty Leaflet No. 4, Child Poverty Action Group, January 1972.

27 R. M. Titmuss, 'The Social Division of Welfare', Rathbone Lecture delivered in 1955 and published in *Essays on the Welfare State*, Allen & Unwin, 1958. Titmuss was not the first person to draw the analogy between the systems but stimulated a more general interest in it.

28 Allowances are amended annually by the Finance Acts and details can be obtained from Inland Revenue departments.

29 In general there has been a tendency for Labour Chancellors to remove these concessions for family trusts and interest on loans other than mortgages. Conservative Chancellors have tended to reinstate them.

30 For a discussion of the disadvantages of rates and the difficulties of replacing them see *The Future Shape of Local Government Finance*, Cmnd 4741, HMSO, 1972.
31 A brief historical account is given in G. D. Gilling Smith, *The Complete Guide to Pensions and Superannuation*, Penguin, 1967.
32 *Occupational Pension Schemes 1971—Fourth Survey by the Government Actuary*, HMSO, 1972, and earlier surveys.
33 Beveridge Report, *op. cit.*
34 *Ibid.*, para. 17.
35 *Ibid.*, paras 292–5.
36 Under the National Insurance Act, 1959.
37 The National Insurance Act, 1966.
38 Richard Drabble, Mark Rowland and Nicholas Warren, *Guide to Contributory Benefits and Child Benefit*, Child Poverty Action Group, November 1978.
39 Beveridge Report, *op. cit.*, para. 308.
40 *Ibid.*, paras 369 *et seq*.
41 National Assistance Act, 1948.
42 Ministry of Social Security Act, 1966. An excellent if somewhat bland account of the administration of supplementary benefits is provided by Olive Stevenson, *Claimant or Client? A Social Worker's View of the Supplementary Benefits Commission*, Allen & Unwin, 1973.
43 But for evidence of the extent of variation in tribunal decisions see Kathleen Bell *et al.*, 'National insurance local tribunals', *Journal of Social Policy*, vol. 3, no. 4, vol. 4, no. 1, October 1974 and January 1975.
44 Kathleen Bell, 'Supplementary benefit appeals tribunals', *Case Conference*, November 1968. Also *Guide to Supplementary Benefit Appeals*, Child Poverty Action Group, undated. Obtainable for 5p, from CPAG, 1 Macklin Street, London, WC2.
45 The DHSS Annual Reports no longer give information on progress in this respect. For a discussion of early difficulties that almost certainly still continue see Anne Lapping, 'Social security: how new a Ministry?', *New Society*, no. 245, 8 June 1967.
46 See, for example, M. Clark, 'The Unemployed on Supplementary Benefit', *Journal of Social Policy*, October 1978.
47 *Annual Abstract of Statistics*, HMSO, 1969.
48 Summarised, except 1956 figures, in the 4th survey, *op cit.*, para. 3.1.
49 DHSS, *National Superannuation and Social Insurance*, Cmnd 3883, HMSO, 1969. The Bill was based on proposals formulated in Opposition, see *National Superannuation*, Labour Party Publications, 1957. See also Brian Abel-Smith and Peter Townsend, *New Pensions for Old*, Fabian Society, 1955; *National Superannuation: A Critical Review of the Labour Party Proposals*, Association of British Chambers of Commerce, 1958.
50 DHSS, *Strategy for Pensions: The Future Development of State and Occupational Provision*, Cmnd 4755, HMSO, 1971.
51 See *Observer*, 20 January 1980.
52 Introduced under the Family Income Supplement Act, 1970, and the Family Income Supplement (Computation) Regulations.
53 Originally the supplement was payable without reclaiming for six

months. This period was extended by the Pensions and Family Income Supplement Payments Act, 1973.

54 Central Statistical Office, *Social Trends*, no. 9, HMSO, London, 1978.

55 The tribunals are those set up by the Industrial Training Act to hear appeals from employers against training levies imposed by the Industrial Training Board.

56 S. Mukherjee, *Through No Fault of their Own*, Macdonald (for PEP), 1972.

57 These points are vividly made in R. M. Titmuss and B. Abel-Smith, *Social Policies and Population Growth in Mauritius: A Report to the Governor of Mauritius*, Methuen, 1961.

58 See Ministry of Labour, *Sick Pay Schemes*, HMSO, 1964, for information about existing arrangements and discussion of the questions raised.

59 Home Office, *Report of the Working Party on Compensation for Victims of Crimes of Violence*, Cmnd 1406, HMSO, 1961; *ibid.*, *Compensation for Victims of Crimes of Violence*, Cmnd 2323, HMSO, 1964. The work of the Criminal Injuries Compensation Board is reviewed in its annual reports published under the auspices of the Home Office from 1965 onwards.

60 Henderson and Gillespie's *Textbook of Psychiatry*, 9th edn, revised by Sir David Henderson and Ivor R. C. Batchelor, Oxford University Press, 1962, pp. 170–2. For a full discussion of the weaknesses of the legal system for settling compensation including its expense see Terence A. Ison, *The Forensic Lottery*, Staples Press, 1968.

61 For an account of the setting up and administering of the fund by the director of the Joseph Rowntree Memorial Trust see Lewis E. Waddilove, 'The Family Fund', in Kathleen Jones (ed.), *The Year Book of Social Policy in Britain, 1973*, Routledge & Kegan Paul, 1974, chapter 12.

62 The maximum rates for an order for the maintenance of a wife or child were abolished by the Maintenance Orders Act, 1968, on the recommendation of the report of the Committee on Statutory Maintenance Limits, Cmnd 3587, HMSO, 1968.

63 Ministry of Social Security, *Annual Report, 1967*, HMSO, 1968.

64 For a study of the situation of women without male support and living on supplementary benefits, see Dennis Marsden, *Mothers Alone: Poverty and the Fatherless Family*, Allen Lane, 1969; see also Margaret Wynn, *Fatherless Families*, Michael Joseph, 1964.

65 Victor George and Paul Wilding, *Motherless Families*, Routledge & Kegan Paul, 1972.

66 DHSS, *Report of the Committee on One Parent Families* (Finer Report), Cmnd 5629, HMSO, 1974.

Notes to Chapter 5

1 R. Lawton, 'An age of great cities', *Town Planning Review*, 43, 1972, pp. 199–224.

2 O. Hill, *Homes of the London Poor*, Macmillan, 1875.
3 *Royal Commission on the State of Large Towns and Populous Districts: First Report*, HMSO, 1844: *Second Report*, HMSO, 1845.
4 The Public Health Act, 1848.
5 By the Labouring Classes Lodging Houses Act, 1851.
6 In the Housing, etc., Act, 1923 (Chamberlain Act).
7 Housing (Financial Provisions) Act, 1924.
8 T. Young, *Becontree and Dagenham*, Becontree Social Survey Committee, 1934.
9 R. Durant, *Watling: A Study of Social Life on a New Housing Estate*, London, King, 1939.
10 In the Housing Act, 1935.
11 *Report of the Royal Commission on the Distribution of the Industrial Population* (Barlow Report), Cmd 6153, HMSO, 1940; *Report of the Commission on Land Utilisation in Rural Areas* (Scott Report), Cmd 6378, HMSO, 1942; *Report of the Expert Committee on Compensation and Betterment* (Uthwatt Report), Cmd 6383, HMSO, 1942.
12 Statistics are provided in the *National Dwelling and Housing Survey*, Department of the Environment, HMSO, 1978, and a discussion of housing needs and priorities is given in *The Assessment of Housing Requirements*, Department of the Environment Housing Services Advisory Group, HMSO, 1977.
13 Housing preferences were investigated and reported by the British Market Research Bureau in *B.M.R.B. Housing Consumer Survey*, National Economic Development Office, HMSO, 1976.
14 Under the Housing (Financial Provisions) Act, 1958.
15 *Housing Policy: A Consultative Document*, Cmnd 6851, HMSO, 1977.
16 A simple guide to the scheme is *Your Guide to the Option Mortgage Scheme*, HMSO, 1967.
17 A number of guides to this Act are available of which one is *The Community Land Act Explained*, Boisot Waters Cohen Partnership, 1976.
18 See, for example, Department of Social Science, 'A Norris Green Study', *Journal of the British Association of Social Workers*, July 1971.
19 For example, Kirkby near Liverpool; see K. G. Pickett and D. Boulton, *Migration and Social Adjustment*, Liverpool University Press, 1974.
20 *Report of the Committee on Local Authority and Allied Personal Services* (Seebohm Report), Cmnd 3703, HMSO, 1968.
21 R. N. Morris and J. Mogey, *The Sociology of Housing*, Routledge & Kegan Paul, 1965.
22 See *Council Housing Purposes, Procedures and Priorities*, Ninth Report of the Housing Management Sub-Committee of the Central Housing Advisory Committee, HMSO, 1969.
23 Report of the House of Commons Environment Committee, July 1981.
24 J. English and C. Jones (eds), *The Sale of Council Houses*, University of Glasgow Discussion Paper 18, 1977.
25 *Op. cit.*, July 1981.
26 A useful account is given in Department of the Environment, *Housing Associations*, HMSO, 1971, a working paper of the Central Housing Advisory Committee.

27 A comprehensive account of slum clearance legislation is provided in J. English and P. Norman, *One Hundred Years of Slum Clearance in England and Wales—Policies and Programmes 1868 to 1970*, University of Glasgow Press, 1974.
28 M. Woolf, *The Housing Survey in England and Wales, 1964*, Government Social Survey, HMSO, 1967.
29 *Face the Facts*, a Shelter Report, 1969.
30 Gillian R. Vale, *Is the Housing Problem Solved?*, Housing Centre Trust, 1971.
31 *Whatever Happened to Council Housing?*, a report prepared by National Community Development Project workers, CDP Information and Intelligence unit, 1976.
32 *Slums on the Drawing Board*, Benwell Community Project, Final Report Series No. 4, 1978.
33 *This Year, Next Year, Sometime, Never*, Shelter (N. Ireland), 1981.
34 Ministry of Housing and Local Government, *Our Older Homes: A Call for Action* (Denington Report) and *Old Houses into New Homes*, Cmnd 3602, HMSO, 1968.
35 For a general account, see J. Trevor Roberts, *General Improvement Areas*, Saxon House/Lexington Books, 1976.
36 The definition of these terms is given under the section entitled 'Rent control and security of tenure'.
37 *Housing Action Areas*, Department of the Environment, Housing Improvement Group, HMSO, 1976.
38 *'As Good as New', Housing and Area Improvement Policy in the U. K.*, Department of the Environment, 1976.
39 *The Poverty of the Improvement Programme*, C.D.P. Political Economy Collective, Tyneside Free Press, revised edn, 1977.
40 A. Nevitt, *Housing, Taxation and Subsidies*, Nelson, 1966, argues that in fact decontrol of rents leads to a lower supply of rented accommodation because a better return can be obtained from the commercial sector.
41 Rate rebates had been available outside the National Assistance scheme since 1966.
42 D. Griffiths, 'Whose Feather bed?', *New Society*, 4 July 1981.
43 *Local Authorities and Building for Sale*, Department of the Environment Housing Development Directorate, 1977.
44 The best known is M. Young and P. Willmott, *Family and Kinship in East London*, Routledge & Kegan Paul, 1957.
45 Ministry of Housing and Local Government, *The Needs of New Communities*, HMSO, 1967.
46 An account of the difficulties imposed by such flats is provided by E. Gittus, *Flats, Families and the Under-5s*, Routledge & Kegan Paul, 1976.
47 The Housing Subsidies Act, 1956.
48 *Interim Report of the New Towns Committee*, Cmd 6759; *Second Interim Report*, Cmd 6794; *Final Report*, Cmd 6876; all HMSO, 1946.
49 No doubt the committee had been influenced by *Becontree and Dagenham*, Becontree Social Survey Committee 1934.

50 See *The Ownership and Management of Housing in the New Towns*, report submitted to the Minister of Housing and Local Government by J. B. Cullingworth and V. A. Karn, HMSO, 1968.
51 See R. Berthoud and R. Jowell, *Creating a Community*, Social and Community Planning Research, 1973.
52 *Where Homelessness Means Hopelessness*, Shelter, 1978.
53 *Housing in London—the Continuing Crisis*, SHAC (London Housing Aid Centre), 1977.
54 *Where Homelessness Means Hopelessness, op. cit.*
55 A history of this movement is given in R. Bailey, *The Squatters*, Penguin, 1973.
56 An account of a Birmingham zone in transition is given by J. Rex and R. Moore, *Race, Community and Conflict*, Oxford University Press, 1967.
57 See N. Deakin and C. Ungerson, 'Beyond the ghetto: the illusion of choice', in D. Donnison and D. Eversley (eds), *London: Urban Patterns, Problems and Policies*, Heinemann, 1973.
58 See *Colour and the Allocation of G.L.C. Housing*, the report of the GLC lettings survey 1974–5, Research Report 21, GLC, 1976.
59 R. Skellington, 'How blacks lose out in council housing', *New Society*, 29 January 1981.
60 See R. E. Pahl, *Whose City?*, 2nd edn, Penguin, 1975.

Notes to chapter 6

1 National Health Service Act, 1946, Section I, (1), repealed and replaced by the consolidating NHS Act in 1977.
2 1388, 12th Richard II. See Karl de Schweinitz, *England's Road to Social Security*, Barnes, New York, 1943, chapter 1.
3 M. W. Susser and W. Watson, *Sociology in Medicine*, Oxford University Press, 1971; A. Cartwright, *Patients and their Doctors*, Routledge & Kegan Paul, 1967, chapter 11; M. E. J. Wadsworth, J. W. H. Butterfield and R. Blaney, *Health and Sickness—The Choice of Treatment*, Tavistock, 1971.
4 See studies such as Thomas Ferguson and A. N. MacPhail, *Hospital and Community*, Oxford University Press, 1954, and Robert Kemp, 'The golden bed', *Lancet*, 14 November 1964.
5 *General Report on the Sanitary Conditions of the Labouring Population of Great Britain*, HMSO, 1842, p. 144: 'In the great mass of cases . . . the attack of fever precedes the destitution, not destitution the disease.'
6 *Report of the Royal Commission on the National Health Service*, Cmnd 7615, HMSO, 1979.
7 W. M. Frazer, *A History of English Public Health 1834–1939*, Bailliere, Tindall & Cox, 1950, p. 451.
8 One of the three working parties set up in 1971 by the DHSS to consider aspects of reorganisation of the National Health Service.
9 DHSS, *The Future Structure of the NHS*, HMSO, 1970 (the Second Green Paper).
10 National Health Service Reorganisation Act, 1973, Clause 10.
11 Local Government Act, 1972, Section 112.

12 See the *First Report of the Working Party on Collaboration between the NHS and Local Government*, HMSO, 1973, for further discussion of the plans for environmental health services.
13 *Fit for the Future, Report of the Committee on Child Health Services*, Cmnd 6684, HMSO, 1976 (Court Report).
14 *First Report of the Royal Commission on Environmental Pollution*, Cmnd 4585, HMSO, 1971.
15 See Brian Abel-Smith, *The Hospitals 1800–1948*, Heinemann, 1964, and Ruth Hodgkinson, *Origins of the National Health Service*, Wellcome Medical History Library, 1967.
16 *Minority Report of the Poor Law Commission*, part I, chapter 5, HMSO, 1909: 'The Poor Law Infirmaries are growing in popularity ... skilled artisans and the smaller shopkeepers are coming to regard [them] as a municipal institution paid for by their rates and maintained for their convenience and welfare [they] are fast becoming rate-aided hospitals.'
17 The White Paper, *A National Health Service*, Cmd 6502, HMSO, 1944, Appendix A, 'Existing services'.
18 See Kathleen Jones, *A History of the Mental Health Services*, Routledge & Kegan Paul, 1972, for a full and lively account of developments in the mental health field.
19 Olive Keidan and Zuzana Hughes, 'Roots', *Social Work Service*, DHSS, November 1979.
20 See the *Report of the Royal Commission on the Law relating to Mental Illness and Mental Deficiency*, Cmnd 169, HMSO, 1957.
21 It is interesting to note that while a great deal has been written on the development of services for the poor there appears to be little collected information on the care of the well-to-do. This is of particular importance in the health service as many of the services made available for all were based on the kind of care that the middle classes usually paid for.
22 See the *Minority Report of the Poor Law Commission*, HMSO, 1909, for a description of the medical policy and practice of the Boards of Guardians; also Ruth Hodgkinson, *op. cit*.
23 See *Minority Report*, chapter 2: 'Phthisis cases are maintained in crowded, unventilated homes where there are unrestrained facilities to convey the disease to their offspring. Diabetes cases live on the rates and eat what they please.'
24 *Health Service Financing*, British Medical Association, 1970, gives a good account of the negotiations.
25 For a very full and clear account of the complaints machinery see Rudolf Klein, *Complaints Against Doctors*, Charles Knight, 1973.
26 In the first three years of the National Health Service nearly 5 million full dentures were supplied, to about 1 person in 10 of the total population (figures from the Ministry of Health Information Service).
27 See W. M. Frazer, *op. cit*., and Madeline Rooff, *Voluntary Societies and Social Policy*, Routledge & Kegan Paul, 1957, Part 2, 'The maternity and child welfare movement'.
28 Dr Truby King, a pioneer in the field of infant welfare at the beginning of this century, applied the principles of successful stock breeding that he developed on the hospital farm to the care of human infants. In a paper

to the Farmers' Union he stated that if the same care and attention were given by the government to instructing mothers in how to rear their babies as was then being devoted to the rearing of stock, they would soon save infant lives.

29 See Ministry of Education, *Report of the Committee on Maladjusted Children* (Underwood Report), HMSO, 1955, for a description of the growth of child guidance.

30 *Interdepartmental Report on the Future Provision of Medical and Allied Services*, HMSO, 1920. Other reports of the inter-war years include the *Royal Commission on National Insurance* (1926), which suggested that medical services should be separated from the insurance system and maintained from public funds. The PEP reports on *Public Social Services*, 1937, and on the *Health Services*, 1937, suggested that there should be a clear separation between the essential health services, which are housing, nutrition, education and insurance, and the sickness service. The sickness service should be centred on the GP, suitably trained, who would act as educator, co-ordinator and counsellor. The BMA reports of 1930 and 1938, *A General Medical Service for the Nation*, suggested the regional organisation of hospital services.

31 R. M. Titmuss, *Problems of Social Policy*, HMSO, 1950, chapter 5.

32 *Social Insurance and Allied Services*, Cmd 6404, HMSO, 1942, Part 6, para. 427.

33 Set up by the BMA and Royal Colleges in 1940.

34 See Sidney and Beatrice Webb, *The State and the Doctors*, Longmans, 1910. They note that one-sixth of all doctors worked as district medical officers for the Poor Law boards. There were perhaps as many or more working for public health authorities.

35 For interesting accounts of the negotiations that took place see Gordon Forsyth, *Doctors and State Medicine*, Pitman, 1973; Arthur Willcocks, *The Creation of the National Health Service*, Routledge & Kegan Paul, 1967; and *Health Service Financing*, BMA, 1970.

36 This antagonism may not have been as widespread as the BMA suggested; nevertheless, an Amendment Act was passed in 1949 which prevented the introduction of full-time salaried service for GPs and dentists except by Act of Parliament. The NHS Act of 1966 was just such an act.

37 *Report of the Poor Law Commissioners*, HMSO, 1842, p. 41. Dr Duncan, the Medical Officer of Health of Liverpool, reported to the Commissioners: 'It is found that the faculty of perceiving the advantage of a change is so obliterated as to render them incapable of using, or indifferent to the use of, the means of improvement which may happen to come within their reach.' The same problem of apathy remains, and contrasts sadly with Beveridge's idea that the 'individual should recognise a duty to be well and to co-operate with all steps which may lead to diagnosis of disease in early stages'. Robert Kemp, 'The golden bed', *Lancet*, 14 November 1964, noted that among certain groups of patients 'apathy is all too common'.

38 *The Administrative Structure of the Medical and Related Services in England and Wales*, HMSO, 1968.

39 *Report on the Cost of the NHS*, Cmd 9663, HMSO, 1956.
40 From the first Ministry circular to the new regional hospital board, in 1947.
41 The first Green Paper, 1968, for example, noted that the respective roles of the regional hospital board and hospital management committees were not clear. Of the boards it said: 'Their primary task as originally conceived was planning and co-ordinating development; their intervention in matters of management has grown out of their responsibility for allocating financial resources'.
42 The Seebohm Committee's Report, *Local Authority and Allied Personal Social Services*, appeared in July 1968 and the Redcliffe-Maud Committee on *Local Government in England* reported in June 1969. The latter report suggested that local government could be responsible for all health services, but this idea was rejected for reasons discussed in the Green Papers.
43 Ministry of Health, *National Health Service: The Administrative Structure of the Medical and Related Services in England and Wales*, HMSO, 1968.
44 DHSS, *National Health Service: The Future Structure of the National Health Service*, HMSO, 1970.
45 See the DHSS *Annual Report* for 1972, chapter 2.
46 The Management Study Group were assisted by a firm of management consultants (McKinsey & Co.) and by the Health Services Organisation Research Unit of Brunel University. The steering committee supervising the study group had members from the DHSS and wide representation from the health services. For its terms of reference see the White Paper on National Health Service reorganisation, Cmnd 5055, HMSO, 1972.
47 *Democracy in the National Health Service: Membership of Health Authorities*, HMSO, May 1974.
48 Royal Commission on the NHS, 1979, Cmnd 7615.
49 See *Care in Action*, HMSO, February 1981 for an account of NHS staffing and financing.
50 *Patients First*, HMSO, December 1979.
51 See the NHS Act 1977 Schedule 4 for information on membership.
52 The Grey Book, *Management Arrangements for the Reorganised NHS*, chapter 2, p. 21.
53 Central Health Services Council Annual Report 1972.
54 See Schedule 5, Part II, 1977 Act, for membership.
55 *Management Arrangements for the Reorganised NHS*, Exhibits VI and VII, gives diagrams of the two different structures. The area team of officers and the district management team combine functions in the areas without districts and are called Area Management Teams.
56 Problems are created when three teams of officers have to be reduced to one.
57 The White Paper, Cmnd 5055, para. 45. See HRC (74) 23 for lists of districts.
58 See the HRC Circulars (73) 4 and 74 (32).
59 *Management Arrangements for the Reorganised NHS*, para. 2, p. 47.

60 *Report of the Committee on Senior Nursing Staff Structure* (Salmon Committee), HMSO, 1966.
61 Ministry of Health, *Management Functions of Hospital Doctors*, HMSO, 1966; a paper prepared by a sub-committee of the Advisory Committee for Management Efficiency in the National Health Service, Ministry of Health, *First Report of the Joint Working Party on the Organisation of Medical Work in Hospitals*, HMSO, 1974.
62 See the White Paper, Cmnd 5055, HMSO, 1972, HRC (74) 4, and the Labour government paper *Democracy in the NHS*, HMSO, 1974.
63 The Voluntary Agencies are selected by the regional health authorities.
64 The Working Party on Collaboration was set up by the DHSS in 1972 to examine matters of common concern to local government and the NHS following reorganisation. Their first report in 1973 recommended that there should be a statutory duty to collaborate.
65 *Care in Action*, DHSS, 1981.
66 House of Commons Report of the Social Services Committee 1979–80, July 1980.
67 DOE, Cmnd 6845, HMSO, 1977. See also *The State of the Public Health*, 1977 report published 1978, p. 62, 'Primary Health Care'.
68 *Sharing Resources for Health in England: Report of the Resources Allocation Working Party*, HMSO, 1976. See also M. Buxton and R. Klein, *Allocating Health Resources: A Commentary on the Report of the RAWP*, HMSO, 1978, a study commissioned by the RC on the NHS, Research Paper No. 3.
69 *Royal Commission on Medical Education 1965–68*, Cmnd 3569, HMSO, 1960.
70 The Royal Commission refers to the fact that the average age of hospitals (based on floor area) was over 61 years in 1971.
71 Ministry of Health, *Hospital Plan for England and Wales*, Cmnd 1604, HMSO, 1962, presenting schemes to be started in the period up to 1971. See also the Central Health Service Council, *The Function of the District General Hospital* (Bonham Carter Report), October 1969. The DHSS Information Office reported that by 1969, 8 district general hospitals had been completed, 83 more were partly complete and 45 more were in progress.
72 Three nucleus hospitals were planned for 1978. The 1977 DHSS Annual Report gives details of capital projects: 25 hospital schemes were started and 117 were already in progress.
73 For instance *The Report on the Cost of the NHS*, Cmnd 9663, 1956 (the Guillebaud Committee) and note 54.
74 Ministry of Health, *Report of the Committee on Senior Nursing Staff Structures*, HMSO, 1966 (Salmon Report).
75 See note 61.
76 See R. G. S. Brown, *The Changing National Health Service*, Routledge & Kegan Paul, 1973, and Rudolf Klein, *op. cit.*, for the useful discussion on the professional role and responsibility.
77 *Third Report of the Hospital Advisory Service, 1972*, HMSO, 1973, para. 115.

78 DHSS, HM (71) 97, *Hospital Services for the Mentally Ill.*
79 DHSS, HM (72) 71, *Services for Mental Illness related to Old Age.*
80 The annual reports of the Chief Medical Officer, *On the State of the Public Health*, give an account of the plans and discussions in the section on mental health. See the report of the conference of the Royal College of Psychiatrists and the DHSS on services for the mentally ill and handicapped, *Approaches to Action*, ed. F. McLachlan, HMSO, 1971. Criticism of the Hospital Plan in the PEL report *Psychiatric Services* in 1975 by G. F. Rehin and F. M. Martin, 1963, drew attention to the dependence of hospital usage on community provision, and their second broadsheet, *Towards Community Care*, 1969, commented on the inadequacy of information on which services are based.
81 See the *Annual Reports of the DHSS* for 1969 and 1970. Also, *Better Services for the Mentally Handicapped*, Cmnd 4683, HMSO, 1971.
82 E. R. Bransby, 'Mental illness and the psychiatric services', *Social Trends*, HMSO, 1973.
83 *Ibid.*
84 The Act followed the publication in 1957 of the *Report of the Royal Commission on the Law Relating to Mental Illness and Mental Deficiency*, Cmnd 169, HMSO.
85 DHSS, *A Review of the Mental Health Act 1959*, HMSO, 1976.
86 *A Review of the Mental Health Act 1959*, Cmnd 7320, HMSO, 1978.
87 See Henry Rollin, *The Mentally Abnormal Offender*, Pergamon Press, 1969.
88 *Report of the Committee on Mentally Abnormal Offenders*, Cmnd 6244, HMSO, 1975.
89 There are four Special Hospitals catering for patients who appear to need a high level of security because of their dangerous, violent or criminal propensities. These are directly managed by the Secretary of State.
90 See for instance the *Report of the Committee of Inquiry into Whittingham Hospital*, Cmnd 4861, HMSO, 1972. Also the *Annual Reports of the Hospital Advisory Services.*
91 *Better Services for the Mentally Handicapped*, Cmnd 4683, HMSO, 1971, outlines the existing services and the possible ways of improving them. The lack of information on numbers and needs was being remedied by DHSS-financed surveys. The report of the 1970 census of mentally handicapped patients was published in 1972. The DHSS also publishes reports on the facilities and services of psychiatric hospitals, unfortunately with rather a long time-lag, but trends can be seen and regional differences in facilities are made apparent. Pauline Morris's study, *Put Away: A Sociological Study of Institutions for the Mentally Retarded*, Routledge & Kegan Paul, 1969, drew attention to the inadequacies of institutional care, and Barbara Robb's *Says Everything*, Nelson, 1967, made a dramatic impact in its exposure of conditions in geriatric hospitals.
92 *Report of the Committee of Enquiry into Mental Handicap Nursing and Care*, Cmnd 7468, HMSO, 1979.
93 See Fig. 1, DHSS, *The Way Forward*, September 1977.

94 *The Mobility of Physically Disabled People*, HMSO, 1974.
95 See Appendix G, Principles and Practice in Rehabilitation, Mildred Blaxter, *Royal Commission on the NHS*, HMSO, 1979.
96 The Constitution of the Executive Councils is found in Schedule 5 of the Act, 1946.
97 Set up in April 1972 to safeguard the interests of staff during reorganisation, advise on the transfer of staff, and keep them informed of progress.
98 Rudolf Klein, *op. cit.*
99 Set up in 1962 on the recommendation of the *Royal Commission on Doctors' and Dentists' Remuneration* (Pilkington Committee), Cmnd 939, HMSO.
100 See Pauline Gregg, *The Welfare State*, Harrap, 1967, Appendix A, V, for a short clear account of the system of pay; also Gordon Forsyth, *Doctors and State Medicine*, Pitman, 1966, and *Health Service Financing*, BMA, 1970.
101 See the Minister's *Annual Report* for 1966.
102 Under the Health Service and Public Health Act.
103 Central Health Services Council, *Report of the Committee on General Practice within the National Health Service*, HMSO, 1954, pp. 2–3 and para. 12.
104 Central Health Services Council, Standing Medical Advisory Committee, *The Field of Work of the Family Doctor*, HMSO, 1963 (Chairman: Dr Annis Gillie).
105 Royal Commission on Medical Education, Cmnd 3569, HMSO, 1968.
106 Paula Cook and R. O. Walker, 'The geographical distribution of dental care in the UK', *British Dental Journal*, vol. 122, nos 10, 11 and 12, 1967.
107 Government Social Survey, *Survey of Adult Dental Health in England and Wales*, HMSO, 1970. Over one-third of the population had no teeth of their own.
108 'Methods of remuneration', Report of the *Ad-hoc* Sub-committee of the General Dental Services, *British Dental Journal*, vol. 117, 20 October 1964, p. 331.
109 See note 74 and *Report of the Working Party on Management Structure in the Local Authority Nursing Service* (Mayston Report), HMSO, 1969.
110 *Report of the Committee on Nursing*, Cmnd 5115, HMSO, 1972.
111 Ministry of Health, *An Inquiry into Health Visiting* (Jameson Committee), HMSO, 1956.
112 *Report of the Working Party on Social Workers in the Local Authority Health and Welfare Services*, HMSO, 1959.
113 *Report of the Committee on Local Authority and Allied Personal Social Services*, Cmnd 3703, HMSO, 1968, para. 380.
114 See Rudolf Klein, *op. cit.* This is a very readable and lively account of what would appear to be a dull subject.
115 *Report of the Committee on Hospital Complaints Procedure* (Davies Committee), HMSO, 1973.
116 He has power to investigate complaints 'that an individual has suffered injustice or hardship through maladministration or failure to provide

treatment and care' (DHSS, *Annual Report*, HMSO, 1972). See also the reports of the Health Service Commissioner.

117 See Michael Lee, *Private and National Health Services*, Policy Studies Institute, 1978. House of Commons Expenditure Committee, fourth Report 1971–2, *NHS Facilities for Private Patients*.

118 See COHSE, *Memorandum of Evidence to the Royal Commission on the NHS*, April 1977.

119 *Private Practice in the NHS Hospitals*, Cmnd 5270, HMSO, 1973.

120 DHSS, *Common Waiting Lists for NHS and Private Patients in NHS Hospitals*, Cmnd 6826, HMSO, 1977.

121 Of the 31,500 private beds in England 22,500 are long-stay and mainly used by the elderly. There are about 2,500 amenity or pay beds in NHS hospitals. *Care in Action*, HMSO, 1981.

122 The Health Service Commissioner reported that difficulties have arisen over TV, noise and smoking.

123 Royal Commission on the NHS, chapter 18. Subscriptions may cover a family. In 1978 2,390,000 people were covered.

124 Under the Nursing Home Act, 1975

125 See David Widgery, *Health in Danger*, Macmillan, 1979.

126 *Report of the Committee of Inquiry into the Regulation of the Medical Profession*, Cmnd 6018, HMSO, April 1975.

127 *Prevention and Health: Everybody's Business*, HMSO, 1976, chapter 3.

128 *Royal Commission on Population*, Cmd 7695, HMSO, 1949.

129 *Report of the Interdepartmental Committee on Abortion*, HMSO, 1939, reprinted 1966.

130 Ministry of Health Circular, 1937.

131 Cmnd 5258, para. 43, 1973.

132 See note 129.

133 *Report of the Committee on the Working of the Abortion Act*, Cmnd 5579, HMSO, 1974. Section B of this report gives a very good survey of the many areas of disquiet.

134 *Care of the Dying*, HMSO, 1973 (proceedings of a National Symposium, 1972).

135 Ann Cartwright *et al.*, *Life before Death*, Routledge & Kegan Paul, 1973.

Notes to Chapter 7

1 Relieving Officers could take the certificate of the Poor Law Examinations Board set up in 1910.

2 See the accounts of training in Eileen Younghusband, *Report on the Employment and Training of Social Workers*, Carnegie UK Trust, 1947, and Marjorie Smith, *Professional Education for Social Work in Britain*, Allen & Unwin, 1953.

3 See Kathleen Woodroofe, *From Charity to Social Work*, Routledge & Kegan Paul, 1962, and Madeline Rooff, *Voluntary Societies and Social Policy*, Routledge & Kegan Paul, 1957.

4 Chiswick Women's Aid Centre was set up in 1971 to provide a

temporary home for battered wives and their children. With increasing recognition of the problem, centres in other parts of the country are being established. See Erin Pizzey, *Scream Quietly or the Neighbours will Hear*, Penguin, 1974.

5 *Report of the Royal Commission on the Poor Laws*, HMSO, 1909. Also Una Cormack, 'The Welfare State', Loch Memorial Lecture, Family Welfare Association, 1953, reprinted in A. V. S. Lochhead, *A Reader in Social Administration*, Constable, 1968.
6 Julia Parker, *Local Health and Welfare Services*, Allen & Unwin, 1965.
7 *Report of the Working Party on Social Workers in the Local Authority Health and Welfare Services*, HMSO, 1959.
8 *Report of the Committee on Children and Young Persons*, Cmnd 1191, HMSO, 1960.
9 *Report of the Committee on Local Authority and Allied Personal Social Services* (Seebohm Report), Cmnd 3703, HMSO, 1968, para.32.
10 'The home help service, a day nursery, nursery school or a residential nursery might all provide means whereby a motherless child could be cared for providing in the first three instances the father was able to take charge at night. But these services are the responsibilities of three different committees and departments, which look at the problems from somewhat different points of view, have rather different methods of trying to solve it, and different orders of priority in deciding how much of their total resources should be devoted to the particular service required' (*op. cit.*, para. 98).
11 Central Training Council in Child Care, Council for Training in Social Work, and the Advisory Council for Probation and After-care.
12 Seebohm Report, para. 482.
13 Local Authority Social Services Act, 1970.
14 *NHS—Future Structure*, February 1970, paras 29–41.
15 See Home Office Circular no. 294/1970.
16 Seebohm Report, paras 640–3.
17 The Council was set up by the Health Visiting and Social Work (Training) Act, 1962, as amended by Statutory Instruments 1221 and 1241 of 1971.
18 See Local Authority Social Services Act, 1970, Schedule I.
19 This model of a Social Services Department has been compiled by the authors from several different local authority structures. Individual Social Services Departments will vary in matters of detail.
20 NHS Reorganisation Act, 1973, Section 10.
21 *The Way Forward*, HMSO, September 1977, Appendix I. *Care in Action*, HMSO, February 1981.
22 See Chapter on Health Services.
23 The Central Health Services Council and the Personal Social Services Council.
24 *Fit for the Future. Report of the Committee on Child Health Services*, Cmnd 6684, HMSO, 1976.
25 *Collaboration in Community Care*, HMSO, 1978.
26 *Care in Action. A Handbook of Policies and Priorities for the Health and Personal Social Services in England*, HMSO, 1981.

27 Seebohm Committee, para. 2.
28 *Report of the Boarding out of Dennis and Terence O'Neill* (Monckton Report), Cmnd 6636, HMSO, 1945.
29 *Report of the Care of Children Committee* (Curtis Report), Cmnd 6922, HMSO, 1946.
30 *Children in Care in England and Wales*, HMSO, 1979.
31 'Short term care matters because it provides the means of entry to a family that has hoisted a signal of distress', H. R. and E. B. Schaffer, *Child Care and the Family*, Occasional Papers in Social Administration no. 25, Bell, 1968.
32 See Barnardo Social Work Papers No. 2, 1976, *Leaving Care*.
33 Children Act, 1948, Section 1 (3), (a) and (b).
34 *Report of the Committee on Children and Young Persons*, Cmnd 1191, HMSO, 1960.
35 J. S. Heywood and B. K. Allen, *Financial Help in Social Work*, Manchester University Press, 1971.
36 Social Services Departments have a responsibility to investigate where necessary the circumstances of children from 0–17 years.
37 Children Act, 1948, Section 13 (1) (a).
38 Children and Young Persons Act, 1969, Section 49.
39 *Report of the Departmental Committee on the Adoption of Children* (Houghton Report), Cmnd 5107, HMSO, 1972.
40 *Report of the Committee of Inquiry into the Care and Supervision provided in relation to Maria Colwell*, HMSO, 1974.
41 The Child Care Act 1980 is consolidating legislation bringing together parts of a number of statutes ranging from the Children and Young Persons Act 1933 to the Children Act 1975. Only the Children Act 1948 has been repealed in its entirety. See Alan S. Holden, *Children in Care*, Comyn Books, 1980.
42 See Eileen Holgate and Tony Neill, 'In Practice', *Community Care*, January 4, 1978, and *Who Cares*?, National Children's Bureau, 1977.
43 The custodianship section introduced a new concept in family placement, allowing for the transfer of the legal custody of the child without changing his name or cutting his links with his parents. Unlike an adoption order, it is revocable.
44 The court may appoint an independent person (guardian *ad litem*) to act for the child. Section 64.
45 Children Act, 1975, Section 14.
46 Ibid., Section 26. See also Tony Hall (ed.), *Access to Birth Records*, BAAF, 1980.
47 See Joan Cooper, *Patterns of Family Placement*, National Children's Bureau, 1978.
48 W. Clarke Hall and A. C. L. Morrison, *Law Relating to Children and Young Persons*, Butterworth, 7th edn, 1967, p. 640.
49 A consolidating Act, the Adoption Act, 1976, is not yet implemented.
50 J. Seglow, M. Kellmer Pringle and Peter Wedge, *Growing up Adopted*.
51 Robert Holman, *Trading in Children*, Routledge & Kegan Paul, 1973.
52 Foster Children Act 1980.
53 Brian and Sonia Jackson, *Childminder*, Routledge & Kegan Paul, 1979.

54 For nursery schools see chapter 2 on Education.
55 Ministry of Health Circular, 221/45, 1945.
56 S. Yudkin, *0–5, A Report on the Care of Pre-School Children*, National Society of Children's Nurseries, 1967, p. 10.
57 See Joyce Moseley, 'Other people's children, the childminder's role', *Social Work Today*, 3 April 1979.
58 Margaret Bone, *Pre-School Children and the Need for Day Care*, HMSO, 1977.
59 *Services for Young Children with Working Mothers*, HMSO, 1978.
60 M. Fry *et al.*, *Lawless Youth*, Allen & Unwin, 1947.
61 *Children in Trouble*, Cmnd 3601, HMSO, 1968.
62 The Children Act, 1908, defined a child as a person under 14 and a young person as one who is 14 but under 16. The upper age limit was raised to 17 years by the Children and Young Persons Act, 1933.
Since the Children and Young Persons Act 1963 the age of criminal responsibility is put at 10.
63 The Children and Young Persons Act, 1933, Section 44(1) states: 'Every court in dealing with a child or young person who is brought before it, either as being in need of care or protection or as an offender or otherwise, shall have regard to the welfare of the child or young person.'
64 Regional Planning Committees, first mentioned in the White Paper, *Children in Trouble*, were established under the Children and Young Persons Act, 1969, Section 35, to prepare plans for a system of community homes in their areas and to prepare schemes for intermediate treatment.
65 *A Future for Intermediate Treatment*, Personal Social Services Council, 1977.
66 See the Eleventh Report from the Expenditure Committee. *The Children and Young Persons Act, 1969*, HMSO, 1975.
67 *Youth Treatment Centres*, HMSO, 1971.
68 See note 40.
69 See *The Central Child Abuse Register*, British Association of Social Workers, 1978.
70 Maureen Oswin, *The Empty Hours*, Pelican Books, 1971.
71 Maureen Oswin, *Children Living in Long Stay Hospitals*, Spastics International Medical Publications Research Monograph no. 5, Lavenham Press, 1978.
72 See the Chief Medical Officer's Report covering the war years 1939–46.
73 From a speech by Pethick-Lawrence when the bill was debated in the House, quoted Karl de Schweinitz, *England's Road to Social Security*, Barnes, New York, 1943.
74 Peter Townsend, *The Family Life of Old People*, Penguin, 1963; D. Cole and J. Utting, *The Economic Circumstances of Old People*, Occasional Papers in Social Administration no. 4, Codicote Press, 1962.
75 About two-thirds of local authorities had separate welfare committees.
76 In 1957 an attempt was made to assign responsibility but shortage of places in hospitals and homes still sometimes prevented care being given in the appropriate place. See the Annual Report of the DHSS, *Ten Year Review*, HMSO, 1958.

77 Ministry of Health, *Health and Welfare: the Development of Community Care*, Cmnd 1973, HMSO, 1963.
78 See Fig. I in *The Way Forward*, September 1977.
79 Audrey Hunt, *The Elderly at Home*, HMSO, 1978.
80 Amelia Harris, *Handicapped and Impaired in Great Britain*, Office of Population Censuses and Surveys, HMSO, 1971.
81 See Julia Parker, *Local Health and Welfare Services*, Allen & Unwin, 1965, chapter 5.
82 Peter Townsend, 'The disabled in society', Lecture given to the Royal College of Surgeons, May 1967.
83 DHSS, 12/70 August.
84 See the article by Walter Jaehnig, 'Seeking out the disabled', in Kathleen Jones (ed.), *Year Book of Social Policy*, Routledge & Kegan Paul, 1972.
85 *Mobility of Physically Disabled People*, HMSO, 1974.
86 Kathleen Jones in *A History of the Mental Health Services*, Routledge & Kegan Paul, 1972, points out that only 1 per cent of the Medical Research Council's funds had been spent on mental health in the early years of the National Health Service, while in the hospital service, where mental disorders take up nearly half the available beds, only about 16 per cent of capital expenditure in the first five years went to mental hospitals and institutions.
87 J. K. Wing, *Reasoning about Madness*, Oxford University Press, 1978.
88 See chapter 6.
89 *Report of the Committee of Social Workers in the Mental Health Services* (Mackintosh Report), Cmnd 8260, HMSO, 1951.
90 See note 7.
91 Reporting in 1957, Cmnd 169.
92 Kathleen Jones, in *A History of the Mental Health services, op. cit.*, discusses the influence of Dr A. F. Tredgold's *Mental Deficiency*, the first clinical textbook on the subject. He thought that mental deficiency was a clearly distinguishable condition—'between the lowest normal and the highest ament, a great and impassable gulf is fixed.'
93 Madeline Rooff, *Voluntary Societies and Social Policy*, part 3, Routledge & Kegan Paul, 1957.
94 The 1899 and 1914 Elementary Education (Defective and Epileptic Children) Acts, and the 1921 Education Act.
95 There was a 55 per cent increase in residential places (or work in progress) between 1971 and 1972. Altogether 8,000 places for adults, including foster homes and lodgings, were available, but as the target proposed in 1969 was 37,000 places it would have taken 30 more years to reach at this pace.
96 White Paper, Cmnd 4683, HMSO, 1971, para. 166.
97 *Ibid.*, para. 26.
98 *A Review of the Mental Health Act, 1959*, HMSO, 1976.
99 *Review of the Mental Health Act 1959*, Cmnd 7320, HMSO, 1978.
100 *Report of the Committee on Mentally Abnormal Offenders*, Cmnd 6244, HMSO, 1975.
101 Olive Keidan and Zuzana Hughes, 'Roots', *Social Work Service*, no. 21, November 1979.

102 P. Burgess, 'Rights of man in welfare', *New Society*, 13 September 1973.
103 See John Spencer *et al.*, *Stress and Release in an Urban Estate*, Tavistock, 1964, and E. U. Goetschius, *Working with Community Groups*, Routledge & Kegan Paul, 1969.
104 For an overview of community work see Peter Baldock, *Community Work and Social Work*, Routledge & Kegan Paul, 1974.
105 See Seebohm Report, para. 2 and chapter 16.
106 See David N. Thomas and R. William Warburton, *Community Workers in a Social Services Department: A Case Study*, National Institute for Social Work and Personal Social Services Council, 1977.
107 See Gene Pack, 'The Family Clubhouse Project' in Mary Marshall (ed.), *Social Work in Action*, British Association of Social Workers, 1979.
108 Seebohm Report, chapter 15.
109 For instance, Portsmouth Social Services Department and Portsmouth Polytechnic established a joint Social Services Research and Intelligence Unit in 1972.
110 F. V. Jarvis, *Advise, Assist, Befriend, A Brief History of the Probation and After-Care Service*, National Association of Probation Officers, 1972.
111 Children and Young Persons Act, 1969, Section 14: 'it shall be the duty of the supervisor to advise, assist and befriend the supervised person'.
112 *Non-custodial and Semi-Custodial Penalties*, HMSO, 1970.
113 Seebohm Report, para. 704.
114 See D. Haxby, *Probation: A Changing Service*, Constable, 1978, and A. E. Bottoms and William McWilliams, 'A non-treatment paradigm for probation practice', *British Journal of Social Work*, Summer 1979.
115 For a discussion on marriage, marriage counselling and the contribution of the National Marriage Guidance Council, see *Marriage Matters*, HMSO, 1979.
116 See the Wolfenden Report, *The Future of Voluntary Organisations*, Croom Helm, 1978.
117 *The Voluntary Worker in the Social Services*, National Council of Social Service, Allen & Unwin, 1969.
118 See Anthea Holme and Joan Maizels, *Social Workers and Volunteers*, British Association of Social Workers, 1978.
119 See Barnardo Social Work Papers no. 3, *Barnardo's Channel Voluntary Family Counsellors*, 1973–7.
120 K. Slack, *The British Churches Today*, SCM Press, 1970.
121 Lindsay Knight, 'Bringing welfare to the shop floor', *Community Care*, 12 January 1977.
122 J. West, *Company Day Nurseries*, Institute of Personnel Management, 1970.
123 TUC Working Party Report, *The Under-Fives*, TUC, 1978.
124 Brian and Sonia Jackson, *Childminder*, Routledge & Kegan Paul, 1979.
125 Equal Pay and Opportunity Campaign Report, *Work and Parenthood*, 1978.
126 See chapter 3 on the Employment Services.

Notes to Chapter 8

1 Lon L. Fuller, *Anatomy of the Law*, Penguin, 1971, p. 9.
2 See Dennis Lloyd, *The Idea of Law*, Penguin, 1977, chapter 1, 'Is law necessary?'
3 See chapter 1, p. 1 in this volume.
4 A. V. Dicey, *Law of the Constitution*, Macmillan, 1885.
5 Martin Mayer, *The Lawyers*, Dell, New York, 1967, p. 261.
6 See H. H. Gerth and C. Wright Mills (eds), *From Max Weber*, Routledge & Kegan Paul, 1948, p. 185.
7 Anthony Lester in Lord Devlin and others (ed. Michael Zander), *What's Wrong with the Law*?, BBC, 1970, p. 22.
8 Thus most European languages make one word serve for both 'law' and 'justice'—*jus, droit, recht, diritto*. Anglo-Saxon usage seems to emphasise their distinctiveness.
9 Thus JUSTICE (the name adopted by the British section of the International Commission of Jurists) has contented itself with particular causes, often with considerable effect.
10 A useful short discussion of the argument appears in the first edition of Peter Worsley (ed.), *Introducing Sociology*, Penguin, 1970, chapter 8, by W. W. Sharrock.
11 'English' law has been that of England and Wales since the conquest of 1535: Scotland and Northern Ireland have separate systems.
12 Time is of the essence: thus abortion, homosexuality and divorce law reform took decades, land law reform centuries.
13 Sir William Anson, *The Law and Custom of the Constitution*, Clarendon Press, 1922, p. 1.
14 Sir Alfred Denning, *The Changing Law*, Stevens, 1953, p. 6.
15 *Central London Property Trust, Ltd* v. *High Trees House, Ltd* [1947], K. B. 130.
16 But there is overlapping: thus magistrates' courts have civil as well as criminal jurisdiction.
17 Sir William Blackstone, *Commentaries on the Law of England*, Cadell, 1793, vol. 4, p. 443.
18 See chapter 1 in this volume.
19 Law Reform (Personal Injuries) Act, 1948; Law Reform (Contributory Negligence) Act, 1945; Fatal Accidents Acts, 1846 and 1864, and Law Reform (Miscellaneous Provisions) Act, 1934.
20 Trade Union Act, 1871; Trade Disputes Act, 1906.
21 E. g. Contracts of Employment Act, 1963, Redundancy Payments Act, 1965, Industrial Relations Act, 1971; and see chapter 3, in this volume.
22 See chapter 5 in this volume.
23 Ministry of Social Security Act, 1966; and see chapter 4 in this volume. See also Harry Calvert, *Social Security Law*, 2nd edn, Sweet & Maxwell, 1978.
24 Sex Discrimination Act, 1975.
25 See, e.g., Chris Smith and David C. Hoath, *Law and the Underprivileged*, Routledge & Kegan Paul, 1975.

26 Legitimacy Act, 1926, Adoption of Children Act, 1926: see Margaret Puxon, *Family Law*, 2nd edn, Penguin, 1971, chapter 10.
27 Matrimonial Causes Act, 1937, Divorce Reform Act, 1969: see Puxon, *op. cit.*, chapter 3.
28 Administration of Estates Act, 1925; Inheritance (Family Provisions) Act, 1938; see Puxon, *op. cit.*, chapter 13.
29 Crown Proceedings Act, 1947.
30 R. v. *Bourne* [1939] 1 KB 687.
31 *Donogue* v. *Stevenson* [1932] AC 562.
32 *Rookes* v. *Barnard and Others* [1964] AC 1129.
33 The so-called 'crime rate' is the number of indictable (i.e. generally more serious) offences reported to the police, and recorded by them.
34 The distinction is well settled at law, though not everyone accepts its morality.
35 *Russell* v. *Scott* [1948] AC 422.
36 Sir Leslie Scarman, 'Need the Law be obscure?', in Michael Zander (ed.), *op. cit*.
37 Terence Ison, *The Forensic Lottery*, Staples Press, 1967.
38 See, e.g., JUSTICE, *No Fault on the Roads*, Stevens, 1974.
39 Quarterly publication *Rights* and occasional other publications.
40 Sir Robert Mark, *Policing a Perplexed Society*, Allen & Unwin, 1977.
41 See, e.g., Lord Hailsham, *The Times*, 18 June 1974.
42 Sir Robert Mark, *loc. cit.*
43 See, e.g., J. Baldwin and M. McConville, *Negotiated Justice: Pressures on Defendants to Plead Guilty*, Martin Robertson, 1977.
44 See, e.g., Brian Harris, *The New Law of Bail*, Barry Rose, 1978.
45 See, e.g., *Balogh* v. *St Albans Crown Court*, reported in *The Times*, 4 July 1974.
46 See, e.g., Dennis Chapman, *Sociology and the Stereotype of the Criminal*, Tavistock, 1968.
47 Home Office, *Children in Trouble*, Cmnd 3601, HMSO, 1968.
48 Richard M. Titmuss, *Essays on 'The Welfare State'*, Allen & Unwin, 1958, chapter 2.
49 See Sir Leslie Scarman, *Law Reform: The New Pattern*, Routledge & Kegan Paul, 1968.
50 See G. Wootton, *Pressure Politics in Contemporary Britain*, Lexington, 1978.
51 E. Ehrlich, *Fundamental Principles of the Sociology of Law*, Harvard University Press, 1936, p. 199.
52 Criminal Justice Act, 1972.
53 Home Office, *Final Report of the Royal Commission on Legal Services* (Chairman: Sir Henry Benson), Cmnd 7648 and 7648–1, HMSO, 1979, chapter 4.
54 The suggested programme is a product of the positivist view of law; natural law thinkers would desire a different approach: see Dennis Lloyd, *op. cit.*, chapters 4 and 5.
55 Though one barrister supporter of the *status quo* has retorted to this criticism that, 'The same could be said of Woolworths or Burtons.'

56 Whereby a prisoner in the dock, if he has £2.22½p, may choose any barrister present in court to represent him; dock briefs have become less common (though by no means obsolete) since the growth of legal aid.
57 Home Office, *Report of the Committee on Legal Aid and Advice in England and Wales* (Chairman: Lord Rushcliffe), Cmnd 6641, HMSO, 1945.
58 'Legal aid' officially means assistance in litigation, 'legal advice' being on matters apart from litigation; but in general usage (and in this chapter) the term 'legal aid' is used to cover both.
59 See E. J. T. Mathews and A. D. M. Oulton, *Legal Aid and Advice*, Butterworth, 1971, with supplement, 1978.
60 Lord Chancellor's Office, *Legal Aid and Advice: Report of the Law Society and Comments and Recommendations of the Lord Chancellor's Advisory Committee, 1972–3 (Twenty-third Report)*, HMSO, 1974.
61 *Report of the Royal Commission on Legal Services*, 1979 (see note 53, above), chapter 2.
62 *Ibid.*, chapter 11.
63 *Ibid.*, chapter 15.
64 Brian Abel-Smith, Michael Zander and Rosalind Brooke, *Legal Problems and the Citizen*, Heinemann, 1973.
65 *Report of the Royal Commission on Legal Services*, 1979 (see note 53, above), chapter 9.
66 *Ibid.*, chapter 8.
67 *Ibid.*, chapters 5 and 16.
68 See H. G. Hanbury and D. C. M. Yardley, *English Courts of Law*, 5th edn, Oxford University Press, 1979, or R. M. Jackson, *The Machinery of Justice in England*, 7th edn, Cambridge University Press, 1977.
69 See *The Times*, 29 January 1974 and the *Guardian*, 4 October 1979.
70 Harry Street, *Justice in the Welfare State*, 2nd edn, Stevens, 1975, and Kathleen Bell, *Tribunals in the Social Services*, Routledge & Kegan Paul, 1969, offer the fullest accounts of administrative tribunals to date, though both are incomplete: see too R. M. Jackson, *op. cit.*, chapter 6, and *Report of the Royal Commission on Legal Services*, 1979 (see note 53, above), chapter 15. Surprisingly, in view of the importance of tribunals, the literature on the subject is meagre and there is as yet no single comprehensive work.
71 Harry Street, *op. cit.*, chapter 3.
72 Home Office, *Report of the Committee on Administrative Tribunals and Enquiries*, Cmnd 218, HMSO, 1957. The chairman was Lord Franks.
73 See Home Office, *Report of the Royal Commission on Assizes and Quarter Sessions*, Cmnd 4153, HMSO, 1969. The chairman was Lord Beeching.
74 See the *Guardian*, 21 September 1979 and subsequent issues.

Notes to Chapter 9

1 T. H. Marshall, *Social Policy*, Hutchinson, 1967, pp. 28–30, 96.
2 T. H. Marshall, 'Value problems of welfare capitalism', *Journal of Social Policy*, vol. 1, no. 1, January 1972.
3 One of the difficulties of reading on this subject is that conventional

textbooks are often uncritical of the theories they present. Radical textbooks which present and criticise neo-classical theory are often better in this respect, but not without their own bias. One of the easiest to read is E. K. Hunt and H. J. Sherman, *Economics: an Introduction to Traditional and Radical Views*, 3rd edn, Harper International, 1978.

4 J. M. Keynes, *The General Theory of Employment, Interest and Money,* Macmillan, 1963 edn. But see any economic textbook for an account of this theory.

5 Monetarist theories are not generally covered very well in economic textbooks. A fairly readable exposition of the monetarist view of the relationship between money supply and the business cycle can be found in W. Poole, *Money and the Economy: a Monetarist's View*, Addison-Wesley, 1978, chapter 4.

6 The title of a book by F. A. Hayek on this subject (Routledge & Kegan Paul, 1944; reprinted 1976).

7 R. Pinker, *The Idea of Welfare*, Heinemann, 1979.

8 R. A. Nisbet, *The Sociological Tradition*, Heinemann, 1970, chapter 1.

9 R. Mishra, *Society and Social Policy: Theoretical Perspectives on Welfare*, Macmillan, 1977, pp. 47 ff.

10 R. E. Dowse and John A. Hughes, *Political Sociology*, John Wiley, 1972, chapter 5.

11 P. Hall, A. Land, R. Parker and A. Webb, *Change, Choice and Conflict in Social Policy*, Heinemann, 1975.

12 Chapter 4.

13 Central Statistical Office, *National Income and Expenditure*, published annually by HMSO, includes a table showing personal income before tax according to source over the previous ten years. While the figures may be subject to error, most of the errors will tend to result in over estimates of the proportion of personal income that comes from state benefits.

14 *Report of the Royal Commission on the National Health Service*, Cmnd 7615, HMSO, 1979, para. 8.23.

15 For the decline in the post-war period see *Social Trends*, HMSO, 1979 edn, Table 8.27, p. 144.

16 In the supporting papers for the DHSS review of the Supplementary Benefits system in 1978 there is a *Report on Research on Public Attitudes towards the Supplementary System* submitted by the Schlackman Research Organisation to the Central Statistical Office which makes this point. The report is interesting for the light it throws on many of the points made in this paragraph. It is (or was) available free on request to the DHSS.

17 *The Perception of Poverty in Europe*, working document of the Commission of the European Communities, 1977, Table 29.

18 Unemployment tends to come high on the list of problems that people think governments need to deal with in opinion polls. Reaction to factory closures also produces appeals to government for support.

19 For a brief discussion of the issues see A. Forder, *Concepts in Social Administration*, Routledge & Kegan Paul, 1974, pp. 120–1.

20 For a brief discussion and further references see Anthony Forder, *Concepts in Social Administration*, Routledge & Kegan Paul, 1974, pp.

129–37. For a fuller discussion see T. Johnson, *Professions and Power*, Macmillan, 1972 and Brian Heraud, 'Professionalism and social work' in Open University, *Social Work, Community Work and Society*, Course DE 206, Unit 26, Part 1.

21 See p. 50.
22 See pp. 173, 184.
23 See pp. 272–5
24 See pp. 17–18.
25 D. S. Lees, *Economic Consequences of the Professions,* Institute of Economic Affairs, Research Monograph, 1966.
26 Ralph Harris and Arthur Seddon, *Choice in Welfare 1970*, Institute of Economic Affairs, Research Report, 1971. A. C. F. Beales, H. Blaug, E. G. West and D. Veale, *Education: a Framework for Choice*, Institute of Economic Affairs Readings, 1967.
27 Brian Heraud, *op. cit.*
28 P. Halmos, *The Personal Service Society*, London, 1970.
29 *Op. cit.*, Table 29.
30 B. Seebohm Rowntree, *Poverty: A Study of Town Life*, Macmillan, 1901.
31 Pp. 93, 106–7.
32 See W. Jordan, *Poor Parents: Social Policy and the Cycle of Deprivation*, Routledge & Kegan Paul, 1974 for an account of Keith Joseph's expression of this theory and for a critique of it.
33 M. Rutter and M. N. Rutter, *Cycles of Disadvantage: a Review of Research*, Heinemann, 1976.
34 O. Lewis, *Culture of Poverty*, Freeman, 1966.
35 J. Higgins, *The Poverty Business*, Blackwell, 1978.
36 J. Bennington, 'The flaw in the pluralist heaven—changing strategies in the Coventry CDP', chapter 19 in R. Lees and G. Smith (eds), *Action Research in Community Development*, Routledge & Kegan Paul, 1975.
37 D. Miller, *Social Justice*, Clarendon Press, 1976.
38 W. G. Runciman, 'Social justice', *Listener*, 29 July 1965, reprinted in Eric Butterworth and David Weir (eds), *The Sociology of Modern Man*, Fontana/Collins, 1970. See also W. G. Runciman, *Relative Deprivation and Social Justice*, Routledge & Kegan Paul, 1966.
39 Cited by Karl Marx in 'Critique of the Gotha Problem' in Karl Marx and Frederick Engels, *Selected Works*, vol. II, Moscow, Foreign Languages Publishing House, 1955, p. 24.
40. J. Rawls, *A Theory of Justice*, Oxford, 1972. Rawls is writing to oppose the utilitarian view that the highest value is the greatest happiness of the greatest number, which of course has no real place for social justice.
41 *Op. cit.*, p. 303.
42 *Op. cit.*, p. 302. The omitted words are 'consistent with the just savings principle' and are concerned with inter-generational justice.
43 *Op. cit.*
44. *Op. cit.*, pp. 40–51.
45 R. A. Dahl and C. E. Lindblom, *Politics, Economics and Welfare*, Harper & Row, 1950.

Index